Date Due

Blyth			
JUN 2 1981			
BC4Mar84			

Our Own Voice

R. E. McConnell

OUR OWN VOICE

Canadian English
and how it came to be

gage PUBLISHING LIMITED
Toronto·Vancouver·Calgary·Montreal

To Dr. R. J. Gregg, scholar, teacher, and generous friend

Printed and bound in Canada

Designed by Michael van Elsen

Maps by Margaret Kaufhold

Canadian Cataloguing in Publication Data

McConnell, Ruth E., 1915-
  Our own voice

Bibliography: p.
Includes index.
ISBN 0-7715-9904-8

1. English language in Canada.   I. Title.

PE3208.M24   427'.9'71   C78-001384-0

Preface

This book is an attempt to bring to the non-specialist some of the informed insights of the scholars who have studied Canadian English. The aim is to tempt the readers to do what these scholars do: to wonder about and to examine the varieties of the English language used in this country.

Because interest in one's own language helps one to gain some insight into all human language, the text is organized to reveal something of the workings not only of English in Canadian communities but also of English as a whole. By fostering informed attitudes to language, such knowledge may help alleviate, in at least a small way, the distress that is caused by misunderstanding and ignorance about the differences among people.

Contents

Symbols of the International Phonetic Alphabet as used in this book

Consonants

The following consonants have their familiar values:
b d f g h k l m n p r s t v w z. Others are:

[j] *y*et	[ʃ] *sh*ip	[θ] *th*in	[ʒ] gara*g*e
[ŋ] si*ng*	[tʃ] *ch*urch	[ð] *th*en	[dʒ] *j*u*dg*e

Vowels

[i] b*ee*t	[ɪ] b*i*t	[e] b*ai*t	[ɛ] b*e*t
[æ] b*a*t	[a] b*a*r	[ɑ] b*ough*t	[ɔ] p*o*rt
[o] b*oa*t	[ʊ] f*oo*t	[u] b*oo*t	[ʌ] b*u*t
[ə] (schwa) sof*a a*bove			

Diphthongs

[iu] *few*	[aɪ] b*uy*	[aʊ] h*ow*	[ɔɪ] b*oy*

Note:

These are approximations only. Canadians, for example, use for the final part of the diphthong in *buy* and *boy* a vowel intermediate between [ɪ] and [i]. Most Canadians also use the same vowel for f*a*ther, c*augh*t, and c*o*t; the quality of the vowel used, shown here as [ɑ], is variable.

Stress marks precede the syllable affected.

Two dots *e.g.* [i:] indicate greater length.

Abbreviations Used in this Book

DA   *Dictionary of Americanisms on Historical Principles.* Ed. M. M. Mathews. Chicago: University of Chicago Press, 1951.

DAE   *A Dictionary of American English.* Ed. William A. Craigie and James R. Hulbert. 4 vols. Chicago: University of Chicago Press, 1938–44.

DARE   *Dictionary of American Regional English.* Ed. F. G. Cassidy. To be published about 1980.

DC   *A Dictionary of Canadianisms on Historical Principles.* Ed. W. S. Avis, C. Crate, P. Drysdale, D. Leechman, M. H. Scargill. Toronto: Gage, 1967.

DCE   *Dictionary of Canadian English: The Senior Dictionary.* Toronto: Gage, 1967; revised and updated, 1973, with alternative title *The Gage Canadian Dictionary.*

DNE   *The Dictionary of Newfoundland English.* Ed. G. M. Story, W. Kirwin, and J. D. A. Widdowson. In final stages of preparation.

EDD   *English Dialect Dictionary.* Ed. Joseph Wright. 6 vols. London: Henry Frowde, 1898–1905.

IPA   International Phonetic Alphabet

OED   *The Oxford English Dictionary.* 12 vols. plus Supplement. Oxford University Press, 1933. (Originally *A New English Dictionary on Historical Principles.* 10 vols. 1888–1928.) New supplements: A–G, 1974; H–N, 1976.

SCE   Survey of Canadian English, 1972. A survey of Grade 9 students and their parents across Canada. See Scargill and Warkentyne 1972 and Scargill 1974 in bibliography.

SSB   Standard Southern British. A dialect, in origin the speech of educated Londoners, and now associated with a higher social or educational background, the BBC (though regional dialects are heard also), and the professions—*standard* as opposed to dialectal; *southern* as opposed to northern standards; and British as opposed to other regional varieties, North American in particular.

Part 1

x

Chapter 1

From the Old Country to the New: An Introduction to Canadian English

We were struck, as every newcomer is, by the new meanings put by Canadians on words, the new connections in which they used them, and the extraordinary way in which some were pronounced. Of course, we heard people 'guessing' at every turn, and whatever any one intended doing, he spoke of as 'fixing'. You would hear a man say, that his wagon, or his chimney, or his gun, must be 'fixed'; a girl would be ready to take a walk with you, as soon as she had 'fixed herself'; and the baby was always 'fixed' in the morning, when washed and dressed for the day. 'Catherine', said a husband one day to his wife, in my hearing pronouncing the last syllable of her name, so as to rhyme with line, 'I calculate that them apples'll want regulatin', referring to some that were drying in the sun. They 'reckon' at every third sentence. A well-informed man is said to be 'well posted up' in some particular subject. Instead of 'what', they commonly say 'how', in asking questions. A pony was praised to me as being 'as fat as mud'. In place of our exclamations of surprise at the communication of any new fact, the listener will exclaim, 'I want to know'. Any log, or trunk of a tree, or any other single piece of timber, is invariably a 'stick', even if it is long enough for a mast. All the stock of a timberyard is alike, 'lumber'. An ewer is 'a pitcher'; a tinpail is a 'kettle'; a platform at a meeting is 'a stage'; children are 'juveniles'; and a baby is 'a babe'. In pronouncing if you would imitate a Canadian, you would need to open your mouth very wide, and make as much of each sound as you can. Of course, I speak only of the country folks, native born.

John C. Geikie, George Stanley; or, Life in the Woods (1864)

In England, *lumber* means 'disused furniture, and the like', thus 'useless odds and ends'; this is the sense in which Pope uses the word in 1711:

> The bookful blockhead, ignorantly read,
> With loads of learned lumber in his head.

Alexander Pope, *An Essay on Criticism* (1711)

Canadian English is different

Canadians have become used to hearing and identifying various dialects of British English (including Scottish and Irish), Australian English, American English, and other 'Englishes', but seldom give much thought to their own 'Canadian English'. Only when they travel or when strangers comment do Canadians begin to notice the features which mark their own variety of the language. Many Canadians can relate stories similar to the following ones.

Canadian (in a store in the U.S.): Where is the department that sells chesterfields?

U.S. clerk: Cigarettes are on the ground floor, sir.

Canadian (outside a residence of a California university): If a phone call comes for me, I'm here, just outside.

American (inside): Where's the Canadian?

Canadian: How did you know I'm Canadian?

American: From the way you said *ootside*. Canadians say *aluminium* for *aluminum*, too, don't they?

Canadian: No, we don't, and we don't say *ootside*, either.

American: Well, that's the way it sounds to me. And you say *hoos*, too. I have worked with Canadians, and that's how I tell them from Americans.

Two people at a conference are standing in the rain waiting for a taxi.

Canadian: Are you going to Jefferson Hall?

American: Yes, I am.

Canadian: Then let's go together, eh?

American: Fine. What part of Canada are you from?

Canadian: Manitoba. But how did you known I'm a Canadian?

American: From the way you said "eh?" at the end of your sentence. I'm from Michigan, and we always recognize Canadians when they say that.

Canadian: You do, eh? Well, I'd never noticed that before.

Canadian (in a souvenir shop in Holland): Will you take American money?

Dutch clerk: Certainly—or Canadian, if you wish.

Canadian: How do you know I'm a Canadian?

Dutch clerk: Well—there is something about the way you speak that is different from the American way. I don't know what it is, but I can always tell. By the way, a Canadian lady in here the other day said that my little son is *skookum*. What did she mean by that?

Canadian: *Skookum?* I've never heard of the word. Are you sure she was a Canadian?

But curiously, these examples of speech do not by themselves set apart Canadian English; in fact, most of them can be found in other parts of the English-speaking world. For instance, the word *chesterfield*, meaning 'settee' or 'sofa', originated in England and was used in the early part of this century to refer to an extremely large sofa. But now the word is only rarely used there. In Canada, however, it has widened its meaning to become the general word for several types of this kind of furniture. Some Canadian stores now advertise *chesterbed*, one that converts into a bed, and Canadians commonly use the compound *bed chesterfield*. Oddly enough, some natives of San Francisco and the northwest California counties also use the word *chesterfield* to mean 'settee' or 'sofa'—though no one knows how it happens to occur there or what connection there is, if any, with the Canadian use (Reed 1954).

A Vancouver newspaper, 1976

Eaton's Archives

The word *skookum*, which puzzled the Dutchman and at least one Canadian and means 'big, strong, fine', is a regionalism, a language feature confined to a specific geographical area—in this instance not only the west coast of British Columbia but also the region from the Alaska coast to the mouth of the Columbia River in the United States.

Similarly, what is known as the "Canadian *ou*" in *outside* and *house* may be heard in the speech of a few Americans, those from eastern Virginia or the South Carolina-Georgia Tidewater area. Even the tag *eh*? is not limited to Canadians.

Indeed, except for many words which are particularly Canadian, most of the language features of Canadian English are found in either British English or American English, and sometimes in both. **It is the particular combinations of these features which set apart Canadian English.** The U.S. Immigration and Naturalization Service is said to have a quick border test to give to people claiming to be

Americans but thought to be Canadians. The test, which is shown in the margin, uses not one but several pronunciation features of Canadian speech, some that are patterns and some confined to individual words.

The test is far from conclusive, as American and Canadian pronunciations overlap and the variants may be found on both sides of the border, but the combination of features does provide some indication of one's origin. Moreover, the many regional, social, and sometimes personal differences within Canadian English further complicate matters—and these are always changing. No living language, that is, a language being spoken and used, is static; no living language is geographically and socially uniform.

Nevertheless, for a country whose population comes from such diverse sources and is strung out so thinly across three thousand miles with barriers of water and mountain, the English language spoken by Canadians is remarkably homogeneous—probably more homogeneous than the language of any other country of a considerable size. A Torontonian's speech, except for a few terms and perhaps subtle differences in intonation, is much like that of a native of Winnipeg or Vancouver.

Some Pitfalls in Speaking the Same Language

What is the problem of communication in the following instances? Can you recount similar incidents?

Two Britishers on arrival in Canada were standing by their baggage wondering where a friend, who had promised to meet them, might be. A porter asked if they wanted to check their bags.

"They're all here, thanks," they replied.

London telephone operator: "Are you through, New York?"
New York operator: "No, London. One moment, please!"

What is going on?

When Canadians speak in the British Isles, they frequently find themselves taken for Americans. In the United States, on the other hand, they may be asked—though perhaps with some hesitancy—if they are English (meaning 'from England'). Occasionally in either country they may have the pleasure of being recognized by their speech as being Canadian. Just where is Canadian English placed in relation to these two large regional varieties of English? And how did the Canadian variety come to be?

To speak of British English, American English, or even Canadian English is, of course, to speak in broad generalizations, because each of these geographical varieties (British English more than the others) has within it many further regional variations. Nevertheless, the general terms can be useful if one remembers the relativity of the statements. British English here means Standard Southern British, usually referred to as SSB; American English refers to those features that are generally prevalent in the United States; and Canadian English means that variety of English heard generally in Canada, particularly from Ontario westward. In all three, the reference is to the speech of educated people—in North America, of the educated urban population.

One way to discover something about the Canadian variety of English is to compare it with American English and British English. Such a comparison may be made of all aspects of language: pronunciation, grammar, vocabulary, and semantics (meaning).

Differences within a language arise mainly from separation. Groups of speakers of a language become separated, either regionally or socially. The varieties of the language they speak then evolve in their own ways. If the separation continues, the varieties may change enough to become different languages. For example, French, Spanish, Portuguese, and Italian were all at one time varieties of Latin, but they are now discrete languages. If, however, the differences are not great enough to prevent mutual intelligibility, the varieties may be called *dialects* of the same language.

A dialect, therefore, is a variety of a language that has recognizable features that distinguish it from other varieties of the same language. These features may be in pronunciation, grammar, vocabulary, and semantics (meaning). The study of such variations within a language is called *dialectology*. In the past century dialectologists have developed special techniques to examine and describe dialects and to trace their history. These techniques involve sampling, usually by oral or written questionnaires, and mapping the results. For those interested in knowing more about the methods of dialectology, special attention to this topic is provided in Chapters 3 and 4.

The English language today, which is spoken as a first language by over three hundred million people, has hundreds of varieties within it. Canadian speakers of English use a variety known as Canadian English.

Each of these major varieties of English has within it features of vocabulary, grammar, and sound that set it apart from the other varieties; yet each also contains sub-varieties, the special usages of smaller regional and social groups. Canadian English, for example, has a set of features used by most Canadians and not used by speakers of British English, American English, Australian English, and others; but it also has within it the regional differences found in Newfoundland, the Maritimes, the North, the Pacific coast, and so on. Strictly speaking, if a variety of a language has recognizable features that set it apart, it may be called a dialect. But for clarification we shall use the term *dialect* for the sub-varieties only. The methods of studying these differences within a language apply to all varieties, both large and small.

The greatest barrier between the English and the Americans is that they speak the same language.

Oscar Wilde, *Notes on a Tour of the United States* (1883)

```
                              English
        ┌──────────┬────────────┼────────────┬──────────┐
     British    American     Canadian     Australian    Other
     English    English      English      English      "Englishes"
                           ┌────┼────────┐
                    Newfoundland Maritimes Western Canada  etc.
                       dialect    dialect     dialect
```

Language, be it remembered, is not an abstract construction of the learned or of dictionary-makers, but is something arising out of the work, needs, ties, joys, affections, tastes, of long generations of humanity, and has its bases broad and low, close to the ground.

Walt Whitman, *November Boughs* (1888)

The study of the distinctive features of Canadian English and its regional dialects is a recent development. With the exception of the work of A. F. Chamberlain in the 1890's and of Henry Alexander in the 1930's, the systematic examination of Canadian English has taken place only in the last twenty-five years. Our knowledge about our own variety of English is therefore still incomplete. Since the formation of the Canadian Linguistic Association (CLA) in 1954, progress has been considerable, particularly in identifying the questions that will help us explore this dimension of Canadian life. There are, therefore, more questions than answers in this book —but questions that can make us more aware of how Canadians really use their language and of the close relationship between a language and the experiences of its speakers.

Where did Canadian English come from?

How British is our variety of English? How American? How much our own?

Reprinted by permission of The *Toronto Star*.

Two views of the English language about 1600; which one is true now?

The English tongue is of small
reache, stretching no further
than this island of ours, nay not
there over all.

   Richard Mulcaster (1592)

And who, in time, knows whither we may vent
The treasure of our tongue, to what strange shores
This gain of our best glory shall be sent,
T'inrich unknowing nations with our stores?

   Samuel Daniel, "Musophilus" (1602)

The First Great Separation: English Goes to North America

The first great division in the English-speaking peoples was the seventeenth century migration across the Atlantic Ocean to the "New England" and other North American colonies. The emigrants brought with them their regional and local varieties of Elizabethan English. Although there continued some contact with the home country through trade and by officials, this first great separation of English speakers occurred when travel was slow and difficult. Thus each North American colony along the Atlantic coast developed, within a few generations, its own kind of English, retaining much from the original varieties and adding its own innovations.

When, one and two centuries later, the North American people moved westward, the speech which had already been established in the Atlantic seaboard colonies determined the various regional dialects of the present-day United States. Dialectologists find, in general, three clearly marked speech areas, differing in pronunciation, grammar, and vocabulary: the *Northern* area, from western New England into the Great Lakes area; the *Midland* area, from Pennsylvania to Ohio and the southern Appalachians; and the *Southern* area. The differences among the three areas were more marked on the eastern seaboard and became more mixed as settlement pushed west, but even on the Pacific coast many variations in speech can be traced to the areas from which the main group of settlers came. (See map p. 134.)

The origins of these regional dialects, however, were in seventeenth century British English—either the general language of that time or regional variations. Certain changes that have occurred in southern British English since the departure of the colonists account for many of the modern divergences between the American and the British varieties of the language. In other words, many features of North American English are relics of an older form of the language. A few differences—especially in vocabulary—are North American innovations.

The Second Separation: To Canada

When Canada became a British possession in 1763, it had almost no English-speaking settlers. (The term *Canada* as used then would not, of course, include the British colony of Newfoundland. Acadia, a French-speaking area, had officially become a British colony in 1713.) In 1783, with the end of the American Revolutionary War, the picture changed abruptly. A mass migration of civilian and military refugees—the United Empire Loyalists, as they came to be called—moved from the new "United States" to the two provinces of "Nova Scotia" and "Canada." In 1784, New Brunswick and Cape Breton received such an influx of Loyalists that these two areas were divided from Nova Scotia (Cape Breton to be re-annexed in 1820). These settlers were largely from the New England and New York seaport areas, with a few from the southern states. Within a few years "Canada" (meaning central Canada) received at least 10 000

Let any English-speaking Canadian sit down in his corner and divest himself of whatever is American in origin and impulse and culturally and intellectually he'll look like a half-skinned rabbit.

Arthur L. Phelps, *These United States* (1941), quoted in Hamilton (1952)

The speech of a colony is conservative. It is in the language of the mother country that innovations are made.

Cleanth Brooks (1937)

In the heart of the Canadian of English speech there will be found, if he will confess it, as he often will, one profound spiritual wound, the division in the race, the American Revolution.

A. R. M. Lower, *Colony to Nation* (1946)

settlers, mainly from western New England, New York, and Pennsylvania. After the Loyalists, settlers continued to move into British North America, and within a generation after 1783 the area that would later become Ontario had a population of over 90 000—largely land-hungry settlers from the United States, with a sprinkling of British and German soldiers and other immigrants. It has been estimated that by 1813 fully eighty per cent of the inhabitants of Upper Canada were American in origin.

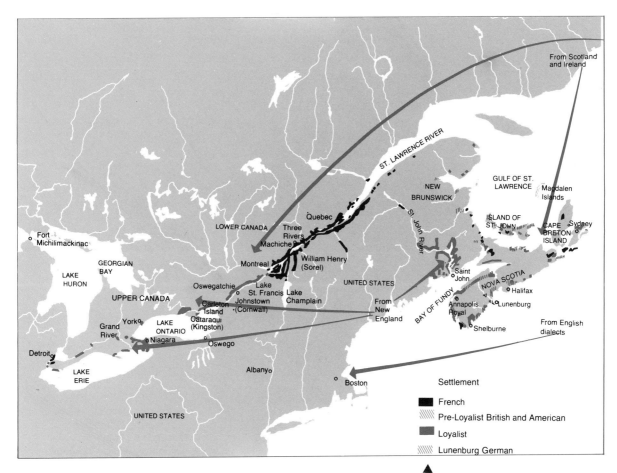

▲
Early sources of Canadian English

In the 1830's and 1840's—several generations after the first Loyalists—came a flood of immigrants from England, Ireland, and Scotland. These people, too, have left their mark upon Canadian speech, particularly in certain regions. Political and economic ties, the anti-American and pro-British sentiments of the Loyalists, and the prestige of British English have always influenced the language of Canadians. **But the base of Canadian English is the North American English spoken by those first settlers of the 1780's and 1790's.** Their migration to Canada was, however, a physical separation. In spite of continued influence from usage in both Great Britain and the United States, Canadian English began to develop in its own way.

Thus Canadian English has within it much of what had developed in the American colonies from the 1600's, something of late eighteenth and early nineteenth century British English and of local and regional variations brought from different parts of the British Isles, and something of its own making.

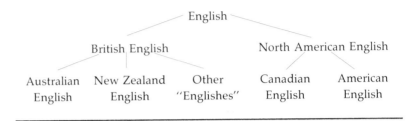

An immigrant from England to Upper Canada in the 1830's noticed these "American" (meaning North American) expressions in the speech of his neighbors in Canada. The husband, Mr. Root, was a "genuine Yankee" by birth, his wife, Irish. What is your reaction to these expressions?

The hostess was intently busy making large flat cakes; roasting them, first on one side, then on the other; and alternately boiling and frying broad slices of salt pork, when, suddenly suspending operations, she exclaimed, with a vivacity that startled us, "Oh, Root, I've cracked my spider!"

Inquiring with alarm what was the matter, we learned that the cast-iron pan on three feet, which she used for her cookery, was called a "spider," and that its fracture had occasioned the exclamation. . . .

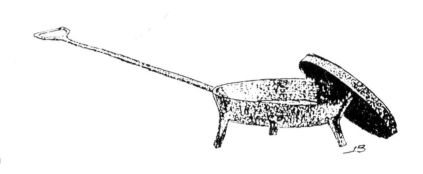

A spider

It was now day-break. As we were newcomers, Root offered to convoy us "a piece of the way," a very serviceable act of kindness, for, in the dim twilight we experienced at first no little difficulty in discerning it. Pointing out some faint glimmerings of morning, which were showing themselves more and more brightly over the tall tree-tops, our friend remarked, "I guess that's where the sun's calc'lating to rise."

Samuel Thompson,
Reminiscences of a Canadian Pioneer for the Last Fifty Years: An Autobiography (1884)

Spider is a northern American term; *a piece of the way* is generally a midland expression; *I guess* and *calculate* are examples of old British meanings preserved in North America and early recognized as Americanisms.

Her potato cakes were compounded of mashed potato and boiled red salmon; and, cut into round patties, were fried in a black spider with a long handle.

Patrick Slater, *The Yellow Briar* (1933)

Also being manufactured once more are cast-iron spiders, footed griddles, cast-iron tea kettles and skillets, stewing pots, and muffin pans. Most of these are exact replicas of utensils once considered outmoded, but invaluable to anyone cooking over coals.

Spiders, familiar to antique buyers, are frying pans or skillets with long legs. They may have dished covers designed to hold live coals, or plain flat or domed tops. The purpose of the legs is to allow them to be used over a thin layer of coals for slow sautéing, or the coals may be heaped high, until they contact the bottom of the spider, for quick frying.

Mel Marshall, *Cooking Over Coals* (1971)

North American differences: vocabulary

It is not always easy to disentangle the threads of North American English. The appearance of a feature in both the American and Canadian varieties may be a North American innovation, or it may be traceable to a common British or British dialectal root; or it may come from another language through either American or Canadian. For example, many Canadians use such expressions as:

I want off.

The cat wants out.

The dog wants in.

This omission of *to go* or *to get*, which sounds strange to the ears of many English speakers, occurred in older English and is preserved in some Scots-Irish dialects. It is also common in the speech of the American Midland, a region settled by Ulsterites and by Germans. German speakers would accept the structure readily when they learn English, because it corresponds with German grammar. The expression, therefore, may have come into Canadian English as a relic, or from Midland American (into western Ontario, where many Pennsylvanian people settled), or directly from Scots-Irish or from German—or from all of these. Canadian English is complicated in its relationships.

Do you use these expressions?

I plan to go back to school in the *fall*.

The lamp attracted many flying *bugs*.

I'm going to ask for a *raise* in pay.

I like my steak *rare*.

Put the steak on the *platter*.

I'm *mad* at you.

It'll rain soon, *I guess*.

The term *fall* meaning 'autumn' was originally a fuller phrase *the fall of the leaf*. The gardener in Shakespeare's *Richard II* uses the phrase in talking about the fall of the king:

He that hath suffered this disordered spring
Hath now himself met with the fall of leaf.

Similarly, about 1600 Sir Walter Raleigh played upon the potential meanings within *spring* and *fall*, using the latter word to refer to autumn:

A honey tongue, a heart of gall,
Is fancy's spring, but sorrow's fall.

"The Nymph's Reply to the Shepherd"

The punctuation and comment in the following excerpt, published in 1817, indicate that the term *fall* for 'autumn' was strange to this British writer and probably would have been to his readers in England:

Whilst we stood contemplating the varied objects in this interesting scene, a flock of geese flew screaming past; and a gentleman, who knew the country well, immediately observed, that we should have an "early fall"; thereby intimating that the winter would soon make its appearance.

Lieut. Edward Chappell, R. N., *Narrative of a Voyage to Hudson's Bay in His Majesty's Ship Rosamond* (1817)

North America as a Relic Area

Canada shares with the United States many words and expressions that were current in the seventeenth century when the colonists came to America but have since disappeared or changed in meaning in Standard Southern British (SSB). For instance, Shakespeare used both *fall* and *mad* in the senses shown in the examples on the previous page, but present-day Britishers do not.

The expression *I guess* meaning 'I suppose' or 'I judge' was used by Chaucer before 1400, just as it is used in North America today. Criseyde, for example, says of Troilus in *Troilus and Criseyde:*

> But yit to me his sorwe is muchel more,
> That love hyme bet than he hymself, I gesse.
> (ll. 899–900)
> (But yet his sorrow is much more to me,
> who loves him better than he [loves] himself.)

This use of *guess* has moved out of SSB. Indeed, in 1821 Lord Byron used the expression *I guess* as a "marker" of North American speech in his poem "The Vision of Judgment." When witnesses of various nations testify at King George III's bid to enter heaven, Byron has the American "Jonathan"* testify in this way:

> The voice of Jonathan was heard to express,
> "*Our* President is going to war, I guess."
> (ll. 471–2)

Thomas Pyles (1952) lists the following as some of the archaisms preserved in North American speech. Do you use them? Do you recognize any of them as being usage problems—that is, words used in various ways or of doubtful status?

to loan money—once standard British, but now changed to *lend* in SSB

a well man—not used now in SSB

to peek—used by Chaucer (late 1300's) to mean 'look furtively', but not so used now in SSB

trash   'rubbish', (as in Iago's "Who steals my purse steals trash," Shakespeare's *Othello*); used now by SSB speakers only figuratively, for worthless artistic or literary work

deck   'pack', of cards (but *deck* normal in Irish)

gotten   (though SSB keeps this older form in some frozen phrases such as *ill-gotten gains*)

Henry Alexander (1940) found such survivals and others in both the vocabulary and pronunciation of rural people in New England and Nova Scotia: *cuffs* were often *wristbands*, pronounced *rizbans*; the upper part of the house was the *chamber; Mrs.* was often *Mistress*, especially in areas settled by Scots; *waistcoat* was pronounced *weskit*,

---

* In the 1800's *Jonathan* (in Canada often *Brother Jonathan*) meant 'American'. The name seems to have been given by the British soldiers to the Americans during the Revolutionary War, probably because the colonists so frequently used Biblical names (a Puritan practice).

fortnight as *fortnit*, and *deaf* as *deef*—all well-established forms in older British English.

Some North American terms are British regionalisms, perhaps brought over by original colonists, perhaps reinforced by later settlers from these areas, or perhaps "relics" that all outlying areas have kept while SSB has changed. Here are two often noticed in North America:

pond—To most Britishers *pond* means an artificial pool only, except in Surrey, where it may refer to a natural small lake. This Surrey use seems to have been brought or extended to the colonies. Its use and meanings are very wide in Newfoundland.

druggist—This term (originally from French) changed to *chemist* in England only in the nineteenth century; but *druggist* is still used in Scotland. The Scottish influence would, of course, be strongly reinforcing in Canada.

North American Innovations

Faced with new conditions in a new land, the colonists naturally created new terms. Sometimes these terms were created by extending or changing the meaning of old words, transferring *robin*, for instance, to a bird much larger than the English robin. The colonists borrowed many words from the Indians (*moose, muskeg, skunk*); some from the French (*prairie, levee, butte, depot, cache*); from the Spanish (*canyon, tornado, mosquito, cafeteria*); the Dutch (*Santa Claus, boss, cookie*); the Germans (*hamburger, sauerkraut, semester*); and other peoples (*ravioli, matzo, smorgasbord, chow mein*). Or they made new compounds from old words (*log house, bluenose, panhandler*). Sometimes the colonists coined new words—the racy picturesque "slanguage" for which North America is noted. The inventiveness and exuberance in such words as *rubberneck, galoot, ripsnorter, highbrow*, and *blurb* may come from the tendency of any frontier area toward exaggeration, metaphor, and humor.

The Industrial Revolution, bringing the need for new terms, came after the separation of North American English. Often the two areas chose different "old" words to name the new technological changes. When railways came in, the British borrowed *carriage* and *coach* from earlier methods of transportation and used them in ways different from those in North America. The British *railway coach* is a *railway car* on the other side of the Atlantic; but a long-distance *bus* is a *coach* in Britain, the word *bus* being limited to urban and suburban transportation. A North American visitor to Britain soon learns to get a *railway* ticket at a *booking office*, and, in a city, to ride on the *underground* or *tube*, but to walk in a *subway* under a street. Such a visitor must also learn new terms for such common objects as the parts of an automobile and for everyday activities such as using the telephone.

Other reasons for differences

Some differences between North American and British usage have historical and social explanations. North Americans count city dis-

What is a *pond* here?
You can come out of a gulch in the land to higher ground and find buildings clustered around the approaches of an iron bridge. Under the bridge a creek slips down to lose itself in the brackish water of the pond, a narrow salt lagoon lying inside the Channel beach. The tides find their way in and out at the pond's eastern end. . . .

Charles Bruce, *The Channel Shore* (1957). A novel set in Nova Scotia.

Do you know what these British automobile terms mean?
the accumulator
a lay-by
an articulated lorry
on the nearside
a roundabout

tances in *blocks*, but Britishers do not because many of their cities were generally laid out in medieval times and not in the later square pattern. The British use *plot* to refer to the piece of land upon which a town-dweller builds a house, but this word is associated by Canadians and most Americans with gardens and graveyards; the *lot* of North America is an older use, and may have been reinforced by the word *allot* or *allotment* because of the way in which land was often given out to new settlers. In Prince Edward Island, a *lot* originally meant a township of 20 000 acres. The island was surveyed and divided into 67 "lots," which were distributed by lottery in 1767 to the king's grantees. It is interesting that such a piece of land is a *section* in New Zealand and a *block* in Australia. Each British colony adapted the language differently for its own needs.

The British use of *dust bin* for what North Americans call the *garbage can* is a reminder that until recently the main refuse in such containers was the ash of coal fires. There may also be historical and physical reasons why most North Americans walk on the *sidewalk*, while the British walk on the *pavement* (which would mean the roadway to most North Americans), or the *footway* or *footpath*. The *Oxford English Dictionary* (OED) lists *sidewalk* as an old word referring to a raised foot passage: in early North American settlements, and still in many Canadian towns, the first walks were boards raised above the mud and dust. Robert Harlow's description in *Royal Murdoch* (1962) of a pioneer town in British Columbia uses the image of "the hot summer dust whirling along wooden sidewalks." The material of the "sidewalk" has changed with progress; the term has not.

Rather similar to *sidewalk* is the North American use of *store* when most Britishers would use *shop* (though *shopping* is the term used everywhere for the actual activity). The earliest "store" in a new colony would be a general store or storehouse; this word, often in the plural form *stores*, is still used in parts of Great Britain in the same sense. In North America its meaning became extended to any store, *e.g.*, a grocery store, a drug store. Catherine Parr Traill (1836) explained in a letter to her mother in England that in the "backwoods" of Peterborough in 1832 a storekeeper can be a member of "a very genteel society":

Though a store is, in fact, nothing better than what we should call in the country towns at home a "general shop," yet the storekeeper in Canada holds a very different rank from the shop-keeper of the English village. The storekeepers are the merchants and bankers of the places in which they reside. Almost all money matters are transacted by them, and they are often men of landed property and consequence, not unfrequently filling the situations of magistrates, commissioners, and even members of the provincial parliament.

In both Australia and New Zealand the word began in the same way but became "a country word" until recently when, from Ameri-

Glenbow-Alberta Institute

General store in Crossfield, Alberta

can influence, the *chain store* came in and with it the expression "a big city store."

North American settlers soon needed new topographical terms. Some words such as *creek* (pp. 104, 146) and *bush* were extended from their British meanings, as happened later in Australia and New Zealand also. Other words, such as *coulee, mesa,* and *portage,* were borrowed from other languages. But all the colonial areas lost some British words. W. K. Hancock, writing about Australia (quoted in Baker 1966), says:

> The Australian has rejected, almost at a blow, the beautiful names of an intimate countryside—fields and meadows, woods, copse, spinney and thicket, dale, glen, vale and coomb, brook, stream and rivulet, inn and village. But in their place is a new vocabulary of the bush—billabong, dingo, damper, bushwacker, billy, cooee, swag, swaggie, humpty, drover, never-never, outback, back blocks.

For most North Americans, too, many British topographical terms are literary words only: the concept of a *moor* learned from *Wuthering Heights*, of a *heath* from Hardy's novels, of *fens* from those of Dickens, and of a *lea* from poetry. And how many Canadian children understand the words when they sing "The farmer in the dell"?

It is a long journey on foot to Mollineux, to one unacquainted with a blazed path in a bush road.

Susanna Moodie, *Roughing it in the Bush* (1852)

South Africans have lost *field* except in the sense of 'sports field', e.g. a *rugby field*. They use *land* or *lands* to refer to an area on a farm suitable for cultivation.

Differences in Semantic Range

Because differences in the meanings of words occur regionally and sometimes suddenly, over-generalizing about meaning is always a dangerous practice. Nevertheless, we know that some words, though used in both the mother country and North America, have acquired differences in the *range* of their reference. The following is but a sampling from a long list.

Wider range in North America

candy—To North Americans, *candy* is a generic term, referring to a large class.

To the British, *candy* is a hard sugary fudge (compare the verb *to candy*); *sugar candy* means a bar of 'rock candy'.

The British have no generic term, except *sweets*; although a *sweet* can also refer to what North Americans call a *dessert*. Britishers wanting "candy" ask for a specific kind, *e.g.* toffee or mints.

bug—This word originally meant 'insect' but in England has narrowed to mean 'bedbug'—so our older and wider use of the word could raise the eyebrows of a visiting Britisher.

raise—Once wide in its use, the word has become differentiated in Britain into such words as *rise* (in pay), *grow* (plants), *breed* (animals), and *rear* (children). North Americans use all these terms too, but can also use *raise* in place of any of them. Britishers would consider the term *a raise in pay* as substandard and use *a rise in pay*—but all areas use *a rise in prices*.

sick—In English use (not Scottish or Irish) *sick* usually means 'nauseated' only, whereas North Americans keep the older and wider use of being in ill health. Britishers do keep the older idea in the phrases *sick leave* and *sick bay*. The older use is heard in South African English also, though frowned upon.

potato chips—Britons divide the term, reserving *chips* for 'French fries' (as in *fish and chips*), and *crisps* for the packaged type; most Canadians still flounder in the ambiguity of *potato chips*, though commercial products are beginning to add other terms. (Look in your local supermarket.) The short form *fries* is also seen and heard now in Canada.

Narrower range in North America

corn—Most Canadians have learned from the accounts in their history books of the Corn Laws that *corn* in Britain is the generic term for 'grain', or the prevalent grain of an area; that is, in England *corn* would usually mean 'wheat', and in Scotland or Ireland *corn* would mean 'oats'. Germans use the word *korn* in the same wider way.

In North America, *corn* is a shortening from the original *Indian corn*, meaning 'Indian grain'. In England, *maize* is the specific word, but people now use *corn on the cob* as an importation.

biscuit—A larger class for the British, referring to both (North

". . . . My 'usband often talked of you and wondered how you were getting on in that outlandish place, and if your poor wife could put up with it. . . . I suppose it's all according. Some people don't mind. Some people are brought up to it, raised, as they say 'ere. I do so 'ate to 'ear slang. . . ."

Frederick Niven, *The Flying Years* (1935). The speaker is an Englishwoman whose husband had been the Indian agent on a reserve near Calgary.

American) *crackers* and, as *sweet biscuits*, to *cookies* (a word given to the North Americans by the Dutch).

Shopping for clothes in Britain requires some caution; for example, a British *waistcoat* is equivalent to the *vest* in North America and a British *vest* is an 'undershirt'. Canadian women may be surprised to learn in England that a *jumper* is a *pullover sweater* (though a *pullover* is not unknown and seems to be used for men's wear), and that the Canadian *jumper* or *jumper dress* is a *pinafore dress* to the British. Sometimes men in England use the word *jumpers* to refer to overalls.

Differences in Connotations

The meaning range of words includes the fringes of their meaning, the connotations that people attach to them. These sometimes subtle but socially important differences that have grown around a word can cause misunderstanding. What North American telephone company would use this slogan, now current in England?

IT'S SO CHEAP TO PHONE YOUR FRIENDS AFTER SIX OR AT WEEKENDS!

Mother Tongue
Richard Armour *The New Yorker* (1955)

Oh, to be in England
  If only 'arf a mo',
Where, when they speak of wireless,
  They mean a radio,

Where private schools are public
  And public schools are snobby
And insurance is assurance
  And a cop is called a bobby,

Where a traffic hub's a circus
  And up is down the street
And a sweater is a jumper
  And candy is a sweet,

Where a cracker is a biscuit
  And a trifle is dessert
And bloody is a cuss word
  And an ad is an advert,

Where gasoline is petrol
  And a stone is fourteen pound
And motorcars have bonnets
  And you take the Underground,

Where, holding up your trousers,
  It's braces that you use
And a truck is called a lorry
  And boots are really shoes,

Where a druggist is a chemist
  And the movies are the flicks
And you queue up on the pavement
  For a stall at three and six. . . .

There is no language barrier
  The tourist needs to dread
As long as he knows English
  From A to Z (no, zed).

Note:
The British pronunciation *zed* is favored everywhere in Canada except Newfoundland. Consider British children who watch American television shows such as *Sesame Street*. Which forms will they use? Will American terms become permanent items in their language? Why?

Inexpensive Not Cheap

A Canadian advertisement—which "makes sense" to a North American but probably not to a Britisher.

To table a motion?
In [British] parliamentary language, this means to put down for discussion, the exact opposite of the American meaning, to set aside. At the 1962 Geneva Disarmament Conference, the American and British delegations spent a large part of an afternoon locked in argument about whether to table a certain British motion before they found out they were on the same side. The Americans kept saying, to the Britons' confusion, "But it's a very *good* motion. Why do you want to table it?"

Norman Moss, *What's the Difference?* (1973)

The ultimate test of knowing a language is to be able to share the linguistic jokes made in the language.
    How many North Americans would "get" the point of this British cartoon? They would have to know that the British term for a 'roast of meat' is *joint*. *Pricey*, as one might guess, is colloquial in Britain for 'expensive'.

The word *cheap*, originally from a word meaning 'trade, market' as in the place name *Cheapside*, means merely 'inexpensive' in England and does not conjure up sub-meanings of miserliness. Note, too, that most North Americans would use *on weekends*.

There are subtle differences in other sets of words, for example, *scent*, *odor*, and *smell*:

scent—in North America can refer to perfume and carries favorable connotations.
    —in England refers to cheap perfume; though when used with flowers, etc. may carry the idea of 'pleasant smell'.
odor—in England carries only unpleasant connotations, but is more neutral in Canada, and in fact can be a euphemism for 'foul smell'.
smell—is neutral in England, but carries rather negative connotations for Canadians.

'Blimey! Beef must be pricey.'

The Listener, June 15, 1972

NO LANGUAGE BARRIER. NO DICTIONARY REQUIRED.
Advertisement of British Travel Association.

Canadian differences: vocabulary

So far, we have seen that Canadians share much vocabulary, both old and new, with the people of the United States. Canadian English is basically of the North American variety. But Canadians also share in the innovations and usages of the British. Most Canadians, in fact, are bi-dialectal in at least *knowing* many of the variations, because they frequently hear or read them. They learn to shift between such items as *first floor/ground floor, pants/trousers, suspenders/braces, absorbent cotton/cotton batting/cotton wool*—and to recognize that *ladders*, as well as *runs*, can occur in stockings, and that *boaters* and *bowlers* can be hats.

The prestige of British English varies within regions and certainly within families. It is also true that across Canada there exist pockets of English, Scottish, Irish, American, and other peoples, in which linger remnants of the original speech.

But Canadian experiences and customs have their own character, and Canadians have developed new words and phrases and have changed the meanings of many old words and phrases. What would a Britisher make of the following sentence? How much would an American understand?

> The separatist from the Maritimes, a product of the separate school system, defaced the NDP poster on the boulevard when he saw that it was signed by the reeve of the municipality, who had just been elected by acclamation.

The vocabulary of Canadian English is, indeed, both different enough and large enough to warrant a separate chapter (Chapter 2). The following examples are given to whet the appetite.

A Sample of Canadian Vocabulary

Here is a sampling of Canadianisms—that is, words and expressions that either originated in Canada or are used in Canada with special meanings. These are taken from the novel *The Vanishing Point*, a novel about Alberta and the relations between the whites and the Indians, by W. O. Mitchell (1973). All are listed with their origins, histories, and meanings in *The Dictionary of Canadianisms* (DC). A few words are regionalisms, used mainly in the Canadian West. How many do you know? How many are in your active vocabulary?

1. He could identify it now; a *ruffed grouse* drumming out again and again its invitation to join the living whole. Spring—actual spring by God! (3)
2. He'd recognized it immediately as a gift of contrition for chewing *snoose* in reading period that morning. (4)
3. Thick and white the smoke rolled over Esau's roof, curled down and around the eave, was carried off low by the *chinook*. (5)

An older use of a word:
. . . He grasped Kevin's shoulder and shook him. "You mind Estelle Blaine, Kev?"

Kevin looked blank for an instant before he recalled that in Lockhartville "mind" could be a synonym for "remember." "Yes, sure," he said. "I think I remember her. Sure."

Alden Nowlan, *Various Persons Named Kevin O'Brien: A Fictional Memoir* (1973). Short stories about life in a village near Windsor, N.S.

4. Quite often Victoria used to come down here, to snare *grayling*, to cut *kinickkinick* for old Esau to peel and roast in his oven, to mix half and half with fine-cut tobacco. (12)

5. Archie Nicotine stood before the Ladies and Escorts entrance of the Empress *beer parlour*. (45)

6. ''They come into this city from five different *reserves*—and there's a lot aren't *treaty* any more and it's a big city. We're just a small *band* and there isn't anybody like that in our Stony band.'' (53)

   (On the same page, an American uses the term *reservation*—evidence that the author is aware of the difference between Canadian and American usage.)

7. Archie Nicotine drove up in a *bob-sleigh* pulled by a woolly bay team, his Christmas present to Carlyle, a lynx hide. (165)

8. . . . Carlyle opposite Old Esau with his death's head festive under a red *toque* pulled down over his ears. (166)

9. The first severe spasm of winter—mid December—with a *wind-chill factor* of sixty *below* . . . . (105)

10. . . . and then Carlyle caught water glint through *pin cherry* and *saskatoon*. (129)

Both *reserve* and *homeland* are used in South Africa for areas set aside for Black Africans. In Rhodesia the term is a *restriction*.

The sounds of the language: British, North American, Canadian

Note:
This section becomes rather technical. Some readers may prefer to move straight to p. 35 and to return to this section later.

It has long been known that the sound system of any language changes, sometimes slowly and imperceptibly, and sometimes within a generation of speakers. A change may start in a large or prestigious centre and then spread outward, leaving the older form only in remote areas, which thus become "relic areas." A change in London speech, for example, often did not reach Ireland, Scotland, or some rural areas in England. Some changes are confined to certain social classes. Others affect the whole sound system of a language, one shift making another one necessary, and then another, and so on. Such a chain effect took place between approximately 1300 and 1700 with all the tense vowels of English, a shift which left the "back" tense vowels (*i.e.* those made with the back of the tongue raised) quite unstable and the resulting forms in modern English often unpredictable. Do these sets of words, for example, all rhyme in your speech:

broom room boom doom?
roof hoof?
boot root soot foot loot?
book look took nook?

Vowels in English are *tense*, like the [i] and [u] in *feel* and *fool*, or *lax*, like the [ɪ] and [ʊ] in *fill* and *full*. In pronouncing such vowels as [i] and [u], the tenseness can be felt in all the organs of speech, but particularly in the tongue.

Most Canadians would say *broom* and *room* with the vowel sound of *too*, but many Maritimers, like eastern New Englanders, would use the vowel of *book* for these words and also for *roof* and *hoof*. The word *soot* has at least three variants all across Canada.

Tracing such patterns and variants in pronunciation is one of the most important tasks of dialectologists. Because the sound system is probably that part of the language system that a person uses least consciously, it is therefore a good "marker" of the sources of one's language and the influences upon it.

To treat adequately the sound systems that Canadians use and to compare them with other varieties of English would be difficult to do in an introductory book such as this. Nor is everything known about the speech of Canadians. To identify sounds, we will use the symbols of the International Phonetic Alphabet (IPA)—a system in which a given speech sound is consistently represented by the same written or printed symbol (see p. viii for a chart of the symbols used). The symbols are enclosed in square brackets to distinguish them from ordinary letters of the alphabet. But we will use the IPA system in a general way only, and we will give (in spite of the obvious room

What evidence suggests that the writer of these lines is an American, not a Britisher?

> The turtle lives 'twixt plated decks
> Which practically conceal its sex.
> I think it clever of the turtle
> In such a fix to be so fertile.

Ogden Nash, *Many Long Years Ago* (1945)

for error on the part of the reader) some key words for identifying the symbols.

Dialectologists use the IPA, but with finer distinctions. They may also use in their questionnaires the devices of rhyming (*e.g.* "Does *genuine* rhyme with *fine* or with *fin*?") and, of "sames" and "contrasts" (*e.g.* "Is *cot* pronounced the same as *caught*, or differently?" "Is *hoarse* said the same as *horse*? Is *whine* the same as *wine*?"). These devices may be useful to you if you wish to test some of the items in this section with people in your part of Canada.

North America as a Relic Area: Pronunciation

A few differences in pronunciation immediately mark off most North American speech from nearly all other English dialects. These are certain features of seventeenth and eighteenth century English speech which were retained in most of North America, including Canada, but changed in SSB. Because Australia, New Zealand, and other countries were colonized after the changes in the home country, these phonological differences set North American English apart.

1. So-called broad a

North America (generally) has retained the older [æ] (the vowel of *hat*) in words such as *dance, half, path, pasture,* whereas SSB has adopted [a:], somewhat like the vowel in *father* or that in *farm*. This use of [a:] was a dialect feature in Great Britain and was considered "vulgar," or substandard, up to the end of the eighteenth century, when the fashion rather suddenly changed.

In neither area is the pattern complete. North Americans generally do not use [æ] before [r] in words like *far, farm,* and *dark,* nor before [l] in many words, such as *palm,* nor in some frequently used words such as *father*. In England, the change did not affect all words: *bass* (the fish) and *mass* have [æ] while *grass* has [a:]; the newer word *plastic* has [æ] but *plaster* has [a:]. As English pop singers of imported American lyrics have discovered, *dance* and *romance* do not rhyme in SSB. Many an imitation of southern British speech puts an [a:] into words that do not have it, *e.g. gather,* which should have [æ] and does not rhyme with *rather*.

Here are the results of one question in the Survey of Canadian English (SCE), a written questionnaire (1972) given to Grade 9 students and their parents across Canada.* The results shown are in percentages and are for students and parents born in Canada. Examine the results. Can you explain the regional differences?

Is this still true of some Canadians?

Mrs. Bilbeau came up. . . . She spoke nasally and with one of those accents common to eastern Canadians of "good family": she would say "bawths" and "I cawn't" in one breath, relapse into common Canadianese the next.

Selwyn Dewdney, *Wind Without Rain* (1946). A novel about a schoolteacher in a small town of southern Ontario; Mrs. Bilbeau is the wife of the principal.

* Pronunciations of *aunt* for Nova Scotia are on the dialect map on pp. 114-5.

87) Do *ant* and *aunt* rhyme? (A) yes; (B) no.

	male parents		female parents		male students		female students	
	A	B	A	B	A	B	A	B
Nfld	61	38	56	44	71	27	62	36
PEI	50	49	40	59	39	57	41	58
NS	41	58	28	71	43	57	31	68
NB	29	71	23	77	27	70	19	80
Que	84	13	79	20	81	16	82	15
Ont	87	13	85	13	80	15	82	17
Man	77	21	83	16	79	19	82	17
Sask	77	21	82	17	78	19	81	18
Atla	87	12	87	12	86	12	86	13
BC	86	13	87	12	84	14	82	16
Total	63	36	58	41	65	32	63	36

2. Loss of r

North America has retained the post-vocalic [r] (that is, [r] after a vowel) before a consonant as in *farm* and *court* or before a pause (*i.e.* in final position, as in *far* and *core*), whereas SSB has dropped the [r], so that *far*, for example, sounds to Canadians like *fah* [fa:]. There is abundant evidence that in Elizabethan English all dialects articulated **r** in all positions. The dropping of [r] in the positions mentioned was an innovation in SSB, completed by the end of the eighteenth century. The change also affected certain areas of the United States, especially eastern New England and parts of the South. These areas, which kept closer contact with the mother country, either changed to the British pattern or were settled by people from the southern and eastern counties of England, where the **r** change (and in some cases the "broad a" change) may already have taken place before these settlers emigrated. The Midland area of the United States was settled by many Ulster Scotch-Irish people, who kept a strong final [r]. The Scots and Irish influence has also been strong in Canada.

It is interesting to note how many *r*-less variants have crept into dialects of English—some seeming substandard or perhaps folksy even though the *r*-less varieties of English enjoy a certain prestige. Here are some examples: *cuss* (a variant of *curse*), *gal* (*girl*), *hoss* (*horse*), *bust* (*burst*).

How do these two fairly recent changes in SSB—the change to "broad a" [a] and the loss of [r] in certain positions—explain why speakers of SSB say *calves* and *carves* as homophones, while most North Americans do not?

In any variety of English, all vowels are affected in quality when followed by **r**, and both British and North American dialects display a bewildering variety of pronunciations for certain words. Listen, for example, to various dialect speakers say *car, poor, pure, clerk, bear, more*, and the surname *Moore*.

3. A Relic Stress Pattern

North American speech usually retains a seventeenth-century stress pattern in many polysyllabic words, a pattern probably used by Shakespeare but since changed in SSB. The difference is especially noticeable in words ending in **-ary, -ery,** and **-ory**. North Americans use a secondary stress on the second from last syllable, while the British tendency is to keep the strong stress on the first syllable but to reduce the other syllables, thereby changing the sound of each vowel to a schwa* or omitting it altogether. Some examples are:

How do you pronounce *dictionary?* *territory? cemetery? necessary?* Do you give the full vowel sound to the second from last syllable?

U.S.A.	British	
sécretàry	sécretary	(as if sécret'ry)
millinèry	millinery	(as if millin'ry)
obligatòry	obligatory	(as if obligat'ry)
mónastèry	mónastery	(as if mónast'ry)

Some other words show similar differences. For example:

interèsting	interesting	(as if int'risting)
médicìne	médicine	(as if médsin)

For some words, American dictionaries record both pronunciations—the British one often being assumed to be the more elegant. It is also apparent that the North American stress pattern (and perhaps the influence of the spelling) may be affecting British speech; the pronunciation *sécretàry*, for example, is now commonly heard in England. Canadians choose from both these major patterns of stress placement but, like Americans, tend to follow the older pattern. This major difference in stress placement gives the two large varieties of English markedly different speech rhythms.

In Robertson Davies' novel *Fifth Business* (1970), set in a small town of Ontario about a generation ago, one character (a Canadian) expresses his emotional reaction to a word pronounced with a different stress. (How do you pronounce the word?)

I used to hear him abused by some of the junior masters at the school. They were Englishmen or Canadians who had studied in England, and they were full of the wisdom of the London School of Economics and the doctrines of *The New Statesman.* . . . it amused me to hear those poor fellows, working for terrible salaries, denouncing Boy and a handful of others as "ca-*pittle*-ists"; they always stressed the middle syllables, this being a fashionable pronunciation of the period, and one that seemed to make rich men especially contemptible.

A recent change in British speech is the converse of the movement described above. The main stress in some four- and five-syllable words in British speech is now moving from the initial syllable to the second or third syllable. Simeon Potter (1969) notes that *labóratory* has replaced the former Cambridge pronunciation *láboratory*, that *kilómetre* is competing with *kílometre*, and *contróversy* is gaining upon *cóntroversy*. He observes that in many four-syllable words such as *applicable, commendable, comparable, despicable, formidable, illustrative, intricacy, migratory, pejorative,* and *reputable,* usage remains unsettled; but he decides that the initial stress still "bears the cachet of elegance" and, even in England, will probably prevail.

Within Britain, the United States, and Canada, there are many other slight variations of stress, and thus of pronunciation of vowels; some of these variations are social in range and some are regional. Little wonder that Canadians, who are exposed to many kinds of English, often consult dictionaires to find out the "correct" placement of stress in words such as *centenary, compensatory,* or *predicative,* or to see if other Canadians' final vowel in *program* or *record* (noun) is more "correct" than their own—only to discover that more than one pattern is acceptable.

Do you say ['prógræm] or ['prógrəm]? ['rɛkɔrd] or ['rɛkərd]?

"Would you mind repeating that?"

Try taping various speakers saying this question, including British speakers if possible. The intonation pattern that many British speakers use to mean merely "Please repeat that" often suggests anger or disbelief to North Americans.

4. Intonation Differences

Few people realize that the intonations of a language or dialect, that is, the musical aspects of speech, marked by the raising and lowering of *pitch*, carry a great deal of message. In fact, intonation is so

---

* Schwa, also called the "neutral vowel" and represented by [ə] in IPA, refers to the unstressed vowel sound heard, for example, in the first syllable of *above* and the last syllable of *circus*.

highly patterned and so basic within a language—and even within a dialect of a language—that a good mimic wishing to copy a language or dialect learns the intonation patterns as the first, and perhaps the most important, step. Because we frequently tie emotional meanings to changes in intonation, misunderstandings can occur with unfamiliar patterns. The main intonational difference between the two large varieties of English—British and North American—shows itself in the question or request pattern.

Generally, the North American intonation for a question or request demanding a yes/no answer is a long, continuous rise in pitch. The British pattern begins at a high pitch, then falls, and rises again on the last syllables only. A recent study of the intonations used by Toronto teenagers, however, shows that many variations exist, some related to the sex and class differences of the speakers— enough differences to suggest that more research must be done before generalizations may be made about Canadian speech. (C. Seguinot, in P. R. Léon and P. Martin 1976). There may also be subtle differences between and within regional areas of Canada. If, for instance, we say that prairie speech is "flatter" than Ontario speech, what exactly do we mean? Is Maritime intonation different again? In what way?

Canada as a Relic Area: A Canadian Diphthong Rule

Canadian English differs from most British and American dialects in the pronunciation of two diphthongs.* In fact, the two variations can be seen as one systematic "sound rule."

Nearly every non-Canadian notices the way in which Canadians pronunce the "ou" sound in words such as *house, out, shout,* and *south.* The diphthong is not [aʊ] as in most other dialects but [ʌʊ]; that is, it begins with, not the vowel sound of *father* or *balm,* but a centralized vowel (*i.e.* made more in the central part of the mouth) like the [ʌ] in *love,* or a stressed form of the [ə] at the beginning of *above.*

Similar, though less noticeable, is the Canadian diphthong in such words as *white, life, type,* and *mice.* It follows the same pattern in that it is pronounced [ʌɪ], with a centralized first vowel, rather than the southern British and the American [aɪ] with a glide from the vowel sound of *cart* to that of—approximately—*sit* [sɪt].

Yet in words such as *how, houses, housing, rowdy, loud,* and *wide, alive, tidy, knives,* and *high,* Canadians regularly use the diphthongs [aʊ] and [aɪ], as do speakers of the other two major varieties of English. What, then, is this system that Canadians are unconsciously using?

A Canadian can hear the different diphthongs in pairs such as the following. (Caution: don't let the spelling fool you; listen to the *sound* of the vowel before voiced or voiceless consonants. You can also feel the change in the opening of your mouth.)

---

* A diphthong is the blending of two different vowels into one syllabic unit, so that the native speaker hears one vowel sound; examples are the "ou" sound in *house* and *how,* the "oy" of *boy* and *toil,* and the "ay" [aɪ] of *die* and *tile.* Say them very slowly and you can hear the gliding from one vowel sound to another.

Here is how Pyles (1964) contrasts the intonational patterns ("roughly indicated") of "Standard British English" (SBE) and American English (AE):

SBE:
Where are you going to be?

AE:
Where are you going to be?

SBE:
Are you sure?

AE:
Are you sure?

SBE:
Let me know where you're going to be.

AE:
Let me know where you're going to be.

SBE:
Don't tell me that you're sure.

AE:
Don't tell me that you're sure.

Thomas Pyles, *The Origins and Development of the English Language* (1964)

What differences do you hear between the vowel sounds in each of these pairs?

grouse   browse
ice   eyes

	voiced		voiceless
knives: knife	([v]	-	[f])
hide: height	([d]	-	[t])
rise: rice	([z]	-	[s])
loud: lout	([d]	-	[t])
lousy: louse	([z]	-	[s])
how: house	(zero	-	[s])

The Rule
The first part of each diphthong becomes centralized before a voiceless* consonant.

The general English language often marks a switch from noun to verb by voicing the final consonants; when this happens, Canadians also change their diphthongs.

noun (voiceless)	verb (voiced)
my *house* [hʌʊs]	I'll *house* them for a week [haʊz]
my *mouth* [mʌʊθ]	Don't *mouth* your words [maʊð]

Plurals, too, follow a similar pattern, as in *wife: wives, house: houses*, when these also involve voicing.

When words are run together, a diphthong may follow the same rule. Canadians usually say *high* (alone) or *Hi!* with the [ai] sound, but in *high school* (fused, or pronounced as if one word) they probably switch to the [ʌɪ] diphthong (before the voiceless [s]).

Many Canadians use the regular [aɪ] when pronouncing *diaper* with three syllables, ['daɪəpər], as the diphthong is before a vowel, *i.e.* a voiced sound; yet they change to [ɪ] if they drop a syllable, ['dʌɪpər] (as if rhyming with *viper* or *wiper*), because the diphthong now is followed by a voiceless consonant, [p].

Unconsciously, Canadians are following a complicated yet systematic rule.

Where did this feature of Canadian pronunciation come from? There is evidence to show that in Shakespeare's time—the period in which the first British settlers came to North Ameriaca—*all* the front glide diphthongs were pronounced [əi]. Though probably already changing in the seventeenth century, [əu] was also an early pronunciation of the back glide diphthong in all positions. Dialect surveys reveal that scattered instances of these earlier centralized pronunciations still occur in rural parts of New England and in some parts of western New York State. Only in three widely separated areas in North America, however, does the systematic alternation of the diphthongs occur: in Canada and (with some slight differences) in eastern Virginia and a part of South Carolina.

Therefore the [ʌʊ] of *out* and *house* and the [ʌɪ] of *white* and *ice* in Canadian speech are probably relics, reflecting an earlier stage in English pronunciation. These relic features are retained only partially (that is, before voiceless consonants), but systematically.

How Do You Pronounce "khaki"?

One unique Canadian pronunciation illustrates what can happen when a people conscious of their British and North American linguistic backgrounds borrow a word—in this case, the word *khaki* (from India, the Urdu word for 'dust'). Involved are both the loss of

* A *voiced* sound is one in which the cords vibrate; a *voiceless* sound is articulated without this vibration. You can hear the difference by covering your ears and articulating [z] (voiced) and then [s] (voiceless). Vowels are regularly voiced. The difference is important in the phonological system of the English language, in which there is a meaningful contrast between the members of such pairs as [b] – [p]; [z] – [s]; [g] – [k]; [v] – [f]; [d] – [t]; and [ð] – [θ] (e.g. *wreathe/wreath*).

[r], and the [ɑ] versus [æ] difference. The English pronounce the word as [kaː'ki] (that is, no [r]); the Americans use a spelling pronunciation, with [æ], rhyming with *tacky*. Canadians probably first heard the word through Britishers and, accustomed to the Englishman's omission of **r** before consonants, inserted an **r** sound, and made the word [kar'kī] (to rhyme with how a Canadian says *snarky*). A unique pronunciation which, of course, implies a preceding [a], for [ɑ], and not [æ]. At present, with less frequent use of the word *khaki* and with the power of mass media from the United States, there is a movement toward the American pronunciation—that is, if younger people know the word at all. The results of recent surveys suggest that few of them do.

How Do You Pronounce "tomato"?

Sometimes a prestige pronunciation extends to one or two words only. In *aunt*, *rather*, and *tomato*, for example, the [æ] may give way to the British sound [aː]. In fact, *tomato* may have three variations: the vowels of *hate*, *hot*, and *hat*. A survey of the Kootenay area in British Columbia showed definite trends away from the British forms:*

		Adults		Teenagers	
tomato	[e]	(like *may*)	92%	[e]	100%
	[ɑ]	(like *hot*)	8%		
	[æ]	(like *hat*)	none		
rather	[æ]	(like *hat*)	83%	[æ]	96%
	[ɑ]	(like *hot*)	17%	[ʊ]	4%

I was standing on a log in my caulked boots only we call them cork boots. . . .

Henry Pennier, *Chiefly Indian* (1972). Pennier's life story.

Three or four times Mace rushed in to stomp him, finished him off with his calked lumber boots. But each time the smaller man squirmed away, somehow survived.

John Craig, *The Clearing* (1975). About a boy growing up, at a summer cottage in Ontario.

Does the same misunderstanding of a British "r-less" dialect lie behind these two Canadian pronunciations of *caulked*? The two pronunciations have persisted since at least the turn of the century. (See *caulked boots* in the DC for further examples.)

Practical Observations

One can train the ear to tune in to Canadian speech, and one can also listen for some sound changes that are happening right now.

1. How Canadians treat t

(a) In many parts of Canada and the United States, a **t** sound in certain positions may be voiced to a **d** or to almost a **d**. Listen to how people around you, in ordinary running speech, say:

butter (like *budder*?)
kitty (like *kiddy*?)
patio (like pa*dio*?)
teeter-totter (like *teeder-todder*?)

* Courtesy of Dr. R. J. Gregg and his students James Polson (written questionnaire) and Howard Woods (field work), 1970.

Listen to how Canadians pronounce *Ottawa*.

If asked to pronounce pairs, *e.g. bleating/bleeding, better/bedder, waiting/wading*, and the like, such speakers can readily put back the **t**; but in unconscious, informal speech the movement toward or actually to the **d** can be heard.

Canadians also use the correct "Canadian" variants of *i* and *ou* diphthongs in words such as *writer/rider* and *pouter/powder*.

This voicing of the **t** is not "sloppy speech"; it dates back to Elizabethan English or earlier, and is heard also in some dialects of Anglo-Irish and southern English (other relic areas for this sound feature). The spreading of this voicing in North America has been observed and recorded since the late nineteenth century.

How is the local pronunciation of *Toronto* affected by this sound change?

(b) Also widespread in Canada and the United States is the deletion of a **t** in certain positions, especially after an **n**, so that *winter* sounds like (or almost like) *winner*, *centre* like *cenner*, *twenty* like *twenny*, *international* like *innernational*, and *interested* like *innerested*.

Speakers can—as in (a) above—recapture the **t** in conscious or formal speech as, for example, in differentiating between meanings of *an inter-city express* and *an inner city express*, but the deletion is becoming increasingly noticeable in Canada. A Canadian television ad about a dental product insists that the product was "invenid by a denist."

"I dont steal, n' I dont stool. I eat like most a the boys, a twenny-eight cents a day meal scrip, and what I can bum. The Canadian Noo Deal."

A working man in Earle Birney's novel, *Down the Long Table* (1955). Note how the novelist catches the loss of **d** or **t** after **n**, and gives a pronunciation of *new* which is often considered non-standard.

(c) On the other hand, an intrusive **t** may occur between **l** or **n** and **s**—that is, in the sequences **ls** or **ns**—so that *else*, for example, may be pronounced likes *elts*, and *once* may sound like *wunts*. This explains why *dance* is sometimes spelled *dants*.

Barry berry bury

Do you differentiate these in speech?

2. *Mary merry marry*

Do you and the people in your area say all these words in the same way?

Speakers of SSB and of most other British dialects have three distinct vowels in these words. Many older Canadians say *Mary* and *merry* in the same way but *marry* differently. Dialectologists are finding, however, that many younger Canadians are merging these vowel sounds before **r** (when the **r** comes between two sounded vowels) so that all three words sound alike. This change, which happened long ago in the northern and north midland parts of the United States, is now taking place in many parts of North America.

Try testing this item in your area, and see if there is a generation gap, or if the change has already occurred.

Some Other General Patterns in Canadian Speech Sounds
1. *cot/caught, don/dawn, collar/caller, holler/hauler*
Are these pairs homophones for you (that is, do they sound exactly alike)? Most Canadians have merged these two vowels sounds, which SSB speakers and many (but not all) Americans differentiate.

2. *horse/hoarse, morning/mourning*
Are these pairs homophones for you? They are pronounced alike in most parts of North America. But in many parts of the English-speaking world, including the American South, parts of the Midlands, sections of New England and, possibly, parts of the Canadian Maritimes, these words are clearly differentiated, as are the vowels of *forty* and *four*. To know this is to understand why the spelling differentiation is sensible for many English speakers.

Some Other Divided Usages in Canadian Pronunciation

The speech forms of all three large regions—the British Isles, the United States, and Canada—have within them a wide variety of vowel patterns besides the main differences mentioned above. It is not surprising, therefore, to find that Canadian speech sometimes follows a dominant American pattern (especially northern), sometimes the British (SSB) usage, sometimes a mixed pattern, and sometimes its own. Here are some of the main variations:

1. Are the following pairs homophones in your speech?
(Do not be fooled by the spellings!)
   wine/whine, witch/which, Wales/whales, weather/whether, wear/where.
Few speakers of SSB now distinguish between members of these pairs. The older use of [hw] to begin *which, whale*, and so on is now considered old-fashioned or provincial. This change in SSB came about in the late eighteenth century.

How many of these words do you differentiate in speech?

where wear were

In the United States, usage varies: the New England area is evenly divided in usage, but the northern area overwhelmingly keeps the older pattern.

Surveys in Canada show that the pattern is unsettled, some Canadians using [hw] consistently, some using only [w], and others using either—depending on the stress or on the word. For example, a Canadian may differentiate between *weather* and *whether*, yet pronounce *Wales* and *whales* as homophones and use either [w] or [hw] for *wheat* or *wheel*. Sometimes teachers have insisted upon different pronunciations to match the spellings, resulting in people either thinking they differentiate the sounds or differentiating only a few pairs of words.

Our students go and play hockey with their stoodents and our tourists going out meet their toorists coming in.

Stephen Leacock, "I'll Stay in Canada" (1936)

2. Are these words homophones in your speech: do, due, dew?
In both the United States and Canada, the pronunciation of the vowel in words such as *student, news, tune*, and *duke* has long been a speech marker and a social shibboleth. The British generally use a glide (that is, a sound beginning like the **y** of *yes* or the **ee** of *see*, followed by the **u** sound), especially after **t, d** and **n**: this pronunciation, as contrasted with the simple [u] usually found in educated North American, carries much prestige. Surveys of educated people in Ontario show wide individual variation and much inconsistency. Listen carefully to the usage in your area, especially in words like *Tuesday, news, dew, duke, due, tune, student*, and *suit*.

Old Man Hunter spat a stream of tobacco juice over the side of the wagon-box, and wiped his mouth with his coat sleeve. "Any noos from town?"

Edward McCourt, *Music at the Close* (1947). A novel set in a small Saskatchewan town.

How do you pronounce *missile*? to rhyme with *thistle*, or with the last syllable rhyming with *file*? Or either way?

In the 1972 Survey (SCE), from 74 per cent to 88 per cent of the Grade 9 students and their parents chose the pronunciation like *thistle* (generally American), rather than the *file* pronunciation (SSB). (See also page 21 for the example of the rhyme *fertile/turtle* used by the American poet Ogden Nash.)

3. *How do you pronounce the italicized syllable in these patterns? Are you consistent within a pattern?*

(a) *process progress* (noun, verb) *produce* (noun, verb) *profane proceeds*

(b) *agile docile facile fertile futile hostile missile textile virile sterile servile puerile fragile reptile*

It is interesting that, although Americans tend to weaken or even eliminate the vowel of the -**ile** while SSB speakers keep it (so that the example words all rhyme with *mile*), American speakers usually keep it in *gentile, exile, crocodile,* and *domicile*. Canadians have mixed usage, often rhyming most such words with *mile*, but perhaps using the American pronunciation for a few words, such as *missile* or *futile*.

(c) *quinine genuine bovine iodine feline*

Here is how some modern dictionaries describe the pronunciations: AHD is *The American Heritage Dictionary*, 1969-70; OALD is *Oxford Advanced Learner's Dictionary of Current English*, 3rd ed., 1974; DCE (1967 or 1973). The three possible pronunciations are -*in* (rhyming with *fin*), -*ine* (rhyming with *fine*), and -*een* (rhyming with *teen*).

	AHD	OALD	DCE
quinine	-*ine** (Br. -*in*)	-*een* (U.S. -*ine*)	-*ine* or -*een*
genuine	-*in*	-*in*	-*in* and -*ine* (the latter with the warning that it may be "considered vulgar")
bovine	-*ine* and -*een*	-*ine*	-*ine*
iodine	-*ine* -*in* -*een*	-*een* (U.S. -*ine*)	-*ine* -*in*
feline	-*ine*.	-*ine*	-*ine*

Variations occur in all regions. The pronunciation of *genuine* with the last syllable rhyming with *nine* is widespread in Canada, but is considered by many to be vulgar. Walter S. Avis (1973b) points out how persistent this attitude has been in Canada:

> That this shibboleth has a long history in Canada may be inferred from the following bit of doggerel reported by Captain Marryat, an English traveler, in his *Diary in America*, London, 1839 (Vol. 1. p. 217):
>
> To the Ladies of the City of Toronto [1837]
>
> Our ladies are the best kind,
> Of all others the most fine;
> In their manners and their minds,
> Most refined and *genuine*.

Avis comments:

> The italics of the last word reflect the attitude of Marryat toward

---

* This pronunciation of *quinine* stresses the front syllable, which has the vowel of *eye* ('kwaɪ naɪn)

this sample of Torontoese. I personally see no reason whatever for disowning this pronunciation, especially in view of its obvious acceptance by a substantial number of educated Canadians.

This pronunciation is also heard in the Midland area of the United States. Here are the relevant results of the SCE (1972). What differences do you see?

26) *Genuine* rhymes with (A) *fin;* (B) *fine;* (C) either way.

| | male parents | | | female parents | | | male students | | | female students | | |
	A	B	C	A	B	C	A	B	C	A	B	C
Nfld	27	62	7	26	61	7	21	62	16	23	60	16
PEI	19	72	7	23	69	5	17	66	13	17	68	13
NS	25	68	7	33	62	4	24	58	16	24	63	12
NB	24	67	7	34	58	6	23	56	19	22	63	15
Que	31	61	5	41	49	8	37	43	18	37	48	14
Ont	36	58	5	41	51	7	31	53	15	29	53	17
Man	24	73	2	22	72	4	27	53	19	26	56	17
Sask	16	78	5	24	67	8	19	63	16	20	62	17
Alta	18	79	3	27	63	8	24	58	17	28	58	14
BC	31	62	4	40	54	5	34	48	17	40	46	13
Total	24	69	5	31	62	6	26	56	17	27	58	15

What is your own attitude toward the pronunciation of this word?

4. anti- semi- multi-
Most Americans use ['sɛmaɪ] (ending with the vowel of *my*); Canadians generally prefer ['sɛmi] (ending with the vowel of *me*), though the other form is also heard. The two other prefixes follow the same pattern.

Avis reported in 1956 that Ontario teenagers, noticing the pronunciation south of the border, referred to Americans as "the semi's" ['sɛmaɪz].

Variants: Individual Words
There are many words used quite correctly in Canada with various pronunciations. A glance through the *Dictionary of Canadian English* (DCE) will reveal how commonly such variant pronunciations appear in Canadian speech. Here are a few items that people often ask about.

1. How do you pronounce *vase?*
   rhyming with *pause?* (based on SSB, but used by many Canadians and a few Americans)
   rhyming with *face?* (U.S., not often heard in Canada)
   rhyming with *faze?* (widespread in Canada)
   rhyming with *has* or *jazz?* (occasionally in Canada)

2. Do you say *blouse* with an [s] (U.S.) or with [z] (Br.)?

3. Do you use [sk] or a **sh** sound [ʃ] at the beginning of *schedule*? The American pronunciation, beginning like *school* or *scat*, is an older pronunciation: in fact, SSB adopted the **sh** only in the early 1800's. The CBC official use of the **sh** form has helped to advance this British choice in Canada, but the American pronunciation is also strong. Some Canadians now amalgamate the two, beginning the word with **shk**.

4. Do you say *zebra* with [i] (as in *bead*) or with [ɛ] (as in *bed*)? Most dictionaries now give [i] (as in *bead*) as the more common form, and some give *only* this form.

   Avis gives for Toronto (1950's) 52.3 per cent [ɛ] (as in *bed*) and 47.7 per cent [i].

Pronunciation of *drought* in the Maritime Provinces

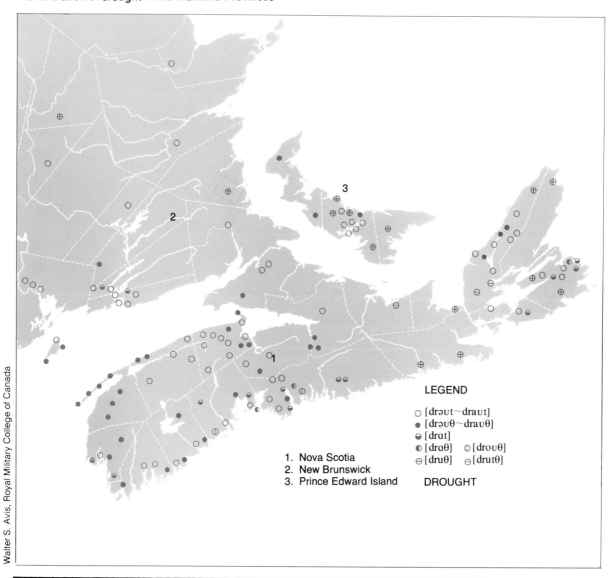

LEGEND

○ [drəut~draut]
● [drəuθ~drauθ]
◒ [drɑt]
◐ [drɑθ]   ◍ [drouθ]
⊕ [druθ]   ⊖ [drutθ]

1. Nova Scotia
2. New Brunswick
3. Prince Edward Island

DROUGHT

Check the Speech Around You

Avis's research suggests that Canadian speech shows these general preferences between British and American usages. What are the preferences in your own area?

been—rhymes with *bean* (U.S. with *bin* or *ben*)

ration—rhymes with *fashion* (U.S. with *nation*)

Z—rhymes with *bed* (U.S. with *bee*)

lieutenant—begins with *left-* (U.S. with *loo-*)

drought—mainly rhymes with *out* (U.S. mainly rhymes with *mouth*; in Pennsylvania, a Scotch-Irish form rhyming with *tooth* may be heard. Variants occur on both sides of the Atlantic.)

again—rhymes with *gain* (Br., and a late change) or *den* (U.S.). (But *against* may be different!)

evolution—begins with [i] (Br.) or [ɛ] (the vowel of *bed*, (U.S.). Compare the two pronunciations of *Evelyn* and of *economical*.

either, neither—have [i] (U.S.) or [aɪ] (the vowel of *ride*, Br.) in the first syllable, but both pronunciations occur in both areas. The British preferred form seems to have become popular as late as the nineteenth century.

nephew—with an [f] rather than [v] (Br.). Here the older form, based on French *neveu*, is the British preference, while the American [f] is probably based on spelling.

Of course, not everyone uses all of these forms, yet all are used regularly by educated Canadians in large numbers. Who can deny that ri zôr'sǝz [rɪ'zɔrsǝz] and (spe'sēz) ['spisiz] are more often heard at all levels of Canadian society than (ri sôr'sǝz) [rɪ'sɔrsǝz] and (spē'shēz) ['spiʃiz], the pronunciations indicated in nearly all available dictionaries? Surely, when the evidence of usage justifies it, forms such as these should be entered as variants in any dictionary intended to reflect Canadian speech.

W. S. Avis, "Why a Canadian Dictionary?" (1966b)

Canadian Innovations

In arguing for a Canadian dictionary (which he eventually edited), W. S. Avis pointed out (1960) that educated Canadians use pronunciations seldom listed in either British or American dictionaries. Here are some of his examples:

absolve [æbzalv]	jackal ['dʒækǝl]	prestige [prɛs'tidz]
arctic [artɪk]	longitude ['laʒgǝ,tud]	resources [rǝ'zɔrsɪz]
chassis [tʃæsi]	official [,o'fɪʃǝl]	senile ['sɛnaɪl]
culinary ['mʌlǝ,nɛri]	opinion [,o'pinjǝn]	species ['spisiz]
finale [fǝ'næli]	placate ['plæket]	
fungi ['fʌŋbi]	plenary ['gsæket]	

How do you pronounce these words? Find their variations (some of which are spelling pronunciations) in various dictionaries:

herb forehead Arctic
against family February

Try some of these words on people you know, and see what pronunciations you hear. If you used one of these pronunciations and an American or British speaker suggested that you were wrong, how would you answer?

Spelling Pronunciations

The spelling of a word may eventually change its pronunciation. The word *often*, for instance, is now frequently heard with the **t** pronounced, although **t** in this position has generally been lost in the language (cf. *soften, listen, Christmas*). Similarly, some Canadians far from the oceans may pronounce the l in *salmon* (cf. *calm, palm, psalm, almond*).

Place names often retain an older pronunciation in their own area but take on a spelling pronunciation for outsiders; *Nanaimo*, B.C., has the vowel of *time* for its second syllable, but may be pronounced with the vowel of *same* by visitors. Port *Dalhousie*, near Toronto, keeps its older sound (as if *Daloozie*), but *Dalhousie* University usually receives the **h** and **ou** sounds of *house* (verb). Place names borrowed from other languages often become changed to their "spelling pronunciation," *e.g. Pouce Coupe* (French 'cut thumb') of the Peace River District is called locally [pusi'kupi]—something like Poosie Coópie. Similarly, the local inhabitants of Bien Fait, a town near the Cypress Hills in Saskatchewan, use the pronunciation "Bean Fate."

Conclusions

Canadian speech in general is much the same as that of the Northern dialect area of the United States, particularly in its use of [æ] in *dance, class*, and the like and in its strong final and preconsonantal **r**. But it also has many Midland American features, many British features, and some features of its own. Its varied settlement history and its ties with the British Isles make inevitable many divided usages, and there is a broad tolerance of such differences. Nevertheless, there does seem to be emerging something like an educated Standard Canadian English, with a grouping of features and choices that marks it as being Canadian. Slowly dialectologists are finding out the Canadian choices.

Grammatical differences

There are very few grammatical differences between British English and American English, particularly when the language is written. The printed word and schooling help to keep the two varieties parallel. Those differences that do exist, however, may cause problems, or at least hesitation, about "correct" usage for Canadians, who are continually exposed to material from the two varieties.

Some differences are scarcely noticeable. The British, for example, nowadays tend to use the article *the* less frequently with institutions as: *He went to hospital* (not *the hospital*) or *He is in hospital*, a pattern North Americans use with only a few words, such as *school, college,* and *university*. This loss of the article in British English is a modern change that seems to be spreading. It is worth investigating in Canada.

British usage also seems to retain the possessive form where North American usage merely compounds the nouns: *barber's shop* rather than *barber shop*, and *grocer's shop* rather than *grocery store*. On the other hand, Americans have kept a very old "adverbial genitive" in expressions like *He works nights*— not a plural form originally but an **s** form to mean 'by night'. This is now seldom heard in England. Its use in America may be reinforced by analogy with the similar structure in modern German, *e.g. nachts* 'nights' or 'at night' (recurring), *morgens* 'in the mornings'. Britishers also notice the colloquial use in Canada of *anyways* ("I'm going to try it, anyways")—though they themselves use the similar form, *always*, which long ago supplanted *alway* in general use. British usage also has social differentiation between *anyway* (no prestige) and *anyhow* (high prestige). There may be a slight meaning difference as well, a point that needs investigation.

There are only a few, usually minor, differences in the use of prepositions. Which of these do you use? If both are in your vocabulary, do you make distinctions?

U.S.	SSB
He lives *on* Thompson Street.	He lives *in* Thompson Street.
There's nothing *to* the rumor.	There's nothing *in* the rumour.
all *of* the dishes	all the dishes
on weekends	*at* weekends

It may be a comfort to Canadian students to know that many of the bedevilling preposition problems, such as choosing *between* or *among*, and *different from* or *to* (*different than* is not British), are also usage questions for British students.

On the other hand, Britishers are often repelled by the North American tendency to use postpositional adverbs with the verb, as

A Canadian six-year-old recently placed in a British school found difficulty with some sentences in her British primer—some involving prepositions and some involving other words, *e.g.*:

"The lorry was standing in the road." The meaning was 'on the road', not 'in the way'. (The latter is a metaphor used in northern England, but not in London.)

We looked in at the windows of the shops.

The children played in the back garden. ('backyard')

They were playing in the wet. ('in the rain')

Have you my biro? ('ballpoint pen')

A similar problem of "two countries separated by the same language" arose when a Canadian teacher told a British schoolchild, "Go and stand in the hall," meaning 'the corridor', and was shocked to find him later, meekly standing in the school auditorium!

How do you use these expressions?
    She's at school.
    She's in school.
Could either, or both, mean 'She is attending school'? British English uses *at* for this meaning; and *She's in school* would mean that she's actually inside the building.

Would you use:
    She's at/in university.
    She's at/in Queen's (Dalhousie, Simon Fraser, etc.).

in *visit with*, *head up a committee* and *refer back to* old business, *meet up with* a friend and *study up on* a subject. The British writer Sir Ernest Gowers (1954), while acknowledging that phrasal verbs can enrich and extend the vocabulary (as, for example, *measure up to*, *face up to*), quotes the following as undesirable Americanisms: *drown out*, *points up*, *sound out*, *lose out*, *rest up*, and *miss out on*. British English is reported to be using this grammatical device with increasing frequency, but there seems to be no comparative survey made of its occurrence in, for example, newspapers of the three areas, Canada, Britain, and the United States. A British observer may also be missing some of the subtle differentiations made possible by this very old device available in English. One writer complained, for example, about someone *sitting in on a committee* when, he said, *sitting on a committee* would have done; obviously he did not realize the difference in meaning.

Some North American/British differences have become textbook shibboleths. The differences between *shall* and *will*, for example, apply only to southern British and not to Scottish or Irish dialects, and have never been transferred to North American English. Yet they still appear as rules in textbooks. Gowers, repeating the old story of the drowning Scot who was misunderstood by English onlookers and left to his fate because he cried: "I will drown, and nobody shall save me," reports that not only does American practice follow the Celtic areas, but "the English have taken to imitating the American"—in other words, the distinction between *shall* and *will* is breaking down. But some distinctions between the two have not disappeared from either variety of English. The truth is that the differences are more subtle than is shown in most textbooks. For example, the difference in meaning between

Shall we adjourn at noon? and *Will we adjourn at noon?*

is not a matter of futurity versus determination but one of polite suggestion versus direct question. It is far better to observe modern usage, in speech and in writing, than to believe outdated textbook shibboleths.

Like North Americans, the British may choose between a plural or singular verb according to the context when the subject is a collective noun (*e.g.* the committee, the council, the team, the government *is* or *are*), but they are much more likely to use a plural than are North Americans. The following British advertising slogan, for instance, seems odd to a Canadian:

BE FUSSY ABOUT YOUR SHERRY
SANDEMAN ARE

This tendency to use the plural verb (and pronoun) came into SSB about the middle of the eighteenth century; North Americans use the older practice of the *idea* governing the choice.

Variant Verb Forms

Like most dialects of English in any area, British and American sometimes go separate ways with verb forms. Canadians often use either, or both. Here are a few examples:

t/d forms

The British often prefer a [t] form (sometimes with a vowel change) where Americans use the regular [ed] form of a past tense or past participle, *e.g. spelt/spelled; dreamt/dreamed; leant* (rhymes with *bent*)/*leaned; knelt/kneeled*. But usage certainly varies within the United States. Sometimes the difference is merely in spelling, not in sound.

Of course, in all varieties of English -t is now the only standard form of the past and past participle of many verbs, *e.g.: crept, felt, kept, left, meant, slept, swept*. Sometimes a differentiation is made according to the use of a past participle, *e.g.:*
  I have *burned* (*burnt*?) the toast.
  The toast is *burnt* (*burned*?).
  I like *burnt* (*burned*?) toast.

do—have—got

Americans tend to use *do* with *have* for questions and negatives, *e.g. "Do you have* a cigarette?" SSB speakers use this for only a habitual action ("Do you have a cigarette every day before breakfast?") and otherwise use only *have* ("Have you a cigarette?").

Canadians may use either of these, or, as some Britishers and many Americans, they may add *got: "Have you got* a cigarette?" Some northern British dialects use *do you have*, and these have doubtless added to the mixture in Canada. Americans have subtle distinctions of meaning between *have* and *have gotten* (see p. 98).

Would you say this? *I wish I could have gotten here earlier.*

Gotten itself is a relic, the usual form in English 200 years ago. Canadians generally use *have got*, but because of American influence the relic form *have gotten* seems to be spreading.

These differences cause other interesting patterns, especially in the spoken idiom. Notice, for example, the following change going on now in SSB, involving *do* in answers to questions.

England (recent, and colloquial):
  Will you help me with this?   Yes, I will do.
  Have you read this book?   Yes, I have done.
  Could you have eaten this?   Yes, I could have done.

The change in meaning occurred in North America, as this anecdote from Newfoundland suggests:

Even three miles across the harbor at Bordeaux the inhabitants used certain phrases which could cause merriment at Arnold's Cove.

Once, when the 'flu was rampant, Great Uncle Tom Eddy rowed down to the cove and, of course, the first question was "And how is all your crowd, Uncle Tom?"

"Only poorly, men. Only poorly. Maggie is all knocked up and Triffle is knocked up and I'm knocked up meself."

In the progressive community of Arnold's Cove the phrase, used by Queen Victoria herself to indicate any complaint or illness, had already become a euphemism for pregnancy.

Ray Guy, *You May Know Them as Sea Urchins, Ma'am* (1975). Selections from columns published in *The Evening Telegram*, St. John's, Nfld. The anecdotes reveal much about the language of the outports.

North America (and possible also in British English, which includes Irish and Scottish):

Will you help me with this?	Yes, I will.
Have you read this book?	Yes, I have.
Could you have eaten this?	Yes, I could have.

There are many other verb forms in which usage varies, *e.g. dived/dove* and *has drunk/has drank*, and even more in the speech of rural areas. Sometimes Canadians follow the British pattern. Canadian parents, for example, usually *bath the baby* more often than they, like Americans parents, *bathe the baby*. Other forms, such as *has drank*, linger on the tongues of many in spite of the strictures of teachers. Most Canadians and most Americans also *sleep in* late rather than *lie in*. The term *sleep in* is "provincial" (that is, Scotch and Irish and outlying dialects) in England. Britishers are also puzzled when North Americans talk of *leafing through* a book. North Americans are amused (or shocked) when an English hotel desk clerk offers not to "call you" but to "knock you up" in the morning. Americans, on the other hand, are sometimes puzzled when a Britisher or Canadian says he or she will "ring up"; and the North American use of *call* for 'telephone' may puzzle a Britisher, to whom *call* means a 'visit'.

North American—but not American

Although Canadians share many features of language with Americans, particularly with those in the northern and midland dialectal regions, they do not share all words and usages. The following lists (adapted from dialect surveys) indicate only a few of the expressions not generally used by Canadians but common in certain regions of the United States.

Do you know what these words mean? All are used in certain regions of the United States.

bonny clabber
cade
ponhaws
croker sack
eace worm
suppawn
milking gap
middlins

Vocabulary

paper container for groceries, etc.	—*poke* (midland), *sack, toot* (from German)
large insect around water (dragonfly)	—*snake feeder* (midland), *snake doctor* (southern), *sewing bug* (*darning needle* or *devil's darning needle* is used in the North.)
doughnut	—*crull, cruller, fat-cake*
to miss school	—*bag school, cook jack, flick, flake school*
tap (British)	—*faucet, spigot, spicket* (But advertising has made *faucet* well known and some Canadians may use it. The word, now American, is a relic, going back to the Middle Ages (from French), when it meant the tap for drawing liquor from a barrel.)

a quarter *till* six (midland and southern; some northern Americans use *of*.)

She isn't *to* home.

They named the baby *at* (or *from*) him.

He's sick *on* his stomach. (midland; also uses *at, in, with*; southern is *of* or *at*; northern is *to*.)

She came over *for to* tell me.

This is *all the further* I can go.

You *hadn't ought* to do that. (northern; southern and midland often use *oughtn't; might could* also occurs in places.)

I *used to didn't*. ('didn't used to')—(south midland)

Non-standard Dialects as Relics

Many of the above grammatical items—and hundreds of others—recorded as existing in American speech are slowly disappearing because they are not supported by the written standard form of English—the language of books, magazines, newspapers, government, and literature. Yet, in spite of the effects of schooling, many of these variants linger in the speech of educated people, even though such speakers may not write the local and regional variants in situations where formal standard English is expected.

So far there has been little study done on non-standard language within Canada, though everyone knows of its existence. What is your attitude toward a speaker who, in a formal situation, says:

I *seen* it (or *seed* it) with my own eyes.

It *don't* really matter.

He did it quite *good*.

To know what is considered standard and what is labelled non-standard is important—though not always simple. In forming *attitudes* about non-standard forms, however, it is salutory to remember that most non-standard features are very old in the language, and are frequently relics of former standard or regional speech. Here are a few North American examples:

get pronounced as *git*—the standard English form in the eighteenth century

boil pronounced as *bile*—the standard English form in the eighteenth century

final *-ing* pronounced as *in*—correct in standard English in the eighteenth century and still heard in British upper class language. The new pronunciation (now standard) is from spelling.

have drank—widespread in North America. Still used (though non-standard) in many parts of southern and midland England.

it don't—used orally until very recently by many well-educated people in the British Isles, and still used in the rural speech of central and southern England. The form *doesn't* was northern

"You git another rock and chuck underneath. We wanta save what we got, she's riz some. . . ."

Ernest Buckler, *The Mountain and the Valley* (1952). Nova Scotian farmer and son, lifting a large rock. The older forms *git* and *riz* are relics and still heard in parts of the Maritimes and New England.

See on page 214 an example of the northern English dialectal form *-s* for the *plural* (present tense) verb in Sir Alexander Mackenzie's journal (1789): "the natives *does*"; this form may still be heard in parts of the Maritimes.

Look at the language of Lord Peter Wimsey, the detective hero of many stories by Dorothy Sayers; he uses *it don't* habitually.

English, at one time limited to the Danish area established by treaty between the Danes and King Alfred in the late 800's. This usage difference has a long history indeed!

In Canada generally, *he ate* (rhyming with *gate*) is the standard pronunciation, and *he "et"* (rhyming with *get*) would be considered non-standard. Yet the latter form is SSB and, though rapidly yielding ground, is current in many parts of the Atlantic states and thus probably occurs occasionally in the Atlantic Provinces of Canada.

Non-standard speech, therefore, need not be termed substandard. One form is *inherently* as good as any other, though one form may lack the prestige of another. But when language is in *use*, the speaking or writing of it becomes a social act—a person or persons expressing a message to other people by means of words—and the use dictates the form to be chosen: the sensitive speaker or writer chooses the language most appropriate to the audience, the situation, and the social context, knowing that the choices made become part of the message.

To label someone else's speech as incorrect or substandard merely because it is different from one's own, however, may be linguistic snobbery based upon ignorance about the variations possible within a language. Differences in speech can be more fruitfully studied as matters of historical, social, and linguistic interest than as items for outright condemnation.

Changes in All Regions: A Reminder
North America has never been completely isolated from the mother country or its literature, and has shared many British major sound shifts, as well as other changes. Shakespeare's language, and therefore the language of many of the first colonists to America, would have pronounced *meat* like present-day *mate*, for example, and both areas have shifted this sound, *e.g.* in *beneath, rear, dear,* and so on. (But the older sound is retained in parts of Newfoundland.) A look at the language of Shakespeare or the 1611 Bible will reveal that many changes in both sound and grammar are shared by all English-speaking areas: *e.g.* the -**eth** to -**s** (*hath* to *has*, *cometh* to *comes*—a change that was going on in Shakespeare's time), the dropping of the syllable **e** in -**ed** (*confinéd* to *confined*), the dropping of some pronouns and verb forms (*e.g. thou art*), and the loss of many words (*e.g. forsooth, nay, thence, wot, yare, usance*). Over three hundred million people, though speaking different varieties of English, nevertheless do share a written language, and even orally their varieties are mutually intelligible.

Susanna Moodie, writing in the 1830's catches some of these archaisms in the speech of the "Yankee" settlers around her. The following is her reproduction of the speech of a young girl:
    . . . No: I just stepped over to see what was going on. I see'd the teams pass our'n about noon, and I says to father, 'Them strangers are cum; I'll go and look arter them.' 'Yes,' says he, 'do—and take the decanter along. May be they'll want one to put their whiskey in.' 'I'm goin' to,' says I; so I cum across with it, an' here it is. But, mind—don't break it— 'tis the only one we have to hum. . . .'

Roughing it in the Bush (1852)

The written language in Canada

Canadian teacher: Spell "color."
Canadian pupil: Which way—British or American?

Canadian Spelling

Canadian spelling, like Canadian vocabulary, is a mixture of British and American practices (or is it *practises*?), and most Canadians are aware of the two systems.

The American changes were largely, though not entirely, initiated by Noah Webster in the early 1800's. Some of his innovations were eventually adopted also by the British; dropping the **k** from such words as *musick, traffick*, and *publick* is an example. American English did not accept all of Webster's suggestions: his 1828 dictionary recommended, for example, *hiz* (his), *giv*, and *proov* (though the **e** after final **v** is quite regular in English), *wel, hed, ruf*, and many others, but none of these caught on with the American people. The British can also innovate occasionally: *tyre* (as on a wheel), for instance, was once spelled *tire* in England. Today (or *to-day*?), with mass media and more direct communication, the two spelling systems are influencing each other extensively. Nevertheless there do exist differences, and from these Canadians make their choices.

Problems in Surveying Spelling Practices

Fortunately, most words of the language are spelled the same throughout the English world. The standard written language is the "broadest" form of English—an *interlingua* that leaps over the barriers of oral dialects, and the one form that all educated English-speaking people and millions of others learn in order to benefit from the knowledge stored in this world of words.

But who sets the standard for disputed spellings? Newspapers, with their millions of words daily, designed for hurried (and space-saving) reading? Government publications? Advertisements, with their many functional innovations in spelling (for advertisements are certainly an influential part of the world of written English)? Books, by different publishers (and many Canadian companies are owned and directed by American firms)? How do even the publishers decide?

Most people in doubt about a spelling consult a dictionary, but frequently do so without checking the date or place of its printing, the source of the editors' decisions, or, least likely, the aims and policy of the dictionary-makers. Such people treat the dictionary as if it were infallible. In Canada many use the OED as the standard, for it carries the prestige of British English and is a truly great historical dictionary, probably the world's greatest. Yet it is several generations old—a new supplement is now being issued in four

cen·tre or cen·ter (sen'tər)
hon·or or hon·our (on'ər)
skil·ful or skill·ful (skil'fəl)

Entries in *Dictionary of Canadian English: The Intermediate Dictionary* (1972)

cen·tre or cen·ter ('sen tər)
hon·our or hon·or ('on ər)
skil·ful or skill·ful ('skil fəl)

Entries in *The Winston Dictionary of Canadian English: The Intermediate Edition* (1970)

volumes (*Vol. 1, A-G,* 1972; *Vol. 2, H-N,* 1976)—and it does not necessarily reflect Canadian practice.

In the United Kingdom, although the OED is the base, the ultimate spelling authority for most printing houses is *The Authors' and Printers' Dictionary,* edited by Frederick Howard Collins. It has gone through ten editions and sixteen impressions since being first published in 1905—a reflection of changing usage and attitudes in Britain. The most recent edition of G. H. Vallins' *Spelling* (1965) devotes 34 pages to showing deviations in the practices of the main publishing houses, newspapers, and dictionaries of Great Britain.

In the United States, there are many excellent dictionaries but, as several scholars have recently demonstrated, these list alternate spellings for over two thousand words and do not always agree on preferred spellings. For example, in five recent dictionaries there are altogether six spellings for *caliph, naivete,* and *parakeet,* eight for *finicky,* and nine for *jinni*; and *disk jockey* is the preferred spelling in two major dictionaries but is not given at all in another. These facts serve to remind us that in the United States, as in Great Britain, there is frequently more than one "correct" way to spell a word.

Canadian Dictionaries and Spelling

The investigation of spelling practices in Canada has been done mainly by members of the Dictionary Committee of the Canadian Linguistic Association, who wanted as much objective and soundly-based evidence as possible for the editors of the new dictionaries that began to appear in the 1960's for use in Canadian schools.

By 1965 Walter Avis reported that, whereas certain American or British forms are "well-entrenched,"

> the degree of preference for one form or the other in such cases varies from word to word, from age group to age group, and from province to province. On the whole, Canadians probably respond to such variants with equal ease, although *connexion* (with an **x**) would doubtless give them more pause than *traveler* (with one **l**).

Because Canadians are largely aware that people sometimes react violently to a variant spelling—to an extent far out of proportion to its importance—they may spell differently for different occasions. A complete Canadian survey, therefore, would involve *who* uses *what form* and *for what function*—an immense task.

The makers of the DCE series use a code to show the more frequently used of the variants, the order being based on the studies and observations made of actual usage in Canada. Even *The Junior Dictionary* gives *woollen or woolen, color or colour, paralyse or paralyze; The Intermediate Dictionary* and *The Senior Dictionary* explain the Canadian spelling situation and elaborate upon this code. The editors did, however, find it necessary to make some arbitrary decisions in order to keep patterns internally consistent (unless there is evidence for exceptions, of course). These are noted in the discussions below.

The editors of *The Winston Dictionary of Canadian English* (Intermediate Edition, 1970), a school dictionary, decided to record "all variant American and British forms" but also to use questionnaires to find "the current styles approved by Departments of Education and educational publishers generally" rather than "those of the news media." Dictionary editors do sometimes set themselves such specific terms of reference. When they do, it is important for the reader to have this information and to take it into account when using the dictionary.

The following summary shows the findings thus far acquired from investigations into Canadian spelling practices. It is important, however, to remember that these investigations are far from being complete or up-to-date. One must also remember not only the wide variation within Canada mentioned by Avis, but also the fact that in neither the United States nor Britain is spelling completely uniform. Even within a well-established pattern, exceptions can occur for psychological reasons: for instance, while the -**or** pattern is almost exclusively used in the United States, *glamour* and *Saviour* persist as the dominant forms.

American Forms in Canada

In the following patterns, which are discussed in detail, Canadians use American forms almost exclusively:

(a) -**ction** (Br. -**xion**)
   connection, reflection, inflection, deflection, and so on (rather than the Br. *connexion* (but see comment below), *reflexion, deflexion,* and so on)
(b) -**ize** (Br. -**ise**)
   recognize, realize, criticize, civilize, and so on (rather than the Br. *recognise, realise, criticise,* and so on)
(c) *some individual words*
   curb, jail, sceptic, tire (rather than the Br. *kerb, gaol* (but see comment below), *skeptic* (becoming rarer), *tyre*)

(a) -**ction** (Br. -**xion**)
This pattern is not completely consistent in British English (Vallins (1965) gives the details, pp. 154–5), and some British dictionairies accept both spellings. The power of analogy favors (or *favours*) the -**ction** spelling, which relates the noun to the verb and often to the adjective, *e.g. connection, connect, connective.* In fact, *connexion* is becoming rare. But *complexion* is standardized in all areas (check the advertisements), perhaps because of *complex.* Britishers (and perhaps Canadians) sometimes use *reflection* for certain senses of the word and *reflexion* for others; compare the adjectives *reflective* and *reflexive.*

(b) -**ize** (Br. -**ise**)
This is a complicated and far from consistent pattern in any area. The problem was created by the English having borrowed this suffix (ultimately from classical Greek verbs ending in -**izein**) through several different sources, especially post-classical Latin as -**izare**

and French as -**iser**. Today -**ize** is a highly productive suffix, being added to almost any stem to form words meaning 'make' or 'become', as *Canadianize, naturalize*, and then their derivatives in -**ation**, as *Canadianization, naturalization*. The DCE records that Canadians use -**ize** for most new words, *e.g. atomize, transistorized*—an indication of the power of this pattern. In fact, the editors of the OED in the 1930's commented that, because nearly all the words derive ultimately from Greek and because -**ize** fits the pronunciation, there "is no reason for special French forms," that is, for -**ise**. Similarly, the *Pocket Oxford Dictionary of Current English* (1969) gives long lists of -**ize** words, and *The Times* follows this pattern generally. Yet many British printing houses prefer the -**ise** forms.

The persistence of the -**ise** spelling may be due partly to the presence in English of many words ending with an **ise** that is *not* a suffix (or in some cases no longer felt to be a suffix). Examples are *surprise, advise, exercise, chastise, comprise, despise, disguise, excise, franchise, supervise*, and *merchandise*. Even *advertise* is frequently found in the United States; in Canada it is the usual, though not exclusive, spelling; and *advertisement* nearly always has the **s** form in both Canada and the United States. Britishers and Canadians also share some **ize** words, *e.g. recognize, size*, and *assize*, but these are fewer in number. Where there is uncertainty, the trend seems to be toward **ise**. Both *surprize* and *enterprize*, for example, were the regular British forms up to the end of the eighteenth century.

Canadians also hesitate between the American-**yze** in words such as *paralyze* and *analyze* and the British **s** forms, *paralyse, analyse*. The latter pattern has the virtue of keeping the connection with the nouns: *paralysis, analysis*.

(c) Individual words

Newspapers and advertisements are probably strong influences toward spellings such as *curb, jail*, and *tire* in Canada. It is interesting that both *tire* and *curb* are the older spellings, which were changed in Britain for their specialized meanings but not in America. Only official British, not books or newspapers, retains *gaol*, just as the official army term in the United Kingdom is *serjeant*, contrary to the ordinary usage of *sergeant*; so neither of these British forms (*gaol* or *serjeant*) is really used or even seen by Britishers in general.

How do you spell the machine that dries clothes—a *dryer* or a *drier*? And does it make your clothes "*dryer* than *dry*," or "*drier* than *dry*"? Do you make any differentiation in the spelling of *flyer/flier* for the various meanings of the word?

Many **y** forms, where most Americans and some Canadians use **i**, are slowly moving out of British usage: examples are *cider/cyder, siren/syren* (some make differentiations for meaning), *siphon/syphon*, and *cipher/cypher*. All areas hesitate between *gypsy* and *gipsy, pygmy* and *pigmy, sylvan* and *silvan*—but most Canadians write *syrup*, not *sirup*. The editors of the DCE decided on the **y** form generally, except for *dike* and *tire*; they also give *pyjamas* as preferred to *pajamas*.

British Forms in Canada

For a few words the British spelling is the only established form in Canada. Unlike Americans, Canadians find it useful to separate *cheque* and *check*, though *exchequer* is universal, and most Canadians would play *checkers*, not *chequers*; and Canadians generally use *axe, catalogue, plough*, and *programme* more often than *ax, catalog* (and other **-og** words), *plow,* and *program*—but the other forms do occur and, influenced by *snowplow*, the shorter form *plow* may be increasing in frequency. The retention of *programme* as a prestige form is interesting, as the word came into English directly from Latin as *program*. The DCE gives the shorter form as the preferred one, to be in line with the other *gram* words and with the recommendation of the OED. Nevertheless, because of bilingualism, it is sometimes an advantage to Canadian printers to use the French form, *programme*. (*Program* is impossible in French.)

Variant Forms in Canada

In other patterns, and in many individual words, the Canadian spelling varies. Writers and publishers choose between the American and the British forms according to the situation (formal or informal; what the audience expects; area; age group), or even the whim of the moment. At one time many Canadian schools taught the British forms of these variables as "the only correct" spellings. Today, knowing more about language change and the history of spelling, and being more sophisticated about the variations within the English spelling system, teachers tend to show Canadian students the choices open to them and suggest that the knowledgeable writer uses the form expected by the audience and is consistent when choosing among variables; such a writer does not, for example, use in the same work both *color* and *colour* or even *honour*.

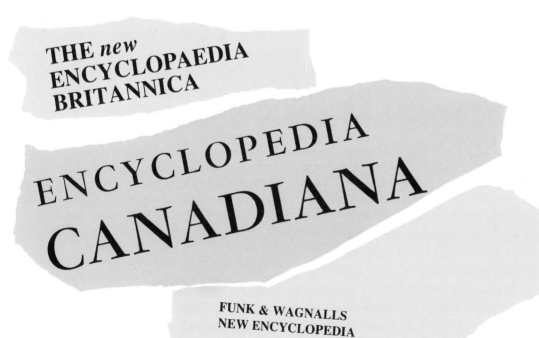

THE *new* ENCYCLOPAEDIA BRITANNICA

ENCYCLOPEDIA CANADIANA

FUNK & WAGNALLS NEW ENCYCLOPEDIA

Main Patterns of Variable Spelling

Following are samples of the main patterns of difference between British and American spelling practices, both or either of which may be used by Canadians.

	BRITISH	AMERICAN	YOURS
(a)	**-our** *colour, honour, flavour, neighbour*	**-or** *color, honor, flavor, neighbor*	
(b)	**-re** *centre, theatre, fibre*	**-er** *center, theater, fiber*	
(c)	**-ence** as a noun ending *defence, offence, pretence, persistence*	**-ense** *defense, offense, pretense, persistense*	
(d)	double l before adding suffix *traveller, travelled, jeweller, grovelled*	single l unless stress is on final syllable *traveler, traveled, jeweler* but *propel, propellor, propelled*	
(e)	usually keeps *digraphs* from other languages *anaemic, oesophagus, mediaeval, manoeuvre, aesthetic, diarrhoea, encyclopaedia*	usually simplifies to **e** *anemic, esophagus, medieval, maneuver, esthetic, diarrhea, encyclopedia*	

(a) **-our/-or**

In Great Britain the **-or** is the shibboleth that marks American. In his discussion of this spelling difference H. W. Fowler is worth quoting at length (1940, 1965).

> The American abolition of *-our* in such words as *honour* and *favour* has probably retarded rather than quickened English progress in the same direction. Our first notification that the book we are reading is not English but American is often, nowadays, the sight of an *-or*. "Yankee" we say, and congratulate ourselves on spelling like gentlemen; we wisely decline to regard it as a matter of argument. The English way cannot but be better than the American way; that is enough. Most of us, therefore, do not come to the question with an open mind. Those who are willing to put national prejudice aside and examine the facts quickly realize, first, that the British *-our* words are much fewer in proportion to the *-or* words than they supposed, and, secondly, that there seems to be no discoverable line between the two sets so based on principle as to serve any useful purpose. By the side of *favour* there is *horror*, beside *ardour pallor*, beside *odour tremor*, and so forth. . . . it would need a very open mind indeed in an Englishman to accept *armor* and *succor* with equanimity.

British spelling already uses many agent nouns in -or: *author, doctor, tailor, sailor, orator, governor*, and others. Moreover, when adding suffixes to -**our** words British English usually omits the **u** before -**ation**, -**ous**, and -**ary** (all Latin), giving *colour, coloration; humour, humorous*, and so on, yet retains the **u** before an English-derived suffix, as: -**hood** (*neighbourhood*), -**less** (*flavourless*), -**ful**, -**ish**, and -**ly** (thus *odorous*, but *odourless*). Before other prefixes, *e.g.* -**able**, -**ism**, -**ist**, custom varies: one might find, in spite of *honorary*, either *honorable* or *honourable* (though in both Britain and Canada the **u** is retained in the official title). Clearly the American use of -**or** could simplify all this.

Canadian newspapers and magazines usually prefer the -**or**, and the DCE gives this as the preferred form. Canadians who do use the base -**our** form are likely to simplify to -**or** when adding a suffix, without regard for the British rules.

A similar pattern of **o/ou** alternatives may occur in words such as *mold: mould, smolder: smoulder, molt: moult*, in which the **u** is usually dropped in the United States but more often kept in Canadian and British practice. *Webster 3* notes that in no area does this pattern extend to *molten* (from *melt*). It is also probably useful to keep *boulder* separated from *bolder*.

(b) -re/-er

The American use of -**er** does not apply after **c**: all areas use words such as *acre, massacre, mediocre*, to preserve the [k] pronunciation. Oddly, this does not apply to the **g**, a pattern with little consistency: Br. *meagre*: U.S. *meager* (usually); all use *eager*, yet *ogre*.

Webster's Third New International Dictionary (1966) points out that, whereas both *theatre* and *theater* are in general use within America, New York City (the centre of the industry) usually employs the -**re** in names and signs.

Some British usage makes complicated differentiations between *metre* for either verse rhythm or the actual unit of measurement and *meter* for the instrument, *e.g. a gas meter*, or its combining form, *e.g. thermometer, hydrometer, diameter, hexameter*. Indeed, this is the pattern indicated by the preferred spellings of the DCE, though the alternative use of *meter* is allowed for in all cases.

Besides carrying the prestige of British, the -**re** form is also useful in Canada because it usually matches the French form. The fact that the Federal Government's Metric Commission has stipulated the spelling *metre* for the unit of measure, and for all its compounds, will undoubtedly help move Canada even more toward the -**re** pattern. Because the -**er** pattern is firmly entrenched in the United States, the possible influence of metrication on American spelling is less predictable.

The -**er** pattern suggests the power of analogy with other English -**er** words. The -**re** pattern, on the other hand, seems to fit better with the adjectival forms, as *central* (not *centeral*), *lustrous, metrical, theatrical*. Two patterns in the language are clashing, and the result is mixed usage.

A survey of the advertisements in a recent issue of *Chatelaine* showed that Kraft cheese has *flavour*, while Kraft marmalade has *flavor!*

What do you think of the following, printed in *Maclean's*, February 1970?
DON'T LABOUR THE POINT! In a bold blow against Americanization, the *Labor* Council of Metropolitan Toronto has asked Bell Canada to change the spelling of its phone-book listing to Metro *Labour* Council, saying the *or* spelling detracts from Canadian cultural identity.

Discuss the spelling used in this Canadian bilingual sign.

INTERPRETIVE
CENTRE
d'INTERPRETATION

Find similar examples. You might, for instance, want to look at the labels on cans and other food containers.

Tire Centre

Only in Canada could this sign appear. Why?

A Canadian university renamed a department as the "_____Center," using the -**er** spelling. The director was amazed at the reaction to this choice of spelling—a reaction ranging from irate phone calls about this "perverse spelling" to one professor's refusal to teach a course he had taught regularly for this department. Eventually, the president of the university decreed a return to the *Centre* spelling. What attitudes may lie behind such reactions? How would you, if you were the director, answer these angry people?

The hard or soft **-g** problem (mentioned above) recurs with variants such as *judg(e)ment, acknowledg(e)ment, abridg(e)ment*, which are in turn like the variants *lik(e)able, liv(e)able, mil(e)age*. In all of these, usage is divided about evenly in Great Britain, and Canadians incline towards the shorter form, though usage may vary with each word.

What attitudes to spelling are revealed in this letter to the editor of a Canadian newspaper?

How disappointing—not one kiss!

Sir—Please note the following entries in the 1972 edition of the Concise Oxford Dictionary:

"bus . . . (plural -es) . . . omnibus."

"buss . . . (archaic) . . . kiss. From the French baiser."

If anyone wants a kiss on the cheek or feels an aching need for a peck upon the forehead then follow the directions kindly provided on several B.C. Hydro bus signs pertaining to "busses."

What disappointment for the eager crowd waiting by the Fourth Avenue-Granville "busses" sign whose nearest thing to a little closeness is the lurching "smack" of the Dunbar tram.

Telephone calls to a variety of B.C. Hydro departments revealed that the head of the sign department, much to his credit, believes strongly in the use of a dictionary. I was told that his research shows either plural usage of bus is correct.

My question is: how long do Canadians have to put up with the kind of schizophrenic attitude evident in not having a uniform standard of proper English, spoken north of the 49th parallel?

I'm sure that I speak for a large, chagrined minority who abhor the way in which our language is being butchered by such commercial monstrosities as "kleen", "hi-life" or "ezway". There is no law penalizing those who cannot or will not spell correctly but as taxpayers and citizens we can expect a crown corporation like B.C. Hydro to spell in a way acceptable to the populace.

At best the sign saying "busses turn here" is a joke, at worst an insult to everyone's intelligence. How can we expect children to respect our language when we adults wallow in our apathetic mudholes blinking stupidly at the signs around us?

Let's keep it "on the buses" and let's start with that sign on the Granville Street bridge.

The *Vancouver Sun*, Jan. 5, 1974

Buses will be rerouted

Headline in same newspaper

(c) **-ence/-ense**

This, too, is not a perfect pattern in any area. Both British and American authorities give, for example, *suspense* and *recompense*, but *experience*; also, the British **c** changes to the **s** before a suffix beginning with a vowel, as in *defensive, offensive, pretension* (cf. Br. *defenceless*).

Some Americans and most Candians differentiate between *practice* as a noun and *practise* as a verb (cf. *practicable*); most Canadians also use *licence* as a noun and *license* as a verb. This tendency toward c as the noun-marker may be by analogy with those (in all varieties) where the sound also changes: *advice/advise; device/devise; prophecy/prophesy*; or possibly with other nouns such as *justice* and *service*.

(d) doubling final l

This is another complicated and not completely consistent rule in British spelling. Generally, the DCE gives both forms as alternatives, with the double l preferred (except that *medalist* is more common than its British counterpart). To make for further confusion, the British often drop an l in verbs if the accent is on the final syllable, whereas the Americans are more likely to keep it, as in *enrol(l), enthral(l), fulfil(l)*, a pattern sometimes extended to derivatives, *enrol(l)ment, fulfil(l)ment*, and so on. All areas have divided usage for some words ending in **s**, e.g. *bias(s)ed, focus(s)ing, bus(s)es, bus(s)ing*, and a few in **p**, as in *worship(p)ed*.

(e) reducing or keeping digraphs

encyclopedia	esthetics	esophagus	diarrhea	fetus	gynecology
or	or	or	or	or	or
encyclopaedia	aesthetics	oesophagus	diarrhoea	foetus	gynaecology

From Latin and Greek comes a set of words which, in the classical languages, were spelled with **ae** or **oe**, often run together as **æ, œ**. Many of them have been reduced to **e**, and some divided usage remains for others. But, as these are usually technical words, both forms are found in all areas. The prestige of the digraph form is also an important factor in choice. The DCE gives the shorter form as the preferred one, except for *manoeuvre* (a word that involves two patterns of difference; note also the convenient tie-in with French).

It is interesting that Canadians who now use the spelling *airplane* rather than the older *aeroplane* often retain in their pronunciation the three syllables of the older spelling. The *aer(o)-* is also used in every area for the combining form, as with *aerate, aerial, aeromechanics, aerosol*, and so on—but *airline*.

Some Individual Variants in Canada
There are many words with variants in both England and the United States, as well as in Canada. The following are the usual British spellings. Find out what the American dictionaires give; examine your own practice; then check with the Canadian dictionaries.

BRITISH	AMERICAN	YOURS
moustache	_____	_____
better or bettor (one who bets)	_____	_____
mileage (usually)	_____	_____
liquorice	_____	_____
employe (for male)	_____	_____
peddler	_____	_____
storey (of a building)	_____	_____

Some other variants for Canadians as listed in the DCE are:

aluminum	aluminium
veranda	verandah
bazaar	bazar
coconut	cocoanut
enclose	inclose
gray	grey
blond (a man)	blonde
curtsy	curtsey
disk	disc
whisky	whiskey

"The study of language is one of the best ways in which a narrow belief in the rightness of one's own way of doing things, and the wrongness of every other way, can be broken down."

Nelson Francis, "Some Dialect Isoglosses in England" (1959)

It is not surprising that Canadians, and Canadian teachers, in particular, welcomed the publication of Canadian dictionaries showing variant forms used by educated writers in Canada. A good dictionary reflects the world of its users, and the linguistic world of Canadians is a complex one. Probably, too, with faster communication, both British and Americans are becoming—as are informed Canadians—more used to and more tolerant of varied spellings. But, because writing is a much more conscious activity than speech, change is more rigorously resisted in spelling than in any other part of a language.

Punctuation

The Canadian writer can be confused also by several differences between North American and British practices in punctuation. These practices differ widely among publishers and printers. They also change rapidly, influenced partly by more and faster communication demanding greater clarity and speed, partly by typographical improvements, and lately by the conventions used in computer programming. Simeon Potter suggests that many recent changes in Britain's Fleet Street were brought about by the influence of the late Lord Thomson, who renounced his Canadian citizenship to obtain his peerage.

In *Changing English* (1969) Potter notes the increasing omission of the period after an abbreviation (unless, of course, needed for clarity), especially after the letters forming acronyms (*i.e.* words made from initials, as UN, UNESCO, CARE, CBC). This practice is an extension of the well established British custom of omitting the stop (*i.e.* period) after an abbreviation when its final letter is the same as that of the full form. Potter uses, for example, *Gk* for *Greek* (but *Lat.* for *Latin*). Potter also approves the simplification of punctuation in postal addresses (though some Britishers still use a comma as in 27, Wells Road). He notices the reduced use of the apostrophe in shortenings and possessives (especially in possessive plurals like *Teachers College, boys shirts*), the disappearance of the hyphen whenever feasible, and a continuation of the trend to reduce capitals to lower case. Americans and Canadians share in all these shifts.

But any change in custom involves a state of flux and thus a problem of correct usage. Some Canadian school texts, for instance, still insist on the hyphenated forms of *to-day, to-morrow*, and *to-night* as the only correct forms, although *today, tomorrow*, and *tonight* are preferred in major dictionaries and are used in most of the print the students read every day. The widespread belief that any change in the language, especially one toward a simplifed form, is an Americanism and a corruption of pure English seems to inhibit change in many Canadian practices.

One difference between British and American practices often sends Canadians to handbooks: the comma before the *and* that closes a series. The British, following the logic that a comma replaces an *and*, usually omit the comma when the *and* appears (unless there is a possibility of ambiguity):

At the meeting were Jones, Fife, Smith and Stuart.
as opposed to:

At the meeting were Jones, Fife, Smith, and Stuart.
Many (but not all) American style books prefer the comma, particularly for academic and reference material. Canadian usage also varies, but tends to include the comma.

Look also for these changes in punctuation practices:

1. A period for a question mark in polite requests:
   "Would you mail this letter for me."
2. Various devices to avoid the clumsiness in the system of quotation marks.
3. A decline in the use of the semi colon.

Chapter 2

From Aboideau to Zing-ping: How Canadians Make Words

QUIZ

Do You Speak Canadian?

All these words are Canadianisms: words made up or developed by Canadians in a unique way. All are described in the DC. How many of these Canadian words do you know? The answers are given at the end of the quiz.

1. A *McIntosh red* is:
   (a) a communist Scot   (b) a special tartan developed in Nova Scotia
   (c) a berry used for pies
   (d) an apple.

2. A *bombardier* is a:
   (a) military officer   (b) ski-mobile   (c) French Canadian canoe   (d) Canadian politician.

3. A *boondoggle* is a device to:
   (a) whistle at girls   (b) fish through ice   (c) whistle for your dog without annoying your neighbors
   (d) take up the slack of a chin-strap.

4. If you win *The Brier* in Canada, you win a contest in:
   (a) pipe-smoking   (b) land-clearing   (c) curling   (d) making blackberry jelly.

5. If someone gives you a *shivaree*, you have just:
   (a) won a prize at bingo   (b) got married   (c) started a garden
   (d) started a zoo.

6. A *four-pointer* is a:
   (a) heavy blanket   (b) demerit for double-parking   (c) reliable hockey player   (d) teacher heavy on discipline.

7. To *jacklight* means to:
   (a) take on an extra job   (b) hunt or fish at night with a light   (c) smoke illegally   (d) start a fire with twigs cut with a knife.

8. The slang term *hootch* meaning 'homebrew, liquor' was originally:
   (a) a Scottish dialect word   (b) a word meaning 'steal'   (c) the name of an Indian village   (d) an Irish term meaning 'drink'.

9. *Larrigans* are:
   (a) toboggans   (b) hoodlums, toughs   (c) substandard horses   (d) moccasins that reach to the knee.

10. A *go-devil* is a:
    (a) facetious term for a preacher
    (b) wild driver   (c) crude sled used for hauling   (d) small sturdy airplane.

11. A *mackinaw* is a word that originated in:
    (a) an Indian name   (b) a Scottish name   (c) a corruption of "Mackenzie King"   (d) a British firm's name.

12. To be elected by *acclamation* means in Canada that you are elected:
    (a) with no opposition   (b) with a great shout   (c) because you are famous   (d) with a huge majority

13. To call someone a *Bluenose* is to say he or she is:
    (a) a teetotaller   (b) a hockey fan
    (c) a Nova Scotian   (d) a puritan.

14. A *camp robber* is:
    (a) a packrat   (b) a Canada jay
    (c) a transient pickpocket
    (d) a tax inspector.

15. *Frazil* is:
    (a) how you feel after a party
    (b) a shelter for ice-fishing
    (c) ice crystals on water
    (d) a fish stew.

ANSWERS

15. (c)	12. (a)	9. (d)	6. (a)	3. (d)
14. (b)	11. (a)	8. (c)	5. (b)	2. (b)
13. (c)	10. (c)	7. (b)	4. (c)	1. (d)

New words for new surroundings

What do people do when, placed within a new environment, they come upon plants and animals unknown to them, unfamiliar features of landscape, and (as they begin to form a society) new customs and new ways of thinking? How do they adapt and expand the language they brought with them so that it will express what is happening in their changed lives?

Faced with this need to give names to new objects, experiences, and ideas, Canadians have built up a large vocabulary of their own. Some of these words and expressions are native to Canada; others, though not exclusive to Canada, carry special Canadian meanings or are distinctively characteristic of Canadian usage. Scholars have already collected these Canadianisms which have appeared in print and described them in the DC—a book with about 12 000 entries. It is the main source for this chapter. Such a dictionary is not merely a list: it is a record of the unique experiences of the English-speaking people in Canada.

A study of the meanings of the word *Canada* itself, for example, reveals almost an encapsulated history: the origin of the name obscure but probably from the Iroquois language to French; the earliest known use of the name in print in 1536; and its meanings expanding with settlement and Confederation. *Canadian* at first referred to an Indian or an Eskimo, and until well into the nineteenth century to a French Canadian, revealing similar changes of meaning according to time and place. As late as the 1970's, a Nova Scotian talking (in Broadfoot, 1973) about his childhood during the Depression in the 1930's, uses the word *Canadian* with a special regional sense:

> I was hidden in the pantry off the kitchen and heard him say to my mother that the banker had said there were no loans left, especially for shore people, us, with no fish markets, and on and on and on. Dad was really ferocious about that banker, let me tell you, and he called him a 'damn Canadian'. He meant the man was from Ontario, an Upper Canadian, and that was not good. He wasn't from Nova Scotia. He didn't understand our ways. . . .

The ways in which Canadians have made their own words are those employed by the speakers of any language. For, whether a person is ingenious or trite as a word-maker, that person has only so many linguistic devices or "operations" to work with. There are thirteen main methods of making vocabulary, which may be grouped into three:

A. extending the use of words already in the language;
B. creating new terms from the resources of the language;
C. borrowing from other languages.

"Language fulfils its role to no small extent by the very fact that its users are able to change it."

Randolph Quirk, *The English Language and Images of Matter* (1972)

A. Extending the Use of Words Already in the Language

1. Extension of Meaning

A quick and easy way to name a new object is to give it the term used in the home country for something similar. It is often easier to use an existing word than to make up a new one. An example of such extension of the meaning of an old word, one noticed by every Britisher on coming to North America, is the use of *robin* to name a bird that is really a large thrush, different in size and color from the European bird but similar to it in having a red breast.

Examples of Canadianisms that are extensions of previously existing words are:

> *crocus* (on the Prairies) for 'anemone'; sometimes *prairie crocus* to differentiate, and also called *prairie smoke* (not a Canadianism), *sandflower*, and *windflower*
>
> *band* 'group of Indians in a given area and recognized by the government as a group'; hence such compounds as *band list, band constable*, and *band council*
>
> *bridle* 'loop of a snowshoe in which the toes are placed'

One could make a long list of words borrowed from regular English and given different meanings to name aspects of Canadian government systems: *reeve* (almost a lost word in the home country), *county* (used in various ways within Canada), *by acclamation, confederation, sessional indemnity, sheriff* and *sheriff's sale*, and of course all the phrases made with *province*—enough old words used in new ways to make our political and legal systems sometimes seem strange to both Britishers and Americans.

The Canadian use of the word *riding* to mean 'an electoral district' is unique. Historically, it was used in Upper Canada at first to mean a subdivision of a county, a meaning in line with its British counterpart, where it was applied in particular to Yorkshire, whose three ridings were originally *thridings*, from Norse meaning 'a third part'. The **th-** of *thriding* became assimilated with the preceding **t-** or **th-** in the compounds *East Thriding, North Thriding*, and *West Thriding*, reducing the word to *riding*. In England the term had nothing to do with national politics; but in Upper Canada the word referred first to an administrative division and was later extended to an electoral district. From Upper Canada this extended meaning spread to the whole country.

The word *bush*, which in England means merely a shrub or clump of shrubs, illustrates how circumstances in new countries can bring about extensions of meaning. In both Canada and Australia *bush* was applied to the unsettled, uncleared areas, the "back country" whether wooded or not, as opposed to the "town." In Canada it was extended further to mean the forested wilderness. In the two colonies there thus developed scores of phrases and compounds, *e.g. take to the bush, bush fire, bush telegraph, bushman* (with a special meaning in Australia), *bushranger*, and *bushwhacker*. Often *bush* gathered connotations of 'anti-town' or 'peculiar' or 'unsophisti-

Royland came to the door, looking old as Jehovah. Wearing his plaid wool bush jacket and heavy denims.

Margaret Laurence, *The Diviners* (1974)

56

cated'. To be *bushed* may mean to either an Australian or a Canadian 'lost in the bush' or 'lost' generally; but to Canadians *bushed* may also mean 'crazy', 'terrified', 'exhausted', 'alienated', or 'acting strangely as a result of being isolated from other people', 'confined to the wilderness', or 'living in the wilderness by choice'. A *bushed* Australian wants to get out, but a *bushed* Canadian may not want to return to civilization at all. The various special Canadian meanings of the term lie behind Earle Birney's poem "Bushed" (1951), and behind Joyce Marshall's story "The Old Woman" (Weaver and James 1952) in which this dialogue occurs:

Bush jacs: they take the bite out of winter

> "What do you mean?" he demanded.
> "Just that you had three years here alone," she began.
> "I have never been bushed," Toddy interrupted furiously. "How dare you suggest that such a thing could ever happen to me? . . ."

In New Zealand *bush* more specifically suggests 'forest', and the word *backblock* or *back country* (the latter also in Canada) is used for 'non-town'. (For a fuller discussion of *bush*, see G. W. Turner (1966) for Australia, and the DC for Canada.)

Any special activity demands a special vocabulary, much of which may be created by extension. In the context of hockey (*ice hockey* outside Canada) almost any Canadian knows the special meaning given to otherwise ordinary words such as *boarding, blueline, icing, cushion,* and *crease*. Some such special terms may be extended to ordinary life: a Canadianism in mining circles, *hardrock* 'mining in solid rock, usually in quartz', has been extended by Canadians to describe any tough or stubborn person, *e.g.* a *hardrock player*, or a *hardrock Protestant*. One word may also be extended in different ways in different regions, *e.g. range* as used in various parts of Canada.

Note the extension, in sports slang, of the meanings of *homebrew* and *import* to the special Canadian meanings.

In this newspaper headline, *homebrew* is extended to refer to racehorses. (The British Columbia government allows a bonus for horses bred in the province.)

Homebrew bonus incentive

The *Vancouver Sun*, Dec. 20, 1976

2. *Personal and Geographical Names*

Words may become deliberately or casually linked with the name of the originator, inventor, or place of origin. Such words are usually compounds.

McIntosh apples—from John McIntosh, born 1777, of Dundas County, Upper Canada, the original grower of these famous apples

Menzies spruce—from the man on Captain Vancouver's 1792 expedition who discovered the species

Peterborough canoe (or *Peterboro*)—after the place

Quebec heater—a famous type of heating stove

Winnipeg goldeye—from the lake in the region of which the fish are found

Madeira fish—in Newfoundland, second grade codfish, once used to supply the Spanish and Portuguese markets

Digby chicken—in the Maritimes, named after Digby, N.S., and referring to a small smoked herring; the salted fillets are *Digby chips*.

Some proper nouns may be replaced and almost forgotten as

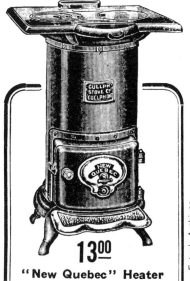

13.00
"New Quebec" Heater

names yet continue as common nouns. Although *Ottawa*, since 1855, has replaced *Bytown* (named after Colonel By, who built the Rideau Canal) the word *Bytowners* is still used, and the mineral *bytownite* (a form of feldspar) remains in the language.

A Red River cart

The workmen wore red and black mackinaws and caps . . .

Hugh MacLennan, *The Watch That Ends the Night* (1959)

Do you know what these are? A cake plate that was Mother's, heaped with softening Nanaimo bars, sits on Algertha's kitchen table. . . .

Merna Summers, "The Blizzard," in *The Skating Party* (1974). Stories about Alberta.

Well known in B.C., *Nanaimo bars* are a confectionery made with a chocolate-coconut-biscuit mix as the base, a layer of a creamy mixture, and iced with chocolate.

A proper noun may become a common noun by frequency of use. The ordinary *mackinaw* that a Canadian wears (a short, belted coat or jacket made of heavy felted woollen cloth) has a long history, going back to fur-trading times in the area of Michilimackinac Island at the head of Lake Huron—when *mackinaw* could also refer to a blanket, a fur-trading company, or a boat—and coming originally through Canadian French from an Ojibwa expression meaning 'Great Turtle', which described the shape of that island. This movement from a proper to a common noun is really a special form of extension. Other Canadian examples are:

Cabbagetown—once a depressed area in Toronto, but now generalized, referring to any rundown urban area

Grit 'Liberal', from the American expression 'clear grit', 'obstinate', 'unflinching', a term given to an 1840 reform group in Upper Canada and then generalized to any Liberal

albertite—a hydrocarbon used for oil and gas in the nineteenth century and named after Albert County, N.B.

stanfields 'long underwear', from Stanfields Limited, a knitting manufacturing firm in Truro, N.S.

bombardier—a winter vehicle with skis at the front and caterpiller tracks at the back, at first a trade name, after Armond Bombar-

dier, the inventor; now any road used by these vehicles is a
bombardier trail

shediacs—famous oysters from Shediac, N.B.

Names frequently become the source for slang terms for a general
class of people. Some, like *dogan* (from the surname) for 'Irish
Roman Catholic', are at least mildly derogatory. The name *John*
is especially productive in English, and has produced some
Canadianisms, *e.g.*:

Jean or *Jon Baptiste* (also *Joe*)   'French Canadian'
Johnny Canuck   'Canadian'
John Company   'Hudson's Bay Company'

The name *Jack* has long been a form denoting 'humanness', 'male-
ness', or 'male worker' in the English language (witness *steeplejack*,
jack-o'lantern, and *Jack Frost*) and some Canadianisms follow this
pattern: *jackfish* (also called *jacks*), *jack salmon*, *jack herring* (B.C.), *jack
rabbit*, and *lumberjack*.

3. Metaphor
In some ways a metaphor is another subset of extension. A metaphor provides a basic and often vivid way to project the meaning of
one word to something else that is quite different yet similar in one
way; a metaphor therefore involves the power of an image. Some
Canadian examples follow:

A corduroy road

corduroy road, a road made by putting down logs, making a bumpy
   surface like that of ribbed corduroy cloth. (In Australia a corduroy is a rut across a road.)
fiddleheads, not strictly a Canadianism, as it is used also in parts
   of the U.S.; but for Canadians, fiddleheads are associated especially with New Brunswick: 'edible, tightly-curled heads of new
   fern fronds'—so named because of their shape
fairy shoe small pink orchid that grows wild
boiler 'a stretch of seething water, as below a waterfall'
lilypad ice 'small rounded cakes of ice, about 45 cm in diameter'
   (North). A *lily pad*, in B.C., may be a "round" (slice) cut off a
   large log.

Canadian weather seems to produce many metaphorical terms; a
few representative ones are:

frost boil (or, simply *boil*), an eruption in a road produced by frost
skin ice, (North) 'thin, new-frozen ice'
black ice, transparent ice formed on roads after rain, especially
   in B.C.
silver thaw, a thaw that leaves frost hanging from trees—known in
   Newfoundland as *glitter*

An example of a vivid metaphor (1971, on radio) related to function is *bird-dog plane*, 'a plane that leads a water-bomber to the
correct position over a forest fire'. (This is not in DC, and may have
originated in the U.S., but the context was a Canadian story.)

Much slang and humor can be expressed in metaphorical coinages. In Canada some seem to have been based on a need to make life more bearable under harsh pioneer conditions. Typical are:

homesteader's fiddle or *misery fiddle* 'crosscut saw', (before the days of the power saw)

homesteader's Bible 'mail order catalogue' (also known as *The Book*)

jawbone 'store credit' (in the West especially), presumably because of the necessary persuasion

beanery 'cheap eating-place'

skypilot or *sky agent* 'missionary or clergyman'

chain lightning 'cheap whisky'

talkie-tooter lumber camp slang for an electronic device that blows the danger signal

Canadians also use metaphor to find facetious names for people living in various regions:

Bluenosers, Nova Scotians, sometimes extended to those from New Brunswick. The origin of this well-known term is uncertain.

Spud Islanders, people of P.E.I.—famous for its potatoes

Herring Chokers, Maritimers, but usually those from N.B.

Slackers, naval slang for 'Halifax', probably because of the relaxation from discipline when a ship is in port.

Saw-off—a term of Canadian politics

A. F. Chamberlain (1890) noted the Canadian invention of this metaphor (used as a noun or verb) to describe a particular manoeuvre of politicians:

. . . this is used when, in the same constituency, a member of one political faith having been elected to the local legislature, and one of the opposite faith to the federal parliament, or *vice versa*, and petitions alleging corruption, etc., having been entered in the courts, it is agreed by the parties concerned to withdraw all petitions, the Liberal member for the local legislature retaining his seat, and the Conservative being allowed to occupy his seat in the federal chamber. This expression was especially current in 1887-8; further back I am not able to trace it.

An early Canadian novel has a political "saw-off" as a central episode:

"It's the most natural thing in the world that you should want to clear yourself definitely . . . . On the other hand, I think it quite possible that you exaggerate the inference that will be drawn from our consenting to saw-off with the other side on the two principal counts.

Sara Jeanette Duncan, *The Imperialist* (1904)

Later this slang term came to be used for, in the words of the DC, "an arrangement between two political parties by which one agrees not to enter a candidate in a certain riding if the other agrees not to enter a candidate in a different riding."

Now the term is used for any kind of trade-off—even for a draw in a hockey game:

Canucks Manage Sawoff

Vancouver Sun, Jan. 23, 1978

B. Creating New Terms from the Resources of the Language

4. Compounds

Do you know what these Canadianisms mean? Do you use them?

(a) Six o'clock in the evening, there's a CPR *dayliner* stops at Hainesville.

    Alden Nowlan, "The Girl Who Went to Mexico" (1968)

(b) When a *crown fire* struck down the far side of the river . . . firefighters felled the tree by the barn.

    Roderick Haig-Brown, "Autumn" (1950)

(c) If signs are to be trusted, the *ice-run* for the last 500 miles of river must have been terrific.

    Jack London, "From Dawson to the Sea" (1899)

(d) 'I was sitting in a *beer parlour* with a crowd of total strangers, we were glued to the set, and the moment Bannister pulled out to pass, everybody in the room picked up his rhythm.'

    Hugh Hood, "The End of It" (1962)

(e) The Wheatsheaf's *beverage room* is gloomy and functional but it is distinguished from other gloomy and functional *beverage rooms* by the quality of its floor.

    Harry Bruce, *The Short Happy Walks of Max MacPherson* (1968)

and every teamster with such a pride
before God and Life in himself
that he piled his log load as near the sky
as he dared go and not touch heaven
on earth he called it the "brag load"

    Al Purdy, *In Search of Owen Roblin* (1974). About his grandfather, who at eighteen ran teams near Renfrew, Ontario.

A speaker faced with the problem of naming a new object or situation may merely combine words already known, making a compound term that seems appropriate. This is probably the most frequent way in which Canadians create the new terms they need.

Often the first word of the compound is a modifier that gives the new term a specific meaning within the general meaning of the second word, or head word. From the French Canadian word *prairie* have come dozens of new terms: *prairie crocus, Prairie Provinces, prairie wool* (a grass), and *prairie squint* (characteristic of farmers who have worked years in the sun) are but a few on a possible list. Any Canadian can make other lists of compounds using as either the modifier or the head word such important words as *snow* (e.g. *snow blindness, black snow*), *ice, canoe, beaver, buffalo, moose, log, river*. Or one can make compounds with a proper noun or its adjective as the modifier, for example:

Hudson's Bay *blanket, start, style*
Canada *lynx, stove, thistle*
Canadian *balsam, boat-song, honker*
Indian _____
Western _____
French _____

. . . Then about eight P.M. he would make a Hudson's Bay start for Namko, pausing for a partial night's sleep about one hundred miles west of town.

    Paul St. Pierre, *Breaking Smith's Quarter Horse* (1966)

Most of the terms so made would be phrases peculiar to Canada.

Many Canadian combinations of words which seem ordinary enough to Canadians are unfamiliar elsewhere. Here are a few; do you know them?

fishing banks, staking rush, bush pilots (who sometimes go on *mercy*

A NEW WORD?

flights), *interdiction list* (also called *interdict list*, or *Indian list*, and in B.C., *Siwash list*), *mosquito-smudge*, *sugaring-off*, *swim-ups*, *tar-sands*, and *moose-deer berry*

Once a compound is accepted, another may be coined by analogy. In Canada a town owned by a company is called a *company town*; its opposite has come to be known as an *open town*. When an injunction prevents union members on strike from forming a picket line, non-union sympathizers sometimes form a *citizen picket line*, or become (in British Columbia, at least) *mystery pickets*, which "mysteriously" come and go.

Customs peculiar to Canada or one of its regions may produce compounds motivated by a need for euphemistic alternatives. Canadian drinking laws, for example, have produced *beer parlors* or *beverage rooms* in hotels. The same regulations helped to extend the meaning of *hotel*, so that in informal speech "Let's go to the hotel" means "Let's go to the beer parlor and get a beer." In some provinces a room given a temporary licence for serving liquor at a "wet" social occasion may be called the *hospitality centre*.

The term *New Canadian* probably arose as a euphemism to avoid *immigrant*. Australians use the similar compound *New Australian*. In Canada (and possibly elsewhere) a rather curious euphemism has come into use recently, the word *ethnic* as a noun, *e.g.* "Being married to an *ethnic* gives you a new perspective on your own background."

Some compounds reveal other human motivations for special naming. The lumber industry, for example, had its *sawdust nobility*, *lumber kings*, and *timber barons*, and the annual loggers' convention in British Columbia is known as the *Loggers' Parliament*.

Slangy compounds often "stick" because they involve repetition of sounds: *sin bin* and *rink rats* are part of Canadian hockey vocabulary; *Sea Flea* was the name given to a tiny speedboat. *Baby Bonus* for the Family Allowance and the *funny money* of Alberta's Social Credit Party are now "historical" for many young Canadians.

5. Blends

Parts of two words may be run together, usually deliberately, to coin a new term. When Canadian biologists created two hybrid fish, they gave them the hybrid names of *splake* (from *speckled* and *lake* trout) and *muspike* (from *muskellunge* and *pike*). An experimental cross between prairie buffalo and domestic cattle resulted, of course, in *cattalo*. The naming of a hybrid normally involves taking the first half of the new name from the name of the female parent, the second half from the name of the male parent.

Between his winter jobs and school back in Edmonton he managed to acquire status as a likeable "rink rat". In exchange for sweeping the ice and the stands he got free ice time.

From a story about John Bucyk by Andy O'Brien, *Weekend Magazine*, Nov. 2, 1974

STALKING THE EDIBLE CHEASANT, CATTALO

GUELPH, Ont. (CP) — Cheasants and cattalos might be main dishes on future Canadian menus.

Both are hybrid animals being developed by University of Guelph researchers, one a cross between a chicken and pheasant and the other the offspring of a cow and bison.

Prof. P. K. Basrur of the department of biomedical sciences is investigating hybrid problems to better understand genetic aspects of cross-breeding. But the researchers also hope to develop two commercially-viable animals for consumption as well.

Prof. Basrur first heard of cheasants when she read that ancient German monarchs bred them for feasts. But she is facing the same problems as the old kings—sterility in the male hybrids and lack of functional reproductive organs in the female.

Several breeding projects involving cattalos have been carried out in North America since the turn of the century, but none of these produced a commercially-viable animal because of sterility and difficulty at calving time.

The Canadian Press, November 22, 1974

Another "Cheapstakes" planned

BURNS LAKE — The Burns Lake Rotary and Kinsmen Clubs will jointly sponsor a new "Cheapstakes" lottery to raise money for the Burns Lake artificial ice fund.

Burns Lake Mayor John Baker said tickets will go on sale in July with the drawing of the winners set for some time in December.

Cash prizes will continue at $2 500 for first, $500 for second and $200 for third.

The *Vancouver Sun*

Some Canadian blends are old: in Newfoundland, *fishocracy* described for at least a century the well-to-do merchants and officials who held the money and power. (New Zealand had a *squatocracy*.) A more recent blend, Saskatchewan's *Medicare* Plan (1962), has developed to a common noun *medicare*, and *denticare* has been formed by analogy. The term *medicare* has spread into the United States, but usually with the narrower sense of a government health program for the aged. *Medicaid* (for the poor) is another term used south of the border. A similar term *judicare* 'provision of legal services to persons of low income' seems to have been coined in the United States. Another well accepted Canadian blend is *permafrost*.

A few blends begin as slang or derogatory terms, but become accepted because of repetition, particularly in newspapers. Examples are *Socred* for 'Social Credit' or 'Social Crediter' and *boxla* for 'box lacrosse'. Some begin as trade names: the romantics may be distressed by the appearance in our North of a fibreglass igloo, named a *Polygloo*. Some blends arise from the sheer fun of coinage: *e.g. bruck* 'a bus and truck, carrying both people and freight' in the North; or an Edmonton blend of ping pong and badminton, named *pingminton* (apparently players use large table-tennis bats to hit a badminton bird over a volleyball net!); or the invention by the people of Burns Lake, British Columbia, who, finding that their announced sweepstake would be limited by law to small prizes, decided to run a *cheapstakes* instead. A coined word such as *cheapstakes* may be used only once—a nonce word—and may never be entered in a dictionary.

Floatathon set for centennial

ENDERBY — Residents of Grindrod will float down the Shuswap river later this month to raise funds for a new community hall.

The community has decided on the floatathon as a means of raising money for its centennial project, a new hall to replace one destroyed by fire in 1968.

The object will be to float from the launch site near Enderby in any type of home-made craft except a boat, and float downstream to Grindrod. The winner will be presented with the "Huck Finn" award.

Sweepstake tickets will be sold on the race which will start at 10 a.m. on Sunday, June 20th. The same day, a centennial picnic and old-fashioned fun day will be held in Grindrod Park to coincide with the floatathon.

In the evening, a bonfire will be lit to dispose of all rafts used in the event that owners don't want to take home.

Plans call for the purchase of the Women's Institute hall with the proceeds and have it renovated for a community hall.

The *Vancouver Sun*, June 2, 1971

Create for yourself an endurance "event" and give it a name ending in **-thon**.

onomatopoeia — Gr. *onomata* 'word, name' + *poios* 'making'

Canadians also follow fashions in blends: plays upon the word *marathon* resulted in a *rockerthon* in Montreal, and a *floatathon* in a British Columbia town, by which competitiors floated down the river in anything but a boat.

6. *Onomatopoeia*

Occasionally a word or blend seems to be imitative of some specific sound. A *rattle*, 'small waterfall in a mountain stream', seems to be a Newfoundland coinage of this type. Another Newfoundland word is *sish*, 'ice scum', which was probably influenced by *slush* and *swish*. Some Canadian birds and animals have received special names imitative of their calls, *e.g. chewee* (or *cheweek, chewink, pewee*) for the eastern towee, and *chickaree* for a species of squirrel that chatters. One must be careful, however, in assigning sound symbolism as the basis for the creation of a word for which we already know the meaning, as the relationship may be only in our own minds. (See Folk Etymology below.)

7. Acronyms

SPEC, NATO, UNICEF, CARE. . . . The twentieth century seems to delight in creating words, especially "catchy" names of organizations, by using initials. Though more conservative than the United States in this word game, Canada has a few such coinages that are nationwide, as well as numerous local ones. The *SARAH* beacon (Search and Rescue and Homing), a safety device used for aircraft, is a forced but typical example. The *DEW Line* (Distant Early Warning) is now obsolete. Some initial groups are used so often that they are almost words: from *CBC* and *NDP*, for example, Canadians form derivatives such as *NDPer*, *CBC-types*, or *CBCite*.

Both computers and the recent explosion of government agencies have added to the bewildering number of acronyms. *CANUNET*, the computer acronym for 'Canadian University Computer Network', a pilot project for a cross-Canada electronic postal service, and *LIP* grants, 'Local Initiative Projects', are Canadian examples.

Perhaps more common, especially in Canadian slang, is the opposite process, the making of phrases to match well-known initials: the Hudson's Bay Company has been given many humorous nicknames, *e.g. Here Before Christ* (or *Columbus*), *Hungry Belly Company*, *Hell's Blackest Curse*, and *Heaven's Bad Charter*. The CNR and CPR are two other favorite victims of this naming game.

acronym—Gr. *akro* 'tip' + *onyma* 'word, name'

—George Diack Photo

CANUNET: un "service postal" électronique de Halifax à Vancouver

Newspaper headline, Regina, April 30, 1973

Vancouver Sun Photo

◄ TOUGH, TINY STEEL-HULLED dozer boats, as manoeuvrable as quarter horses, ride herd on log booms all over the B.C. coast. On Burrard Inlet below Barnet Highway, east of the Texaco plant the seagoing bulldozers slam into logs of all sizes.

The *Vancouver Sun*, Nov. 13, 1975

8. Shortening

To make the language simpler or to show familiarity, speakers often shorten a word. The new word may remain merely slang, or it may be used generally and accepted as a word in its own right. Canadian examples are numerous:

Mountie 'North West Mounted Police' (1873); then 'Royal North West Mounted Police' (1904–1920); then the 'Royal Canadian

Note the two shortenings of the word *muskellunge*. What is the effect?

> There was the narrow, weedy channel between the two rocky islands up near the head of the lake where he had seen the monster muskie. As long as a paddle that 'lunge had been, as it tore through the lilypads, its huge predatorial head twisting from side to side, gulping voraciously at the schools of minnows.
>
> John Craig, *The Clearing* (1975). About Ontario.

Eaton's Archives

A hydro jacket

Mounted Police'; also shortened to the acronym MP or, more commonly in recent years to RCMP. (What is happening to the name now, especially the word *Royal*?)

keg 'muskeg'

Vets Affairs for the government department (which sometimes runs *rehab* centres)

bulker 'bulk carrier' on the Great Lakes

chix 'chicken halibut' (plural)

dozer 'bulldozer', extended to *boom dozer* and *dozer boat* in logging. This boat is known in B.C. also as a *log bronc*, a shortening of *bronco*. (See pp. 145-6.)

storms 'storm windows'

roto-thresh combine 'rotary combine', a trade name of a machine invented and used in Manitoba in the 1950's

Macs 'McIntosh apples' (see p. 57)

Expo 'exposition internationale, or world fair', a successful term coined for the 1967 World Fair at Montreal that has since been transferred elsewhere.

Some shortenings are compounds which please by their repetition of sounds: a caterpillar tractor in the North and West is called a *cat-track* or simply a *cat*. Other shortenings are amusing puns, as when the long drawn out and increasingly expensive Bilingual and Bicultural Commission (the *B & B*) became dubbed the *Bi-Bi Commission*.

Some are compounds which have become so familiar that one part is dropped: *plaza* or *mall* for 'shopping plaza' or 'shopping mall' can be heard now in many Canadian towns and cities (though not necessarily of Canadian origin).

The growth in meaning and respectability of the Canadian *hydro* illustrates how quickly a word may change and become accepted. At first the term seems to have been an informal shortening of 'Hydro-Electric Commision of Ontario', formed in 1906. Then it extended both to similar corporations in other provinces and, in many areas, to the actual power or electricity distributed by that corporation, so that Canadians can speak now of the cost of *hydro service* (which may, in many places, include natural gas) or say that the *hydro* has been cut off. They can even buy a *hydro jacket*.

There are holes here and there for
  a gold-mine or a hydro-plant.
But the tartan of river and rock
  spreads undisturbed,
The plaid of a land with little desire
  to buy or sell.

> Douglas Le Pan, "Canoe-Trip" (1948)

I did not see the old man being rolled into the grey-black hydro blanket or watch the body being carried to the back of Rolly's pickup. . . .

> James Demers, *The God Tree* (1974). A novel about the Cobalt–Kirkland Lake region.

He and Sonny and Roy cut a lot of ice in the winters. There was no hydro then and the cottagers used ice-boxes to keep their food.

> John Craig, *The Clearing* (1975). Set in Ontario.

Companies may deliberately shorten their names for psychological reasons: *B.C. Tel* and *Sasktel* (a blend) are typical (perhaps, too, with some intended pun upon *tell*).

A special kind of shortening is *back formation*, from a longer word to a new "root word," as with *edit* from *editor* in general English. A Canadian example may be heard in the North: the pronunciation *link* for the singular of 'lynx'—a natural confusion for someone who has not seen the word in print.

9. Grammatical Shift

Like other users of the English language, Canadians may extend the usefulness of a word by making it act as another part of speech. This may be a simple shift (when, of course, the word takes on the regular inflections of the new part of speech):

> We *corduroyed* the swamp. (from noun to verb)
> The store will *grubstake* you. (from noun to verb)
> We will need some *over-snow* vehicles. (from phrase to adjective)

By the same process, the verb *scoot* 'go suddenly and fast' probably suggested the nouns *scoot* and *snow-scoot*, the Canadian words for a craft driven by an aircraft engine to travel over northern ice or water.

The grammatical shift may involve the addition of the usual English derivational suffixes or prefixes. In the eastern fisheries, a boat that uses long lines is called a *longliner*; this kind of fishing is called, therefore, *longlining*, and the fisherman is a *longlinerman*. The *-er* suffix is especially productive. A Hudson's Bay *four-point* blanket is called a *four-pointer*. A *homer* to a hockey fan is either a 'supporter of the home team' or a 'player or team that does well at home games'. Winter in some parts of Canada makes necessary a shoe attachment with caulks or spikes known as *ice-creepers* or, by shortening, *creepers*.

Some of these shifts have interesting bits of Canadian history attached. When the Canadian prairies were being surveyed, the men used as markers a square pit with a mound of earth, because there was a shortage of wood for the usual stakes and, besides, the Indians picked up any wood there was to use for their fires. The surveyors thus became known as *mounders*.

But, as *over-snow* illustrates, almost any group of words may suddenly function as a new word. In some parts of Canada the legal phrase "those found in such. . ." has become the source for the noun *found-ins* 'those arrested in an illegal establishment'. Similar in construction are the Canadianisms *breakup*, 'spring thawing of the ice on rivers and lakes', *ice-out*, 'the movement of the melting ice', and the hockey term *face-off*.

Once a word is made and used, new ones may be formed by analogy. From the general English word *mule-skinner* 'driver of a mule team' (who, figuratively, "skins" his animals with his whip), comes by analogy *catskinner*, the driver of the *caterpillar tractors* (*cat tracks*) in the North.

Truck logger hits "gyppo" label

Do you know what this headline means? It is from a B.C. newspaper. Can you guess? You can check your guess with the DC.

Grey Cuppers face a chill day

The *Vancouver Sun*, May 1, 1975

10. Coinages

Even if limited to words of one syllable, any speaker of English can coin thousands of new words that conform to the English sound system; *flib, blift, brut, brupe* (but not *srip, lbift, rtub*) suggest some of the possibilities. Yet deliberate coinage of completely new words, unrelated to any other words in the language, is rare in English and probably in most languages. Canadians have created a few. One of the most commonly used is *kerosene*, coined by Dr. Abraham Gesner of Halifax (1797–1846), who developed a profitable method for distilling from coal this valuable material, known also as *kerosene oil* and *coal oil*. But the word is really a borrowing, from Greek *keros*, 'wax', and **-ene** (a suffix used in chemistry for certain hydrocarbons). The DC lists *insulin* as a Canadianism (from *insula*, 'island', and **-in**); Sir Frederick Banting's original choice was *isletin*, and both terms are based on the islets of Langerhans, a group of cells in the pancreas. Other Canadian coinages are mainly trade names, some of which, like *Ski-doo*, have become generalized to a class; but even these names are usually designed to suggest some other word or words. Perhaps to relieve the load upon memory, a language tends to enlarge its storehouse of words mainly by re-using elements already within it rather than by coining new items "out of the air."

C. Borrowing from Other Languages

11. Loan Words

Many new English words have been made by borrowing from other languages. Some examples in Canada are:

> *muskeg* from Algonkian (Cree *muskak* 'swamp')
> *mukluk* from western Eskimo *muklok* 'large seal' (source of the material)
> *voyageur, lacrosse,* and *concession* 'grant of land', all from Canadian French
> *snoose* (or *schnoose*), from Modern Scandinavian *snus*, a shortening of *snustobak* 'a kind of snuff'
> *keta*, originally Russian, a 'chum or dog salmon'—renamed for marketing reasons

Occasionally only part of a borrowed word is used. In the Maritimes the Acadian French term *tarte rappée*, literally 'grated pie', a nourishing meat and vegetable dish, survives as *rappé pie*. Sometimes it is spelled *rawpi, rapee,* or *rappie*, illustrating how the anglicization of a borrowed word may distort its sound and spelling, that is, reshape it to fit the English language system. The change from the French *bête de la mer* 'sea beast' to *bedlamer*, the Newfoundland name for the young harp seal, is the result of similar processes.

Because borrowings from those who were in Canada before the British—the Indians, Eskimos, and French—form a major part of the unique Canadian vocabulary and reflect important aspects of the experience of the Canadian people, each of these is given a separate and fuller treatment at the end of this section.

The cattle-and-horse-ranching areas of western Canada have borrowed many words from Spanish and the Indian languages of Mexico and California, but most of these are North American in scope, shared by all in the great stretch of drylands east of the Rockies. A few, such as *stampede* (Am-Sp. *estampida*), *lasso* (Sp. *lazo* 'noose'), and *ranch* itself (Am-Sp. *rancho* 'small farm') are used now in general English. Others have been changed or adapted by western Canadians. (See sections on Regionalisms.)

A few words also slip into the language from other English-speaking areas. Australians are represented, for example, by the term *damper* 'scorched balls of dough',* which appears in a Stephen Leacock story, "The Speculations of Jefferson Thorpe," in his *Sunshine Sketches of a Little Town* (1912):

> He knew what it was to eat flour-baked dampers under the lee side of a canoe propped among the underbrush, and to drink the last drop of whisky within fifty miles. Mr. Smith had mighty little use of the North.

Though *damper* is still used, the item is more commonly called by its Scots Gaelic-derived word *bannock*, or its French Canadian counterpart *galette*, from French *galette* 'pancake'. Other names are the compounds *river cake, stove cake, bush bread*, and *trail biscuit*. A Canadian slang term for a skilful bachelor cook is *bannock puncher*, probably by analogy to *cowpuncher* (just as, in lumbering slang, the operator of the donkey engine may be called the *donkey puncher* or merely the *puncher*).

12. Folk Etymology

When people borrow a foreign word they not only shape it into their own sound system (as we have seen with *rappée*) but also may change its form to fit what they mistakenly believe to be its origin. Often a familiar term somewhat similar in meaning influences this reshaping. The word *bedlamer*, for instance, may have evolved because of some connection in the speakers' minds between *bedlam* and the noise produced by the seal. This process is called *folk etymology*.

Another Canadian example is the adaptation of an Algonkian term (possibly Cree *weskuchanis*) meaning something like 'little blacksmith' for the bird found all across Canada and known generally as the *Canada jay*. The Indian word came from the bird's sooty color. The English adaptation of this Indian sound sequence took the forms of *whisky-jonas*, then *whisky-john*, and then *whisky-jack*, all of which are still used. In some areas where the bird frequents lumber camps, the name has changed again, to *lumberjack*. The bird has at least thirty recorded names, many of which can be found in bird books and government booklets.

A whisky-jack

* The shorter OED lists *damper* as an Australianism—perhaps incorrectly, as Boy Scouts use the term to mean 'strips of dough made from flour, water, and salt wound spirally round a stick and baked over a campfire'. The Australian entry in the OED is dated 1833, so perhaps the Scouts have borrowed it or perhaps it is a British dialectal word.

An example of the original meaning of *skid road*:

> The foreman came to me. 'To-morrow,' he sez, 'I'll take you off swamping and give you a job barking up at the head of the new skid-road.'
>
> M. A. Grainger, *Woodsmen of the West* (1908)

"Fall ball"
Is this an example of folk etymology? Is the expression general in Canada or parts of Canada, or peculiar to one person? As it appears twice in the story, it is not a misprint. Perhaps *fall ball* makes more sense to children than does *foul ball*. Folk etymology by children can change words and expressions in the language.

> except for Austin who got out for the second time on Wednesday with a fall ball one of the girls caught behind third base. . .
>
> Miss Ralston hit it at an angle so that it fell sideways, a fall ball, toward George Fowler's outstretched hands.
>
> Ann Hart, "The Friday Everything Changed" (1976)

The newer spelling also appears in this poem, written before 1900; the internal rhyme (with *dale*) suggests the pronunciation as *vale*.

> From intervale and swampy dale
> Are wafts of fragrance blown,
>
> Margaret Gill Currie, "By the St. John"

Note: *sourced* as an instance of grammatical shift.

A rocky islet followed
With one lone poplar and a single nest
Of white-throat-sparrows that took no rest
But sang in dreams or woke to sing,
To the last portage and the height of land:

Duncan Campbell Scott, "The Height of Land" (1916)

The development of *skid road* provides another interesting example, this time from an English rather than from a foreign base. Originally, in lumbering, a skid road was a greased road or chute made for hauling logs ("skidding" logs) out of the forest. In Seattle and Vancouver, districts grew up near the terminus of such a road and here loggers would congregate for lodgings and entertainment in town; here too, their money gone, they would wait to be taken back to work. These areas kept the name of *skidroad*, and the term was then generalized to refer to any such area of "down-and-outs," with its missions, soup-kitchens, cheap lodgings, and so on, even though the town might not have been a lumbering centre. Because *skidroad* now refers to an area rather than a road, by folk etymology it frequently becomes *skid row*.

An even more obvious example of folk etymology is the frequent change in the Atlantic Provinces of *interval* 'an area near rivers that is rich in alluvial deposits of soil' to the term *intervale*, a variant probably suggested by *vale*. This word is not a Canadianism but was brought to colonial Canada from New England by the Loyalists or pre-Loyalists. It is still widely used in the Maritimes. The older spelling is used by Thomas Haliburton in *The Clockmaker; or, The Sayings and Doings of Samuel Slick, of Slickville* (1836):

> "If I was to tell them in Connecticut there was such a farm as this away down East here in Nova Scotia, they wouldn't believe me. Why there ain't such a location in all New England. The Deacon has a hundred acres of dyke"—
> "Seventy," said the Deacon, "only seventy."
> "Well, seventy; but then there is your fine deep bottom, why I could run a ramrod into it"—
> "Interval, we call it," said the Deacon, who though evidently pleased at this eulogium, seemed to wish the experiment of the ramrod to be tried in the right place.
> "Well, interval, if you please—though Professor Eleazer Cumstock, in his work on Ohio, calls them bottoms—. . . ."

But a more recent book about Nova Scotia uses the spelling of the form created by folk etymology:

> . . . aimless brooks and stillwaters in which are sourced the creeks that slip through hidden intervales and narrow valleys . . .
> Charles Bruce, *The Channel Shore* (1957)

13. Loan Translations
Because of Canada's history, there are many Canadianisms created from a word or phrase originally Indian or French and translated directly into English. The Canadian phrase *height of land* 'watershed', or, as a proper noun, 'the high watershed between Lake Superior and Hudson Bay', is probably a translation of Canadian French *hauteur des terres*. The term *dead waters* for 'area of sluggish muddy steams and muskeg' is a translation of the French metaphor *eaux morts*; and the intriguingly descriptive phrase *strong woods* for a

heavily forested area is a translation of the voyageurs' *bois fort(s)* and has entered into compounds such as *strong woods country, strong woods buffalo,* and *strong woods reindeer.*

Many attractive place names in Canada are translations of Indian phrases or names; some examples are: *Medicine Hat*, the *Land of Little Sticks* (from Chinook Jargon, pp. 226 ff.) *Sweetgrass Hills* (Alta.), and *Bow River*. In northern Canada the north wind is called *The Coldmaker*, a translation from the name of the spirit in Indian mythology.

Often an Indian name is adopted by people who do not understand the meaning of the original word, causing some tautologies, such as *Atlin Lake* and *Muncho Lake*, both meaning literally 'Lake Lake'; and *Etzikom Coulee*, literally 'Coulee Coulee'. (The word *coulee* is from French.)

Sometimes both French and English names survive: *Pouce Coupe* in the Peace River country was named after a trapper given this nickname by the French Canadian voyageurs because he had lost his thumb in a gun accident. (Simon Fraser mentions this Sikanni trapper in 1806.) Not far away is *Cut Thumb Creek*, a translation. Folk etymologies involving names also abound across Canada. The science of studying the origin of names, called *onomastics*, is closely related to the study of dialects but can be a fascinating study in itself.

Summary

This classification of the methods of creating vocabulary must allow for cross-classifications. For example, a metaphor is a form of extension, and it may also be a compound or a translation from another language. As no living language is without continual change, one word or phrase may in time be subjected to several processes. The development of the Yukon and British Columbia slang term *hootch* 'a kind of homebrew liquor' shows a typical cluster of word-making methods at work. Originally it was a borrowed word, from the Tlingit Indian word *khutsnuwa*, literally 'grizzly bear fort', the name of an Indian village and its people on Admiralty Island, where the liquor was first made. Anglicization made it into *hootchinoo*. This in turn shortened to *hootch* or *hooch*. Then the meaning of the word widened to include any alcoholic drink, especially homebrew or whisky.

khutsnuwu 'grizzly bear fort'	INDIAN PLACE NAME
hootchinoo	BORROWING
hootch 'a local drink'	SHORTENING
hootch 'any alcoholic drink'	EXTENSION

The classification above is, therefore, flexible. Nevertheless it gives some insight into the methods by which the users of any language may create words to meet new needs. Any adoption or adaptation must fit a pattern known to the speakers of the language. Coinage goes on continually, but because it is patterned to the language, a new coinage is usually understood immediately. Any Canadian understands such phrases as "He *out-Trudeaued*

And the process of word-making still goes on, as this 1972 newspaper item reveals:

'YUKON HOOTCH' RUM GOES ON THE MARKET

WHITEHORSE, Y.T. (CP) — Scotland has scotch. Kentucky has bourbon.

Now the Yukon Territory has its own special liquor — Yukon Hootch.

A blend of Canadian and imported rums, Yukon Hootch went on sale last week throughout the territory in conjunction with Klondike '73, a year-long celebration marking the 75th anniversary of the Klondike Gold Rush.

Produced solely for distribution by the territorial government, Hootch has an alcoholic content about the same as most standard brands of rum and is being sold in 12- and 25-ounce bottles.

Rollie Thibault, Yukon director of liquor control, said the brew originated during Gold Rush days.

The *Vancouver Sun*, Dec. 26, 1972

Trudeau" or "The camp . . . was in accord with the best traditions of *haywiredom*" (quoted in the DC) because one understands not only the meaning of the base words (*Trudeau*, and how he acts; *haywire*, a slang extension to mean something poorly and inefficiently organized) but also the grammar and the methods of such coinages. The speaker and the listener unconsciously share a system, certain rules or conventions from which they create and recognize a new piece of language.

To expand its vocabulary to meet the special needs of its speakers, Canadian English—like all other languages—uses three basic processes:

A. extending the use of words already in the language
   1. extension of meaning
   2. personal or geographical names
   3. metaphor

B. creating new terms from the resources of the language
   4. compounds
   5. blends
   6. onomatopoeia
   7. acronyms
   8. shortening (and back formation)
   9. grammatical shift
 10. coinages

C. borrowing from other languages
 11. loan words
 12. folk etymology
 13. loan translations

Canadian borrowings:
French, Indian, Eskimo

When the first English-speakers came to Canada, they met at once three peoples who lived here and had given names to places, objects, and experiences: the Indians, the Inuit (Eskimos), and the French. From all of these the English-speaking Canadians have borrowed so many words that this method of making new vocabulary in Canadian English merits an expanded discussion.

Canadian Words from French
Do you know the italicized words in the following? Do you use them?

Gull Lake set in the rolling *prairie* —
    Duncan Campbell Scott, "At Gull Lake: August 1810"

The pinelands whose limits seem distant as Thules
The millions of lakes once *cached* and forgotten, . . .
    Douglas Le Pan, "Canoe-Trip" (1953)

Far across the *brûlé* they could see her standing on a big pine stump near the bars . . .
    Ralph Connor, *The Man From Glengarry* (1901)

This powerful stream, against which they also had to paddle, led them to the Methye *Portage* (or Portage LaLoche), a very tough one with a sharp height of land at the end of it.
    Hugh MacLennan, "The Rivers that Made a Nation" (1961)

If overtaken, as was often the case, in a long *traverse* from point to point, or across large bays in the big lakes, the heavy parla used to be thrown over the goods as a storm deck . . .
    Peace River: A Canoe Voyage from Hudson's Bay to Pacific by the late George Simpson, in 1828; Journal of the Chief Factor, Archibald McDonald (1872)

All are Canadianisms borrowed from the French Canadians. The Canada Census of 1971 reveals that French is the native tongue of nearly 27 per cent of the Canadian population, and English is the native tongue of 60 per cent. Many English-speakers are bilingual in the sense of knowing both English and French, and most have some contact with the French language—even if it is as peripheral as the bilingual cereal box on the breakfast table or the "other side" of a federal government form.

It is natural to expect that the English vocabulary of Canada should contain words from French, the other official language and the tongue of Canada's first European explorers and settlers west of the Maritimes.

But long before the English had settlements in Canada, the English language of all North America was absorbing terms from the French Canadians, who had penetrated by the water routes well

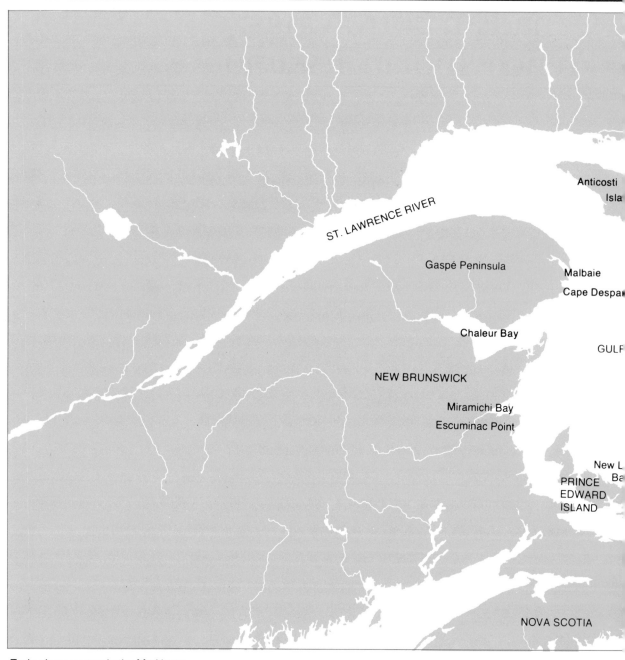

Early place names in the Maritimes

into the centre of the continent. Therefore Canada shares with the United States a special vocabulary derived from the French Canadian language. Adopted very early were such geographical and travel words as: *bat(t)eau, portage, prairie, rapids*. Only a little later entered: *coulee, cache, crevasse, chute, bayou* (lumbering areas), *depot*. The word *cache* has added meanings in North America, particularly in Canada, that are not known in the mainstream of French. It is really a case of reborrowing, as the OED lists *cache* in English as early

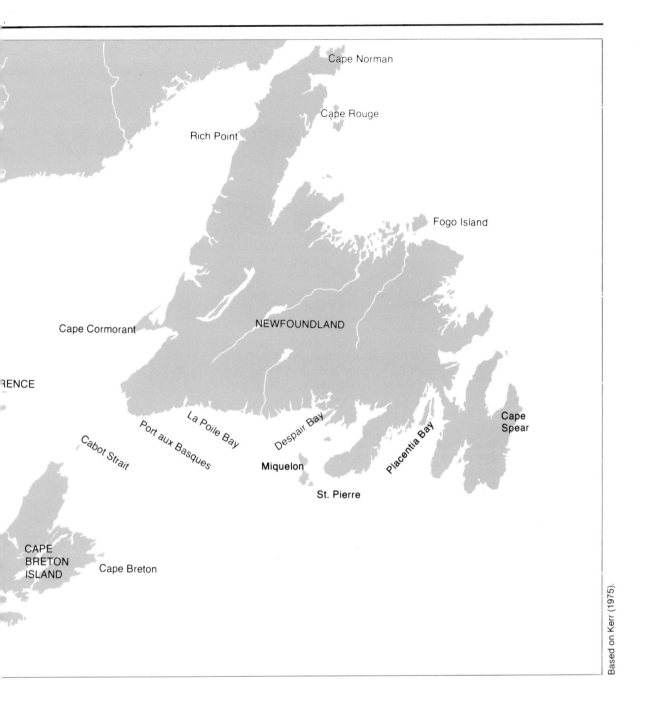

Cape Norman

Cape Rouge

Rich Point

Fogo Island

Cape Cormorant

NEWFOUNDLAND

RENCE

La Poile Bay

Despair Bay

Cape
Spear

Port aux Basques

Cabot Strait

Placentia Bay

Miquelon

St. Pierre

CAPE
BRETON
ISLAND

Cape Breton

Based on Kerr (1975).

as 1595. Apparently it "died" in ordinary English until borrowed again in North America from Canadian French.

Many French Canadian words are recorded all across the continent as parts of place names. Some examples are: *sault, dalles, grande, ronde, bois, butte.*

The word *sault* 'leap, jump', therefore 'waterfall or rapids', is found in many names (*Sault Ste. Marie, Sault au Mouton*) and preserves a seventeenth century spelling (Mod. Fr. *saut*). Frequently

. . . they shared in the celebrations of New Year, instituted by French and Scottish fur-traders, whose regale for the Indians was far more potent than the mission's tea and currant scones.

Ruth Matheson Buck, *The Doctor Rode Side-Saddle* (1974)

Oddly, the word *canoe* is not French but came into English in the sixteenth century through Spanish from the West Indies. Nevertheless, the French Canadian word *canot*, as applied to the Indian birchbark canoe and adaptations of it for the fur trade, undoubtedly added Canadian meanings to the word. A study of the compounds of *canoe* listed in any Canadian dictionary reveals a vital part of our history.

the anglicized or changed spelling of place names may hide their French source; some good clues of possible French origin are:

1. the root word—*e.g.* Detroit 'strait, channel' (Fr. *étroit* 'narrow')
2. the pronunciation of **ch** as **sh** (though spelling may change it to a **ch** sound for some speakers)—Cache Creek, Chaleur, Champlain,
   or of **i** as English **ee**—Lachine (originally La Chine—see p. 176).
3. French word order—Montreal (Mount Royal), Lake Superior (What's happening today, *e.g. Air Canada*?)
4. (less surely, but common) use of *Saint* or, especially, *Sainte*—Ste. Agathe

But folk etymology does strange things to names. As an illustration, here is the history of *Malbaie* on the Gaspe Peninsula, to the north of Chaleur Bay. In Champlain's time, it was *La baie des molues* (*morues* 'cod'); then it became *Moley Bay*; then *Mal Bay*, then *Malbaie* — no remaining relationship with the original. Nearby, Jacques Cartier in 1534 named *Le Cap d'Espoir*, which turned into its opposite, *Cape Despair!* In Newfoundland, similarly, *Bay d'Espoir* is regularly pronounced *Bay Despair*, but the Spanish-named *Capa de espera*, a little south of St. John's, has long since become *Cape Spear*.

Occasionally a Canadian translation of a French Canadian term has added a new sense to an English word. An example is *kettle*, or sometimes *cauldron*, a translation of Canadian French *chaudière*, used to describe and name the round basin worn at the foot of a waterfall by swirling "boiling" water. Canada has many *Kettle Rivers*, *Kettle Creeks*, and *Kettle Portages*.

Sometimes the slang of the voyageurs was translated literally: the jail or guardhouse at forts or posts into which unruly men were placed to cool off was nicknamed *pot-au-beurre* by the French, and thus became for the English the *butter-tub* or *butter-vat*. Unfortunately, a translation of a French term can make the original obsolete: the white and red *pomme de neige* (also known as *Fameuse*) is now a *snow apple*, a term which retains the original image; but *pomme de glace* 'apple of ice' is merely a *Transparent*.

The student of history can add vivid images to many Canadian terms. Behind the phrase *The Long Trail*, a euphemism for 'death', is the old fur-trading *Longue Traverse*, the cruel punishment meted out by the factors of the big fur companies whereby intruders or thieves were sent with no food and little or no ammunition to make their way hundreds of miles through forest to civilization—a virtual sentence of death. The custom was also known as *The Death Trail*. All these terms are marked "historical" in the DC, but *The Long Trail* and the *Long Traverse* may still be heard in Canada.

Many North American terms have entered the general English of this continent through French from Indian languages, either by translation or by an imitation of the Indian words. The word *caribou* (formerly pluralized in Canada with the addition of **-x** in the French manner) is probably from the Algonkian word for the animal, which originally meant 'scratcher, pawer' from its habit of scratching in snow to reach the moss; *carcajou* 'wolverine' and *toboggan*, both from Algonkian, and *mackinaw* from Ojibwa have similar histories. The DC gives a long list of the extensions and compounds that Canadians have given to *caribou*: to name a bird, an airplane, an Eskimo group, a fly, a moss, a plain, and with a slight change in spelling, a mountain range and a large region in British Columbia—and in Quebec a potent drink.

From Canadian French itself come:

gopher—probably from *gaufre gris*, Fr. *gaufre* 'honeycomb' (because of the structure of its burrow; in French the word has been extended to mean 'waffle')

many fish names in Canada, *e.g. doré (doree, dory)*—from *poisson doré* 'gilded fish', a pike

brochet 'great northern pike'

conny (connie)—a reduction of *inconnu* 'unknown', a large northern fish.

French Canadian customs have left their mark upon the general North American language. Generations of Canadians and Americans have danced 'square dances' to the calls of *dos-à-dos* (with various spellings), originally 'back to back', and *promenade*, probably without realizing that they were using French Canadian terms. The person who calls or chants the movements is a *caller-off*, a Canadianism, and the word *sashay* (French *chasser*) has become part of the everyday spoken language ("I think I'll sashay on home now.").

The word *shivaree* 'noisy serenade for a newly married couple', through Canadian French from French *charivari*, seems to have spread with the custom itself from the East and the Mississippi Valley to most of the United States as well as to much of rural Canada. This is an interesting item on many dialect surveys; other names for the custom are: *serenading, tinpanning, bull band, belling, dishpanning, skimmelton, callathump, reception, horning, drumming,* and *salute*.

A Charivari

"Do tell me," I cried, "the meaning of this strange uproar?"

"Oh, 'tis nothing," she replied, laughing. "You and Mary look as white as a sheet; but you need not be alarmed. A set of wild fellows have met to charivari Old Satan, who has married his fourth wife tonight, a young girl of sixteen. I should not wonder if some mischief happens among them, for they are a bad set, made up of all the idle loafers about Port H____ and C____."

"What is a charivari?" said I. "Do, pray, enlighten me."

"Have you been nine months in Canada, and ask that question? Why, I thought you knew everything! Well, I will

In telling about a village in southern Ontario in the early 1900's Robertson Davies describes a shivaree organized to deride a man and his wife:

It was Cece, with some of his crowd, and the Harper boys (who ought to have known better) who organized the shivaree when the Dempsters moved. . . .

At midnight a gang with blackened faces beat pans and tooted horns outside the cottage for half an hour, and somebody threw a lighted broom on the roof, but it was a damp night and no harm was done.

Robertson Davies, *Fifth Business* (1970)

tell you what it is. The charivari is a custom that Canadians got from the French in the Lower Province, and a queer custom it is. When an old man marries a young wife, or an old woman a young husband, or two old people, who ought to be thinking of their graves, enter for the second or third time into the holy estate of wedlock, as the priest calls it, all the idle young fellows in the neighbourhood meet together to charivari them. For this purpose they disguise themselves, blackening their faces, putting their clothes on hind part before, and wearing horrible masks, with grotesque caps on their heads, adorned with cocks' feathers and bells. They then form in a regular body, and proceed to the bridegroom's house, to the sound of tin kettles, horns and drums, cracked fiddles, and all the discordant instruments they can collect together. Thus equipped, they surround the house where the wedding is held, just at the hour when the happy couple are supposed to be about to retire to rest—beating upon the door with clubs and staves, and demanding of the bridegroom admittance to drink to the bride's health, or in lieu thereof to receive a certain sum of money to treat the band at the nearest tavern.

"If the bridegroom refuses to appear and grant their request, they commence the horrible din you heard, firing guns charged with peas against the doors and windows, rattling old pots and kettles, and abusing him for his stinginess in no measured terms. Sometimes they break open the doors, and seize upon the bridegroom; and he may esteem himself a very fortunate man, under such circumstances, if he escapes being ridden upon a rail, tarred and feathered, and otherwise maltreated. . . ."

Susanna Moodie, *Roughing it in the Bush* (1852)

Also Canadian but well known in all America are:
mush — (French *marche*) as used as a command to dogs in the North;
lacrosse — (*la crosse* 'hooked stick');
tuque — a dialectal variant of French *toque* 'knitted stocking-type cap'.

Like words in any language, many French Canadian terms have changed with time and place. The word *cariole* (or *carriole*) was originally a light open sleigh drawn by horses or perhaps by dogs. The term was extended to mean various kinds of winter vehicle. By folk etymology arose the term *carry-all*, and this is now used by the United States Army in the North.

The word *snye (sny, snie)*, from Canadian French *chenail* 'channel', in the Ottawa Valley lumbering region originally referred to a side-channel, natural or artificial, that bypassed a falls or rapid. Such

A tuque

[She] was forced to retire at the sight of the first carryall full of men from the Milburn Boiler Company flaunting a banner inscribed "We are solid for W.W."

Sara Jeanette Duncan, *The Imperialist* (1904). An election parade in Ontario.

channels were used as routes for rafts of timber being floated downstream. In the Canadian northwest the word has become the term for a narrow sluggish side-channel of a river, sometimes the equivalent of a *slough*; it is a *blind snye* if it has a dead end, and a *fast snye* if open at both ends. In the Mackenzie River Valley, planes may use water like this for a landing place, so it becomes a *landing snye* (or *snigh*), sometimes pronounced with a **sh-** sound, a remnant of the original French word.

A borrowed word may undergo so many transformations of form and meaning that scholars have difficulty in ascertaining the etymology. Although the word *shanty* is usually cited as a French Canadian word, from *chantier* (Canadian French, 'logger's camp or cabin', from French 'timber-yard or dock' or 'workshop'), it could also be derived from Irish Gaelic *sean tigh* 'old hut', especially in Upper Canada where the term first seems to have arisen and where there were many Irish immigrants, many of whom worked in the woods.

Hundreds of French Canadian words are marked "historical" in the DC—words seldom used now but known to Canadians through their reading about the past: *voyageur, coureur-de-bois, habitant, seigneury, corvee,* and some lesser known items, such as:

boudet 'folding canvas cot'
hivernants 'winterers at a post'
voltigeur—from French 'horseman, sharpshooter', and thus 'militiaman or bush ranger'

Others linger in the living Canadian English language as regionalisms in areas where French influence was or is strong. The word *coteau* 'hillock' is recognized in most prairie areas as referring to an elevated plateau or ridge; *butte* (pronounced like the first

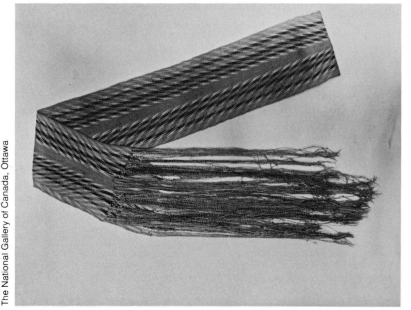

Ceinture flêchée (arrow sash)

I like the winter carriages immensely; the open carriole is a kind of one-horse chaise, the covered one a chariot, set on a sledge to run on the ice; we have not yet had snow enough to use them, but I like their appearance prodigiously; the covered carrioles seem the prettiest things in nature to make love in, as there are curtains to draw before the windows. . . .

Frances Brooke, *The History of Emily Montague* (1769). The first Canadian—in fact, North American—novel; its setting is in Quebec and Montreal between the conquest by Wolfe in 1759 and the American War of Independence of the 1770's. Mrs. Brooke was the wife of the chaplain of the British garrison at Quebec, 1763–1768.

We moved off on to the prairies of the coteau, young men on horseback, women also on horseback but with tepee-poles affixed on each side of their mount[s] and dragging the ground behind. On shorter poles laid across these were the rolls of tenting, the pots and the kettles. As well as the dragged poles, the travois, we had some Red River carts with us. I thought that these made noise sufficient to drive all the buffalo out of the country.

Frederick Niven, *Mine Inheritance* (1940). A historical novel about the Lord Selkirk settlement in the Red River Valley. In this excerpt the hero is joining the Métis in a buffalo hunt.

Among the many other words from Canadian French which Niven uses are *bois brûlés* (extended to mean people of mixed Scots and Indian blood), *capot, caches, régale, coulee, parflèched*. How many do you use or know?

syllable of *beauty*, rhyming with *mute*) is still used in this general way, *e.g.* on the outskirts of Paradise Hill in northern Saskatchewan; and *coulee* is widely used in all the West of Canada to designate a deep dried slough or riverbed. Maple sugar regions know *lateer* (*la tire*, from *tirer* 'to pull'), the name given to the toffee made when boiling syrup is put on the snow.

Words from Canadian French may disappear for economic reasons. A generation ago, at least in the West and North, people went out at night or went hiking lighted by a *bug*, a corruption (with perhaps some folk etymology) of French *bougie* 'lantern, candle'. A *bug* was a candle set in a tin can with a hole punched in one side. Cheaper flashlights have caused the virtual disappearance of the *bug*. The French word is derived from the Arabic, the name of a town Bijiyah in Algeria, which traded in wax.

Do older people in your area know this meaning of the word *bug*?

In the Maritimes, French has a long history and is very much a part of the regional vocabulary: *aboideau* or *aboiteau* 'sluice-gate in a dike', sometimes widened to mean the dike itself, and *anse* 'cove' (common in place names) are but two examples of a rich heritage

Tyron, with Aboiteau Bridge and ▶
Tyron River in the foreground

Public Archives of Prince Edward Island

dating back to the time of the Acadians or further.* From the East to Alberta, and perhaps beyond, is known the term *frazil*, originally from French *frasil* 'cinders', the flaky ice-crystals formed in turbulent water, as well as *frazil-* or *frazzle-ice*, made on the shore by these flakes. The North, of course, has many French Canadian words in

* About half a million Americans in southwestern Louisiana, descendants of Acadians displaced from Nova Scotia in the eighteenth century, still speak French. Some contributions of the *Cajuns* (a form of *Acadian* used by the Acadian French themselves, and a Canadianism) to the North American English language are: *bayou* 'small stream' (a Choctaw Indian word originally); *cush* or *cush cush*, Texas version of Acadian *couche-couche* 'fried cornmeal dough and sugar'; *gumbo*, borrowed by the Acadians from an African term for the okra plant, and used in Canada to mean 'thick sticky mud'; *praline* 'pecan candy'; *armoire* 'wardrobe with drawers'; *banquette* 'sidewalk'; and *lagniappe* 'extra gift given with purchase'.

its special vocabulary, ranging from: clothing, *e.g. capote* 'the Canadian coat'; and picturesque metaphors like *la foule*, literally 'the crowd', referring to the spectacle of the caribou massing for migration; and *poudrerie* or *poudre* 'a fine, hard, drifting snow' (also known as *snow-smoke*); to the ordinary greeting of traders, trappers, Indians, and others, *Bo Jo(u)*, an informal shortening of *bonjour*.

Although this section has given but a sampling of the French Canadian elements in Canadian English, and although the French Canadians are right in claiming that English has affected their language much more than vice versa, the material does perhaps suggest why Hugh MacLennan (1960) feels that Canadians *are* different from Americans. "The true makers of Canada, the forerunners," he declares, "were not like the settlers of the States, not dominantly Anglo-Saxon, but French and Highland Scotch, giving a special tone to Canada":

> Emphatically they were neither respectable nor middle class. They were desperate men, and the story of their fabulous river voyages has no counterpart anywhere in the world, and if anyone wants to known why Canada is subtly different in character from the United States, it is to these men and to this period he should look.

Canadian Words from Indian Languages

How many of the following words do you know? All are Canadianisms derived from Indian languages. You can find them in the DC.

shaganappi (Algonkian)	scuttaywabo (Algonk.)
wanigan (Algonk.)	olallie (Chinook)
sagamite (Algonk.)	pemmican (Algonk.)
pekan (Algonk. No, not the nut!)	pichou (Algonk.— various spellings)
lahal (Chinook)	rogan (Algonk.)
saganash (Algonk.)	rubaboo (Algonk.)
kinnikinik (Algonk.)	sapi (Athapaskan)
saskatoon (Cree)	shishiquoi (Algonk.)

Except for thousands of place-names, including *Canada* itself, and some regional west coast expressions from Chinook, surprisingly few Indian words have entered Canadian English. Even the term "Indian," as every schoolchild knows, is a misnomer. Indeed, in areas where there are many Canadians from India, it becomes a confusing misnomer, giving rise to such odd yet logical terms as *native Indian, Canadian Indian*, and *East Indian*. The term "redskin" is also a misnomer (as well as a poor description), one extended to all natives from the early descriptions of the Beothuks of Newfoundland, who painted their bodies with red ochre.

Most of the words that were borrowed from Indian languages referred to things new to the Europeans, and many words came into Canadian English filtered through Canadian French. Hundreds of

> Once all this mighty continent was ours,
> And the Great Spirit made it for our use.
>
> Charles Mair, *Tecumseh* (1886)
>
> They flow like water, or like wind they flow
> Wymouchcheeching, loon-haunted Manowan
> Far Mistassini by her frozen wells,
> Gold-hued Wyagamac brimming her wooded dells;
> Lone Kamiuraska, Metapedia,
> And Mehtlatahkla ring a round of bells.
>
> Duncan Campbell Scott, "Indian Names" (1947)

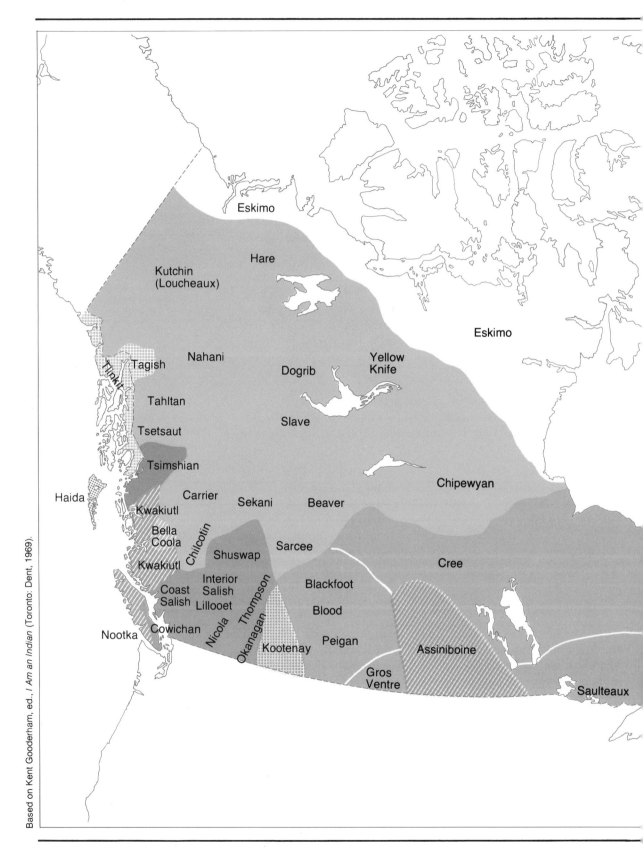

Eskimo

Kutchin
(Loucheaux)

Hare

Eskimo

Nahani

Tagish

Yellow
Knife

Tlkit

Dogrib

Tahltan

Slave

Tsetsaut

Tsimshian

Haida

Carrier

Sekani

Beaver

Chipewyan

Kwakiutl

Bella
Coola

Chilcotin

Shuswap

Sarcee

Cree

Kwakiutl

Interior
Salish

Coast
Salish

Lillooet

Thompson

Blackfoot

Nicola

Okanagan

Blood

Nootka

Cowichan

Kootenay

Peigan

Assiniboine

Gros
Ventre

Saulteaux

Based on Kent Gooderham, ed., I Am an Indian (Toronto: Dent, 1969).

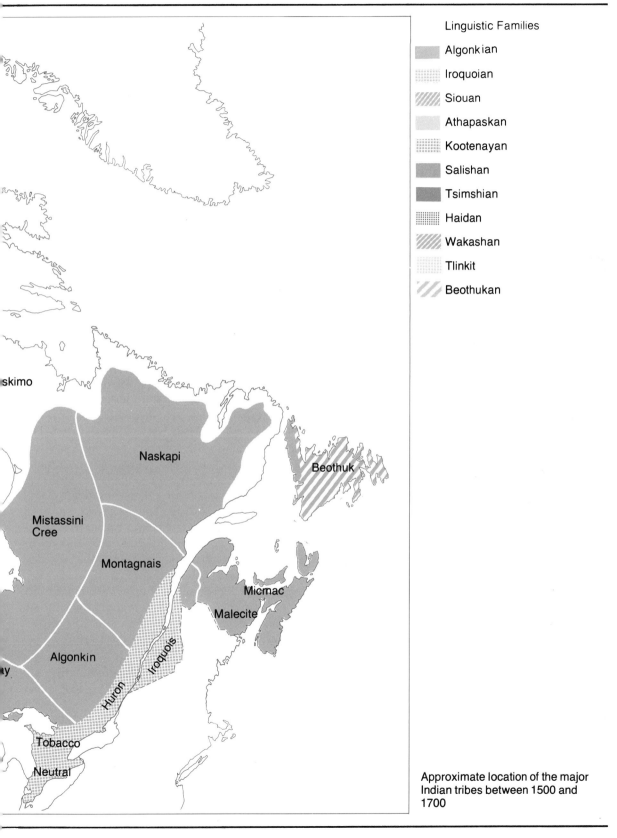

Linguistic Families

Algonkian
Iroquoian
Siouan
Athapaskan
Kootenayan
Salishan
Tsimshian
Haidan
Wakashan
Tlinkit
Beothukan

skimo

Naskapi

Beothuk

Mistassini
Cree

Montagnais

Micmac

Malecite

Algonkin

Huron

Iroquois

Tobacco

Neutral

Approximate location of the major
Indian tribes between 1500 and
1700

Indian words have become so distorted in sound that scholars have difficulty in tracing their exact sources—distorted because newcomers, with no written language to refer to, merely repeat what they think they have heard and change the sounds to fit their own system or, as examples of folk etymology show, to fit their own understandings of the meaning. Misunderstandings were common; many of our terms for Indian tribal groups such as *Salish, Haida*, and *Tlingit*, were originally words meaning merely 'people' in general.

Many Indian words have entered the general vocabulary of all North America and beyond, *e.g. pemmican, papoose, moccasin, pow wow, tomahawk, wigwam, tepee*; it is pointless to claim these as purely Canadian.

Folk etymology is especially apparent in the shaping of the borrowed names of animals. The *chipmunk*, from Algonkian *atchitamon* 'headfirst' (from its manner of descending a tree), was earlier recorded in such forms as *chetamon* and *chitmonk* before the present spelling, obviously tied to a meaning, became standard. Even more apparent is the change to *muskrat* from the Algonkian word somewhat like *miskwasi*; the anglicized version *musquash* is still found, but the "rat" forms are now dominant, including *mushrat* which is possibly a variant of *marsh rat*. In some areas the shortened form *rat* is enough, and hunting rats is *ratting*, sometimes done from a special *ratting canoe*. The journals of David Thompson for the years 1804–5 describe what he and other fur traders called the *Musk Rat* country, or the *Rat Country*, a region about 300 miles wide and about 100 miles inland from Hudson's Bay. The word *sockeye*, by folk etymology from Salish *suk-kegh* 'red fish', is well established. The same linguistic process has made the common northern greeting *wachee*, borrowed from the Cree greeting *wacheya*, mean to many English speakers 'What cheer!'

Moose 'browser, stripper' and *skunk* are other Algonkian words now established in the English language. The southern and midland dialect areas of the United States use *polecat* rather than *skunk* and *ground-squirrel* for *chipmunk*: both are adaptations of old words to the new country, much like the extension of *robin* to the new bird or of *buffalo* to include the bison of the prairie.

Animals and fish, *e.g. muskellunge*, often shortened to *muskie*, are only two groups of new objects that were often given their Indian names. Trees and berried bushes important to Indians and settlers have frequently kept their original names. Examples are:

tamarack   'larch' (from Algonkian, exact origin unknown)
saskatoon—from Cree *misaskwatomin* 'fruit of the tree of many branches'
pembina   'high cranberry bush' (from Cree *nepen* 'summer' and *minan* 'berry')

Both *saskatoon* and *pembina*, like hundreds of other Indian words, have become Canadian place names. Some of these place names in turn become part of compounds for further naming; examples are:

Notice how we got the word *Cree*:

Southward of the above latitude the country is in the possession of the Na-hath-a-way Indians, their native name. . . . The French Canadians . . . call them "Krees", a name which none of the Indians can pronounce; this name appears to be taken from "Keethisteno", so called by one of their tribes and which the French pronounce "Kirsteno", and by contraction Krees ("r", rough cannot be pronounced by any native).

David Thompson, *Travels in Western North America 1784-1812*, ed. Hopwood (1971). This excerpt written 1792–3.

Saskatchewan berry (*Saskatchewan* means 'swift current')
Kamloops trout (*Kamloops* means 'meeting of the waters')
Sitka spruce and *Sitka deer* and *Sitka grouse* (from the Tlingit name)
Malpeque oysters (Micmac 'large bay', through French)
Manitou wheat (Algonkian 'spirit, deity')

Even more productive of compounds is the Algonkian word *muskeg*, from which Canadians, who must cope with the physical fact, have created many terms, a few metaphors, and even a nickname of a railway—the *Muskeg Express* or *Muskeg Special* for the mixed passenger and freight train on the Hudson Bay Railway.

Of course the word *Indian* itself was useful as an easy way for Europeans to name new objects or concepts. The long list of such compounds which are Canadianisms (over one hundred items in the DC) includes:

Indian cup and *Indian rhubarb* (plants)
Indian hen 'marsh bittern'
Indian winter 'cold spell in early spring' (obviously by analogy to the North Americanism *Indian Summer*)
Indian list 'people barred from buying liquor'
Indian price 'exorbitant price for illicit liquor' (because Indians, in many areas, until recently, were not allowed to buy liquor)

Also included are numerous terms for government dealings with Indians, including *Indian reserve*, the Canadian equivalent for the American *reservation*—though either may be heard in Canada.

Many Indian words are regional or occupational in scope. To a northern trapper a *wash* (sometimes *wisch*), probably borrowed from Algonkian, may refer to the den of a bear or the underwater exit from a beaver lodge; its meaning has extended also to the lodge itself, and even to the house of a muskrat.

In the Maritimes a *bogan* or *bogan hole* is a marshy cove or a stagnant pool near a stream, and is probably a corruption and shortening of another Maritime word *pokelogan* or *pokologan*, from Algonkian 'stopping place'. Another *bogan*, meaning 'sled' (for hauling pulpwood logs), is a shortening of a different Algonkian word, meaning 'handsled'. *Bogan* also developed through Canadian French *tabagan(e)* to the English word that every Canadian knows, *toboggan*. This *bogan* has its verb forms, such as *boganning*, and also appears as a compound, *logboggan*. The full word enters into dozens of compounds and now, with motors entering the winter transportation scene, it forms the compounds *motor toboggan* and *autoboggan*. The Canadian child playing in the snow with a toboggan is linked by a word to the eastern Indians who showed the early arrivals from Europe how to cope with the new conditions that they met.

Some customs that Indians taught the European settlers have retained their names: many "outdoor" Canadians use the term *ponasking* (from Algonkian) when they cook their fish or game by holding it on a stick over an open fire. Other customs, such as *jacklighting*, 'luring fish or game at night by using a light', do not

The village of L'Arbre Croche supplies, as I have said, the maize, or *Indian corn*, with which the canoes are victualled. This species of grain is prepared for use, by boiling it in a strong lie, after which the husk may be easily removed; and it is next mashed and dried. In this state, it is soft and friable, like rice. The allowance, for each man, on the voyage, is a quart a day; and a bushel, with two pounds of prepared fat, is reckoned to be a month's subsistence. No other allowance is made, of any kind; not even of salt; and bread is never thought of. The men, nevertheless, are healthy, and capable of performing their heavy labour. This mode of victualling is essential to the trade, which being pursued at great distances, and in vessels so small as canoes, will not admit of the use of other food. If the men were to be supplied with bread and pork, the canoes could not carry a sufficiency for six months; and the ordinary duration of the voyage is not less than fourteen.

Alexander Henry ("The Elder"), *Travels and Adventures in Canada. . .* (1809)

Occasionally when you read old records, journals, travel books, etc., you will find a quotation that pre-dates the ones given in DC. Here is an example:
    We landed upon the bank, kindled a fire, and roasted some venison-steaks after the Indian manner, called by them *ponask*. Having cut a long skewer of wood, they scrape off the bark, and stick the meat upon its point. The other end of the skewer is then forced into the ground, close to the fire; and by turning it round occasionally, the food is soon sufficiently cooked. I never tasted anything more savoury than a venison-steak prepared in this manner.

Lieut. Edward Chappell, *Narrative of a Voyage to Hudson's Bay in His Majesty's Ship Rosamund* (1817)

The Canadian Press

Ogopogo seen by fishermen

KELOWNA (CP) — The first sighting reported this year of Lake Okanagan's famous Ogopogo water monster came Tuesday from two fishermen near Fintry on the west side of the lake. . . .

"It was blue-black in color. We saw the head and tail appear as it moved in a caterpillar-like fashion in the water". . . .

The Canadian Press, July 8, 1976

The Indians called it [the lake] We-cha-ka-skoo-se-ya Sa-ka-ye-kun, the lake of the bad-smelling weed—but the wild onions that grew there had been known to early travellers, and added a change of flavour in hot *rubaboo* or *ruchow*, though pemmican of itself was good enough.

Ruth Matheson Buck, *The Doctor Rode Side-Saddle* (1974). About Saskatchewan in the 1890's.

show their Indian origin in their English names. The Indian game of *baggataway* is now called by its French name *lacrosse* (*la crosse*).

Translations of Indian expressions have added a flavor to the Canadian language (aided, in some cases, by Western movies). Such phrases as *Great Spirit*, a literal translation of *Gitchi Manitou*; *Master of Life*, of similar origin; special meanings of *medicine*, as in *strong medicine, big medicine*, or *bad medicine*; and local phrases such as *strong cold*, all carry special connotations.

Indian folklore has added a few terms to the language, though most are of restricted usage. In the West the "Wild Man of the Mountains" takes the name of *Sasquatch* in Salish areas, including parts of Washington state. The legendary giant of the Ojibwa, a creator-magician and folk-hero, is *Nanabozho*, said to lie now in Lake Superior as the Sleeping Giant. Of the opposite type is the evil giant and cannibal, *Wendigo* (or *Wettigo*). The immigrant imagination has taken over or created others: Victoria's Cadboro Bay sea-monster was given the pseudo-scientific name of *Cadborosaurus* ("*Caddie*"); the Indian *Naitaka* or Lake Demon of Lake Okanagan was rechristened *Ogopogo*—alas, not an Indian word but taken from a song in a British musical comedy that played in that area in the early 1900's! Truly Indian and of much wider circulation is the Algonkian word *totem*, originally meaning 'his brother-sister-kin', which, with its derivative *totemism*, was made popular and given a special meaning by the writings of Sir James Frazer and other anthropologists. On the west coast *totem* also has the restricted meaning of the *totem poles* of that area—a misnomer according to the experts, who point out that these were gate posts or doorposts whose figures have heraldic value.

Along the Pacific coast, from Alaska to the mouth of the Columbia, an Indian trade-language called the *Chinook Jargon* has contributed many words to the English spoken in that area. Chinook is discussed in Part Two (pp. 226 ff.).

Probably the most striking Indian legacy to Canadian English is the long list of intriguing place names and translations of Indian names. *Ponoka* is Blackfoot for 'elk'; *Thunder Bay* is a translation of the Indian name meaning 'Thunder Bird Bay', the folklore bird responsible for thunder. Without knowing that the original name for Regina was *Waskana*, Sioux for 'pile of bones', a reader would miss the allusion in F. R. Scott's lines from "Trans Canada" (1945):

We sprang upward into a wider prairie
And dropped Regina below like a pile of bones.

The area was once littered with buffalo bones because the Indians and Métis gathered there to make *pemmican* (another Canadianism derived from Indian languages) from the plentiful buffalo meat mixed with tallow and berries.

In the early days of Canada the Indian was often the helper and supplier of the exploring and trading Europeans. There was an exchange of language because there was an exchange of information and of cultures. Therefore the French or English speech of the

Olwen Drysdale

A *hoodoo* was "a supernatural creature of dangerous and malignant tendencies" (DC), one of whom terrorized the Indians of the Columbia Valley. The name has been transferred to the strange geological forms shown in the picture.

◀ Weird pinnacles and grotesque forms called "hoodoos."

traders of that era was full of Indian terms—names for animals, sleds, foods, trees, and places—all names they needed. This kind of exchange ended with the coming of the settler.

Perhaps the most damning example of linguistic evidence showing the relationships between the English-speaking Canadian and the Indian lies in the changing meaning of the Algonkian word *nitchie* (with various spellings). At one time *nitchie* meant 'friend' and was used by an Indian to greet another Indian. It came to be used by traders to mean 'an Indian' and was often used disparagingly, so that the term gathered unfavorable connotations, until now it is classified "often derogatory." The west coast counterpart is *Siwash*, derived from the French voyageurs' name for the Indians, *sauvages*, which carried no connotations of the English word *savages*. The term *Siwash* collected so many negative connotations that it, too, is now avoided.

they are all ready
to be found, the legends
and the people, or
all their ghosts and memories,
whatever is strong enough
to be remembered.

John Newlove, "The Pride" (1968)

Canadians Words from Eskimo Languages

The approximately 13 000 Inuit in Canada represent less than one-fifth of the total Eskimo population of the world: there are 35 000 Inuit in Greenland, 30 000 in Alaska, and 1000 in Siberia. All Inuit groups speak the same language, but dialects differ widely enough to cause serious difficulties in mutal intelligibility.

Because of limited contact (until lately), few Eskimo words or expressions have entered Canadian English, and those that are known usually refer to life in the arctic area. Nearly every Canadian understands to what these words refer: *mukluks, oomiak (umiak), kayak, tupek* 'tent of skins', and *komatik*. The meanings of some have been extended by Canadians: a *kayak* may now refer to any boat of

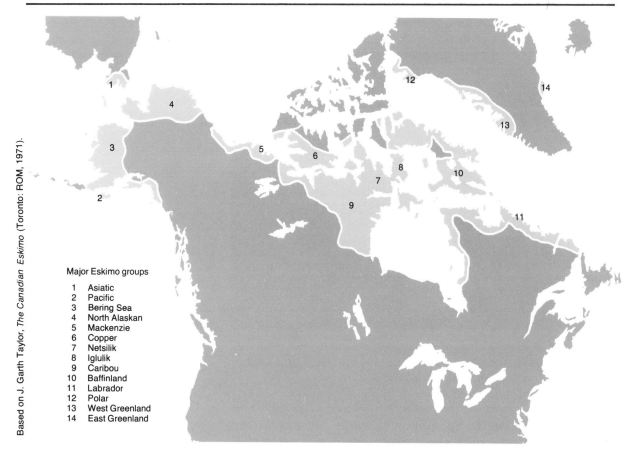

Based on J. Garth Taylor, *The Canadian Eskimo* (Toronto: ROM, 1971).

Major Eskimo groups

1 Asiatic
2 Pacific
3 Bering Sea
4 North Alaskan
5 Mackenzie
6 Copper
7 Netsilik
8 Iglulik
9 Caribou
10 Baffinland
11 Labrador
12 Polar
13 West Greenland
14 East Greenland

Map of the major Inuit language groups

that shape; and a *mukluk* is now any shoe of that traditional type. The Canadian garment industry has also popularized the terms *kuletuk*—a parka trimmed with fur and designed for women—and *sealopack* (from Inuit *silapak*, but the English spelling suggests a pseudo-folk etymology)—a wind-blocking fabric of tightly woven poplin and cotton, used to make an outer garment (Avis 1973b). Many southern Canadians also know the *anorak*, a waterproof outer coat of sealskin, often used by the hunter with the lower edge of the coat fitted tightly around the opening in his kayak (Avis 1973b).

Even wider has been the development of the use in English of *parka*. The word, given several different pronunciations in the North, is not Inuit in origin, but came into the Aleutian dialect through Russian from Samoyed. It was brought into the mainstream of Canadian English by the Klondikers of the late 1890's, and now refers in English everywhere to any coat of a parka style.

The quaint little sealskin figure called *ookpik (ukpik)*, 'snowy owl', was first made by an Inuit woman living in Fort Chimo, and has recently become famous as the symbol of Canadian Eskimo handicrafts. Literature, too, has popularized some terms, *e.g. Nanook* 'polar bear' and *Kabloona* 'person with big eyebrows', the Inuit term for a European. (Duncan Pryde, who knows the Eskimo coun-

Fred Bruemmer Photo

Inukshuk (Esk. 'something acting in the capacity of a man'; compare *inuk*, plural *inuit*, 'people, man') (See the DC for further explanation.)

◀ An ancient, vaguely man-shaped Eskimo stone landmark near the coast of northwestern Hudson Bay.

try well, suggests (1971) that this word really came from Greenland and meant 'a man from the South', thus 'a white man', and that it became confused with a similar word in western arctic dialect which means 'prominent eye-brow ridge'.)

The word *Eskimo* itself, which Canadians and others have used generally for both the people and the language, is probably from an Algonkian word meaning 'eater of raw flesh'. At first the French spelling was more common, *Esquimeau*, with the plural in **-x**, but this has given way to the Danish **k**. Recently the Eskimo people have asked to be called *Inuit* (also, especially at first, spelled *Innuit*), their own name for themselves, the plural of *inuk* 'man', therefore meaning 'the men, the people, mankind', and emphasizing their identity in contrast to Indians, who differ physically, culturally, and linguistically.

One variant of *Eskimo* developed into *Huskimaw* in Labrador and Newfoundland and then shortened to *husky*, now used in the North (with derogatory overtones) to refer to the Eskimo or the language, but in general Canadian usage to refer to the Eskimo sled-dog.

Like some words derived from Indian languages, a few Eskimo words have been distorted by folk etymology to create new English words. One rather amusing example is the change from *atigi* 'shirt of skins, worn with the fur inside', to English *a dickey*.

With the recent "opening-up" of the North, more Inuit terms will probably move into Canadian English. The greeting *chimo*, first recorded in 1748 and still commonly used in the North, is now a piece of slang for Canadian and American young people, and it is commonly used in advertisements. Saskatoon called its Homecoming Festival the *Saskachimo*.

New words were adopted into the language of the Inuit. "Sailor" became *seealar*, a follower; "flour" became *palaugak*; and "Portuguese" became *pautigee*, meaning a brown-coloured person. The Scottish sailors, dirty from stoking steam engines or boiling whale blubber, became known as *pauktut*, "greasies." The European whalers were too lazy to learn Inuit names, and made up their own such as Aivilik Dick, John L. By 'n' By, and Wager Dick. Some of these names are still used by Inuit for dealing with Europeans, though they use their Inuit names at home.

Keith J. Crowe, *A History of the Original Peoples of Northern Canada* (1974)

One wonders how long the native Inuit language will remain as a spoken language in the future.

A Short

Quiz

All the phrases below are taken from an autobiography, *I Nuligak*, written by a member of the Kitigariukmeut tribe of the Canadian Inuit (trans. Metayer, 1966). How many of the words do you know? Can you guess their origins? Some are general Canadianisms; others are Canadianisms that belong to the North.

ANSWERS

1. That *Kablunak*, the *big-brow* who is travelling with you, took him far away last winter.

2. It was said that he had been lost in the river during *break-up*.

3. He tripped on a big rock and fell flat on his face in the pebbles, grumbling like a *bearded seal*.

4. The *kayak* was paddled by a Krangmalerk *inuk*.

5. I started to run after the *tuktuk*, following the low valley between the two ridges.

6. We continued our pursuit by sledge and we soon overtook and killed *nanuk*.

7. The Delta was full of *rats*.

8. *Wolf-dogs* like mine are good runners.

9. We had a *cache* of herring there.

10. I had made a net with seven-inch meshes to take the *inconnus*.

Pitseolak: Pictures Out of my Life (1971)

inconnus: 'large fresh-water fish', "unknown" in the rest of Canada (Cdn. Fr.)

cache: 'hidden store' (Cdn. Fr.)

wolf-dogs: 'sled dogs with wolf ancestry' (Eng. -compounding)

rats: 'muskrats' (by folk etymology from Algonkian, then shortening)

nanuk: 'polar bear' (Esk.); various spellings

tuktuk: 'caribou' (Esk.); also *tuktu*

inuk: 'man' (Esk.)

kayak: 'light sealskin boat, with a small opening for the paddler' (Esk.)

bearded seal: 'kind of seal with large beard-like bristles around the mouth' (Eng.-compounding)

break-up: 'the sudden spring breaking up of ice on lakes and rivers'

Kablunak, Big-brow: 'white man' (Esk.); there are other variants, e.g. *Kadloona*, *Kadluna*, and *Kodlunar*.

90

A Matching

QUiz

How many of these Indian, Eskimo, and French voyageur terms do you know? Try matching the pictures to the words.

1. oomiak (umiak)	6. komatik	11. atigi
2. kayak	7. ookpik	12. chiploquorgan
3. kudlik	8. tumpline	13. parfleche
4. hohoq	9. muskimoot	14. ooloo (ulu)
5. bateau	10. travois	15. toboggan

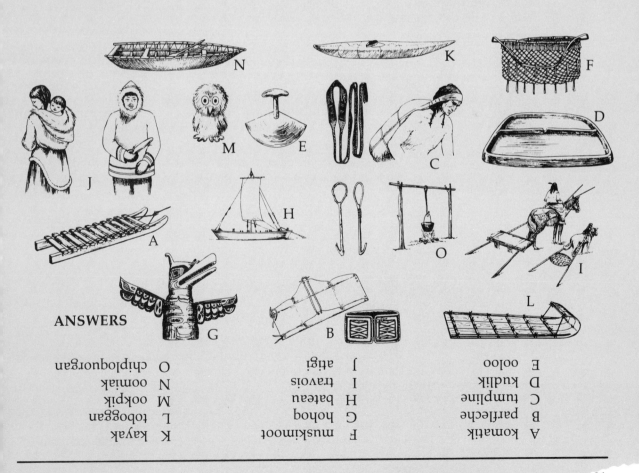

ANSWERS

A	komatik	F	muskimoot	K	kayak
B	parfleche	G	hohoq	L	toboggan
C	tumpline	H	bateau	M	ookpik
D	kudlik	I	travois	N	oomiak
E	ooloo	J	atigi	O	chiploquorgan

91

Canadianisms in literature

Part of the delight of reading Canadian poetry chronologically is watching the gradual emergence of a language appropriate to its objects. I'd say it first began to really happen in poets such as Lampman and Duncan Campbell Scott. For a good example, take a look at A. J. M. Smith's poem "The Lonely Land," which has all the jagged edges of a Tom Thompson jack pine but still manages to affirm.

Margaret Atwood, *Survival* (1972)

No one would claim that diction alone—what J. R. Colombo calls "a garnish of maple leaves"—can make a piece of literature Canadian. But it is apparent that Canadian writers are using their own "voices" and that Canadian words and expressions do appear, often adding a distinctive flavor to a story or novel or poem.

A brief scanning of Robert Harlow's *Royal Murdoch* (1962), a novel with a British Columbia setting, reveals a surprising number of words and phrases marked as Canadianisms in the DC. Here is a sampling:

How many of the italicized words do you use? recognize?

. . . right there, . . . was one of the hundred or more tool and equipment *caches* found along the whole length of the old Grand Trunk Pacific . . . (3)

. . . then it was a notation on a location engineer's map, then a homestead, and finally it became a *townsite* when the railway built a roundhouse . . . and called it a *divisional point* . . . (3)

. . . a *government liquor store*, a detachment of *Mounted Police*, . . . more hotels (. . . all of them with *beer parlours* attached) (3)

She was born in the country that runs along the crest of the *Great Divide* . . . (7)

a band of Indians living in their willow teepees and hunting the moose, the deer, the bear, the *cariboo*, and the elk (7)

they were the best canoe-makers and handlers the *voyageurs* had met (8)

this, for the moment, was the *end of steel* (10)

she went to the bridge-builders' *cook-car* for food . . . she had not been to their *outfit* before (10)

the eastern boundary was spongy with *muskeg* (15)

He nagged the *legislature* until Linden had *provincial government* buildings, where there was a *county court*, a new jail and there he installed a city police force to supplement the *Provincials* (16)

He chaired the *school board* (16)

the first log is raised wetly out of the mill-pond and grunts up the *jack-ladder* to be scaled, rolled, *dogged*, cut, edged, and sent sliding along the greenchain to be piled in the drying yards (19)

through sagebrush to territory covered by fir and *bull pine*, past ranches and open government *rangeland* (61)

he had packed his *duffle* and his only suitcase (61)

A character in Hugh MacLennan's novel *The Watch That Ends the Night* (1959) recalls the Montreal of his childhood. All the italicized words are Canadianisms.

> This pale twilight bathing the city erased time: it called me back to the Montreal which once had been one of the true winter cities of the world, with iced *toboggan slides* on the mountain and *snowshoers* in scarlet sashes and *tuques* and gray homespuns bright against the snow and *shacks* with rank coffee and acrid air where you warmed your half-frozen feet in front of *Quebec heaters* and felt young and clean and untroubled. It was gone now that we were learning to live like New Yorkers.

The *scarlet sashes*, though not listed as a Canadianism, probably refers to the *scarf-belt* or *L'Assomption scarf* (both Canadianisms) associated with French Canada (see p. 107).

One may well ask to what extent the idea or promotion of a distinct Canadian culture has affected our authors. Some have undoubtedly striven for a Canadian flavor, while others have expressed a national distinctiveness less self-consciously. In either case, though, they have provided ample evidence of the kind referred to in this statement by Robertson Davies:

> Our most self-exploratory, and therefore most revealing and individual, art might be music, ... for music is the language of feeling. But I hope it will be literature, and there are evidences in our poetry and some of our novels that this may be so. Those who have not seen the evidence have not been looking hard enough.

"The Poetry of a People" in Wainwright (1969)

To hold in a poem
I would take words
As crisp and as white
As our snow; as our birds
Swift and sure in their flight;

As clear and as cold
As our ice; as strong as a jack pine;
As young as a trillium, and old
As Laurentia's long undulant line;

Sweet-smelling and bright
As new rain; as hard
And as smooth and as white
As a brook pebble cold and
   unmarred;

To hold in a poem of words
Like water in colorless glass
The spirit of mountains like birds,
Of forests as pointed as grass;

To hold in a verse as austere
As the spirit of prairie and river,
Lonely, unbuyable, dear,
The North, as a deed, and forever.

A. J. M. Smith, *A Sort of Ecstasy*
(1954)

Part **2**

Chapter 3
Language and Dialects

People have long been aware of geographical and social differences within a language. The Old Testament gives us an early account of how such differences may mark people off—in this instance, for death. Our English word *shibboleth*, which in Hebrew meant 'ear of corn', comes from this story:

> And the Gileadites took the passages of Jordan before the Eph-raimites: and it was so, that when those Ephraimites which were escaped said, Let me go over; that the men of Gilead said unto him, Art thou an Ephraimite? If he said, Nay; Then said they unto him, Say now Shibboleth: and he Sibboleth: for he could not frame to pronounce it right. Then they took him, and slew him at the passages of Jordan: and there fell at that time of the Ephraim-ites forty and two thousand.
>
> Judges XII (King James Version)

Even a single feature of speech may signal that a person belongs to a certain social group or geographical area.

From the time a West Germanic language (a geographical dialect of Germanic) was first brought to England about 450 A.D., the language which has come to be known as English has had many regional and local dialects. At the end of the 1300's Chaucer amused his courtly audience by giving northern dialectal forms to the speech of the two students who fool the miller in the ribald "Reeve's Tale." When Caxton brought the printing press to England in 1476 and began to translate great books into English and print them, he almost despaired because "the comyn englysshe that is spoken in one shyre varyeth from a nother," and he wasn't sure which "englysshe" to use. It was a matter of comment that Sir Walter Raleigh kept his Devon dialect (a form partially preserved in some Newfoundland dialects) while he was in Elizabeth's court.

Shakespeare could use stereotyped stage dialects to mark not only Welshmen and Scots (see Fluellen and Macmorris in *Henry V*) but also rural characters and people of various social levels, *e.g.* Bottom and his friends in *A Midsummer Night's Dream*. More impor-tant, Shakespeare could rely upon stereotyped reactions of his audience to these voices. Boswell, in the 1700's, laughed at some remnants in Dr. Johnson's speech of his rural origin, and boasted that no Scottish features lingered in his own language. The theme of Shaw's play *Pygmalion*, the basis for the musical *My Fair Lady*, is the complex relationship between dialect and social snobbery. The study of dialects is thus closely related to the study of literature, social history, and social attitudes as well as to the study of language itself.

Language change
and dialects

Every child is born into a speech community, and at an early age begins to learn the language spoken around him or her. There are from three thousand to four thousand languages in the world, some with only a few speakers and others, like English, Chinese, and French, with millions of speakers in many parts of the world. When a language is in constant use, it is also constantly changing. To read the English of King Alfred, for example, needs special training, and to learn to speak as did Englishmen of his time is equivalent to learning a new language; yet King Alfred lived only a thousand years ago. If we could be taken back to the London of 1600 and be fortunate enough to attend one of Shakespeare's plays, we would probably have difficulty in understanding the actors' lines—yet this was the general language taken soon afterward to North America.

Why language changes is not completely understood. We can sometimes see words drop in and out of our language and change their meanings. (What will happen to the words *inch*, *mile*, and so on, when the whole English-speaking world changes to the metric system? And how long will we retain the proverbs and sayings that use these words, such as, "Give him an inch and he'll take a mile"?) But why does the grammar of a language change? And why does the sound system of a language change: merging some sounds in our speech, such as **ea** and **ee** (*dear, deer*) which were once separate; dropping some, such as the **b** at the end of *thumb* and *numb*; and altering others, such as the vowel in *calm* and *palm* (words which now have at least three pronunciations)?

We know that a change sometimes arises from a mixture of dialects. Historians of the English language can show us, for example, that both the spoken language of SSB and the written standard English language which we all use are really mixtures of dialects. They can identify in them features of English from northern England, East Anglia, Kent, and so on, all with their own histories. One form becomes popular and gathers around it the prestige of its speakers, and is generally adopted. But other changes in a language remain unexplained.

All living languages have both regional and social dialects. Regional and social groupings separate some speakers of the language from the others. Therefore change in a language is not uniform, and a language breaks into various varieties and sub-varieties, each continuing to change in its own way.

SUMMARY

A dialect is a sub-variety of a language, either regional or social. It is distinguished from other sub-varieties of the same language by a unique combination of language features:

pronunciation (including stress and intonation)
grammatical forms
words and expressions
meanings of words and expressions.

Because it is not always easy to separate a language from a dialect, it is difficult to give the exact number of languages in the world. Shall we call two very different varieties two languages or two dialects of the same language? A good general measure is *mutual intelligibility:* the ability of speakers to understand one another. Dutch and English are historically related; both are varieties of Low German (the German of the coastal regions). Yet, with the separation of time and distance, they are no longer mutually intelligible, and are now called different languages. But English speakers of London, Edinburgh, Dublin, Toronto, New York, Melbourne, Aukland, Los Angeles, and Cape Town can converse together without a great deal of misunderstanding. Each speaker may use a dialect of English, but all the speakers still share a common language.

The label *language* can, however, become attached to the speech of certain groups because they are separated politically. Norwegian and Swedish are mutually intelligible, but they are usually called languages, not dialects. Flemish and Dutch provide another example. The term *language* may also be applied to the written form: Chinese, for example, has broken up into several major dialects that are not always mutually intelligible when spoken, but when written are mutually intelligible because they all share a writing system (which is based on *meaning* forms and not, like ours, on forms representing sounds). All the varieties, therefore, are still called Chinese. Nevertheless, if we keep in mind these other forces which involve the separation and coming together of people, and if we remember that mutual intelligibility is not an absolute measure but a matter of gradation, then the term is a useful one to separate language from dialect.

Dialect and Standard Dialect

Most European countries have one "standard" spoken dialect associated with education and class, usually the language of the capital city or, if different, of the chief cultural centre. Thus, in Europe the term *dialect* may carry connotations of "rural" or "folk," "provincial," "old-fashioned," and often "substandard" or, erroneously, "corrupted" and "ignorant"—that is, judgments based largely on the social status of the speakers of the dialect. This is less true in North America, where no one type of speech is standard—witness the regional dialects of the last four presidents of the United States or, less obviously different, the speech of Canadian political leaders. On this continent, people are more mobile and their societies have shorter histories. Even so, some of the European connotations of *dialect* have spilled over to affect attitudes on this

. . . precisely because a standard dialect is historically the dialect of a ruling class, history makes it more than that. Generations work to realize its potentialities; and because people everywhere come to expect its use in government, in education, and in literature, it becomes more effective in those uses than dialects which have not been so used. To dismiss these historical advantages is to dismiss civilization. . . .

James Sledd, *American Speech* (1973)

continent toward speakers of regional dialects different from one's own.

It is salutary to remember that a standard dialect of *any* language is merely a local dialect that has spread because it carries the prestige of its speakers, usually those who have power. Inherently, it is no better, no "purer," no more "logical," and no older than any other dialect. Many Europeans use two dialects quite naturally, the standard dialect at work or school, and the local dialect at home.

A typical shibboleth involving English dialects is the use of *gotten* as the past participle of *got*. Many Britishers and Canadians consider *gotten* a deterioration from the "right" language and an unfortunate American innovation. Yet, in fact, *gotten* is an older form of English (a relic form), and *got* is the innovation. Britishers who don't use *have gotten* will use *have forgotten*, and many Canadians would correct a child who says, "I have forgot my book." So neither variety of English is more systematic or "logical" than the other. Moreover, the Americans who have both past participle forms of *get* at their disposal can make a precise distinction that Britishers and most Canadians cannot make. As Albert H. Marckwardt explains in his book, *American English* (1958):

> We've *got* ten thousand dollars for laboratory equipment," means that the funds in question are in our possession—we have them. "We have *gotten* ten thousand dollars for laboratory equipment," means that we have obtained or acquired this particular sum of money. Few Americans would have the slightest question about the difference in the meaning of these two sentences.

Similar is the distinction that some Newfoundlanders can make between a form that marks merely "non-past," but indefinite otherwise in time, and strictly "present" and "now":

Non-past	*Present*
I *bees* sick. (generally)	I'*m* sick. (right now)
He *bees* sick.	She's sick.
They *bees* sick.	They'*re* (or they'*m*) sick.

This useful contrast cannot be expressed in the verb alone by speakers of standard English. The same Newfoundland dialect has at its disposal the double, even triple, negatives of the language of Chaucer and Shakespeare that allow extra emphasis. This is a language device lost to the present-day speaker of standard English because of the attempts of eighteenth and nineteenth century grammarians to make the language "logical" ("two negatives make a positive"—really a confusion between algebraic and linguistic systems). The people of Carbonear, Newfoundland, can say:

> "I don't want no dinner."
> "He don't have neither one."
> (I thought you liked her.) "No more I don't."

Would you use this expression?
"I see you got you some lumber," he said.

Merna Summers, "The Bachelors" in *The Skating Party* (1974)

Shakespeare often used a double negative:
I pray you bear with me, I cannot go no further.

Celia, in *As You Like It* II. iv. 8.

There is no harm intended to your person,
Nor to no Roman else: so tell them Publius.

Brutus, in *Julius Caesar* III. i. 91–2.

Two centuries earlier, Chaucer freely used double, triple, and even quadruple negatives:
O wikke Fame! for ther nys
Nothing so swift, lo, as she is!
(Oh wicked, Fame! For there is not
Nothing so swift, indeed, as she is!)

"The House of Fame," ll. 349–350

He nevere yet no vileynye ne sayde
In al his lyf unto no maner wight.
(He never yet in all his life (not) said (nothing) villainous about (no) kind of man.)

The Knight in the Prologue to *Canterbury Tales* ll, 70–71

Some non-standard forms enter the language by the process of children copying the speech in use around them. An example in Canadian speech is the use of *snuck* as the past tense of *sneak*, e.g. "She snuck up behind me." The older generation used this form facetiously but recent surveys show that many of the younger generation use this as their *only* form. Children also use forms that are similar to others forms. Many Canadians use *dove* as the past tense of *dive*, on the analogy of *drive/drove*; some children take this analogy to its logical conclusion and use *have diven* (to rhyme with *given*). In time, both *snuck* and *have diven* could become standard Canadian English.

To study dialects is to watch change within a language while it is happening.

Your Idiolect

Although language is a code agreed upon by a group of people, every person has a personal set of language habits called an *idiolect*. From the time a person begins to hear and react to language, one's world of language enlarges as one's social world enlarges to include: immediate family, neighborhood, the school where one absorbs the written language (and possibly other forms of the spoken language), occupation, hobbies, travels, the media of radio, movies, and television—the list varies for each person. In other words, each person enters various "speech communities." While an individual does not use all of the language features that he or she encounters, or even understands, other features of language are absorbed, consciously or unconsciously, into one's active repertoire. Over a period of time everyone's language changes, but for clear communication it must still approximate the language in use around one. When a group of idiolects have recognizably common elements of vocabulary, pronunciation, and grammar to distinguish them, we have what we call a dialect.

Then he spotted this mother bear and her two cubs down the slope dining on the blue berries and Frisco snuck down to make the kill.

Henry Pennier, *Chiefly Indian* (1972). Set in B.C.

He snuck over beside her and grabbed a sticky handful of sliced peaches and crammed them in his mouth.

George Bowering, "Time and Again" in Geddes (1975). A story set in B.C.

. . . she learned to accept, even to like, the grim old city of St. John's . . . Even her speech changed somewhat. The drawling, word-champing dialect that came to her naturally from dim origins in Somerset, with modifications added by the isolation and local conditions of Haystack, now became overlaid with the colonial Irish spoken by nearly everyone in St. John's.

Percy Janes, *House of Hate* (1970). Story of Corner Brook, Nfld.

SUMMARY

dia 'through, across, apart'   *-lect* 'speaking'

What a dialect is *not:*
—sloppy, irresponsible usage
—necessarily non-standard language
—necessarily quaint, old, or rural usage
—the same as "accent." The term *accent* refers to pronunciation features only, whereas *dialect* involves other features of language as well.

Every language has varieties within it, called dialects.
Every language is a composite structure of overlapping dialects.
Every speaker of a language uses a dialect.
Every speaker of a language has his or her own set of language habits, an idiolect.

The dimensions of dialect

Before beginning to study the language being used by a group of people, a dialectologist must specify the kind of variation being investigated. A speech community can be a *regional* group or a *social* group; and both groups exist within *time*.

Geographical Dimensions

A geographical dialect is that speech shared by people within a certain area: a language community separated physically by mountains, a river or sea, or by political boundaries. We could, therefore, consider Canadian English, Australian English, and so on as dialects. However, as stated in Part One, it is easier to consider these national divisions as broad *varieties* of English, each capable of containing a number of different dialects. Thus within Canada we can speak of Newfoundland dialects, of an Ottawa Valley dialect, of British Columbia dialects, and so on. Further, within different areas of a country there may occur regionalisms, or even localisms, linguistic features confined to a given region or locality. For example, when North Americans had to differentiate between ordinary highways and the new "limited access" roads, various regionalisms arose; as one drives in different parts of the continent one can be on a *freeway*, a *thruway*, an *expressway*, a *turnpike*, or a *parkway*. What is the term in your part of Canada? Is there any differentiation made between terms?

Similarly, towns and cities in North America have developed localisms for the grass strip between the sidewalk and the curb of the road: *tree lawn, tree belt, tree bank, tree row, boulevard, median, devil strip, grass strip, parking strip* (or plain *parking*), *parkway, city strip, sidewalk plot, neutral ground, terrace,* and *berm*. No doubt there are other local terms across Canada.

Localisms may occur as vocabulary items peculiar to a small area. Ernest Buckler in his fictional memoir *Ox Bells and Fireflies* gives several localisms that flourished in his small Nova Scotian community, among them:

copperosity	'well-being'	How's the state of your copperosity?
defewgulty	'trouble'	What's the defewgulty? (perhaps a form of *difficulty*)
sevaggirous	'wretched'	Every time he gets a chill he has this sevaggirous time with his waterworks, too.

Any social group that is isolated geographically soon uses the language in its own way.

The word *berm* is also used in the United States to refer to the dirt "shoulder" of a road. The State of Ohio has adopted the term officially. In North Dakota, however, it refers to the area between the sidewalk and the road.

It is an old word (from French *berme*, in turn from Dutch and German, and probably cognate with Old Norse *barmr* 'brim') which once referred to the space left between the ditch and the base of the parapet in fortifications; later, in the United States, it referred to the bank of a canal opposite the towing path. From castle to canals to highways: the history of a word can reflect the history of a people.

Time Dimensions

Changes in a language generally occur most rapidly in vocabulary and meanings. Witness how, in 1971 , millions of English-speaking people, while watching or reading about the astronauts on the surface of the moon, assimilated almost immediately a new word *lunain*, made by analogy with *terrain*. Pronunciation and grammar, however, change more slowly and less obviously, but inevitably. The language of one generation is never quite the same as the language of the previous generation. A dialect can therefore be studied historically, that is, from the viewpoint of a time dimension.

The time (or temporal) dimension and the geographical (or spatial) dimension are, of course, intertwined. When people are separated geographically, the consequent differences in language occur within time. It is quite reasonable that Canadian English, which became established and at least partially separated from both American and British English in the eighteenth century, should develop in its own way.

It is also reasonable that within a social group as tightly knit as a family, the language of two people may vary because of age. For example, a member of an older generation often uses forms that are disappearing (called *recessive forms*).

Today, with mass media making new terms and New York slang being picked up almost immediately by the young, the linguistic gap between generations, especially in vocabulary, can widen quickly. A recent survey of the Kootenay area in British Columbia shows, for example, that the high school students tend to use *sofa* for 'the large piece of furniture two or three people can sit on', while nearly all their parents use the more general Canadian term, *chesterfield*. The source of the change, though not certain, is probably American, spreading northward by means of television and perhaps through frequent contact with Spokane, Washington, a centre for shopping. But the 1972 SCE confirms a general trend away from the Canadian term. (See the comments and table below. See also p. 132.)

Question 29   sofa, chesterfield, davenport

The preferred usage in British is *sofa*, although *chesterfield* is also used. The C.O.D. [*Concise Oxford Dictionary*] recognizes *davenport* as a small desk only. *Sofa* and *davenport* are the most commonly used of these choices in American English. The Canadian preference for *chesterfield* clearly sets Canadian English off from the American and British varieties. A large number of students, except in Newfoundland, have chosen answer D, which might represent names like *couch* and *settee*.

The distribution of answers is as follows:

29. What do you call a piece of furniture that seats two or three people in a row and has upholstered arms and back?
    A. *sofa*   C. *davenport*
    B. *chesterfield*   D. by another name

	male parents				female parents				male students				female students			
	A	B	C	D	A	B	C	D	A	B	C	D	A	B	C	D
Nfld	10	82	4	3	9	82	1	3	8	83	3	5	11	79	3	5
PEI	10	75	5	9	9	79	3	8	12	56	3	28	11	61	2	26
NS	9	83	2	5	10	82	2	5	9	62	2	26	8	67	1	23
NB	11	80	3	5	8	83	1	7	8	58	3	30	9	60	1	30
Que	24	71	1	2	21	66	2	9	16	67	1	14	17	63	1	18
Ont	11	86	1	3	11	82	1	5	11	68	3	17	13	61	1	24
Man	13	79	2	4	5	85	3	6	9	74	3	14	12	70	1	15
Sask	7	87	2	3	4	91	1	3	8	69	3	19	7	67	1	24
Alta	9	84	2	4	6	87	0	7	7	76	0	15	6	69	2	23
BC	6	88	1	3	4	90	0	5	8	72	1	16	6	67	1	25
Total	10	82	2	4	8	84	1	6	10	67	2	19	10	65	1	23

Quirk was what our townsfolk call a 'cute young man. Indeed, he was a smart chap; . . .

Thomas McCulloch, *The Step-sure Letters* (1821)

How does the use of the apostrophe in *'cute* suggest its origin? How has the meaning changed?

A man "going up in the world" reacts to the "small town" (Ontario of a generation ago) word usage of his wife; how do you react to these usages? Are they "social markers" in your linguistic and social world?

Nor did she speak English as became the wife of one who had once hobnobbed with a Prince and might do so again. If she positively *had* to use hick expressions, I once heard Boy tell her, she might at least say "For Heaven's sake," and not "For Heaven sakes." And "supper" was a meal one ate after the theatre, *not* the meal they ate every night at half-past seven. Nor could she learn when to refer to herself as "one," or remember not to say "between you and I."

Robertson Davies, *Fifth Business* (1970)

An East London mother was once heard to say proudly of her successful businessman son, "He can talk up or he can talk down." In other words, her son's linguistic competence included more than one dialect which he could "turn on" as the occasion demanded.

A word may die because the image lying behind the word disappears. One example is *spider* for frying pan (a North Americanism, see p. 10). Another, not quite "dead," is the Canadianism *firereels*, which, W. S. Avis reports, was used in Toronto during his boyhood there and was originally the word for the old horse-drawn vehicles equipped with a huge reel of hose. Today the "reel" is less conspicuous, and the term has been largely displaced by the more general expressions *fire engine* and *fire truck*.

Sometimes the clash of old and new meanings can eliminate the use of a word: one hesitates these days to say that one attended a *gay* party; and recently a twelve-year-old, familiar with the current slang meanings of *cool*, was puzzled when he found in a book the older "straight" phrase, "She acted coolly toward him." Will the slang meanings eliminate the older uses of the word? On the other hand, most slang terms belong to the oral language only and are not preserved through time.

Social Dimensions

Groups of people may also be separated by social class; certainly we all recognize and react to social dialects. These may be less important or less obvious in Canada than in England, where the "standard" spoken English has been until very recently a class dialect. Although based historically on the speech of London, this dialect is related more to family and to education than to region. Cockney, for instance, is a dialect of London and southern England, but hardly carries the prestige of SSB. In fact, a speaker of this standard dialect in England or Wales is said to have "no accent," that is, no observable characteristics of the speech of a geographical area.

Canada, too, has its social dialects and, in spite of a hundred years of public education, its lingering linguistic shibboleths. These are more frequently found in grammatical items (some of which have long, often aristocratic, histories) than in pronunciation and vocabulary. Gauge your own reaction, for instance, if someone says, "It don't" or "He done it good."

Social dialects in Canada have not yet been studied to any extent.

But as a Canadian, you know many of the social "markers" in the speech of Canadians in your area.

Sex Differences in Language

Anyone wanting a proper sampling of a community's dialect, especially on the social dimension, must take into account sex differences in language. These are revealed mainly in vocabulary and perhaps in style. Some adjectives, in particular, are used almost exclusively by women (a *darling* hat); and even "Women's Lib" has not freed all Canadian women from certain linguistic taboos. Some of the differences in vocabulary arise from differences in activities. In Newfoundland, for instance, boys have fun at spring *breakup* (a Canadian term meaning 'the time the ice melts and begins to move') by playing the risky game of *copying*, jumping from ice pan to ice pan far out in a cove. In the Carbonear area this game is called *cocking*. A dialectologist received this response immediately from every boy and man asked, whereas few women knew the term at all, and those who did gave *copying*, which they probably learned from print, not from experience (Paddock, 1966).

Other Social Groupings

Nearly everyone in his or her lifetime acquires several special vocabularies, each limited to an occupation, a profession, a sport, a field of scholarship, or any social or shared activity. A good reference library now contains a surprisingly large number of dictionaries listing such special vocabularies; few general dictionaries can include or describe them all. Even Dr. Johnson, for his great *Dictionary* of 1755, decided that he would not be able to list the "many terms of art and manufacture." He explains in his Preface:

> I could not visit caverns to learn the miner's language, nor take a voyage to perfect my skill in the dialect of navigation, nor visit the warehouses of merchants, and ships of artificers, to gain the names of wares, tools and operations, of which no mention is found in books; what favourable accident, or easy inquiry brought within my reach, has not been neglected; but it had been a hopeless labour to glean up words, by courting living information, and contesting with the sullenness of one, and the roughness of another . . .

Some words and expressions from *one* article in a British Columbia magazine for loggers! How many do you know?

booming ground
bunk scales
catch-boom
cat loader
chokerman
cradle
crawler-loader
cunits
deadfalls
faller
heel boom
ring barkers
sinkers
stumpage
stump-to-dump contract
truck bunks
wheel skidders

Sometimes, however, pieces of a "special" language may become part of the general language, either as accepted terms or as metaphors: terms such as *moron* or *IQ* from psychology; metaphors such as *getting down to bed-rock, hitting paydirt*, and *waiting to see how things will pan out* from mining. Because of such "leaks" the study of the special language of any one activity or social group can be an important part of the general study of dialects.

Functional Variations: "Code-Switching" to Fit the Social Occasion

Within any dialect there are functional varieties determined by audience, situation, and occasion. These functional varieties may range from the intimate and the informal to the formal or the ritualistic, and may occur in both the spoken and the written modes. Some of the most commonly recognized varieties are often given labels, such as "colloquial," "literary," "poetic," "religious." A child learns very quickly to suit language to the audience and the occasion: listen to a boy answering a telephone and changing his language to fit the person on the other end; or listen in on small girls playing adult roles of "mother," "teacher," "doctor," or characters from TV.

The school experience can increase one's ability both to know and to use additional varieties: to switch, perhaps, from the home's "I seen" or "I seed" to the school's "I saw"; or to add grammatical structures and vocabulary from the written language of books—so, for example, one knows and may use on occasion *brook*, *stream*, even *rivulet* or *rill*, yet with friends, go fishing in the *creek*, sometimes pronounced *crick*.* Education can widen a linguistic world and eliminate many barriers of space and time, but it can also destroy characteristic features of geographical and social dialects.

Canadian Attitudes to Other Dialects of English

Recently there has been an upsurge of interest not only in the social dimensions of dialects but also in the attitudes of people toward the speech of others. It has been demonstrated that certain non-prestigious dialects, both regional and social, can handicap speakers in education and in advancement in their work. But such judgments of people according to their speech are usually based on false generalizations, stereotypes, and emotional prejudices. One intelligent and well-educated Canadian, for example, confessed that he

---

* See pp. 146 and 182. Some Canadians, particularly in the Maritimes, use *brook* in their regular speech and use *creek* to refer to a salt-water estuary, as do Britishers. For example:

"Creek" applies only to tidal estuaries, and its application on maps above tide level is usually cartographic licence.
"Brook" is the universal term for flowing-water features above tide, with two instances of "run" for similar features.
"Run" is also used for entrances through sandbars, examples being *Tignish Run* and *Miminegash Run*.

Alan Rayburn, *Geographical Names of Prince Edward Island* (1973) "at least half-believed immediately any statement made by someone with a 'cultured' British accent." For others, such a dialect is anathema, carrying connotations of "superiority" and "snobbishness." Until quite recently, in western Canada at least, many employment notices carried the phrase "No Englishman need apply," and local jokes frequently repeated the supposed reactions of Englishmen to the rough conditions of the lumber camp or mining town ("What! No marmalade?"). The nicknames given to immigrants, *e.g. sparrows* or *chirpers* for Englishmen, were also indicators of attitudes.

But the dislike of supposed superiors can also be internal. Susanna Moodie in her chronicles of early Canada, *Roughing it in the Bush* (1852), repeats the then current phrase *to come York over*; "You are not going to come York over me in that way, or Yankee either," meaning 'to play the superior, as if from York (Toronto)'. Some dialects carry favorable connotations; the Scottish dialects, for example, seem to be generally valued in Canada. But all such linguistic judgments, favorable or unfavorable, are based on the false premise that "national characteristics" may be applied to every individual of that national group.

Today, with a better educated and more mobile people, Canada is losing much of this kind of sociological-linguistic folklore—but not completely.

"Avoid awc-cent! Avoid awc-cent!"

Bishop John Strachan's advice to the students of Trinity College, which he founded in 1851. Quoted in Hamilton (1952).

At last he spoke without taking his eyes from the road.
"You from the old country?"
"Yup." (I told you I was getting into the idiom.)

Kildare Dobbs, *Running to Paradise* (1962). About a small town in Ontario.

"Van Horne was called Sparrow Avenue in those days because of the English families living there."

An old-timer of Dryden, Ontario in an interview reported in the *Dryden Observer*, November 10, 1976.

Language in use

I fixed the plow, and told 'em to wear gloves, and helped 'em make a stoneboat. Of course they must have me stay for supper—dinner, they called it. I opened my eyes, I tell you, when they all came to supper dolled up in evening dress, London style; and her ladyship served up a dinner to match, winding up with black coffee and cigars.

H. A. Kennedy, *Book of the West* (1925). The speaker is a native Nova Scotian who had settled in the West, and is describing how he helped some settlers from England.

Here is how a recent immigrant from England heard the word *lunch* used in Saskatoon:

. . . . But there is still a great deal of entertaining in the home, often in a manner which seems very strange to the English immigrant. One has to learn not only new customs, but a new use of one's own language.

The midday meal is called lunch, but lunch is also any snack or form of refreshment which is not a regular meal. So one has lunch after a game of golf, lunch after an afternoon game of bridge, lunch (coffee and cakes) after an evening meeting and lunch after midnight as one watches the late movie. 'To visit' is not to stay with someone (a visitor of the English kind is a house guest); it is to have a little chat with someone, sitting side by side. There is no tea-time.

Elisabeth Gerrard, *We Came to Canada* (1967)

Compare with this usage:

Our tea, as we always called our evening meal, was like a solemn mass compared with the free and easy midday dinner we all enjoyed when the Old Man was at work in the mill.

Percy Janes, *House of Hate* (1970). Newfoundland, a generation ago.

Obviously there are close but never completely definable relationships between geographical, historical, and social variants of a language. The complexity of these relationships becomes apparent when we examine the forces which cause shifts and changes in the language system.

A major force in language change is social prestige. A word or expression or pronunciation takes on the prestige of the people who use it; once an item is considered "superior" it tends to eliminate a variant not so regarded. A *semantic* ('meaning') clash may also wipe out one of a term's meanings. Both these processes working together can be seen in the Canadian use of the word *lunch*, which, on both sides of the Atlantic, has always been used to mean the mid-day meal but in some areas could also refer to 'food eaten between meals'. This second meaning seems to be giving way to *snack* in Canada, for two reasons: the prevalence of *snack* in food advertising and in phrases such as *snack bar*; and changing customs and work patterns which are making the mid-day meal a light one—a *lunch* instead of a *dinner*, so the two meanings of *lunch* are clashing. The term *snack* seems to be filling the need for a word meaning 'something light between meals'.

Sociological changes can cause the referent itself to disappear. The Newfoundland term, which may be found in other places too, a *turn of water* meaning 'a load of two bucketfuls (or pailfuls) carried from a well or pump' is disappearing because water is now piped into the houses. But sometimes a word lingers to take on new meanings in a region: *swamp* in P.E.I. today nearly always refers to a 'wood lot', because all the old swamp lands are now drained. The word remains even when the referent disappears.

Rapid urbanization and changes in rural work and life have made many farming terms obsolete. Here is a sampling of rural terms taken from Ernest Buckler's reminiscences of his Nova Scotian childhood, *Ox Bells and Fireflies*:

steering the share just right to curl over the ribbon of
   greensward
the horse's britchen
cross-laced the headpieces in the groove of the yoke pegs
the heavy double-sled tongue
swiveled the front rocker (of the sled) straight in its bench
in the hardwood chopping, you rugged the oxen
you opened the dinner kettle and saw the food
the grain of the wooden snath
you tripped the load on to the straight . . . windrows

Thousands of Canadians words (many of them French or Indian) are now marked "obsolete" or "historical" in the DC. Some examples are:

terms of the fur trade:	*Montreal canoe, L'Assomption sash, post-house, tripman,*
the settlement of the West:	*ticket of location, harvester-special, settlement duty, colonist car,*
the gold rushes:	*poor man's route, pay gravel, dust ('gold dust'), dump-box,*
the Great Depression:	*Bennett buggy, dust-bowl years* (Sask.), *on the pogey*—although with the rise in unemployment, the term *the pogey* has recently reappeared,
wars and rebellions:	*English party, Exovede, Ross.*

In spite of this continuing change, much of a language, especially in matters other than vocabulary, can remain constant for surprisingly long periods of time. The history of a people can lie embedded in their speech for generations.

What do you call the main room in your house in which you entertain important visitors? *parlor? living room? front room? family room?* A midland U.S. term is *big room*, the South may use *chamber*, and both of these may use *big house*. Have you heard these in Canada?

Note the technical language in this description of the Fraser River goldfields; some of these are listed in the DC as Canadianisms.

The terraces contain vast deposits of gold; and to be worked to advantage the "bench diggings" must command a stream of water supplied from a source higher than their own surfaces, so as to give a fall to enable the miner to apply the water to the face of the "bench" by a hose. The force of the stream is due to the height of the fall. A good strong stream playing upon the face of the hill will disintegrate a great quantity of "pay dirt" in a short time. The floating rubbish, or "dirt," is caught in a long sluice at the base, provided with "riffles" on the bottom, and spread with quicksilver to catch the gold. This mode of mining is called by the miners "hydraulic mining." Such is the wealth of Cariboo that no quicksilver was used, for the miner could afford to lose all the "fine dust" and to be satisfied with the "lumps."

William Carew Hazlitt, *The Great Gold Fields of Cariboo* (1862)

I remember when I wrote *The Stone Angel* what a terrific surprise it was to me to realize that I was actually writing a lot of Hagar's speech in the idiom of my grandparents' generation—which was, I may say, an idiom which I didn't even know I remembered until it came back to me with her, and I knew it was right. It was like tapping a part of your head that you didn't know was there, and it was all there.

Margaret Laurence in Cameron (1973)

Space, time, social and occupational changes, and the various styles adopted for various social roles, plus the levelling influence of education and the media— all the forces that separate people or pull them together can shape and change the language they use. Behind the common phrase "He/she speaks my language" is an intricate network of linguistic, social, geographic, and economic relationships. A variety such as Canadian English therefore can be investigated in many different ways. No matter which "dimension" of the language is chosen, the data can add not only to our knowledge of the dialect itself—and perhaps of all human language—but also to our understanding of the speakers of the dialect and the forces affecting their lives.

Chapter 4
How Dialects are Studied

The scientific study of language variation is called *dialectology*. The branch of dialectology concerned with regional variation is called *linguistic geography*, or alternatively *areal linguistics, geographical linguistics*, and *dialect geography*. Investigations focussing on social variations are a branch of *socio-linguistics*.

The beginnings

The beginnings of the scientific study of dialects lie in the mid-1800's in Europe. Dialectologists were motivated partly by the interest of the times in "folk" ways, but more by the excitement engendered by the discovery of the Indo-European "family" of languages. As linguists traced the sound systems of related languages they discovered that many changes in these systems seemed to be fairly regular. Linguists thus became involved in the whole problem of how languages change, and their search for evidence led to the careful study of various European dialects.

The first modern surveys in Europe show two almost opposite techniques, both of which, with some refinements, are used today. In the late 1800's George Wenker, a German scholar, did one of the widest surveys ever attempted—that of the whole German Empire. He sent out questionnaires for forty-four test sentences to be "translated" by the local schoolmasters into the local dialects of over 40 000 localities. The different varieties of each feature were then plotted on maps to show their geographical distribution. Although the "spelling" method of recording pronunciation was an inaccurate device, the survey did reveal many patterns, some of which could then be investigated further. The project was certainly a major achievement.

A second large survey, done in France and adjoining areas of Switzerland and Italy, used a set of techniques almost opposite from those used in the German survey. The recording was done by one fieldworker, carefully trained in phonetics. There were fewer localities (about 600) and only one person chosen from each locality to be the informant, who answered orally a set of questions from a prepared questionnaire at an interview with the fieldworker. Then one trained dialectologist plotted the answers to each question upon a map, and compiled the maps into a dialect atlas. The great gain was in accuracy, particularly in pronunciation.

Each succeeding survey demonstrated greater sophistication in techniques. A Swiss-Italian questionnaire showed, for example, the value of detailed drawings of items, particularly for helping informants differentiate among various words for somewhat similar items. Would drawings help you, for instance, to answer this set of questions:

What do you call a smaller dressing table, usually with a mirror and with drawers at the sides?
dresser, vanity, vanity table,
other _____ ?

(write in)

What do you call a chest of drawers in which you keep clothing?
dresser, bureau, chiffonier, chiffonrobe,
other _____ ?

(write in)

Dialectology in North America

North American scholars benefited from the European experience. In the late 1920's, the Modern Language Association formed a committee under Hans Kurath to survey the English spoken on this continent. The MLA was particularly concerned that such a survey should be done before the levelling influences of radio, population shifts, and public education could destroy the older differences so vital as evidence in language history. The whole enterprise, which is still going on in various parts of North America, will result in the *Linguistic Atlas of the United States and Canada*.

The Atlantic seaboard constituted the most important area to survey because it was the locale of the first colonies and the main source of the people who later settled the American West. For the first survey the committee chose New England and included six communities in adjacent New Brunswick.

North American surveys must take account of features not always important in European surveys, *e.g.* greater social and geographical mobility; settlement and waves of immigration from various sources; lack of one prestige form established as a "standard"; mass education (illiteracy preserves older forms); mass media of communication; and some cultural insecurity, thus self-consciousness about language. The sampling techniques and methodology were therefore developed with great care, and these procedures have been essentially followed in later surveys in other areas. They may be described succinctly under these headings:

Communities
Because the focus was historical, the "mesh" for sampling was quite fine—more than two hundred New England communities, including towns, cities, and rural areas, about equidistant from one another. The oldest settled areas were given preference, but checks were made by including new areas. A brief history of each community was compiled giving accounts of settlement, later immigration, principal families, and industries.

Informants
Informants were chosen so as to find evidence for differences and changes in the social and time dimensions and to observe possible dialect mixtures.

Social groups:

Type I little formal education, few outside contacts

Type II some formal education (usually high school), more outside contacts and reading

Type III advanced education, more outside contacts (Few of
this category were used.)

Age groups:

Each of these types was further divided by age:

A: aged, or old-fashioned
B: middle-aged or younger

The fieldworkers chose their own informants according to these
guidelines, and compiled both a biographical and a character sketch
of each.

Fieldworkers

All were trained linguists, given special courses in transcribing
speech with the help of a refined phonetic alphabet, and versed in
techniques for eliciting information from informants in a conversational atmosphere. Even with this training, fieldworkers proved to
be remarkably varied in transcribing and in their ability to "hear"
information. Later surveys used special methods to crosscheck, so
that some feature which was peculiar to the worker would not be
interpreted as a geographical one. In order to elicit pertinent information, fieldworkers must be able to ask a question in various ways:
for example, one worker, hoping to find a variant for "frying pan,"
asked his informant, "What do you fry eggs in?" and got the reply,
"Butter."

The personalities of the fieldworkers are all-important. They must
be patient and retain their sense of humor: one informant, when
asked "Were you born here?" answered, "No, across the street."
One of the greatest challenges facing fieldworkers is that of eliciting
a speaker's ordinary, informal language as opposed to the formal
language the speaker reserves for strangers or thinks is "correct."
Investigators must, therefore, be alert to the informant who changes
his or her language either out of shame for it or the wish to be polite
and accommodate to the language of the visitor. A worker will
spend on the average seven or eight hours with an informant, a task
requiring tact and a real interest in people. Our language is so
"ordinary" to us, that an informant can become tired of being asked
questions that seem silly.

The Questionnaire

The dialectologist uses a preliminary questionnaire to gain some
idea of what items will be productive. Worksheets are then prepared
to help the fieldworker record the answers. A general survey attempts to cover variants in all aspects of language: vocabulary,
meaning, pronunciation, grammar, and the attitudes of the informants toward the items.

Vocabulary

Words and phrases are those of everyday life in the family, those
that continue sometimes for many generations and are not learned
from books or in schools. Usually they are grouped under topics,

such as *food, weather, furniture, farm implements*, and so on to enable the fieldworker to introduce them naturally into conversation.

To this basic list a fieldworker may add words of local or economic interest, *e.g.* for Canada, fishing terms in British Columbia and the Atlantic Provinces, mining in northern Ontario and Quebec, or cattle ranching in Alberta and British Columbia.

Pronunciation

This may be the pronunciation of one word—*e.g. slough* is pronounced to rhyme with *how* by speakers in eastern Canada, but west of Toronto it usually rhymes with *glue*. The question may deal with the pronunciation of one sound, *e.g.* the [t] of *writer*, or the quality of the vowel in *home*; or a pattern of sounds, *e.g.* the "Canadian" **ou** in pairs such as *lout/loud, house/houses*.

One aspect of pronunciation still largely unexplored by dialectologists everywhere is intonation—the "music" of speech—unexplored because linguists have not yet devised an easy-to-record description of the phenomena of stress, pitch, and juncture and their relationships.

> Sunshine, sloughs and hawks are what I remember most about our first sight of Saskatchewan. By sloughs I mean shallow stretches of water. We should call them ponds or meres, or even lakes, in England, but we have now learnt to give them their prairie name, which is pronounced to rhyme with 'clues'.
>
> Elisabeth Gerrard, *We Came to Canada* (1967)

Grammar

In Canada grammatical differences are few, but sometimes important, because certain items (*e.g. it don't*) are social shibboleths.

Many grammatical differences are suppressed by schooling and kept only for home usage. The past tense of some verbs, *e.g. dived* or *dove, climbed* or *clumb*, may reveal such differences.

A few expressions such as the Maritimes' and Newfoundland's use of "That's some good" or "Today's some hot" (found also in some British dialects) may be regional variations.

> "... My, 'tis some hot! What have they done with the heat in this place atall?..."
>
> Gordon Pinsent, *John & the Missus* (1974). A novel set in Newfoundland.

Although no survey or questionnaire can reveal *all* differences within dialects, it can provide sample items upon which later surveys will be able to concentrate. For instance, Walter S. Avis has devised a reading passage, called "Harry's House" with a checklist to standardize the study of Canadian speech both in individual words (*e.g. khaki* or *vase*) and in sound patterns (*e.g.* the **ou** sounds in *house* and *houses*). By giving the same reading passage, the investigator can compare the differences found in that style of speech, but it must be remembered that we all change our language slightly for different purposes. A reading style is slower and more careful than running speech, so that some pronunciations may be premeditated rather than spontaneous. Other linguists may be needed later to "chase down" certain words and expressions for which the reading-passage pronunciations seem questionable or unreliable.

Compiling, Editing, and Publishing

The fieldworker uses prepared answer sheets or citation slips on which all the information is written: name or type of informant (usually coded to keep privacy); place; the pronunciation used; the meaning given; and the attitude toward the word or any remarks

Nowadays, the fieldworker may use sheets adapted to the computer. A typical citation slip looks like this:

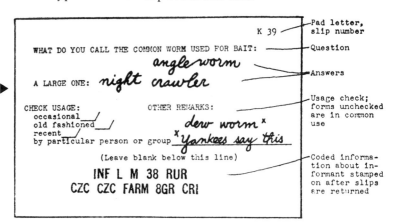

Citation slip from F. G. Cassidy and Audrey R. Duckert, "A Method for Collecting Dialects," *PADS*, No. 20 (University of Alabama Press: 1953). Used by permission.

Source: F. Cassidy, *PADS* 20.

Can you "read" the map? Can you account for the results of the surveys?

An editor then gives each variant form a symbol, and marks its occurrence on a map. A line showing the outward boundary of a form is called an *isogloss*. For example, if a dialectologist plotted on a map how Canadians pronounce *slough*, he or she would probably be able to draw an isogloss somewhere between Manitoba and Ontario—the boundary of the western area which used the pronunciation [slu:] (rhyming with *too*). If the isoglosses for quite a few items fall close together, they are probably marking the division between two dialect areas. Usually, however, such divisions are not clear-cut, because some items "spill over" into the adjoining area.

The making and publishing of a dialect atlas is expensive. Therefore, the results of much fieldwork often remain unpublished, though available in archives as data for analysis.

Below is a map compiled by Avis and based on one item, the vowel of *aunt* as pronounced in Nova Scotia, and as investigated by H. R. Wilson, A. M. Kinloch, M. G. Wanamaker, and (earlier) by H. Alexander.

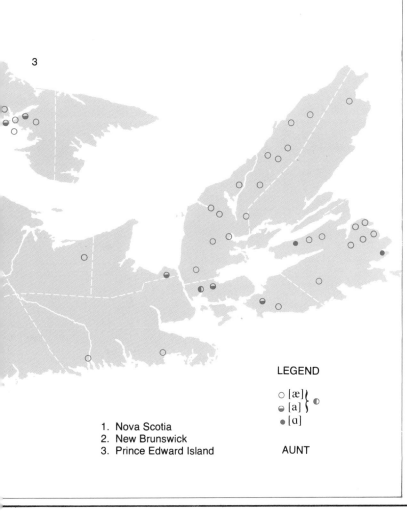

Pronunciation of *aunt* in the Maritime Provinces

1. Nova Scotia
2. New Brunswick
3. Prince Edward Island

LEGEND

○ [æ]
◒ [a]
● [ɑ]

AUNT

Walter S. Avis, Royal Military College of Canada

115

Interpretation of Results

The investigators finally examine the data collected and suggest some hypotheses for the patterns, or breaks in the patterns. The work done so far in the United States is important to Canadians, because the first large group of English-speaking Canadians, except in Newfoundland and parts of the Maritimes, were from the United States. Some of the facts established about American dialects are relevant to Canadian English. For example:

1. Even on the basis of about three hundred vocabulary items, Kurath established that there is no such speech as "General American," as was once supposed, and that the break between North and South linguistically is not the Mason-Dixon line. He found three well-defined major dialectal areas on the American Atlantic seaboard:
   a. *Northern:* New England, the Hudson Valley, the north strip

The westward sweep of American English

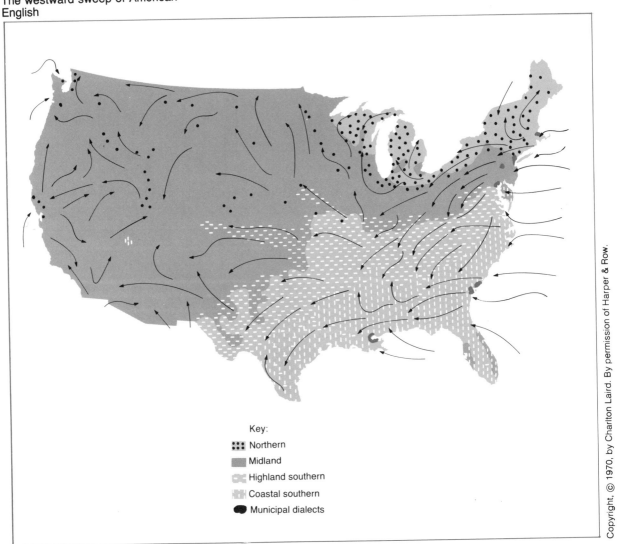

Key:
- Northern
- Midland
- Highland southern
- Coastal southern
- Municipal dialects

Copyright, © 1970, by Charlton Laird. By permission of Harper & Row.

of Pennsylvania, and Greater New York City; then the derivative areas inland: Michigan, Wisconsin, and the northern parts of Ohio, Indiana, Illinois, and Iowa

b. *Southern*: the plantation settlements from Chesapeake Bay to northern Florida

c. *Midland*—divided into two sub-areas: north midland— Pennsylvania and northern West Virginia; south midland —Shenandoah Valley and the southern Appalachians.

2. These three areas spread westward in well-defined migration patterns, sometimes blending as the people moved westward, *e.g.* New Englanders went by sea and influenced the speech of the San Francisco area; people from the Midlands and northerners mingled in the northwestern United States. The speech differences followed the people, and reflect original settlements.

3. These differences in vocabulary are confirmed by many similar demarcations in pronunciation and variant verb forms.

4. Some of the regional differences may be traceable to the British homes of the original settlers in the Atlantic states, *i.e.* to British dialects or to older British usage, though these connections have not been fully proved.

5. There is now a fairly clear picture of social differences within the dialect of each geographical area. The language of the less educated is generally more conservative, retaining older forms.

6. No language differences can be attributed to differences in physiology, race, or climate.

In other words, there is now factual evidence as to the origin and nature of dialectal differences on this continent, with clear implications for those making judgments upon language styles different from their own. Differences in language arise from differences in the experience and heritage of speech groups.

Recent Developments in North American Dialectology

The methods used in studying dialects have become increasingly sophisticated because of new knowledge (especially of statistics and sociology), new technology (computers, better recording, machine analysis of sounds), new theories about language and language variation, and new social concerns. Of course, the problems of time and money can also force investigators to try new methods for collecting data. Even the telephone has been used when only a few items are being surveyed!

The biggest changes, however, have been motivated by the challenge of recent social and educational problems, particularly in urban areas. Many investigators are studying the language of city-dwellers, especially of minority groups, which may reveal the differences arising from racial and social isolation or dialect mixture (*e.g.* families moving into the city from other areas). In cities, because of the greater number of communication links among groups of people, changes in speech may be rapid, and people often shift their usage according to the audience or situation. The early surveys, which had a historical focus, paid little attention to recent innovations and how they spread, or to how language variations are related to the sense of membership in social groups. This interest in the complex social aspects of dialects within a small geographical area has led to new methodologies, and questionnaires have been revised to include urban items, such as the terms used for cuts of meat, for parts of cars, and for different children's games.

The language patterns of non-native speakers and bilingual speakers, neglected by the early surveys, are now receiving attention, for such data can tell us much about how languages are learned. The attention to the sociological aspects of speech differences also has stimulated studies in people's attitudes toward social and regional dialects, especially those features that become "markers" to which people react. Many dialectologists are now active in trying to "translate" their findings into educational action.

Motivated by new theories of language developed by Noam Chomsky and other transformational-generative grammarians, dialectologists have developed a renewed interest in the theories of language variation, particularly in the *system* of a dialect as related to the abstract structure of the language. Indeed, probably the most important result of the recent work of dialectologists is the discovery of the "systematicness" of a dialect; that is, the realization that a dialect has its own grammar, sound, and meaning systems, and that the speakers of a non-prestigious dialect have learned this system and are not using a haphazard, debased kind of English. Speakers of such a dialect are not unintelligent people who cannot "learn grammar." They have already done so, but it happens to be a grammar slightly—but systematically—different from the standard one, and without the social prestige of having been accepted as standard. Even when people "switch codes," that is, change their speech—or in the case of bilingual speakers, change the language—to fit the listener and the situation, they do it not haphazardly, but according to complex social and linguistic "rules." To know more about this human linguistic capacity can lead to better attitudes about language systems different from one's own.

Modern dialectology, therefore, is a far more complex and varied study than it was when the first surveys were made for the *Linguistic Atlas* of this continent.

Dialectology in Canada

The scientific study of Canadian English has been slow in starting. In the 1930's when the *Linguistic Atlas of the United States and Canada* was initiated, fieldworkers did some research in New Brunswick and Nova Scotia. Since the founding of the Canadian Linguistic Association in 1954, however, both interest and research have increased rapidly. Walter S. Avis, in his Preface to *A Bibliography of Writings on Canadian English 1857–1965*, states that of the 168 titles listed, only 16 items appeared before 1900 and 25 before 1930, "an indication of greatly increased interest in the kind of English spoken in Canada." But much work must be done before the *Linguistic Atlas* is fully continental in scope.

Recognizing that the main and most accessible characteristic separating Canadian English from other varieties is its vocabulary, Canadian linguists early formed a Lexicographical Committee to collect authentic data, both contemporary and historical, for Canadian dictionaries. The dictionary projects (described on pp. 125 ff.) in turn have stimulated further interest and research.

More recently, a recognition that the study of Canadian English is worthy of a place in a school curriculum has given impetus to Canadian dialect study. In the spring of 1972, with financial aid from the Canada Council, the Canadian Council of Teachers of English (CCTE) co-operated with the Canadian Linguistic Association to take a wide sampling of the English used across Canada by Grade 9 students and their parents. The resulting *Survey of Canadian English* thus explores two dimensions, regional and temporal (a one-generation gap). The data was compiled by the Director, M. H. Scargill, at the University of Victoria, and the results, along with explanatory material, are published in Scargill and Warkentyne (1972) and, more fully, in Scargill (1974).

It is interesting that this Canadian survey is similar to the first modern survey, by Wenker in Germany, in that they both used teachers and students in order to cover a broad area at one time. Recently Professor Angus McIntosh has asked teachers in Scotland to distribute questionnaires, not to students but to two informants, one Gaelic, and one English-speaking, of their districts. Thus, McIntosh's written questionnaires of about 200 items are evenly distributed throughout Scotland. The information he gets will be important to Canadian dialectologists, who suspect that many Canadian words, such as *droke* or *drook* 'grove of trees', used in the Atlantic Provinces, may be from Scottish or English regional dialects.

Recent Developments in Canadian Dialectology

At present Canadians have been hosts for three international conferences (1972, 1975, 1978) on methods in dialectology. Such

Dialectology has its perils. The following story is told about Henry Alexander, professor of English at Queen's University and a pioneer in the study of Maritimes dialect.

In the early years of World War II, residents of a small Nova Scotia coastal village became suspicious of the activities of a stranger who they thought spoke poor English. They reported the matter to the shore patrol who picked up the man and turned him over to the R.C.M.P. in Halifax. The suspected spy turned out to be a university professor whose cultivated English accent had aroused the mistrust of the Halifax County fishermen. The police were apologetic and to save the professor from any future embarrassment he might suffer on account of his speech, they presented him with an official document certifying him as harmless.

"Speaking as a Canadian," *The Canada Council Bulletin No. 13* (Autumn, 1962)

international co-operation will help in correlating facts about the language in the New World with that of the mother countries. Internally, Canadian dialectologists have broadened their interests to include the study of dialects in all the languages spoken in Canada. A. M. Kinloch and A. B. House, for instance, are investigating the language used in bilingual areas of New Brunswick. The work done earlier in Nova Scotia is developing into a word-geography of southwestern Nova Scotia, an interesting area both historically and linguistically. To prepare for the study of the phonology in this region, Kinloch, M. G. Wanamaker, and H. R. Wilson have been developing a special phonetic system for use on typewriters and computer terminals. A team from Carleton University is doing the preliminary studies for a full survey of the Ottawa Valley, long known as a "dialect pocket." (See Padolsky and Pringle 1977.) In Edmonton, much work is being done on dialects within their social context; and researchers in Vancouver are planning studies of small areas in British Columbia and looking closely at social dialects in the urban area around Vancouver. For example, the latter research (still not fully analysed) suggests that certain items in phonology, such as a voiced [t] between voiced sounds (*e.g. butter* as if *budder*) and the loss of [t] after [n] (*e.g. twenty* as *twenny*), are predictably related to social or educational stratification. Howard Woods, who is working on this study and extending it to other urban centres, suggests that responses to an oral questionnaire may vary also according to the degree of consciousness about speech—for example, whether the informant is asked to say pairs of words (*e.g. latter* and *ladder*), a task which would make the informant very conscious of the difference in sounds, or to read a passage (a semi-formal situation), or to count (*e.g.* saying the words for 20, 21, 22, 23, and so on), or to talk casually. In Ontario, Wilson is working with Ontario teachers to extend and refine the 1972 SCE so as to localize the responses, get more information about alternative forms, and try to alleviate one problem inherent in questionnaires that offer choices—the danger of suggesting certain items that the person doesn't really use. All people interested in dialects are looking forward to the almost-completed *Dictionary of Newfoundland English* (DNE). In short, Canadian dialectologists, though often hampered by the lack of funds and time, are doing the detailed, painstaking work necessary for accumulating accurate information about the English that Canadians use.

Quick

QUIZ

True or False?

1. Every speaker of English speaks a dialect.

2. Most dialects are used by rural and uneducated people.

3. A dialectologist usually wants the careful, formal language of an informant, not unguarded conversational speech.

4. All living languages change.

5. Most languages of the world are really collections of dialects.

6. Most dialectal forms in North America are substandard.

7. A standard arises within a language because it is the best-formed dialect.

8. Dialect areas in the United States are most clearly marked in the East.

9. The differences in speech among North Americans are much greater than those among people in various parts of the British Isles.

10. Differences in vocabulary are usually a much greater social barrier than are differences in phonology or in grammar.

ANSWERS

1. True   3. False   5. True   7. False   9. False
2. False   4. True   6. False   8. True   10. False

121

Evidence and data in language study

Written Evidence: Language Frozen in Print

As well as making surveys of present-day spoken English, dialectologists also examine the written language used within an area. Newspapers, magazines, journals, letters, government records, mail-order catalogues, and literature can give valuable evidence. This interest of the dialectologist in samples of written language ranges from the historical to the contemporary.

Here are some examples of Canadianisms found in the journals of Simon Fraser (Lamb 1960), written when he travelled down the river which now bears his name:

June 24, 1808
. . . Sent some men to visit the rapids, and set out at 8 A.M. After going a mile we came to a *carrying place* of 800 yards. . . .
    Continued — passed a small camp of Indians without stopping and came to a *discharge* with steep hills at both ends, where we experienced some difficulty in carrying the things.

The Canadian French equivalent, *portage*, has also survived, and is probably the one more commonly used now.

In an earlier entry Fraser uses a different spelling of *discharge:*

May 29, 1808
Here we put three bales of salmon into *cache* and carried the rest through a very rugged country. It was late before we had cleared. We called this place *decharge de la Montagne*.

The most common spelling is *décharge*. The French word *cache* is now in every Canadian's vocabulary. Fraser also used many Indian terms now generally obsolete, for example:

June 28, 1808
Their arms consist of bows and arrows, spears and clubs, or horn *Powmagans*. . . . Their hats, which are made of *wattap*, have broad rims and diminish gradually to the top.

Later he uses the spelling *watap*. The influence of Canadian French (or, as in *caribou*, upon the French version of an Indian word) upon the "naming" needed by the early explorers may be seen in such entries as this:

May 30, 1808
. . . their clothing consisted of dressed leather, leggings and shoes with robes of the *Chivirease* [chevreuil 'deer'], *Carribo, Biche* ['doeskin'] and Beaver skins, most of which were dressed in the hair.

English literature has a long history of using dialect for humor or for portraying a person or people belonging to a particular region, class, or age-group.

Dialect in written literature is useful evidence for vocabulary items, but is of dubious value for grammar or for phonology. A writer of fiction, for example:

—is not a dialectologist. A writer may not know or hear a dialect accurately, or may not even realize that a form used is dialectal. Nor is a writer committed to complete factual truth.

—usually deals with idiolects: that is, a writer uses language to create a character, not necessarily a type. W. O. Mitchell in *Jake and the Kid*, for example, creates not only humor but also the character of Jake by having Jake use a certain kind of language; his favorite phrases, such as "It's enough to give one the heartburn," allow the reader to "hear" Jake.

—needs only to *suggest*, not minutely record, a dialect; a writer gives only those markers a reader will react to, not a faithful transcription. Some of these linguistic markers may be mere conventions—stereotypes. Moreover, a writer may choose to represent only one aspect of language, *e.g.* phonology or grammar.

—has only the standard alphabet and punctuation marks to show dialect, limited tools for accuracy, especially in pronunciation. Writers also know that few people will read material that is too far removed from standard spelling.

Many writers use unorthodox spelling, often in stereotyped forms, to suggest that a character is uneducated or is using a non-standard kind of language. Some of these conventionalized spellings, such as *dunno, wimmin, a cuppa coffee, wuz*, represent pronunciations that are much like the actual pronunciations used by educated people in running speech—though literate people are usually so tied to the visual form of the language that they cannot be easily convinced that they do speak in such a way. "Nothing annoys a native speaker of English more," says George Bernard Shaw, "than a faithful setting down to phonetic spelling of the sounds he utters." But the authors who use this unorthodox spelling—a device called *eye-dialect*—are relying upon their readers' reaction, which is based upon common attitudes of people to non-standard forms. Sometimes, as in certain comic strips, the eye-dialect is grossly inaccurate, even in reproducing the grammar of the speaker. Usually eye-dialect is trying to show the social dimension of a language, but the time or geographical dimensions also may be depicted.

Eye-Dialect

Quiz

What pronunciation or other facet of language is the writer trying to suggest in each of the following pieces of written dialogue? Is it accurate? Is it different from normal, running speech? Is it successful? The sources, all Canadian and of this century, and brief comments are given at the end of the samples.

1. "He don't bother bein' lonsome for no one these days. He's gettin' so much pasturin' he looks like a rainbarrel with legs."

2. . . . and Grandpa and I holding our hands to our ears and shouting out at the top of our lungs, "Regs, cloze, botels! Regs, cloze, botels!"

3. "A gentleman 'as been calling you, sir," he said in that voice of his. "Most important 'e said it was, sir, so I left you 'is number in your box."

4. "She could of shut the gate and she didn't. She just open' it up and Flora run out."

5. "You don't deserve to eat anyhow. . . . . You didn't bring nuthin'. Flowers! I saw watcha brung. A buncha flowers. I betcha you stole 'em."

6. Young folks is different now. Cant tell em nothin. They figger more excitement in the city.

7. "Quite a ways. All of thirty mile, we figger. But that really ain't so much in this country. Back east, it's different."

Sources

1. E. G. Perrault: "The Silver King" (1952). Rural B.C. An old man is talking to a boy about a pony.

2. Ted Allan: "Lies My Father Told Me." Montreal. The grandfather is Russian Jewish — not strictly a dialect but a mixture of features from two languages — in Weaver and James (1952)

3. Hugh MacLennan: *The Watch That Ends the Night* (1959). Montreal. Speaker is the college porter, "an Englishman, a former Grenadier."

4. Alice Munro: "Boys and Girls," in *Dance of the Happy Shades* (1968). Western Ontario a generation ago: a boy is talking about his sister, who let loose a horse that was to be shot.

5. John Marlyn: *Under the Ribs of Death* (1957). Winnipeg in the late 1920's; some boys at a girl's birthday party are taunting another boy, a poor immigrant who has followed the custom of his own culture and brought flowers for the girl.

6. Earle Birney: "Prairie Counterpoint" (1947). An old man is talking.

7. Edward McCourt: *Music at the Close* (1947). Farmer in Saskatchewan, early in the century: *back east* is the usual western term for Ontario and Quebec.

124

Lexicography

Canadian Dictionaries: Current Language

The study of contemporary writing is necessary for making accurate, up-to-date dictionaries. The British have had dictionaries of the standard language since the early seventeenth century. A generation after the political separation from England, Noah Webster gave Americans their first dictionaries—a short one in 1806, abridged in 1807, and then in 1828, *An American Dictionary of the English Language* with 70 000 entries, including many words of American origin and definitions illustrating differences between American and English usage.

Both England and the United States have continued to issue new dictionaries of their current language. Canadians, until recently, had no dictionary of their own. Reliance on British and American dictionaries was not too onerous for spelling—though sometimes confusing. But where could a Canadian discover how *Canadians* pronounce *arctic, khaki, lieutenant,* or the meanings of numerous Canadian words that do not appear in available reference books: *barachois, caplin, brulé, snye, kinnikinnick, oolichan*?

The most immediate problem was how to put together a set of general dictionaries for Canadian schools, accurate reference books that would show Canadian words, Canadian meanings of words, the alternative spellings, and the various pronunciations "reflecting the usage of educated Canadians," as well as the needed vocabulary from the general English language. The set was efficiently made by revising the Thorndike-Barnhart school dictionaries, resulting in three volumes of *The Dictionary of Canadian English* (DCE):

The Beginning Dictionary (1962) Grades 3–5
The Intermediate Dictionary (1963, 1972) Grades 6–9
The Senior Dictionary (1967, 1973) High school and adults

Canadians may now find other Canadianized dictionaries.*

To help translation and intercultural understanding, other scholars have compiled a Canadian bilingual dictionary, *Dictionnaire canadien* (1962) edited by Jean-Paul Vinay, which contains the words "normally found in European dictionaries of comparable size," but also "in both languages, those words, phrases, and concepts that are uniquely Canadian."

Written Evidence: The Historical Perspective

Old records, books, journals, letters, magazines, newspapers, and other written material can provide "black and white" evidence of how the language used to be and of the processes of change.

Marked as a *canadianisme* in *Dictionnaire canadien:*

balle au camp 'baseball'
beurre d'arachide 'peanut butter'
bottine de ski 'ski boot'
centre d'achats 'shopping centre'
cour de bois 'lumber yard'
crique 'creek, stream'
école séparée 'separate school'
liqueurs douces 'soft drinks'
luncher 'to lunch'
huile de charbon 'coal-oil'
joueur de hockey 'hockey player'
tire sur la neige '(maple) taffy on the snow'

---

* For example: *The Winston Dictionary of Canadian English* under the editorship of Thomas Paikeday, the *Intermediate Edition* (1970) and the *Elementary Edition* (1975). At a higher level is the revised Canadian edition of *Funk and Wagnall's Standard College Dictionary* (1976), which includes Canadian material and an article, "Canadian English," by Walter S. Avis.

Copyright, © 1924, The Chicago Tribune.

Midway Signs Limey Prof to Dope Yank Talk

Thus a linguist studies older forms of the language for clues as to its nature. Ryhmes, puns, and semi-literate spellings can indicate the changes in pronunciation over the years. M. H. Scargill (1956, 1957), for example, examined some of the early eighteenth century official writings in the Nova Scotia archives, and found that the English used corresponds closely to both British and New England records of the same period, a finding that helps to substantiate his theory that many features of Canadian speech were not necessarily derived from American Loyalists but may be relics of British and American eighteenth century language. One pattern he noticed is **i** [ɪ] where we spell and pronounce **e** [ɛ], *e.g. midle* for *meddle*, *togither* for *together*. This pattern conforms to much speech still heard in North America, and often "seen" in eye-dialect to mark "rural" or "old-fashioned" speech (*e.g. git* 'get', *kin* 'can'). In Ernest Buckler's *The Mountain and the Valley*, a novel about rural Nova Scotia (about 1940), his characters use this pattern repeatedly. They also use **-in** for **-ing** (thus *gittin* for *getting*), a form that was standard English in the eighteenth century.

Historical Dictionaries

All historical dictionaries of English follow the example set by what is probably the greatest scholarly dictionary in the world, *The Oxford English Dictionary* (OED).* The OED does not, however, cite many Canadianisms; neither does it fully explain their background and use.

The American people have two historical dictionaries, derivatives of the OED: *A Dictionary of American English on Historical Principles* (DAE), edited by Craigie and Hulbert (4 vols., 1938), which aims to record words and phrases of American origin, features that set American English apart from the rest of the English-speaking world, and also "every word denoting something which has a real connection with the development of the country and the history of its people" (p. *v*); and *A Dictionary of Americanisms on Historical Principles* (DA), edited by Mitford M. Mathews (1951) and limited to words that originated in America and their histories. Although many words that originated in Canada are included as "Americanisms" (the word *American* has always presented problems!) these dictionaries do not give a clear or adequate picture of Canadian English.

The DC

Therefore, in 1957 members of the Canadian Linguistic Association's Lexicographical Committee began to prepare *A Dictionary of Cana-*

---

* At first, the NED (*A New English Dictionary on Historical Principles*), 13 vols., then taken over by the Oxford University Press. It attempts to record the history and development of every word printed in the English language from about 1000 A.D. to the present, with citations of its first occurrence and of any changes in its use, including spellings, and to give its etymology. The collecting of the over five million quotations began in 1858, and the last volume appeared in 1928, with a Supplement in 1933. Material for revisions are filed, and a Supplement for A to G came out in 1972, and one for H to N in 1976. These new Supplements include Canadian citations and label Canadianisms.

dianisms on Historical Principles (DC). The project was later taken over and completed by the Lexicographical Centre for Canadian English, which was established under the direction of M. H. Scargill, first at the University of Calgary and then at the University of Victoria. The editor, until his death in 1960, was Charles J. Lovell, who had worked on the DA. His collection of over 50 000 Canadian quotations formed the basis of the new dictionary. Walter S. Avis took over as editor-in-chief, and with the help of able linguists and many volunteers—and gifts such as Douglas Leechman's complete manuscript for a dictionary of terms used in the Canadian Northwest—the DC was published in 1967, Canada's Centennial Year.*

The DC does not attempt to record the complete vocabulary of English-speaking Canadians. Nor is it always possible to discover whether a word originated in the United States or in Canada—there are thousands of "North Americanisms" that have moved north and south of the border as the speakers have moved. Indeed, the two countries have shared so many experiences that the DC includes many terms (marked with a dagger, †) that are not originally Canadian at all but have been compounded, have become extended in meaning, or have proved especially significant in Canadian life. An example is *chesterfield* meaning 'sofa', a word not born in Canada, but used widely, and with many compounds, *e.g. chesterfield suite* and *chesterfield table*, that are Canadianisms.

Walter S. Avis

Each unmarked entry is a Canadianism. A "Canadianism," for the editors of the DC, is "a word, expression, or meaning which is native to Canada or which is distinctively characteristic of Canadian usage though not necessarily exclusive to Canada" (p. *xiii*).

With each entry are quotations of the earliest and the latest sources found, and often a variety of chronological and geographical quotations that illustrate its meaning, or changes in meaning or form.

The name *Canada* has a quotation first from 1534, and many later ones to show its various meanings; *Manitou*, "spirit, deity," goes back to the writings of Champlain in 1632; the entry for *sled* quotes *Hakluyt's Voyages* of 1577, "They . . . keepe certeine doggs not much unlike Wolues, whiche they yoke . . . to a sled." But *baby bonus* dates only from 1957, and may become obsolete. Some recent slang terms are too new to have been included: an example is *flight pay* 'extra pay for a beer parlor waiter who must go up and down stairs'.

A superb reference book, the DC is a record in print of the English-speaking Canadians' experience of two hundred years on this continent, of their relationships with the Indians, Inuit, French, Americans, British, and "New Canadians" from many countries, and of their endeavors to settle a land and form a nation. The bibliography of sources in the DC is a useful reference in itself.

---

* It should be noted that the DC was planned as a pilot volume, leading toward a full *Historical Dictionary of Canadian English* that would account for all English words in Canada from colonial times to the present. Collecting is still going on, and materials are kept at the Lexicographical Centre for Canadian English, University of Victoria, British Columbia, under the directorship of M. H. Scargill. Readers of the DC have already contributed new words and quotations.

Handcar pictured at Burnaby's ▶
Heritage Village

Vancouver Sun Photo

A lesson in railway terminology on speeders versus handcars

Re the picture on page 19 of The Sun, of March 16.

It shows two boys using a railway handcar. The caption says the boys are on a speeder. A speeder is a three-wheeled vehicle with a frame, seat and one-man handle that is pushed forward and back.

The handcar can be operated by one man but is usually operated by two or more.

The speeder is used to check track by one man; the seat is less than two feet from roadbed.

A handcar is used to transport men and equipment to a work site, by section crews or railway gangs.

A letter-to-the-editor explains the Canadianism *speeder* by contrasting the meaning with that of a similar object—valuable evidence for the dictionary-maker:

The *Vancouver Sun*, April 6, 1976

Finding Good Quotations for Dictionary Items

A well-chosen quotation for a dictionary collection should help reveal the meaning of a word. A good example is the Canadianism *by acclamation* in Frederick Grove's *Fruits of the Earth* (1933), a novel about the early days in Saskatchewan, in which he shows, both by using quotation marks and by giving an explanation, his awareness that the phrase may be strange to his readers.

Abe was, that winter, elected reeve of the municipality, "by acclamation"; for his candidacy hotly contested for a while, remained unopposed at the last moment.

A fuller account of *Bennett Buggy* is given by a Canadian interviewed by Barry Broadfoot and recorded in his book *Ten Lost Years 1929–1939: Memories of Canadians Who Survived The Depression* (1973)

The Buggy R. B. Made Famous
"You ask me what a Bennett Buggy was? There were hundreds of them, and I wonder if there is even one now in some museum, some farm exhibit somewhere. In the Twenties, farmers bought automobiles, Chevs, Fords, Overlands, Reos, the Hupmobile, oh, a hell of a lot that they don't even make any more. Then came the Crash and the drought and nobody had any money for gasoline, let alone repairs, and they'd thrown out all those fine old buggies every farm used to have, so what was left? A car that wouldn't run.

Somebody got the idea of lifting out the engine and taking out the windshield and sticking a tongue onto the chassis with double trees and that's where old Dobbin and Dolly got back to work again. Two horsepower. Five miles an hour, but those oat burners got you there. Then somebody got the idea, the country was full of wits, to call these contraptions Bennett Buggies. Poor old R. B. Bennett. All over Saskatchewan and Alberta there were these carved up cars, named after him, and a constant reminder that he'd been prime minister when the disaster struck.

Of course, it was wonderful advertising for the Liberals too. Bennett Buggies—there goes the guy who got us into this fix."

An author writing about a region or a former time often explains special terms to his readers. Hugh Garner, in *Cabbagetown* (1968), a novel in which he shows how the Depression ("the Dirty Thirties") affected the Canadian people, frequently has a character or the narrator explain Depression slang, sometimes even how it arose:

"Bennett'll never get in again . . . The farmers out west hate his guts. They've knocked the bodies off their old cars and put a wooden box and shafts on 'em, and now they drive them like a wagon, behind a horse — *Bennett-buggies* they call 'em." (244)

The building ["the House of Industry"] had long been used by the city [Toronto] to house indigents, and was known to its patrons by the tramp's colloquialism for hospital, "pogey." Before the Depression was over this word would also be used as a synonym for city relief and public welfare. (69–70)

Later Garner shows how, by extension, the recipients of relief became known as *pogey stiffs*.

This is the kind of material that dictionary-makers are happy to find while they and their helpers search through vast amounts of print.

Several quotations may be needed to establish the exact meaning of a word in a locality. The following, taken from W. O. Mitchell's *Jake and the Kid* (1961), show something of how *slough* (pronounced [slu] to rhyme with *goo*) is used in Saskatchewan:

You take lard pails, fill her up from the spring sloughs, pour the water down the hole, . . . (44)

We were passing a slough, real white, with alkali lying snowy along her brim. . . . (129)

Even more explicit is the definition of *slough* in a "Glossary of Localisms" provided by Frederick Philip Grove at the end of his prairie novel, *The Yoke of Life* (1930):

'Any depression in the otherwise flat soil, often swampy or filled with water; or merely overgrown with long grass'.

Of course, the dictionary-maker must also look for examples from other Canadian regions because usage may vary. In British Columbia, for example, a slough can be tidal—mud flats at low tide.

Words whose meanings a reader builds up slowly from various contexts are much more difficult. For these the dictionary editor may have to give a definition. A good example is Jake's use of *shaganappy*, a prairie slang expression: Jake talks of "a shaganappy speech" which gives everyone heartburn, and later, when examining an old broken-down couch at an auction, he exclaims, "Thinka anybuddy havin' a shaganappy thing like that in their house!" (W. O. Mitchell, *Jake and the Kid*). The DC editors have traced this word from the Algonkian to its various meanings, first to 'a thong of rawhide', then to 'rawhide' itself, then further widened to a modifer of *horse* or *pony* (sometimes shortened to *shag pony*) in reference to the small and often unkempt ponies often used, and finally to a slang term carrying connotations of 'inferior', 'of little value', 'poorly organized', and 'commonplace'. This excerpt from the same book merely begins to explain a meaning (now historical) of *pound* in Canada:

". . . Say, Jake, did you ever see a pound"?
". . ."

"Not that kind. Like the Indians had, where they run buffaloes so's they can kill a lot and git meat for pemmican." (66)

As the story progresses, the *pound* is seen to be a trap—in fact, a

He picked up the trace, fastening it quickly, one wary eye on Klondike's heels. Then he pulled a short length of shaginappi from his pocket, and tied that about the hook.

Ruth Matheson Buck, *The Doctor Rode Side-Saddle* (1974). A novel about the Prairies at the turn of the century.

buffalo jump, a place where the herd was slaughtered by being stampeded over a precipice. The DC investigators cross-reference these words with others with somewhat the same meaning: *jump, jumping pound, piskun* (Algonkian: the word is *pis'kun*, Blackfoot for 'deep blood kettle', *kettle* meaning 'cauldron' or 'deep hole'), and *buffalo jumping ground* (another term used by Jake and quoted by the DC). The lexicographer becomes a word-detective, tracking down those terms actually used by Canadians and preserved by print.

Catalogues as Sources

Old mail-order catalogues are an excellent source for lexicographers. Not only do these books record the words and illustrate the objects used by former generations, but in their own time they frequently helped to make a term standard. Like all written sources, however, they must be regarded as tentative data only, because, for example, the person making the lexical choices may not have been a native Canadian or may not have been aware of the different usages.

In Canada the most influential catalogue was that of the T. Eaton Company Limited. A re-issue of the 1901 Eaton's Catalogue (Nos. 46 and 47), used when Confederation was only 34 years old and just entering the twentieth century, now makes fascinating reading. As the editor, Jack Stoddart, says in his Introduction:

> . . . the rural and quiet life of Canada comes vividly to life. Some will relive the days of their youth, others will remember the furnishings and equipment they saw stored in their grandmother's attic, and the young will smile and be amused at that very strange and different era.

In it even the amateur dialectologist can find evidence of language change. The catalogue makes clear differentiations among the terms *lounge, couch* (and *bed couch*, which could be converted to a bed), *parlor suite,** *davenport sofa*, and *settee* (as illustrated). How many of these words would you use in the same way?

No. 190. Davenport sofa, quarter-cut oak, golden-finished frame, hand carved and polished, 76 inches long, 31 inches deep, 37 inches high, upholstered spring back and spring-edge seat, buttoned band, in extra heavy figured velour covering.....................................$32.50

Eaton's Archives

* The word was spelled **-or**, not **-our**; also used are *color* and *vapor*.

He went out and sat beside Anna. She was on her knees before the lounge, turning the pages of the catalogue. They played "Which Do You Like the Best?" with the coloured pages. Anna would point to the incredibly beaded silk dress that the girl wore standing in a great stone archway with the sunlight streaming across it, as her choice. He'd say, "Oh, I do, too."

Ernest Buckler, *The Mountain and the Valley* (1952). A novel of a boyhood in Nova Scotia.

Eaton's Archives

We had catalogues—I could have ordered corselettes. The illustrations, considered daring then, pictured swan-necked ladies, shown only from the hips up, of course, encased in lace, boned to a nicety, indrawn waists slender as a wrist, faces aloof but confident, as though they were unaware they faced the world clad only in their underclothes. I used to leaf and ponder, but never did I buy.

Margaret Laurence, *The Stone Angel* (1964)

No. 36. Lounge, hardwood frame, golden finish, neatly carved, upholstered spring seat, covered in heavy satin russe $3.95
Same lounge, upholstered in heavy tapestry.........................$4.75

No 19. This couch is our most popular shape, has beautiful sloped head, upholstered with a fine grade of satin-faced tapestry, spring seat, fringed all around $7.90
Upholstered in figured velours $9.00

No. 15. Parlor suite, 5 pieces, allover upholstered in best Wilton rugs, silk plush trimmed, fringed to match, consisting of sofa, arm chair, arm rocker and 2 reception chairs, spring seats, backs and edges, ...$55.00

No. 304. Hall settee, quarter-cut golden oak, polished, heavy shaped seat, 42 inches wide, heavily hand carved back, upholstered in leather................. .... $12.50

Eaton's Archives

The terms *chesterfield* and *chesterfield suite*, now the usual generic words in Canada for most of these articles, do not appear at all, even in the Index.* Canadians also seemed to have used *window shades*, not *blinds*. Some words are Briticisms: bicycles are listed under *Wheelgoods*; buttons, laces, and other such items are under the heading *Smallwares*—but the Index also lists the more general North American term *Notions*; and the second of the two catalogues gives a double heading *Smallwares and Notions*, suggesting a change, or at least varied usage. Sometimes a listing shows the origin of a term: certain hats, for example, are described as "John B. Stetson's make" (an American company). The Canadianism *mackinaw* is already used as a common noun.

* The DC states that *chesterfield*, now almost a "marker" of a Canadian, was not originally Canadian and is still used occasionally in England and in parts of northern California; the first quotation in the DC is dated 1903; in OED, 1900 'a kind of large, overstuffed sofa'. It may now be going out of Canadian usage. Check recent catalogues and newspaper advertisements, and see results of SCE.

Under *Men's Clothing* the Eaton's 1901 catalogues list these items. How many do you know?

mocha gloves	Fauntleroy suits (boys)
hookdown caps	vestee suits (boys)
celluloid collars	bicycle hose
Prince Albert suits	reefers (articles of clothing)

Ladies Clothing lists these:

silk waists	chipchops (hats)
gimps	widows' caps, with fall
sacques	elastic-side boots
bustles	ottoman capes

How many of these fabrics do you know? Can you guess or discover the source of the names?

albatross cloth	pebble serge
covert cloth	sacque
grenadine	nainsook
brilliantine	cravenette
galatea	cambric
paramatta cloth	henrietta

Note that words may linger in particular senses, even after being removed from common currency: *gimp* 'a braid' is still used as a tightly woven material to put into cracks, and is thus known to carpenters. Though a *waist* is now known as a blouse, women's fashions still use a *shirtwaist dress*. The word *jeans* is old; the OED gives the first date as 1488 and the original source as *Genoa*, then shortened from the form of *jene fustian* to *jean* in England and *jeans* in the United States. In 1901 the word referred to the heavy cotton material from which work clothes often were made.

Comparing lists of various years can reveal changes in Canadian living and Canadian linguistic habits. Comparing catalogues from various regions, *e.g.* a British catalogue or a Sears-Roebuck catalogue from the United States, can uncover evidence for the dialectologist—evidence which, of course, would need further checking with other sources, written and, if possible, oral.

The Time Dimension: A Settler's Journal
The excerpts below are taken from the *Reminiscences* of Samuel Thompson, an English immigrant to Canada, a journalist, a printer, and among other accomplishments, the first editor of Hansard. The book, covering the years between 1833–83, makes fascinating reading.

All the italicized words and phrases are Canadianisms as defined by the DC. Which ones do you recognize as still being in use, and which would you label "historical" or "obsolete"? For the distinction between "historical" and "obsolete," see the DC, p. *xviii*. You can check your decisions with those of the DC (given on the following page).

1. The settlement was called the *Scotch line*, nearly all the people being from the islands of Arran and Islay, lying off Argyle-shire, in Scotland. Very few of them knew a word of English. There were Campbells, McGillvrays, Livingstons, McDiar-mids, McAlmons, McNees, Jardines, and other characteristic names. (62)

2. Here and there, a ravine would be rendered passable by placing across it two long trunks of trees, often at a sharp angle, and crossing these traversely with shorter logs; the whole covered with brush-wood and earth, and dignified with the name of a *"corduroy bridge."* (33)

3. By this time you have cut down trees enough to enable you fairly to see the sky! Yes, dear sir, it was entirely hidden before, and the sight is not a little exhilarating to a new *"bush-whacker."* (43)

4. At length it was whispered that Mary's heart, long hard as *rock-elm*, has become as soft as *basswood*, under the combined influence of the stalwart figure, handsome face and good axe of Johnny, . . . who was born in one of the early Scottish settlements in the Newcastle Districts—settlements which have turned out a race of *choppers*, accustomed from their infancy to handle the axe . . . (42)

5. Eight of the heaviest logs, about two feet thick, had been placed in position as *sleepers* or foundation logs, duly *saddled* at the corners. (57) (See *saddle-notch* in the DC.)

6. Each man gives a day's work to his neighbour, for a *logging or raising bee*; and looks for the same help when he is ready for it. (66)

7. After getting into a better cleared road, the chief difficulty lay with the imperfectly "stubbed" underbrush and the fre-quency of *cradle-holes*—that is, hollows caused by upturned roots—in roughly timbered land. (76)

8. So on I trudged, . . . into the thick dark woods of Innisfil, where the road was a mere *brushed* track. . . . (77)

9. In the first place, you must *underbrush*. With an axe or a strong, long-handled bill-hook, made to be used with both hands, you cut away . . . all the small saplings and under-wood . . . (37)

10. One dark night, in a frontier settlement of the County of Simcoe, a young man was returning through the *bush* from a *township* gathering, when he noticed teams passing along a *concession line* not far distant. (238)

Answers for terms in Thompson's *Reminiscences*

1. *Scotch line*—a *line* was a settlement road in Upper Canada (see *line* (def. 3) in the DC and *concession road*, a term still used in

Ontario). There was an English Line, the Queen's Line, the French Line, the Roman Line (near London, Ontario), and so on. The *Scotch Line*, still used, was near Perth, Ontario, where many Scots settled in the early 1800's. As suggested in the DC, this use of *line* to mean 'road' may derive from older dialectal usage in the British Isles.

2. *corduroy bridge*—still used; the term is a metaphor, the logs making such a road or bridge surface similar to the ribbed cloth called corduroy

3. *bush-whacker*—still used; a person who lives or works in the backwoods; also one who cuts down bush; extended sometimes (but not in this quotation) to mean guerrilla fighter

4. *rock-elm*—still used; a tree, *ulmus thomasi*, of eastern Canada, so called because of the tough wood
   basswood—still used; North American lime or linden tree
   choppers—still used in sense of "skilled axemen," though the form *chop* "clear a farm by removing trees" is obsolete, and *chopping* is marked historical

5. *sleepers*—marked in the DC as an obsolete lumbering term— trunks of trees as "bedding timbers" for a road. People in the Maritimes use the term for a large buried root.
   saddled—still used; the DC gives only the term *saddle and notch*, the "saddle" fitting into a V-shaped notch

6. *logging or raising bee*—historical, though the custom of a "raising bee" is not completely dead in pioneer areas

7. *cradle-holes*—still used; a cradle-shaped hole left when a large tree is blown down; in the Maritimes, a mound of earth caused by such upturned trees is called a *cradle-hill*

8. *brushed*—still used; 'cleared of brush'

9. *underbrush*—still used; the noun *underbrush* is not a Canadianism, though the verb seems to be

10. *county*—still used, but its meaning varies from province to province
    township—historical for Ontario and Quebec; see the DC for various uses of the term
    concession line—still used; a survey line marking the boundaries of a concession, the number of the lot being placed on the posts

Folklore and Sayings

Many dialectologists collect the proverbs and sayings of a community, especially a community "close to the earth," for as well as being interesting in themselves, these sayings give insight into the social life and history of a community, and are sometimes clues to the original homeland. Newfoundland, with hundreds of years of oral culture, is rich in such lore, as are many parts of Canada (see Chapter 5 on Regionalisms for examples). Groups of people who work together develop their own songs, tales, and sayings; part of the Canadian heritage are the songs of the voyageurs, the Paul Bunyan tales and shanty songs of the lumber camps, and the laconic

Helen Creighton (1950) found that many old songs have been preserved orally around the German-settled area of Lunenburg, Nova Scotia. Here is a favorite—about sauerkraut:

Now if you've only listen to phwat ye spake about
I'm going for to toll ye how to make that sauerkraut,
The kraut is not made of leather as effery one supposes
But off that little plant what they call the cabbage roses.

Chorus
Sauerkraut is bully, I toll you it is fine,
Me thinks me ought to know 'em for me eats 'em all the time.

2. The cabbages are growing so nice as it could be,
We take 'em out and cut 'em up the bigger as a pea,
Me put 'em in a barrel and me stamp 'em with me feet,
And we stamp and we stamp for to make 'em nice and sweet. *Cho*.

3. Me put in plenty of salt so nice, don't put in no snuff,
Nor any cayenne pepper nor any of that stuff,
Me put 'em in the cellar till it begins to smell,
So help me Christ me thinks it nice, the Dutchmen like it well. *Cho*.

4. When the sauerkraut begins to smell and it can't smell no smeller
We take it from the barrel that's way down in the cellar,
Me put him in the kettle and it begins to boil,
So help me we can smell her round for 40,000 miles. *Cho*.

Sung by Jupheth Dauphinee Hubbards. "Sauerkraut Song (A)"

Two "folk beliefs" from Waterloo County, Ontario (an area settled largely by people of German origin, many from Pennsylvania):
When the children desired to know where the cows were they would ask the "Daddy-long-legs" spider, which thereupon was supposed to lift one of his long legs and point in the direction where the cows were to be found.

It is believed that the common dragonflies, locally known as "darning-needles," and . . . called *schlanga-dockta* (snake doctors) by the Pennsylvania Germans, will enter the ears of unwary persons.

W. J. Wintemberg, Folklore of Waterloo Country, Ontario (1950)

humor of the western cowboy. Ernest Buckler, in *Ox Bells and Fireflies* (1965), devotes an entire chapter to local sayings. Many are highly descriptive metaphors and, like all such sayings, often humorous, exaggerated, perhaps bawdy—the folk poetry created by the ordinary person. Ordinary language is charged with metaphor. Occasionally one such saying is remembered and passed on orally to become part of the local everyday language. Here is a sampling from Buckler:

a chip in the porridge 'a man who agrees with everyone and has no mind of his own'
a sawney 'a spongy fellow who doesn't stand up for his own rights' (This is an old word, originally a northern English form of *Sandy* (short form of *Alexander*), which developed into a derisive word for a Scotchman, and by 1700 meant 'a simpleton'.)
soft as a punkin 'sentimental'
sounds like a bee under a cup—(said of a singer fumbling for the right key)
quite a moth 'any chronic drain on the purse, *e.g.* taxes'
quite an herb 'any way to make money regularly, *e.g.* getting the local teacher to board at one's home.

Children's Folklore
A. F. Chamberlain records that in 1880 when the children of Peterborough, Ontario, picked up a grasshopper, they recited the rhyme:

Grasshopper, grasshopper gree!
Give me some honey, and I'll let you go free.

(The "honey" is, of course, the yellow substance the grasshopper exudes when pressed.)

An example of local folklore, from W. D. Valgardson's short story "Bloodflowers" (1973). Nearly every one of the ten stories is set in Newfoundland or the Icelandic settlements of northern Manitoba, and involves local folklore and superstition.

> Danny noticed a small, red flower growing from a crack in the rock. When he bent down to get a better look, he saw that the crack was filled with brown stems. He picked the flower and held it up. "What is it?"
>
> "Bloodflower," Mr. Poorwilly replied. "Only thing that grows on the island except lichen. Shouldn't pick it. They say it brings bad luck. If you cut your finger or make your nose bleed, it'll be OK."
>
> Danny laughed. "You don't believe that, do you?"
>
> "Mrs. Poorwilly says it. She knows quite a bit about these things."

Edith Fowke, when collecting old shanty songs around the Peterborough area, discovered a "Depression Days" song created by the men working on a highway being built as a relief project. The lines are bitterly topical for the times:

> It's hailing, it's raining, but during the day
> The Lord works with Bennett to keep clouds away.
> Now if I had Bennett where Bennett's got me,
> The very first morning he'd be weak at the knees.

"Folk Songs in Ontario" (1963)

———

G. M. Story in "St. John's Balladeers" (1971), gives us the following excerpt from a ballad in which the balladeer (Johnny Burke, 1851–1930) delights in a ridiculous catalogue of the ingredients of "The Trinity Cake."

> Glass eyes, Bulls eyes and butter,
> Lampwicks, and linament too,
> Pastry as hard as a shutter
> That a Billy Goat's jowl couldn't chew,
> Tobacco and whiskers of crackies,*
> If you like it or not you should take,
> Oh, it would kill a man dead, if it flew to his head,
> A slice of this Trinity Cake.

> * A *crackie* is a small, noisy dog.

"Folk" metaphors:

> ". . . Then there was the old ram pasture next to the Biggar Hotel. There was usually a game goin' there. Oh, it was an old rooming house. We called it the ram pasture. Biggar was full of roomin' houses 'cause of all the single fellas on the railroad."

Heather Robertson, *Grass Roots* (1973). About life in small towns on the Prairies.

About a wife angry with her husband:

> There was quite a bit of action in the Smith house when he finally came home. She was a hurricane on a ten-cent piece that day.

Paul St. Pierre, *Breaking Smith's Quarter Horse* (1966). Rural B.C.

———

Children's groups have their own dialects, used among themselves. For example:

> What special vocabulary is used by boys or girls playing marbles (or "alleys," a shortened form of *alabaster*)?
> What is solo basketball called in your area? (A B.C. term is *chink*.)
> Different forms of softball?
> What do children say when they come to your door on Hallowe'en?
> What are the rituals for deciding who is "it"?
> What is the place called where one is "safe" in playing tag? (In parts of B.C. it is a *gool*, possibly a form of the word *goal*.)

One important word in children's games is the truce term, used often with a sign such as crossing fingers or feet or raising a hand, to gain relief from tag, fighting, or other boisterous activities. The word map (p. 138) shows the wide variety of truce terms used by children in England, Scotland, and Wales.

Children's truce terms in England, Scotland, and Wales

What about Canada? Are there any terms shown that you used as a child? What do the children of your area use now? An interesting guide, useful for ideas and comparisons, is the study by Iona and Peter Opie, *The Lore and Language of Schoolchildren* (1959).

Postscript

In 1965, under the direction of F. G. Cassidy, dialectologists of the United States began work on the *Dictionary of American Regional English* (DARE), a historical dictionary of usages of local and regional rather than national range. This dictionary will include not only written evidence, gained especially from journals, diaries, letters, and newspapers, but also oral expressions, thousands of which are

"Reflect that it is absurd to set up a standard of *how* English people *ought* to speak, before we know how they actually *do* speak. . . ."

Henry Sweet (1890)

used yet never written down. Fieldworkers, who tour the country in "Word Wagons," use a questionnaire as well as conversation. This is the largest word-gathering project in history.

Here are some words or word sets (excluding the farming items), for which the DARE researchers expect to find many variations. You may like to investigate such words in your own area.

food items, e.g. cuts of meat, pancakes, sandwiches made with a long bun or roll
boats—fishing—transportation—hunting
names of trees, birds, fish, animals
family relationships, e.g. euphemisms for child-bearing
children's games

Some typical questions are:

—What do you call an implement with an X-frame (gesture) to hold firewood for sawing? (About 14 terms are already known, *e.g. sawbuck, sawhorse, sawjack, trestle,* and *woodrack*.)
—What do you call a road that connects a big highway with stores and business places set back from it? (*access road, frontage road, service road,* other)
—Somebody who is *usually* mean and bad-tempered is an awful _____ .

Some items found by DARE not recorded before. Have you ever heard of these words and expressions?
back-family 'one's parents' (as distinct from husband/wife and children) (Maine)
cattail 'small creek' (South Carolina)
cork high and bottle deep 'drunk' (Georgia)
ribble 'small, crinkled bit of dough put into soups' (Maryland) (German is *Ruebel* or *Rubel*, so probably *ribble* is Pennsylvania Dutch; Canadian Mennonites use the term *rivel soup*.)
scope 'stand of trees' (Alabama)
wove—past of *wave* "He wove at me so I wove back." (Wisconsin)

A. W. Read in Sebeok (1973)

What folk poetry is still being created in your part of Canada?

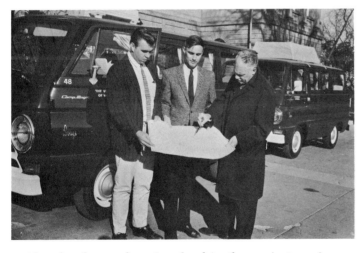

◀ F. G. Cassidy giving instructions to two fieldworkers. Behind them are the two "word wagons," which are equipped for eating and sleeping. The results of the survey of the 50 states will be published soon.

Photo by courtesy of Dr. Cassidy and the University of Wisconsin News Service.

Already, the workers involved in the project are impressed by "the remarkable tenacity of folk speech" and the many new creations, much of it folk poetry.

Similar projects in Canada—the *Dictionary of Newfoundland English* (see pp. 150-152), to be published soon and also based on oral as well as written language, the word geography survey now going on in southwest Nova Scotia (see pp. 120, 164), and future surveys—will reveal the same capacity in Canadians to retain parts of "home language" for generations and to create new words and expressions. "It's great fun," says G. M. Story, director of the Newfoundland project, "to jump from a seventeenth century printed citation to a 1960's tape recording!"

LOBSTICK

cooloo

TILLICUM

MUCKAMUCK

pingo

pemmican

Travois

demoiselle

angishore

ABOITEAU

TAMARACK

PEMBINA

sastrugi

Chapter Five

From Screech to Skookum: Some Regional Variations in Canadian English

. . . the question of Canadian identity, so far as it affects the creative imagination, is not a "Canadian" question at all, but a regional question. An environment turned outward to the sea, like so much of Newfoundland, and one turned towards inland seas, like so much of the Maritimes, are an imaginative contrast: anyone who has been conditioned by one in his earliest years can hardly become conditioned by the other in the same way. Anyone brought up on the urban plain of southern Ontario or the gentle *pays* farmland along the south shore of the St. Lawrence may become fascinated by the great sprawling wilderness of Northern Ontario or Ungava, may move there and live with its people and become accepted as one of them, but if he paints or writes about it he will paint or write as an imaginative foreigner. And what can there be in common between an imagination nurtured on the prairies, where it is a centre of consciousness diffusing itself over a vast flat expanse stretching to the remote horizon, and one nurtured in British Columbia, where it is in the midst of gigantic trees and mountains leaping into the sky all around it, and obliterating the horizon everywhere?

Northrop Frye, Preface to *The Bush Garden* (1971)

sastrugi

LOBSTICK

A Quiz—for Fun

Quiz

How "provincial" are you?

Try the quiz, and see how many regional terms you know. All are Canadianisms, described in the DC. The answers are at the end of the quiz.

1. A *coho* is a:
   (a) bird   (b) fish   (c) type of co-op housing   (d) Chinese eating-place

2. A *Digby chicken* is a:
   (a) smoked herring   (b) good-looking girl   (c) ruffed grouse   (d) duck

3. In Newfoundland a *growler* is:
   (a) a small iceberg   (b) a brown bear   (c) a boss with a short temper   (d) an anchor chain

4. In the North the annual event called *la foule* is:
   (a) the spring break-up of ice
   (b) the arrival of the Canada geese   (c) the migration of the caribou   (d) New Year's Eve

5. A *snye* is:
   (a) a large snow-covered piece of ice   (b) a trap, usually for muskrat   (c) a side-channel in a river   (d) a small evergreen tree in the North

6. The *Scotch line* in Ontario is:
   (a) a mark on a liquor bottle   (b) a concession road near which many Scots settled   (c) The Macdonald family tree   (d) the 49th parallel

7. When told on the Prairies to look for a *bluff*, you would look for:
   (a) a grove of trees   (b) a grain elevator   (c) a high cliff   (d) a moose or caribou

8. The *keta* salmon of B.C. gets its name from:
   (a) Indian   (b) Eskimo
   (c) Russian   (d) Spanish

9. In Newfoundland, if you ask for *screech*, you will get:
   (a) a piglet   (b) a pinch
   (c) a drink   (d) cold ice

10. *Calgary redeye* is:
    (a) an eye-disease from sun and dust   (b) a derogatory term for Social Credit   (c) a drink   (d) a berry

11. You would expect to find a *correction line* in:
    (a) an old-time Ontario school
    (b) B.C. logging camp   (c) the Prairies   (d) the Maritimes, among fishermen

12. In Ontario the *county warden* is the person who:
    (a) is in charge of the jail
    (b) chairs a council of reeves
    (c) supervises game and fish
    (d) supervises all county schools

13. In Labrador a *gasher* is:
    (a) a knife   (b) a boat   (c) a good party   (d) a murderer who has gone mad

14. In Nova Scotia a *fungy* is:
    (a) a fish stew   (b) a foggy day
    (c) an old, unseaworthy boat
    (d) a deep blueberry pie

15. In the North a *pingo* is:
    (a) a float plane that can also use skis   (b) a berry   (c) a large mound of ice covered with soil
    (d) a very large iceberg that is moving

ANSWERS

1. b	4. c	7. a	10. c	13. b
2. a	5. c	8. c	11. c	14. d
3. a	6. b	9. c	12. b	15. c

Some Regional Variations in Canadian English

How much of the following paragraph would be understood by someone from eastern Canada who had not visited the West?

> The chinook and the Stampede are the two most notable events in Calgary and there is a certain madness associated with each. Certainly Calgary goes a little mad in a pleasant sort of way each July. Then the place becomes a cow town, with feed stalls along the main streets and cowpunchers and cowgirls in ten-gallon hats tossing out sourdough flapjacks from the chuck-waggons where they are cooked.
>
> Majorie Wilkins Campbell, "The Prairie Provinces," in *The Face of Canada* (1959)

What would a mainland Canadian make of the following sentences describing the Newfoundland seal hunt?

> A good many of the whitecoats were woggling about on every hand; but not enough to stop us for a rally. Forward we ploughed, looking for more populous nurseries.
>
> George Allan England, *The Greatest Hunt in the World* (1924)

Dialectologists are especially interested in the variations that any region, large or small, develops within its language, and they try to discover the origin of these variants, and why they arise. Within a small geographical area can be found living evidence of language change and language retention.

In any aspect of language, such as grammar, pronunciation, or vocabulary, regional differences may occur. A visitor to some parts of the Atlantic Provinces, and certainly to Cape Breton Island, will notice the expression *"It's some hot today"* (or *some big, some lazy*, and so on), a regional difference in grammar. In other parts of Canada there are subtle differences in intonation—still undescribed systematically. The most common regional differences in Canadian English lie in vocabulary, and this is still the area in which the results of research are most available.

As one would expect from the history of Canada, the greatest number of variations occur in the eastern parts of the country, those that were settled earliest. Some regional differences are inherited from the language of the original settlers. Many of the regionalisms found in Newfoundland, for example, can be traced to either the Anglo-Irish brought by immigrants or to the dialects of southern and western England, the original homes of fishermen who came out to the fishing Banks and then settled on the land. The Newfoundlander's *bultow* 'a handline in fishing', for instance, probably came from the Cornish *bulter* or *bultey* 'a longline'.

Geographic isolation also plays a role. In parts of the Atlantic Provinces each little coastal settlement may retain inherited features and develop its own localisms. Similarly, the mountains and islands of British Columbia isolate some communities and for others set up patterns of communication that can influence the language. The people of Kootenay Valley, for example, are strongly oriented southward toward Spokane for shopping, TV programs, and advertising; and, not surprisingly, recent surveys show that from the choices open to Canadian speakers the teenagers of the Kootenay area show a much greater use of the northern American variants than do the teenagers of southern Vancouver Island or even the Okanagan (unpublished material, Howard Woods and R. J. Gregg).

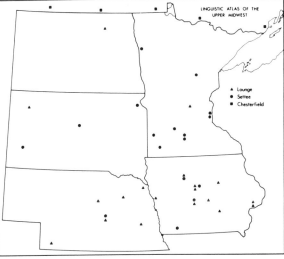

Harold B. Allen (1971)

Above left: The use of *range* in the upper midwest of the United States.

Above right: Note how the use of *chesterfield* seems to stop at the Canadian-American border.

Some variants associated with an area may be occupational more than regional. A special vocabulary may spread throughout a large area and across political borders. Much of the special vocabulary in the Calgary quotation at the beginning of this chapter is part of the language of cattle ranching used in all the foothill country from Mexico north to Alberta, Saskatchewan, and parts of British Columbia. Harold Allen's surveys of the upper midwestern United States show the reality of these north-south lines of communication. He tested words such as *range* 'open grazing land' (still heard in Nebraska but, he found, not used in Minnesota or Iowa) and *corral* (in Nebraska and the Dakotas but not in Iowa, seldom in Minnesota). That is, the differences in vocabulary correlate with the differences between farming in the eastern states and ranching in the dry western prairies. In the Calgary quotation, only two words, *sourdough* and *chinook*, are Canadianisms, and even these occur in Alaska and Washington.

The word *ranch* itself is typical of this wandering of words within an occupation. It came into Canada from American English, in turn from American Spanish, as did many other formerly Spanish words such as *corral, lasso, lariat, bronco* (from Spanish 'unruly', now often

Soon the sage began in good
earnest, and Maggie saw that the
aspect of British Columbia had
changed. They were leaving the
mountains. Hills and great rocky
eminences lay back of the sagebrush. Here and there was an
Indian rancheree.

Ethel Wilson, *Swamp Angel*
(1954)

Other terms used in North America
for a small running stream are:
brook (Northern), *run* (Midland),
branch (Southern), *fork*, *prong*, *kill*
(from Dutch), *burn* (from Scotland
and English-Scottish border areas).
Surveys show many regional variations in England, but neither *run* nor
branch, two dominant forms in the
U.S.A., occurs.

Note Hugh MacLennan's use of the
word *branch* in his description of a
New Brunswick logging camp:
Some of them went swimming in
the water of the branch, water as
cold as melted snow. . . .

The Watch That Ends the Night
(1959)

"In Newfoundland, a gulch is what
mainlanders call a gully. A gully is
what mainlanders call a pond. A
pond is what mainlanders call a
lake.
Fun, isn't it? These verbal musical chairs could go on almost all
day."

Harold Horwood, *Newfoundland*
(1969)

shortened to *bronc*), and *stampede*. The meaning of *ranch* has been extended in Canada, especially in the West, to cover not only estab-lishments for the raising of livestock but almost any kind of large-scale farming, *e.g.* fruit farming or fur farming. A mink, for example, may be described as a *ranch mink*, as opposed to a *wild mink*. The word has been extended also to a kind of bungalow, and one can now buy, in British Columbia and perhaps elsewhere in Canada, a house called a *ranchette*.

On the "time" as well as the geographical dimension of language, the development of *ranch* in British Columbia is interesting. It be-came associated with a similar word *rancherie* (also from Spanish) meaning 'an Indian settlement' and is still used in places to mean 'Indian Reserve'. All these terms and meanings are still part of the language of the Cariboo region in British Columbia.

The word *stampede* similarly has widened in meaning from the original 'unrestrained rush of frightened animals' to such metaphor-ical senses as 'a rush of people'; it also can refer to 'an exhibition of various skills related to ranching', and in Canada to the annual Calgary Stampede.

Apart from differences brought originally by settlers, the two main sources of regional vocabulary are the regular linguistic pro-cesses of borrowing from other languages and broadening or adapt-ing the meanings of ordinary English words.

Different conditions in an area can cause a change in the meaning of a word. Generally in North America, *creek* (often pronounced *crick*) has lost its present British meaning of a 'tidal estuary or saltwater inlet' and has become the name of a freshwater stream smaller than a river, as in:

At the bottom of the gully a small *creek* battled its way through the warp of fallen snags and boulders, like a variegated silver thread.
E. G. Perrault, "The Silver King" (1952)

But in the Altantic Provinces and on the British Columbia coast, areas which both face the sea and have had much British contact, the older sense is occasionally retained, especially in place names. Therefore a freshwater stream in the Maritimes (but not often in British Columbia) is usually a *brook*—a literary word for most other Canadians. Similarly, if someone in Prince Edward Island speaks of a *swamp*, he or she is probably referring to a 'woodlot', for all the land is now well drained.But in Newfoundland, though *swamp* is known, most people use *bog* or *marsh*. In some parts of Newfound-land a shallow pond is called a *gully*, and a *pond* is what other Canadians would call a *lake*.

The following section on Canadian regionalisms is far from com-plete. Too little is known about the regional variations of Canadian English, and for lack of space the DC omitted regionalisms that are not widely used. But the examples and questions may serve to alert us to the possibility of such differences and to their sources in the history and experiences of the Canadian people.

English in Newfoundland

79.   *The foure Elements in Newfound-land.*
To the Worshipfull Captaine John Mason, *who did wisely and*
worthily governe there divers yeeres.
The Aire, in *Newfound-Land* is wholesome, good;
The Fire, as sweet as any made of wood;
The Waters, very rich, both salt and fresh;
The Earth more rich, you know it is no lesse.
Where all are good, *Fire, Water, Earth, and Aire,*
What man made of these foure would not live there?

> From Robert Hayman, *Quodlibets*, "Composed and done at
> Harbor-Grace in Britaniola, anciently called Newfound-Land,"
> 1628. Probably the first piece of English literature written in
> Canada.

Here is a copy of the original title page of *Quodlibets*.

QVODLIBETS, c.25

LATELY COME OVER
FROM NEW BRITANIOLA,
OLD NEWFOVND-LAND.

Epigrams and other small parcels, both
Morall and Diuine.

The first foure Bookes being the Authors owne: the
rest tranflated out of that Excellent Epigrammatift,
Mr *Iohn Owen,* and other rare Authors.

With two Epistles of that excellently wittie Doctor
Francis Rablais : Tranflated out of his French at large.

All of them
Compofed and done at *Harbor-Grace* in
Britaniola, anciently called *Newfound-Land.*

By R. H.

Sometimes Gouernour of the Plantation there.

LONDON,
Printed by *Elizabeth All-de,* for *Roger*
Michell, dwelling in *Pauls* Church-yard,
at the figne of the Bulls-head. 1628.

The Wreckers' Prayer
Give us a wrack or two, Good Lard,
For winter in Tops' il Tickle bes
    hard,
Wid grey frost creppin' like mortal
    sin
And perishin' lack of bread in the
    bin.

    T. G. Roberts, *The Leather Bottle*
    (1934). A collection of poems
    about Newfoundland and the
    Maritimes.

"The Newfoundland fisheries are
more valuable than all the mines of
Peru."

    Lord Bacon, about 1608

Have a look at a map of Newfoundland and enjoy the place
names. Can you imagine how they
might have been created? Here's a
sampling:

Shoe Cove
Witless Bay
Lush's Bight
Snakes Bight
Little Paradise
Famish Gut
Joe Batt's Arm
Doting Cove
Ha-Ha Bay
Muddy Hole
Cow Head

The study of regionalisms in Canada rightly begins in Newfound-land, the earliest part to have been settled by English speakers and the most isolated from mainland Canada. The people of Newfound-land, which was not politically part of Canada until 1949, developed their own linguistic habits without much "contamination" from the mainland.

Even within Newfoundland, many communities (there are more than thirteen hundred outports) were isolated from one another, some for almost 400 years. It is not at all uncommon for New-foundlanders from one outport to comment on the distinctive speech of another community only a few miles away, or even just across a river. Thus there developed not only a particular kind of English but wide varieties of local speech habits—rich material for study by dialectologists as evidence in living speakers of long-retained "home" dialects, of speech mixtures, and of internal changes largely unaffected by an outside "standard."

The existence of a 'special' Newfoundland language was noted as early as 1583, in the account of an expedition of Sir Humphrey Gilbert written by Robert Hay, one of his captains. At that time Newfoundland was a fish-processing station for cod fishermen of many places: France (especially Brittany), southwest England, Ireland, Scotland, the Basque provinces, Portugal, and probably Scandinavia. The variety of people and their languages is par-tially recorded in the geographical names of the coast. Hay noted the special vocabulary which had already grown up around the Newfoundland fishery. Some examples he cites are:

> *green fish*   'fish split and partly pickled' (recorded in the DC as still
>   being in use)
> *corre*   'a kind of fish'
> *skull* of fish   'shoal'
> *gaunts*   'gannets'

Other seventeenth and eighteenth century voyagers, notably a surgeon named James Yonge (on voyages in 1662, 1669, and 1670) and an army officer George Cartwright (1768 and 1777), recorded hun-dreds of Newfoundland words in their journals. Most of these words reflect the highly specialized fishing industry and survive in this day. Some examples are:

Fishing:

> *stage*   'waterside shed for preparing the fish'
> *flake*   'framework for drying cod'
> *header*   'person who beheads the cod'
> *splitter*   'person who splits the cod'
> *water-pup*   'a boil, usually on the hands, caused by an organism
>   in sea water' (also called a *sea-boil*; both terms are now known in
>   all the Atlantic Provinces)

Other:

callibogus   'drink made of rum and spruce beer' (now used in all the Atlantic Provinces)

lords and ladies   'harlequin ducks' (now used on Atlantic and Pacific coasts of Canada)

tickle   'narrow strait between an island and another piece of land', or sometimes 'entrance to a harbor'

tinker   'razor-billed auk'

tilt   'shelter of logs or skins with sloping roof'

◀ A tilt

The progress of settlement of Newfoundland and the coast of Labrador was slow and sporadic. In fact, until the 1700's, to live there was illegal. But as early as 1510 a few people, many of them runaways from fishing ships and, later, from the near-slavery of indentured labor, made homes, intermarried, and stayed to eke out a living in small communities in the myriad coves and bays along the coast. Each year, until the nineteenth century, the fishing fleets from the British Isles and elsewhere visited Newfoundland, and G. M. Story (1965) tells us that "it is recorded that the rurals in the West Country of England reckoned the time by the old Church of England lectionary [a book or list of passages from Scripture to be read at services through the year]: 'Jan! the Parson be in Pruverbs, the Newfanlan' men will soon be a coming whome'."

But some stayed, and, though frequently harrassed by the non-wintering fishermen and the big companies who resented the competition of shore-based residents, the little communities survived. By the nineteenth century, when many Irish poured into Newfoundland, as well as settlers from the English southern counties, the Channel Islands, and France, the differences among the local dialects and customs were quite marked. Story (1965) quotes a 1901 visitor's impression of the "general" Newfoundland language:

Some odd turn of thought makes many of the Newfoundlanders use diminutives. A gale becomes a "breeze," oars are "paddles," an axe is a "hatchet," and schooner is sometimes a "skiff." A two-masted vessel may be called a "punt," a cable is a "string," and a heavy steel hawser is a "wire." The wickedest kind of weather is often only "dirt," while the finest is but "civil." A man sick abed is merely "puckerin'" or "turned over." And yet, when some of these hardy men turn loose, they can draw the longbow with the best.

"Yes, sir," one told me, of a fine day, "dere'm clifts in Europe make ourn look like nothin'. I see 'em on de Mediterranean, nineteen hundurd t'ousand foot high."

"That comes to about three hundred miles," I objected.

"Don't matter, sir. I seen 'em wid me own heyes, an' 'tis sow!"

George Allan England, *The Greatest Hunt in the World* (1924)

A draft item from the projected DNE
Note that a date indicates a printed source, a letter after a numeral is the code to indicate an oral source, and the numerals after an author's name are page references.

LANCH v also launch regional pron [lænʃ] cp OED launch v4 'To cause (a vessel) to move' 1 To move a building or house. [1856] 1966 PITT 65 The spacious old wooden Chapel in Gower Street .. was yesterday launched to the opposite side of the street. T C33-64-0 Some of 'em brought their houses, lanched their houses off of the islands and towed 'em by motor-boats. T C206-65-0 If you wanted a boat pulled, wanted a house lanched, if you wanted to move your house to anywhere, 'tis only go around, 'Boys, I'm going to lanch my house tomorrow; how about coming?'

The language of Newfoundland is one of the most marvellous composites on earth. . . . For the first five minutes you are confident you are conversing with an Irishman—the next five minutes you are highly amused at your mistake. The man is a Scot—probably from Skye or Shetland or some remote community you have never visited. The next five minutes you ask him how long he has been from Devonshire. Sometimes he brings all three nationalities to bear on you in one sentence, as did a Placentia man with whom I climbed a hill. When we had reached the summit, "Aweel, sor, ye're afther being athwart the rudge," he said.

The recent breakout from isolation has made the recording of Newfoundland language and folklore a matter of urgency. Memorial University has met the challenge by helping linguists and students do field work and collect data. Because the researchers at Memorial are in the final phases of preparing *The Dictionary of Newfoundland English* (DNE), much of this regional vocabulary is not in the DC. Unlike the DC, this dictionary will use oral as well as written sources. When published, the DNE will give us a full historical record of the English vocabulary used in the area since the late sixteenth century, with dated citations, spellings, meanings, pronunciations, and etymologies. The university archives also contain valuable material from four centuries of the rich oral culture, including proverbs, children's games, and folklore—material that would eventually disappear if not recorded on tape and in print.

This wide approach, a collaboration of linguists, folklorists, anthropologists, historians, and scientists, is necessary because a language reflects the whole complex of the lives and history of the people, retaining usage hundreds of years old, yet also allowing for inventiveness to fit new circumstances. The work done in Newfoundland quite likely will become the model for future regional studies in other parts of Canada.

Survivals

Here are a few examples of survivals in Newfoundland words from the dialects of the British Isles, generally from the south and west counties, Ireland, parts of Scotland, or from the standard language of seventeenth century England—words which have become obsolete or at least archaic elsewhere.

This list is from an article by G. M. Story in *Encyclopedia Canadiana* (1970). Note too that the DC does not list the "survivals" in vocabulary, as they are not within the definition of Canadianism.

angishore 'weak, miserable person'
bautom 'ball of wool or yarn'
bavin 'brushwood faggot used for kindling' (Shakespeare uses *bavin wits, I Henry IV* III.ii, *i.e.* wits who have a quick, short-lived blaze.)
dean 'a valley' (still used in parts of England)

clever 'strong, healthy' (This word, for which a different meaning occurs on p. 164, has undergone a series of semantic shifts—see OED.)

proud 'inflamed finger' (Extended in the sixteenth century to anything swollen—so *proud flesh* of the 1611 Bible meant 'overgrown flesh around a wound'.) Still present in some dialects of Northern Ireland.

nish 'tender, delicate, sore'

rote 'roar of the sea' (dated 1610 in the OED in this sense and marked "Now U.S.A.")

siche 'small brook'

yesses 'earthworms'

Two well-known words listed as Canadianisms, because their meanings are different in Canada:

brewis (pronounced *brooze*) 'a stew made of ship's biscuit (soaked overnight), salt codfish, and pork fat' (a very old word, retained in many British dialects, meaning 'vegetable and meat broth', *e.g.* used by Sir Walter Scott in his novels as a Lowland Scots word; in northern Irish dialects pronounced [bro:z], *i.e.* to rhyme with *rose*)

screech 'potent dark rum'—a recent adoption (1940's), and ultimately from the Scottish word *screigh* 'whisky' (perhaps coined because of its effect on its consumers) and now widely known in eastern Canada because the liquor is sold there

The well-known word *penguin* seems to have originated in Newfoundland and referred to the now extinct great auk. Probably the term came from a Breton phrase meaning 'white head' (Welsh has related words: *pen* 'head', 'headland' and *gwyn* 'white'). The term was later applied in general English to the antarctic bird.

Occasionally the dialectal pronunciation of an English word creates a new word. The *caa'ing* or *ca'ing* whale of the Atlantic coast seems to have been given its name from the practice of *ca'ing* (Scottish or Scotch Irish for "calling") such whales ashore for killing.

Besides a large vocabulary of words preserved from various dialects, Newfoundlanders often use delightful phrases with an Elizabethan flavor. "I be in the fall of the leaf," says one old fisherman to a sympathetic listener. See p. 11 for Shakespeare's use of this phrase.

Inherited from various British dialects are certain features of sounds and of grammar. Many speakers use a voiced initial [v] for [f], a trait of English West Country dialects (as in the speech of Squire Western in Fielding's *Tom Jones*). Thus *fir* (balsam fir) is, as in all the Maritimes, often called *var* or *varr*. Some Newfoundlanders, usually those with Irish backgrounds, use [t] and [d] where [θ] or [ð] (the two **th** sounds) would be expected, so that *thick* sounds like *tick* and *months* like *monts*, and so on. But recent surveys show that informants are aware of this dialectal feature, and that they use the "th" in careful speech.

1969 MOWAT & DE VISSER 49
When some of the outports were 'closed out,' the people refused to abandon their houses and shifted them [by setting them afloat and towing them across open water] in just this way. Scores of houses were 'launched off'.
2 To transfer from one vessel to another by boat T C144-65-0 We picked up nine men and lanched aboard the "Greenland". T C28-64-0 We picked up eighteen men, dead men, and had them in the boats and lanched them aboard Captain Barber.

LANCH n
1 Hollowed space dug down to soft sand at low tide in which fishing boats are pulled up on shore (P64-0).
2 Organized operation to move a house. C64-31-0 After Uncle's death Peter decided to have the house moved up to the road about a hundred yards away from the garden. In order to move a house a 'lanch' had to be organized. Finally the house was moved up to the road. About two months later another 'lanch' and the house was moved back down to the garden.

Regional Language Studies . . . Newfoundland (2 May, 1975)
Notice the transfer of a "sea word" to a "land" meaning. (See Story's comment on p. 155.)

Pronoun forms are often dialectal or older English, *e.g.* *'tis, 'twas* (*If 'tis found out.*); and possessive forms may be made by adding a syllabic [n], as *hisn*. Also, among some groups (usually of English rather than Irish origin), merely [n] or [ən] may be used instead of *him, her, it*, or *them*, so that the meaning of *"We never got n"* depends on context. Some speakers keep the distinction between *you* and *ye*, and use older past forms of verbs, as *clom* 'climbed', and, like Shakespeare, make free use of double negatives. J. D. A. Widdowson (1964) recorded in central Newfoundland some special uses of *be, e.g.*:

I beez asked out. 'I am asked out'. (habitually)
I do be watching. 'I *am* watching'. (emphatic)
I be into bed but I don't be asleep.

Innovations

But the language of Newfoundland has been a living language for hundreds of years, and Newfoundlanders have both adapted old words to their own use and coined new words, using the usual linguistic processes of the English language. The most common device is to extend the meaning of a word:

tuckamore (also *tucking bushes* and *spruce tuck*) 'a tangled clump of spruce bushes', probably from the British dialectal word *tuck* 'loose, tangled straw'
tolt 'isolated hill, rising abruptly', probably from the British dialectal word *toll* 'a clump of trees'; this change is the converse of that in the use of *bluff* to mean 'group of trees' on the Canadian Prairies.
crop 'equipment and supplies to outfit a voyage'

Some of these extensions are obviously metaphorical:

catch 'to be frozen in'
to raft or *to rafter* 'to pile high in layers', usually of ice hurled up by waves
chute 'a steep, narrow lane'
lolly 'soft, broken up ice', probably from British dialectal *lolly*, originally *loblolly* 'thick soup or porridge'
growler 'large cake of floating ice'

Some words are made by grammatical shifts, often with the help of derivational suffixes:

furrier 'fur hunter'; thus to go *furring* is to go hunting for fur-bearing animals.
to gap 'to cross by boat' (from noun to verb)
sunkers 'reefs and shoals'
flankers 'bright spark from a fire or chimney' (from an obsolete verb *flanker* 'to glow, sparkle')
slink 'undernourished cod' (from dialectal adjective *slink* 'lean, weak')
gaze 'hiding-place from which to shoot seabirds or other game'

152

Some seem to be coinages, often involving sound:

sish ice   'tiny wet "swishing" bits of ice'
slob ice   'densely packed sludgy ice'
crackie   'a noisy barking dog' (in all the Maritimes)
turr   'the razor-billed auk' or 'murre' (probably imitative)

The fishing, sealing, and lumbering industries can supply a long list of Newfoundland terms made by similar methods.

To trace the history of the Newfoundland language requires much painstaking scholarship. For instance, is *liveyere* (or *livere*) 'regular settler' (on the Labrador coast, as opposed to a seasonal visiting fisherman) merely a running together of *live here*, or is this usual explanation just a folk etymology? Is the true derivation from the old French word *livree*, a word that once meant in English villages a manorial worker who had some inherited rights to his cottage and land and was thus a permanent resident? Researchers at Memorial University are trying to answer historical and social questions such as these.

Internal Differences: Regions Within Regions

Typical of the painstaking dialectal studies within Newfoundland is the survey of the Avalon Peninsula (E. R. Seary, G. M. Story, W. J. Kirwin, 1968), which was done between 1957 and 1961. The Peninsula was chosen because, as the oldest settled area and as a focal point of the Grand Banks fishery since 1508, its communities have a long, continuous, yet complex history. The investigators had to go to many fields of study for their information:

cartography: names on old maps
local history: parish registers, Colonial Office surveys, census records, etc.
economics: routes of fishing, sealing, lumbering, mining, etc.— to see when and where people mixed
communication: ships, roads, etc.
sociology, anthropology: the Beothuk and Micmac Indians, religions, schools, folklore, customs, etc.
linguistics: to record on tape and in phonetic script both local and common language, and to correlate with dialect findings in Europe.

The survey shows that the economic history of the island is especially important to linguistic research. The annual seal hunt and the Labrador fishery, by bringing many Newfoundlanders together, exerted the most generalizing effect on the various dialects, spreading vocabulary, grammatical forms, idioms, sayings, and possibly even phonetic features. Informants who *went to the ice* (i.e. on the seal hunt) all used terms such as the following:

ice-claws   'an anchor to hold ship in ice'
they give you a fit-out   'outfit you'
sculp the swoil   'skin the seal'
get a berth to go   'get a place on a vessel and a right to share the profits'

Draft entry for *lolly* in the projected DNE:

LOLLY n also lally cp EDD lolly sb³ D [evon]
'broth, soup' 1777—and loblolly; *Cent* lolly 2; NID lolly 2; DC Soft ice forming in water; loose ice or snow floating in water. [1771] 1792 CARTWRIGHT i 180 There being much lolly in the river, it was with great difficulty that I could cross it in a punt. 1792 CARTWRIGHT Gloss ††† Soft ice, or congealed snow floating in the water when it first begins to freeze. 1842 JUKES i 256 'lolly' . . soft, half-frozen snow, floating on the surface of the water, not more than five or six inches in thickness, and yielding readily to pressure. 1851 *Weekly Herald* 12 Nov. On the 6th January (Old Christmas) the soft ice (LOLLY) made its appearance. 1887 BOND 65 Among the soft slob an' lolly. 1896 PATTERSON 28 ††† This word I have formerly mentioned as used by Newfoundlanders, as by the people on the northern coast of America, and by Arctic explorers, to denote ice broken up into small pieces. 1909 BERNIER 7 ††† Is loose new ice. 1947 TANNER 495 When the anchor ice, or 'lolly', began to form the nets must be taken in. 1955 ENGLISH 35 ††† soft ice beginning to form in harbours. C37-71-0 On the south coast means ice which has been crushed by the action of wind and wave. It has an appearance somewhat like froth on the water. It . . was formed from ice being churned through wave action close to shore.

Regional Language Studies . . . Newfoundland (2 May, 1975)

Informants in areas where people have traditionally gone to the Labrador fishery knew terms such as:

go dun   'become spoiled'
gullidge   'water-barrel'
gib   'take gill out'
till   'salt-box'
bus   'a profit'
brichins   'cod-roes'
to bark   'to tar'
on the bawn   'on the rocky shore'

The survey also revealed at least four major dialect areas within the 3 500 square miles, and many differences within those. Some features of dialect correlate more with religious and ethnic background than with locality—a correlation that suggests how long an "immigrant" dialect feature may linger. Here are the four dialect areas:

1. South Shoreline (largely Roman Catholic settlements)
Some sounds parallel those of Anglo-Irish dialects: a distinctive, clear [l]; a dental [t] and [d] instead of [θ] and [ð] (the **th** sounds); and an [a] sound different from the usual Canadian vowels used in both *odd* and *awed*. In conversation the words *vice* and *voice, kite* and *quoit, tie* and *toy, buy* and *boy, I'll* and *oil,* and so on are homophones, though if pressed to distinguish the pairs, most speakers approach the "cultivated" forms. Distinctive vocabulary items, some of which may be restricted to a few settlements, include: *demmery* 'autumn storm', *gap* 'gate', and *clear a few years* 'except for a few years'.

2. North Shoreline (settlers from the south and west of England)
This area is not as unified in speech; and there are many features like SSB.

3. Bay Roberts
Some features resemble eastern New England speech: *e.g.* loss of [r] in certain positions and the use of an extra low front vowel [a] in words like *bath, dance,* and *can't.* Speakers in this section also omit or insert [h] at random.

Some descendants of settlers from western England substitute *'n* for *him* or *it* ("I often seen 'en.") and use *he* rather than *it* ("inside of he," meaning *it*); these seem to be remnants of a very old English pronoun system.

4. St. John's area
The speech here shows a mixture of influences, some correlating with education, religion, and outside contacts: *e.g.* "Anglo-Irish" [l]; [w], not [hw], to begin words such as *wharf* and *whale* (parallel to SSB and most Canadian usage); two different sounds in *cot/caught, odd/awed,* and the like, patterned as in SSB; an *ou* sound that is not "Canadian," yet [æ] (the vowel of *cat*) in *dance, bath,* and others

(neither in SSB nor in the Bay Roberts area).

Much important work is still going on in the study of Newfoundland speech. Meanwhile the language is changing rapidly. There is little doubt that the influence of SSB will decrease while that of mainland Canadian and American will increase.

But Newfoundland will also retain much of its own—forms of the English language that reflect a long, rich, and often heroic history. As G. M. Story (1965) notes:

> Thus, the main streets of our chief ports are named *Water Street*, houses had, and still have, *bridges* instead of verandahs, guides were called *pilots*, and visits *cruises*. If a new house leaks, a Newfoundlander will shake his head and remark, "She hasn't been *plimed* up yet" as though he were speaking of a boat. Even land words came to have sea meanings, and a *planter*, which meant in the eighteenth century a fishing settler as opposed to a fishing visitor, meant in the nineteenth century—when fishing visitors (other than tourists after salmon or tuna) ceased to come—a shipowner or skipper.

At least partially, the language of the Newfoundland Canadians will remain the "product of nearly four hundred years of growth under conditions which are certainly unusual, and maybe unique, in the English-speaking world."

"Our lives were linked to the sea and to its products, and in due course our language came to mirror our lives."
G. M. Story, "Newfoundland Dialect: An Historical View" (1965)

A Newfoundland
Quiz

Below are some Newfoundland sayings listed in *Historic Newfoundland* (1969), a pamphlet by L. E. F. English, curator of the Newfoundland Museum. How many do you know? How many do you use in the same way? Some are obviously from the Newfoundlanders' original homes and some have been coined or adapted to fit local conditions.

1. All mops and brooms. (untidy hair)

2. An honest man when there are no anchors around. (ironical tribute)

3. A warm smoke is better than a cold fog.

4. A single line may have two hooks. (a dual purpose)

5. Come day, go day, God send Sunday. (applied to a lazy person)

6. Don't cut tails. (Don't be too particular. Fish tails are cut as an identifying mark.)

7. Empty vessels loom biggest.

8. Go to law with the devil and hold court in hell. (The odds are all against you.)

9. In a leaky punt with a broken oar, 'tis always best to hug the shore.

10. Long may your jib draw. (A good wish for the future)

11. Praise the weather, when you're ashore.

12. The devil to pay and no pitch hot. (Unprepared for emergency. To "pay a boat" means to put hot pitch over a seam between the planks.)

Here are some figures of speech heard in Newfoundland. These are from the same pamphlet. How many do you know?

Busy as a nailer
Deaf as a haddock
Dirty as a duck's puddle
Far as ever a puffin flew
Leaky as a basket
Lonesome as a gull on a rock

Like a birch broom in the fits
Rough as a dogfish's back
Smoky as a Labrador tilt
Tick (*i.e.* thick) as tar
Wide as the devil's boots

Newfoundland Terms in Literature

1. Franklin Russell tells us in his book *The Secret Islands* (1965) that he had to learn many Newfoundland terms. All the following italicized terms from his book are listed in the DC. Most of them have been already used in this section. How many of them can you define? If you don't know them, look at their meanings in the margin.

1. The island was locked in ice which, at its periphery, had degenerated into *slob ice*. . . . (84)

2. If Kean did build his schooner, he would have to launch it into the *tickle*. . . . (82)

3. The hitchhiker's uncle had left the outpost and had become the skipper of a *banker*. . . . (43)

4. A deep-sea trip on a *longliner* always had a touch of magic excitement about it. . . . (94)

5. At night, in the lea of the island, with them *turrs* rushing and roaring, you wonder how such an island can be. . . . (99)

6. I felt a pull from the *barrens*, like the hypnotic impulse to fall from a high place. (136)

7. Benny and his sons once collected fifty-five gallons of . . . *bake-apples* (79)

8. In late June, *capelin* appeared, millions strong. . . . (159)

9. . . . the village stood before me, a mere four houses, a couple of stores, two shipways, half a dozen *dead man's hands* driven into the rocks. (76)

Explanation of Terms from The Secret Islands

1. *slob ice*—Russell explains the term as "a tacky mixture of half-ice, half-sludge, which [is] impassable for man or boat." The term originated in Newfoundland, but may be found elsewhere in Canada.

2. *tickle*—'narrow channel between an island and the mainland' or, as in this case, between two islands. The term, which is used throughout the Maritime Provinces, may come from the western British word *stickle* 'rapid, riffle'.

3. *banker*—Russell adds the explanation: "a fishing schooner that worked on the Grand Banks, the great fishing territories southeast of Newfoundland."

4. *longliner*—a Maritimes word for a fishing boat that uses a long line with hundreds of baited hooks.

5. *turr*—Newfoundland for the murre (a bird), and probably an imitative coinage.

A tickle ▶

6. *barrens*—in the Atlantic Provinces an elevated moor-like area of scrub, and/or berry bushes; but this word is used in various ways in Canada according to the region.

7. *bakeapples*—an Atlantic Provinces name for what other Canadians call *cloudberries*, an amber-colored berry on a low-growing shrub, also called the *baked-apple berry*.

8. *capelin*—often spelled *caplin* or *capling*, a small fish used on the east coast for bait; originally from French *capelan* 'codfish'.

9. *deadman's hands*—listed in the DC only as *deadman* and as a general Canadianism, explained as 'any solid object to which a block and tackle might be fixed'; here it is a piece of metal for tying up boats. In the book one Newfoundlander describes it as stuck up "just like a dead man's hand" (74); this may be the origin of the shortened term.

"Silly thing," murmured Faith with a small laugh, as she nudged her husband on their way to the chesterfield where they had their refreshments, which included tea-buns and bakeapple jam.

Gordon Pinsent, *John & the Missus* (1974)

2. Harold Horwood, in his novel *Tomorrow Will Be Sunday* (1966), uses many Newfoundland (sometimes Maritime) regionalisms, and usually explains each such word as it arises. Here is a list of some he uses.

1. He and his companion never called it a village. In Newfoundland it was an *outport*—one of a thousand, all devoted to fishing. (3)

2. The foreshore of the harbor—or *landwash*, as it was called, was crowded with *stages*—rickety wharves just big enough for a *trap boat* to tie up and discharge its cargo of codfish. (5) [Note: a trapboat is a very seaworthy boat about 8 m to 10 m long, with low sides, and equipped with a cod trap—a large netted trap about 30 m square with a door, and a loader to direct fish into it. This term is not explained by the author, but is in the DC.]

3. A little farther back from the sea, with a road separating them from the stores, were the tall, spindly *fish flakes*, platforms built of spruce poles decked with small round sticks called *longers* . . . where the fish were spread to dry in the cool sunshine. . . . (5) [Note: *stores* here are not 'shops' but storage places for the fish.]
   The *flake* where he dried his few fish was built from the thinnest *longers* in the settlement. (12)

4. Mainly the harbor was filled with *trap skiffs* and small motor-boats. (6) [Same as *trapboats*, which are described in No. 2]

5. The small coasters came and went at all times between the treacherous rock shoals known as the *sunkers*, where the sea broke at the harbor mouth. (8)
   . . . the boom of the surf on the *sunkers* at the harbor mouth sounded like continuous thunder threatening death. (31)

6. In winter Eli made trips over that road with his father, travelling on the big *catamaran*—a heavy wooden sled with iron-shod runners. It was just a skeleton of a sled, really: a massive set of runners with two heavy crossbeams and four uprights for holding logs. (13)

7. Most families produced their own lumber, hauling logs from the forest and sawing them on the *halves* at the Gilmore mill. The half that went to the mill provided most of the wood that the Gilmores exported. (14) [Note: *On the halves* means on a half-share basis.]

8. The berries for taking home were the plump yellow *cloudberries*, which were always called *bakeapples* and prized. . . . (19)

9. Maybe a shipowner would purchase a thousand *rinds* of spruce bark, stripped out of the forest, to line the fish holds of his vessel. (20)

10. Unlike most of the fishermen's *swile* guns. . . . (42) [A *swile* is a seal.]

11. *Slob ice* (small thick pans, packed closely together) formed in the harbor that winter. . . . As the year advanced it was joined by northern slob, brought down by the Labrador Current and by the outriders of the field ice from the Arctic. . . . Soon it was possible to walk over the sea . . . or to travel across the Reach by dog team or even with a horse and slide. (42-3)
    . . . he had his trunk unloaded and packed on a horse slide. . . (37) [A *slide* is a catamaran.]

12. Besides the old gun, he had a *wooden dog*—a cross made out of wood, with rows of large fish hooks fastened to both sides of its beam and a light bearing line attached to the upright. You spin a wooden dog around your head until it achieves a great velocity, then let it go so that the line flies out before you. . . . You can . . . use it to retrieve birds from the open water. (43-4)

13. Eli was practising retrieving *ice pans* from the open *lead* with the wooden dog. . . . (44) [An *ice pan* is a large piece broken off from a floe; the *lead* is the open water between the pans.]

14. "Never thought I'd owe me life to a *bedlemer* the size o' ye!" (47) [A young seal—here extended to mean a small boy.]

15. Just below the bridge, where the millrace joined the brook and formed a sort of tidewater estuary—or *barachois* as it was called. . . . (82)
    They were now at the end of the harborless Reach where a tiny sandspit formed a pocket-sized *barachois*. . . . (120) [A small pond near the sea, often separated from it by a narrow causeway; sometimes given to the causeway itself, but not in this case.]

3. E. J. Pratt, in "Memories of Newfoundland," (1936) describes the plight of the mainland Canadian who finds himself with a group of Newfoundlanders gathered together in Toronto:

The conversation, once it has lapsed into dialect, is a closed book to him. He may know that haggis is a Scottish dish, or a particular hybrid of stew is Irish, but has he ever eaten brewis? No. His palate for dried cod is limited to a few tasteless fillets which the proprietor of a meat-and-fish store in the city claimed to have been cut from genuine cod. Has he ever eaten whorts? No, only blueberries—a fundamental error. Or bake-apples or capillaire or partridge berries? Never heard of them. Had he ever been stimulated by the smell of kelp after a north-easter had lashed the shores—a tonic like strychnine to the blood? Or by the smell of caplin three days after the tonnage had been deposited on the cabbage beds? No. Then he was for ever excommunicate, a stranger to the true faith. How did he pronounce the name of the country? With the accent on the second syllable. That was enough, the final heresy.

And for the rest of the evening, while our friendly alien tilted his head over the back of an arm-chair and dozed, we reminisced about Newfoundland dogs, the departure and return of the sealing and fishing fleets, the Gargantuan meals of flippers in the spring, partridge coveys, the size of the trout we almost landed, school thrashings, snow-drifts, fore-and-afters, the late arrival of trains and steamers, and the stories of old salts who knew life as it was in the sixties and seventies. . . .

These are the light and happy memories of Newfoundland, the casual ones which belong to the excursions from the main highway and which form the usual subject of chat when a few of the native-born are grouped around a stove.

English in the Maritimes

but here where heads of Hebridean mould
toss in crusted dories   hard Saxon fingers
sift dour living from the drowned
and drowning Banks

    Earle Birney, "Maritime Faces" (1945)

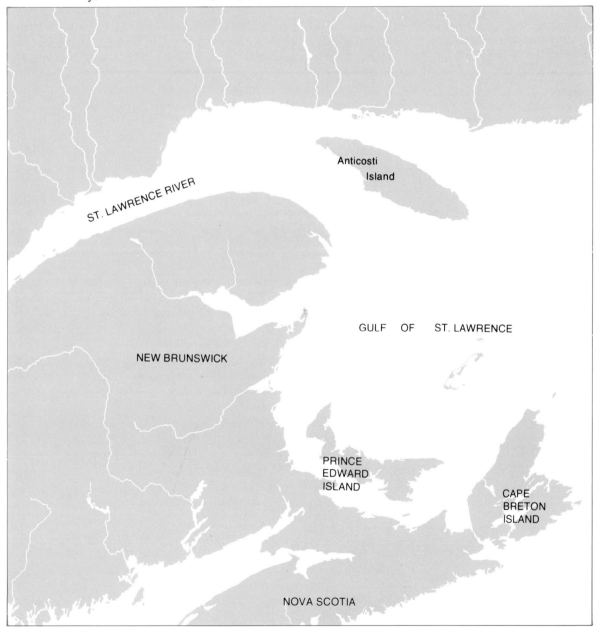

Placed between the French empire on the St. Lawrence and the British colonies of New England, the area now known as the Maritime Provinces and in the seventeenth and eighteenth centuries as Acadia and later Nova Scotia was a strategic region in the long struggle for North America. Settlement at first was slow for, like Newfoundland, the area was valuable to the British mainly for its fishery. Those small settlements that did form were cut off from one another by forests or by water. Thus their inhabitants preserved for a long time much of the speech and customs of their origins: Jersey, Guernsey and west England fishermen, discharged soldiers and sailors of England, Protestant settlers from Germany and Switzerland, farmers from Yorkshire (Chignecto), Ulster (Truro and Onslow), and later Highland Scotland (Pictou, St. John's Island) and, especially around Canso and other harbors of the Acadian shore, many New Englanders—as well as the long settled Acadian French.

The Acadians, descendants of Norman peasants, were expelled in 1755 from their rich Bay of Fundy lands, which were then filled largely by New Englanders. Those Acadians who returned went mainly to the north and east shores of what is now New Brunswick and to the Cape Breton fishery. Many were later moved again to the upper St. John River valley. About one-third of New Brunswick's population today is French speaking.

When the American Revolution broke out in 1775, the population of the whole of the Maritimes area was less than twenty thousand. This figure suddenly and dramatically doubled in the 1780's with the coming of the Loyalists—refugees and discharged soldiers from all classes and from all thirteen colonies, many well-educated and most of them "North American" in outlook. The new province of New Brunswick, "the Loyalist province," was separated in 1784, as was Cape Breton shortly after. Kurath's *Handbook of the Linguistic Geography of New England* gives the background of the settlements chosen in western New Brunswick for the dialect survey, the first phase of the North American atlas project, and notes that the Loyalist groups there came mainly from New York, New Jersey, and western Connecticut, but also from Pennsylvania, Maryland, and various parts of New England—already a mixture.

The British continued the policy of placing reliable soliders in this strategic border and sea area settlement. Later, conditions in Europe of unemployment, famine, and displacement because of new industry added people from the British Isles and Europe to this basic population, frequently (as with the Scots) in group settlements. Such varied ancestry, together with the relative separation of settlements, resulted in a wide variety of dialects and many localisms—truly rich linguistic ore to be mined by the dialectologist.

When Henry Alexander began a survey of Nova Scotia and a few other long-settled parts of the Maritimes in the late 1930's, he identified six main groups of people according to racial origin: (1) English—direct immigrants from England and pre-Loyalists and late Loyalists from the United States; (2) Scots—both Highland

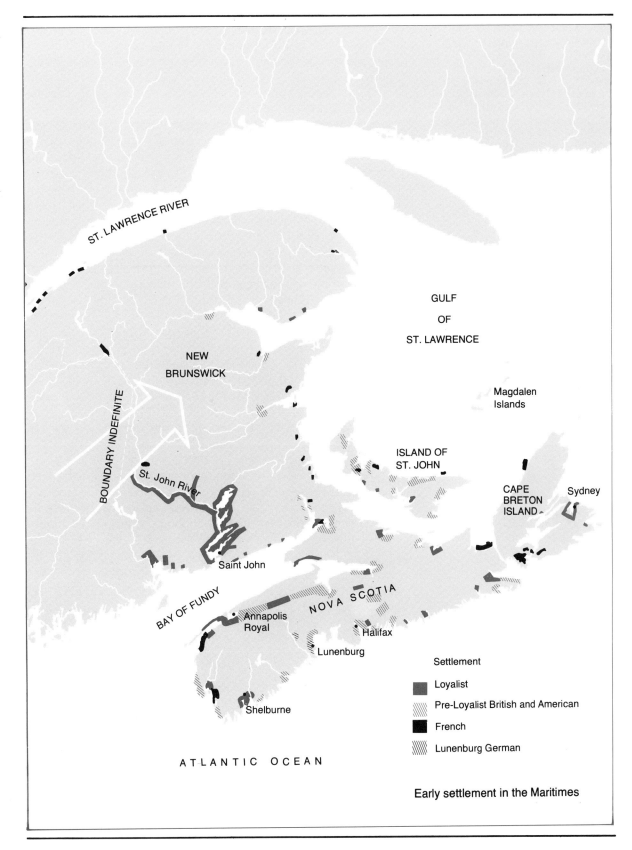

ST. LAWRENCE RIVER

NEW
BRUNSWICK

BOUNDARY INDEFINITE

St. John River

Saint John

BAY OF FUNDY

Annapolis
Royal

NOVA SCOTIA

Halifax

Lunenburg

Shelburne

GULF
OF
ST. LAWRENCE

Magdalen
Islands

ISLAND OF
ST. JOHN

CAPE
BRETON
ISLAND

Sydney

ATLANTIC OCEAN

Settlement

Loyalist

Pre-Loyalist British and American

French

Lunenburg German

Early settlement in the Maritimes

Loyalist blood—those are proud words still in Canada, nowhere more than in Nova Scotia. In our own Pine County to this day, in unexpected places you will hear that musical "heah," "theah," "anywheah," and "Yes, suh!" on the lips of people who never saw the South and never heard of Tarleton's Legion, although they are aware of their Loyalist descent. But if you hunt in the scrub spruce and wire-birch and poplar on the low ridge facing the head of Port Gambier you will find, untouched since 1784, the shallow cedars, the tumbled stone foundations of the huts, the long low boulder walls that Tarleton's Legion built to mark their pitiful "garden plots."

Thomas H. H. Raddall, "A Harp in the Willows" (1959). A story of a southern American legion that came to Nova Scotia in 1784. Raddall, writing in the 1940's, claims that features of the original southern dialect are still heard in the speech of Nova Scotians in that area. Is this true? The results of the surveys now being done in Nova Scotia may throw light on this interesting piece of Canadian linguistic and social history.

"Our family, and the other families in our village, never used the word "friends." People were either *our own* which meant our relatives, or *strangers* which meant everybody else. And this usage prevailed even when the speaker despised or even hated the relatives in question and the *strangers* were old and intimate neighbours."

Alden Nowlan, *Various Persons Named Kevin O'Brien: A Fictional Memoir* (1973)

Do you have special words for "relatives" and "non-relatives"?

Gaelic-speakers and Lowlanders; (3) Irish; (4) French; (5) German; (6) Negros. He especially noted the conservatism of the rural speech. Some older English forms he came upon are : *deef* as the pronunciation of *deaf*, *weskit* (still used) 'waistcoat', *fortnit*, *Mistress* 'Mrs.' (Nova Scotia), and a widespread use of *clever* as used in the eighteenth century meaning 'agreeable, amiable, hospitable', and also recorded in New England dialects. Captain F. Marryat, the novelist, noticed on his visit to America in 1837-8 this American use of *clever* and remarked that "the Americans make the distinction by saying, I mean English *clever*." "Our clever," added Marryat, "is represented by the word *smart*." (For another use of *clever*, see p. 151.)

To illustrate the "striking regional variation," Alexander gives the seven words he found used for the custom of "serenading" a newly married couple: *serenade, salute, celebrate, chivaree, shower, tinpanning*, and *jamboree*. While Nova Scotia has *fungy* 'deep blueberry pie' (origin unknown) as a regionalism, all the Maritimes and New England use *grunt* 'boiled berry pudding'. In Nova Scotia Alexander also heard many of the New England localisms for *see-saw: teeter, teeter board, tippin board, sawman, tilting board, tinter*, and the like, but seldom *teeter-totter*.

Both Wilson and Alexander discuss the difficulty in discovering the "real" language, that is the intimate family style of the older people. Obviously, reports Alexander, there is "a double standard," one style used in spontaneous conversation and a more formalized, careful style. When asked how he refers to his wife, an informant responds, "I call her *my wife*." Later, when questioned about a domestic item, he says, "Oh, I must ask *the woman* about that." To an item of pronunciation he replies *sausages*, but when off guard talks of *sassengers*. Lowman's observations upon the attitudes of the people in western New Brunswick to their speech when he was surveying for the *Linguistic Atlas* in the 1930's are also important data for showing some of the human reasons for dialectal change.

In both the St. John and the St. Croix regions immigrants who came from Great Britain during the nineteenth century have affected New Brunswick speech. For instance, many Irish settlers occupied the region between 431 Woodstock and 422 Fort Fairfield, Maine; and Harvey in York-Sunbury Co. was settled in 1837 by families from the border country between England and Scotland.

Many people in Charlotte Co. have a strong aversion to English, Scotch and Irish types of speech and prefer what they regard as their own Canadian speech, i.e., the speech of the old Loyalist families. The speech of 412 Calais, Maine, they regard as affected. (Kurath, 1939)

All these surveys were done a generation or so ago. It will be interesting to compare these findings with the new materials now being "mined" in the Maritimes by H. Rex Wilson, M. G. Wanamaker, M. Kinloch, and others. Though the surveys are now almost complete, the results are not yet published.

Gaelic Areas

Many older people who use Gaelic as their home speech carry over Gaelic sounds, *e.g.* unvoicing of [v] to [f], of [z] to [s]; some Gaelic words, *e.g. loft* as 'upper part of a house', and *kiry kiry* or *kirsh kirsh* to call sheep (cf. Gaelic *caor(a), caorach, caorich* 'sheep'); and some idioms, *e.g.* the remark of a fisherman, "I ran afoul of him," meaning merely an unexpected but not unpleasant encounter. Cape Breton, which annually has a Mod (Scottish Gaelic for a meeting, an assembly, and in Cape Breton involving sporting events, music, and dancing) and can boast of such Gaelic place names as *Skir Dhu* and *Ben Eoin*, has features of speech different from those in Nova Scotia, many of them going back to the earliest settlement days. Yet Cape Breton, like the rest of the Atlantic Provinces, also has many ties to the "Boston States" (New England).

"We had our church, and there was school, and we had good friends—and they are friendships we still keep to this day—and we had our Highland Dancing, of course, and every summer we'd go to the Gaelic Mod over on Cape Breton Island, and that was just about our life."

P.E.I. speaker in Barry Broadfoot's *Ten Lost Years: Memories of Canadians Who Survived The Depression* (1973).

A Gaelic Mod

Canadian Press Picture Service

(EK8) BOSTON, June 15—SCHOONER VISITS BOSTON—Nova Scotia's smiling schooner Bluenose II arrives in Boston Wednesday for a good will visit. She will visit Portland, Maine, Saturday and Sunday before returning home for the meeting of New England governors and Canadian premiers in Digby and a summer of harbor cruising in Halifax. (AP wirephoto)(the-45iolat-f-Jwe) 1977

Bluenose II

A German-settled Area: the English of Lunenburg County, Nova Scotia

The numerous regional differences of the Maritimes are enriched further by the German heritage of the Lunenburg County area, settled in 1753, named for Lunenburg in Hanover, and home of the famous schooner *Bluenose*. *Bluenose* was the name given to the original pre-Loyalist settlers in Nova Scotia; then it was extended to all Nova Scotians, and later to New Brunswickers. The origin of the nickname is uncertain.

Wilson (1958) recognized this area as presenting a unique opportunity for studying dialect mixture and dialect retention—an urgent task in the 1950's, for even the traces were fast disappearing.

"These Germans of Lunenburg, who early lost their language, are virtually the oldest English-speaking Canadians."

A. R. M. Lower, *Colony to Nation* (1946). Note that this statement was made before Newfoundland entered Confederation.

German origin is apparent in the names of the descendants, though many have been anglicized or, in many cases, "scotchified" so that *Born* has become *Burns*. The original *Weihnacht*, for example, has sometimes become *Whynacht* or even *Whynot*; but in some **Kn-** names, such as *Knickle* and *Knock*, the **k** sound is retained as in German. (See Emeneau, 1935, also.)

Wilson's survey illustrates the superiority of a trained dialectologist to the untrained recorder of speech, who tends "to overhear sounds which differ from his own." For example, Wilson found that the people in this area did not—as popularly supposed—substitute **d** for **th** (*dose* and *dem* for *those* and *them*), but formed a sound intermediate between the two. Similarly, the older speakers use a sound between [w] and [v] rather than [w], [hw], or [v].* In addition, untrained observers do not "hear" certain sound features: the different **r** sound (a velarized [ʀ], articulated with the tongue high in the back of the mouth) of many Lunenburg speakers is seldom mentioned, yet is obvious to a trained worker; and the tendency to unvoice stops, so that [b d g] may become more like [p t k] at the ends of words (as in German), is usually unnoticed.

Many German vocabulary and grammatical features revealed by the survey are not Canadianisms, as they are also found in German-settled areas of the United States, especially in Pennsylvania (the source of much "Midland" dialect), as well as in parts of western Ontario. Some examples are:

snits　'dried apples slices'
hayheap—German *Heuhaufe*
fosnoh or *fosnut* or *fassnack* (from *Fast nacht* 'fast night' or 'night of fasting')　'doughnut'
get awake　'wake up'
The paper wants rain　'predicts'
The road is all　'You've come to the end'
The money is all　'all gone'

This use of *all* for 'all gone' has spread into other parts of Nova Scotia.

Also general, as in Midland American, is *I want off, I want out*, and the like, an idiom which is fairly common across Canada (see page 11). At one time were heard German sentence patterns, such as *Come here once* or *Will you go with*? but these have practically disappeared. Henry Alexander adds to this list *tik of fog* 'very foggy' (thick), and the local calls to animals; pigs, for instance, are summoned with a cry like *woots, woots,* or *wootch, wooth,* or *vootshie*.

Lunenburg is known also for its cookery, and some of the dishes retain their original names and others, such as the *Dutchmess* of Lunenburg (potatoes and salt codfish covered with a dressing of pork scraps and onion), reflect their origin. The word *Dutch* means,

* There are also traces of [v] for [w] or [hw], sometimes in only a few items.

as in Pennsylvania, *Deutsch* 'German'. The names of food form part of that "home" vocabulary which tends to withstand change. Some parts of western Ontario share some of this vocabulary.

Wilson also found much influence from New England, *e.g.* terms such as *sunup, sundown, tempest*, and *portico*. Like many other parts of Nova Scotia, Lunenburg County preserves some relic pronunciations now dying out in New England, *e.g.* [ai] for [oi] in words like *poison* (as if *pizen*) and [æ] (the vowel of *cat*) in *wasp* and *haunted*. Lunenburg itself has also kept the New England term *porch*, in the sense of an addition built onto a house, and *cellar porch* for the little shelter over the cellar entry, whereas the rest of Nova Scotia uses *ell*.

On the whole, the Lunenburg area seems to be "an amalgam of a German substratum with Yankee English." But even these relics are almost gone.

Nevertheless, M. B. Emeneau records, as late as 1940, that at Christmas Eve and New Year's Eve parties, groups of young people still dress in costume or old-fashioned clothes, and often in blackface. On Christmas Eve, a party called *Belsnickels*, a form of *Pelsnickel* 'pelt-St. Nicholas', with one person in a Santa Claus costume, goes to shops and prominent homes playing, singing, dancing, and demanding largesse. Emeneau has traced the word *Belsnickels*, a variant preserved at Lunenburg, to the Palatine region of Germany. Though the users have no knowledge at all of the analysis of the word, he concludes, the young people have preserved an old custom through hundreds of years, and the heritage is revealed in the language.

Shared Features

Besides the many local variations, the Maritimes seem to have a special "Atlantic coast" set of shared features; some, such as technical fishing terms, are known also in the New England coastal area. A few seem to have spread from Newfoundland. Some examples of these regional Canadianisms are:

a *tern*   'three-masted schooner'
a *grayback*   'large ocean wave'
banking   not only fishing on the Banks, but also 'underwater storing of illegally trapped lobsters, until the season opens'
flake   'framework to bleach and dry fish'
fiddler   'Atlantic salmon less than 3.5 kg'
the wind will *breeze up, breeze on*, or *breeze*   'get stronger' (known along the whole Atlantic coast)
make, make fish, or *make cod*   'cure fish by drying in the sun'

The verb to *make* has many specialized uses in regions of Canada; examples from the DC: ice *makes* ('forms') in the North; *make debt* 'draw supplies on credit' (North); *make fur* or *make beaver* (fur trade); *make land* 'cultivate'; *make timber; make track; make good; make good time* (general), and others.

. . . and the lad set to work felling timber in order to make land.

Patrick Slater, *The Yellow Briar* (1933). About Irish immigrants to Ontario.

Shared with some relatively isolated parts of eastern New England is the commonly heard Maritime expression—*That's some good* (or *some bad, some hot*, and the like). This is another relic—an expression very old in English, but lost in most other dialects.

109) Do you say *It's some hot out there*? (A) Yes; (B) No; (C) Known, but not used.

	male parents			female parents			male students			female students		
	A	B	C	A	B	C	A	B	C	A	B	C
Nfld	60	24	15	56	28	14	62	27	10	70	17	11
PEI	49	37	12	44	41	13	48	35	14	42	39	18
NS	55	28	16	50	34	14	58	28	13	56	28	16
NB	57	28	15	51	32	17	53	26	17	61	24	14
Que	11	75	10	7	84	9	7	78	9	5	79	11
Ont	13	72	15	7	79	11	11	74	8	7	80	12
Man	19	40	38	5	88	6	9	84	5	5	88	7
Sask	6	76	17	3	88	8	9	78	9	4	88	7
Alta	7	84	9	6	86	8	7	82	10	5	84	10
BC	10	74	16	5	81	13	8	76	10	6	78	10
Total	32	54	14	28	59	12	28	58	11	25	61	12

The use of *some* followed by an adjective is recorded by the *EDD* for Cornwall, Lincolnshire, and Lancashire in England. Recently a student from East Anglia reported that the expression *some hot* is used by rural speakers of that area. Predictably a high percentage in the Maritime Provinces use this expression. (SCE, 1972)

The historical and economical relationship between some parts of the Maritime Provinces and New England is shown in the sounds of some vowels as well as in shared vocabulary. In 1948 one linguist, Morton Bloomfield, made this general comment:

> The distinctive quality of Maritime speech phonetically comes down largely to its treatment of [a] before medial and final [r] and occasionally elsewhere, which is somewhat more fronted than in General American, somewhat similar to the New England treatment of the sound.

But the newer surveys will probably show that, although New England and the Maritimes undoubtedly share many features, there is also much local variation and many influences.

Some regionalisms of the Maritimes area are derived from Indian terms:

> *pokelogan* or *pokologan* and shortenings: *bogan, logan, bogan hole* 'marshy place or still creek connected with a river' probably from an Algonkian word meaning 'stopping place'
>
> *pung* (also in U.S.) 'low box sleigh, with seats', reduction of *tom pung*, from Algonkian *tow pung*, related to *toboggan*
>
> *malpeque*—name of a famous oyster, from Malpeque Bay, P.E.I., originally from Micmac (through French) 'large bay'

Many regionalisms come directly from French:

> *gaspereau* (various spellings) 'small fish, like herring', from Acadian French (an *alewife* to the British)

aboiteau or *aboideau* 'dike to hold back sea-water, or its sluice-gate', the etymology uncertain

barachois 'small ponds near the sea separated by a narrow causeway', then extended to the causeway itself; from Canadian French *barachoix* 'sandbar'. In Newfoundland, the pond may be called a *barrasway*.

rappé pie 'meat pie', from Acadian French *tarte rappé*, literally 'grated pie'

A few very old words keep meanings because of French influence: a *savannah*, which means in the Maritimes 'tract of peat bog', came into English through Spanish from Indian (Arawakan), but in Canada was probably influenced by French *savane*. Other terms seem to be related to British dialectal words:

slur 'mushy, watery ice', perhaps from British *slur* 'thin washy mud'

droke, drogue, drook 'clump of trees, usually evergreen' (known in all the Canadian Atlantic areas to Hudson Bay), probably a variant of *draw*

Solomon Grundy 'marinated and spiced herring', by folk etymology (possibly influenced by the nursery rhyme) from *salmagundi*, a French dish (the origin unknown) used in England since at least 1674

There are also many others created by extension or metaphor, or just used differently:

sloven (pronounced to rhyme with *oven*) 'long low wagon for hauling'

Mother Carey's (or *Carew's*) *chickens* 'petrel'—various explanations, most of them linked to folklore or some folk etymology. The most likely source is the Latin phrase *Mater Cara* (Portuguese *Matara Cara*) 'Dear Mother', the title of the Virgin Mary as patroness of sailors, who are superstitious about harming the petrel.

We'd go by boat as far as the barachois at the mouth of Wolf Pond Brook. . . . There's an old tilt there.

Harold Horwood, *Tomorrow Will Be Sunday* (1966)

I didn't bother the droke after that—until one morning following a moonlight night in early March when I noticed rabbit tracks. . . . But that was sign enough for me to set a new slip in the heart of the droke. I chopped some birch browse and stuck it in the snow. . . .

Ron Pollett, "The Tongue That Never Told a Lie" in Major (1974). A story about Newfoundland.

I saw shapes whisk against the faint glow of the night: long-winged shapes, sharp-pointed, graceful in their lunging eagerness to cover distance. Only an ornithologist could think of them as petrels. They are Mother Carey's chickens, as sailors believe, truly sea swallows.

Franklin Russell, "A Night with Mother Carey's Children," in *The Secret Islands* (1965)

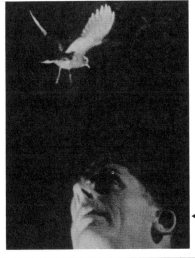

◀ Franklin Russell with a petrel, one of Mother Carey's chickens

crunnicks or *crunnocks* 'dry twisted sticks used for kindling'
crackie or *cracky* 'small yapping dog'
shiretown 'the administrative centre of a county'. In Ontario this
   would be called a 'county town'.
bar harbor—a harbor with its entrance partially obstructed by a
   sandbar
fiddleheads (especially N.B., but also in the U.S.) 'young fronds of
   certain ferns' (from the shape)
fire-barrens 'burnt over land'
crackerhopper or *crackler* (also heard in Ontario) 'grasshopper'
dilworth—(probably historical only) 'textbook', from Thomas Dilworth, an English schoolmaster who died in 1780, whose book
   was long used in the Maritimes.

The previous classification omits many interesting sets of terms,
e.g. forgotten words retained in place names, such as *thrum* or *thrum
cap*, at one time an embroidered cap made of thrums (waste ends of
the warp) and transferred to names of small roundish islands with a
"tuft" of trees in the centre, thus resembling the cap. There is also
the special vocabulary surrounding the maple sugar industry,
shared with parts of the central provinces, and celebrated in Bliss
Carman's lines:

> In rocky groves the sugar maples drip,
> Till the sweet sap o'er brims the shining pails;
> "A Bluebird in March"

Nova Scotian coal-mining gave us the Canadian *draegerman* 'mine-
rescuer', named after the German physicist A. B. Dräger (died 1928),
who invented a mask for gas-filled mines. Probably most influential
of all, especially in New Brunswick, was the rich vocabulary and
folklore of the lumber industry of the 1800's. From the New
Brunswick lumberman Senator John B. Glasier came the term *the
Main John*, which spread across the continent in both countries as a
synonym for 'the big boss' of the woods.

Maritimers also share many customs, such as the annual *Oyster
Day*, a day for visiting, eating oysters, and drinking. The area is also
rich in its inherited and its own proverbial sayings. Helen Creighton
(1950) has collected more than a thousand of such sayings in Nova
Scotia.

Murray Kinloch is presently conducting extensive dialect research
in New Brunswick. The following samples from his questionnaire
are examples of items that are of special importance in the
Maritimes.

21. What do you call a flat-bottomed boat? _____

22. What do you call a pair of men's shoes which do not cover
   the ankle? _____

23. What one word do you use to indicate that a dog is not a
   pedigree dog? _____

With a little help and perseverance, I learned, as you see, to write a tolerably legible hand; and got through my Dilworth without much difficulty.

Thomas McCulloch, *The Step-sure Letters* (1821)

The ramifications of folklore are difficult to unravel, but there is ground for maintaining that the embryo of the Paul Bunyan legends which circulated among the woodsmen of Michigan was brought there by itinerant New Brunswick loggers to whom the idea had been suggested by the Indians of their native province. Superman of the comic strips is certainly a son of Paul Bunyan; almost as certainly, Paul's father is Glooscap, the demigod of the Malicetes of the Saint John River valley.

Fred Cogswell, "The Development of Writing," in *Arts in New Brunswick* (1967)

24. What do you call rural dwellers? _____

25. What single word do you use for the spring flood?

_____

26. What do you call a room with a ceiling shaped like ⌂, and located immediately below the roof of the house?

_____

27. What do you call a room where you keep broken furniture, old clothes, useless tools, etc. and anything you might well throw out? _____

28. What do you call a land-locked stretch of water?

_____

29. What do you call a small house in the country which you live in only in the summer? _____

30. If a room is very untidy, you might say "This room looks like a pig_____".

31. What do you call the white, sweet stuff on top of Christmas Cake? _____

32. What do you say a woman is doing to the cake when she is putting this white stuff on the cake? _____

Prince Edward Island

Recently President R. J. Baker of the University of Prince Edward Island, by running some open-line radio programs, has aroused much local interest in, and gathered data about, the various forms of English spoken on the island (called L'Ile de Saint Jean by Champlain, and by its anglicized form Isle of St. John until 1798).

Constance Cullen, after a pilot survey, has made a lexical survey of four communities, all with long-settled and fairly homogeneous populations:

Kinkora—settled about 1840 by Irish fleeing the potato famine
Post Hill—largely English-settled
North Rustico—French-settled, but now mainly English speaking
Belfast—Scottish-settled

The questionnaire was based on the "Checklist of Regional Expressions" compiled by Alva Davis and Raven I. McDavid, Jr., but to this were added local words, and some variants not mentioned in the list, e.g. potted meat, and the word grate for 'supports for logs in a fireplace'.

The results of the mailed questionnaire show that the vocabulary of the Islanders is still influenced by the speech brought by the early settlers. The answers to the following questions were especially useful.

The Island

Since I'm Island-born home's as precise
as if a mumbly old carpenter,
shoulder-straps crossed wrong,
laid it out, refigured
to the last three-eighths of shingle.

Nowhere that plowcut worms
heal themseves in red loam;
spruces squat, skirts in sand
or the stones of a river rattle its dark tunnel under the elms,
is there a spot not measured by hands;
no direction I couldn't walk
to the wave-lined edge of home.

Quiet shores—beaches that roar
but walk two thousand paces and the sea
becomes an odd shining
glimpse among the jeweled
zigzag low hills. Any wonder
your eyelashes are wings
to fly your look both in and out?
In the coves of the land all things are discussed.

In the fanged jaws of the Gulf,
a red tongue.
Indians say a musical God
took up his brush and painted it,
named it in His own language
"The Island".

Milton Acorn, *The Island Means Minago: Poems from Prince Edward Island* (1975)

40. Are you familiar with the word "snool"?

yes_____ no_____
Do you use it yourself? yes_____ no_____
In what sense do you use it or hear it used:
A. a sneaky, mean-spirited person
B. a mean or unkind person
C. a mealy-mouthed, indecisive person
D. other (explain)

41. Are you familiar with the word "thra"?

yes_____ no_____
Do you use it yourself? yes_____ no_____
In what sense do you use it or hear it used:
A. a tiresome person
B. a procrastinator
C. a bore
D. a long-winded person
E. other (explain)

About 20 per cent of the informants of Kinkora (Irish-settled) used the terms (*snool* in sense A, *thra* in sense E), but none in the other settlements. Similarly, half of the Kinkora informants used and knew *clart* 'dirty, untidy woman or person', and one-third knew *foother* 'awkward, fumbling', terms familiar to only a few in the other communities. The Scottish-Belfast area knew *ceilidh* [keili] (as if *kayly*) 'a session of traditional music and dancing' significantly better than did the others, and still prefer *curds* to the newer *cottage cheese* used in the other three.

All informants used *a time*, a common term in the Atlantic Provinces to refer to any kind of party. Other Prince Edward Island terms are *storm-stayed* 'forced to stay in one place because of heavy snowfalls' and *from away* for non-Islanders, phrases other Maritimers may know or use. The Islanders also used *some* in phrases like *She's some pretty, I was some tired*, already noted as being in common use in Nova Scotia and Newfoundland (see page 144 and the Survey results on page 168).

Cullen also notes recent changes. For example, *widow-woman* (also northern and western Irish) is slowly disappearing in favor of *widow*, and the use of *pa, papa,* and *pop* as family words for 'father' is now less common. In the Irish-settled areas, words like *throughother* 'untidy person' and *sprogs* 'feet', though still recognized, are no longer widely used. Other terms she is investigating are:

> *one hand* (or *arm*) *as long as the other* 'to come empty-handed' (usually to a party). This is also heard in Ireland, as is "Don't stand there with one arm as long as the other!"
> *to put the pigs through it* 'to spoil something going well'

Little, as yet, is known about present-day phonology of the Maritimes, though the early surveys of Nova Scotia gave some data. It is clear that both the dialect surveys now being done and those of

A time: a slightly different use:
"Did she tear her dress?"
"No," he said. "Oh, a little, but she just had to stand there, all humped over, till I got her loose."
"I'd liked to heard her," Charlotte said. "I bet she made some kind of a time."

Ernest Buckler, *The Mountain and the Valley* (1952)

the near future will reveal that the language of the Maritimers, though generally Canadian, is also richly diversified.

Maritimes Terms in Literature

The following italicized words, all from Ernest Buckler's *The Mountain and the Valley* (1952), are terms for items that frequently appear on dialect questionnaires as sources of regional variants. A few of these words, especially the farming terms, are now disappearing; others are still used. How does your dialect fit this Nova Scotian language of a generation ago? (Note that these terms are not Canadianisms.)

Farming and the Land
1. Joseph thrust his fork slowly into the great *cock of hay*, lifting the whole thing.
2. This buck was standing there in the little *swale* where you come round the turn. . . .
3. They dropped an alder branch into the *brook* on one side of the bridge.
4. You could dip out one pailful only, in a quick scoop, before it [the spring] *roiled*.
5. David would thrust the stick ahead on the *sawhorse*.
6. until he heard the crackle of *kindling* in the stove.

The House and Meals
7. the only book was the Bible on the center-table in the *front room*.
8. *Down cellar*, they packed the last pieces of pork into the barrel.
9. "Where do you sleep?" "Over the *ell*."
10. she waited to pull the *blind* down again.
11. . . . doing the *chamber* work—making the untidy waking face of the house orderly again.
12. a *slop pail* held the dirty water.
13. Then his father came into the house with the one magic paper *bag* in the pocket of his bearskin coat.
14. no *boughten* cookies, no *frosting* on the sponge cake.
15. When the day's work was done and *supper* over, the kitchen seemed to smile.
16. And why, when *dinner* was over, did the pines seem as if they had the little torpor of noonday food in them too?
17. She got them a *lunch* at twelve o'clock. He'd never seen midnight before.

Notice that we still keep the word *chambermaid* in general English.

The Cullen survey of Prince Edward Island shows that the informants were nearly unanimous in having "breakfast, dinner, and supper"—but these are rural communities. (See also p. 106 for comments re *lunch*.)

Others
18. David put on his sport shirt and the brand new white *sneakers*.
19. "Look, fuhlas, I'm goona do a *belly-flapper*". (swimming)
20. Letting a woman make a goddam *sawney* out of me.

English in the Central Provinces

Now, o'er rude rocks, rapidly rushing hoarse,
Or through some pent-up pass they speed their course:
Then to the *Utawas* in wedlock bound,
Thy city *Montreal*, the streams surround.
Great mart! where centre all the forest's spoils,
The furry treasures of the hunter's toils:
Within thy walls the painted nations pour,
And smiling wealth on thy blest traders show'r.

Thomas Cary, *Abram's Plains: A Poem* (1789)

Loyalist and French settlements ▶
in Upper and Lower Canada.

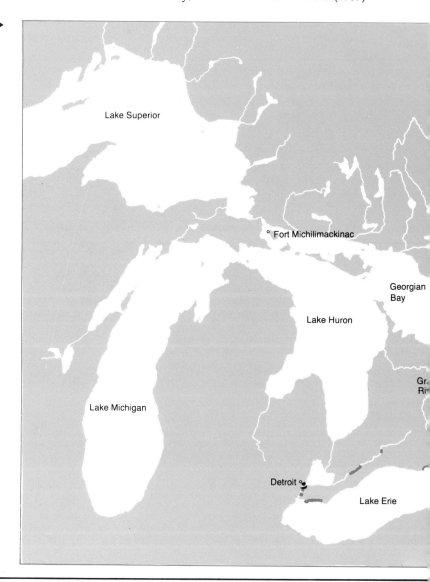

The expression "to make land," common in this province [Quebec], is no mere figure of speech, but the concrete factual description of a living reality. By the axe and plough these early settlers claimed the whole of the St. Lawrence valley for agriculture . . .

Gérard Filion, "La Vieille Province" (1959)

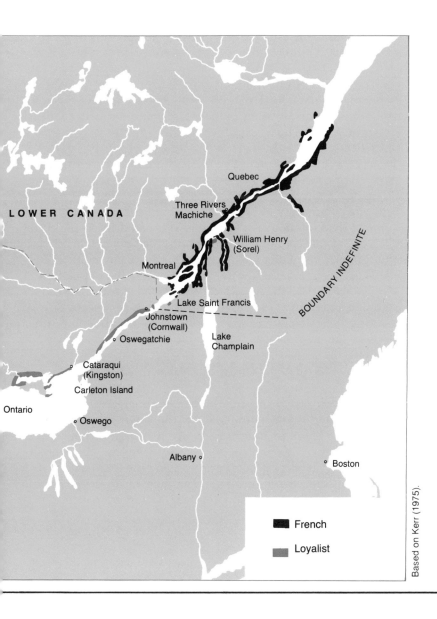

LOWER CANADA

Quebec

Three Rivers
Machiche

William Henry
(Sorel)

Montreal

BOUNDARY INDEFINITE

Lake Saint Francis
Johnstown
(Cornwall)

Lake
Champlain

Oswegatchie

Cataraqui
(Kingston)

Carleton Island

Ontario

Oswego

Albany

Boston

Based on Kerr (1975).

French

Loyalist

Place names
The place names of the St. Lawrence area, the centre of Canada,
reflect Canada's early history.
Some of these names allude to the
early fishermen and whale-hunters
from the Pyrenees, Brittany, and
Normandy:

Chauffaud-aux Basques—recalls
those who built a *chauffaud*
'drying rack for cod' near the
mouth of the Saguenay.
Isles-aux-Basques—where the
Basques rendered the blubber of
the whales.
Forillon (cliff near Gaspé)—once
"stood a structure like a small
lighthouse (*forillon*) where the
fishermen kindled their fires at
night to attract the fish into their
weirs."
Lachine—a derisive name given to
the seigneurie of La Salle, who
returned home empty-handed
from a trip to "China" (*La Chine*).
Cap-Diamant (originally *Cap-aux-
Diamants*, now within Quebec
City)—where "diamonds" were
picked up and sent to France, to
be judged worthless; an incident
that gave rise to the French
expression "Diamonds from
Canada."

The study of the English used in Canada's central provinces, Ontario and Quebec, is essential for understanding many facts about
Canadian English in general, for it is from this region that western
Canada drew most of its English-speaking settlers. In one sense
western Canada was a colony of central Canada. This western
movement of people came mainly after the railways were established; thus the remarkable homogeneity of Canadian speech in
spite of the great breadth of the land.

English-speaking Canada* came into being suddenly and dramatically. Although the Treaty of 1763 brought to Montreal and
Quebec a few British officials and soldiers and some merchants and
traders, Canada was seen as French in population and important
only as the centre of the fur trade. In 1783, at the end of the Revolutionary War, there were almost no English-speaking settlers. In
what is now Ontario there were only a few villages along the Detroit
River settled by disbanded French soldiers.

With the American Revolution had come thousands of its refugees, the United Empire Loyalists, each family with a *location ticket*,
to settle in the Eastern Townships of Quebec or along *the Front* (the
north shore of Lake Ontario, and later, Lake Erie). In 1783 Simcoe
ordered the registration of all those "who had adhered to the unity
of the Empire," and only they or their descendants are truly entitled
to the term U.E.L. Those who followed this first contingent were
often called *late Loyalists*.

These first settlers, a mere five or six thousand, were soon out-
numbered by other newcomers—some British soldiers and German
mercenaries; groups of Glengarry Highlanders (celebrated by Ralph
Connor); a community of Mennonites from Pennsylvania (the beginning of the Waterloo area and other German districts of central
Ontario); a small band of Quakers who settled north of York; but
mainly Americans, either late Loyalists motivated by political con-
victions or others looking for new land. By 1812 the population of
about 50 000 to 80 000 (the figures vary) was made up almost entirely
of former Americans. The eighteenth-century-American base of
Ontario speech—in spite of some small "pockets" of various other
dialects or languages—was well established in this first phase of
settlement.

After the War of 1812, which did much to solidify a sense of
community in the area, the American migration to Upper Canada
and the Eastern Townships continued, immigration to the rest
of Lower Canada being hindered by the seigneurial system of
land-holding. Many of this later group of Americans, especially
those bound for western Upper Canada, were members of the
professions—doctors, teachers, printers, and the like—who would
be leaders in their communities and influential in setting up the
American-type public educational system, so important in its effects
upon the language.

---

* Canada before 1867 did not include the Maritimes. The new province of Quebec
made in 1763 included little beyond the seigneurial area and a corridor along the
Ottawa to Lake Huron.

To counteract this preponderance of Americans, the British government actively encouraged British immigration, and between 1820 and 1850 about 300 000 persons came to Upper Canada (called Canada West after 1841), outnumbering the Loyalists and other American settlers. But the gap between 1783, when the first Loyalists were registered, and the European immigration of the 1820's onward was crucial linguistically, for during that time a certain type of English was generally established to serve as a basis for later development; it is known that immigrant children generally adapt their language to the language that is already there.

The newcomers were: English, many of them army and navy officers; Lowland Scots; Gaelic-speaking Highlanders, who usually settled in groups, as at Argenteuil in Lower Canada and in Bruce, Oxford, and Glengarry counties in Upper Canada; southern Irish, who have marked the English of Quebec City and other eastern ports; and Ulster Irish, who have left permanent traces on the language of whole counties of Upper Canada. The southern Irish, who came in great numbers after the potato famine of 1846, were generally poor and usually went to the lumbering camps, though they often drifted back later to the cities. The language of the people of the Ottawa Valley still has a distinctive "Irish" and "Scottish" flavor, and some Irish and Scottish dialectal features: for instance, a cow barn may be a *cow byre*, and the vowel sound of *calm* may be [æ] as in *hat*.

We have a great deal of written evidence that the newcomers from Great Britain found the language used in Canada quite "Americanized." Catherine Parr Traill, the wife of a British officer, wrote the following letter home to her mother in 1832–3:

> We had heard so much of the odious manners of the Yankees in this country that I was rather agreeably surprised by the few specimens of native Americans that I have seen. They were, for the most part, polite, well-behaved people. The only peculiarities I observed in them were a certain nasal twang in speaking, and some few odd phrases; but these were only used by the lower class, who *"guess"* and *"calculate"* a little more than we do. One of their most remarkable terms is to "fix." Whatever work requires to be done it must be fixed. "Fix the room" is, set it in order. "Fix the table"—"Fix the fire," says the mistress to her servants, and the things are fixed accordingly or arranged in their places.*
>
> I was amused one day by hearing a woman tell her husband the chimney wanted fixing. I thought it seemed secure enough, and was a little surprised when the man got a rope and a few cedar boughs, with which he dislodged an accumulation of soot that caused the chimney to smoke. The chimney being *fixed*, all went right again. This odd term is not confined to the lower orders alone, and, from hearing it so often, it becomes a standard word even among the later emigrants from our own country.
>
> With the exception of some few remarkable expressions, and an

Another commentator notes the free movement of people between the two countries:

> February 9th [1828]. The driver of the sleigh made his appearance much later than he had promised, but was accompanied by the owner, who, by way of apology, told me that I had "the best span of horses in Montreal" for my journey. A "span of horses" means a pair driven abreast, and is one of the many American expressions current in this part of the country. Indeed there is so little bar to the communication along this part of the frontier, that a great similarity consequently exists in accent, manners, and general appearance between the inhabitants on both sides.

George Head, *Forest Scenes and Incidents in the Wilds of North America* (1829)

* A footnote to an 1894 edition says, in reference to *fix*, "The word is now becoming obsolete; we never hear it—nor do we *calculate*."

attempt at introducing fine words in their every-day conversation, the lower order of Yankees have a decided advantage over our English peasantry in the use of grammatical language: they speak better English than you will hear from persons of the same class in any part of England, Ireland, or Scotland—a fact that we would be unwilling, I suppose, to allow at home.

The Backwoods of Canada (1836)

The later editions of Mrs. Traill's book omit a statement (important for our purposes) that "new comers" are "very apt to confound the old settlers from Britain with the native Americans," as they have "certain Yankee words in their conversation"—suggesting that some kind of "Canadian" blend was already taking place.

The large numbers of Ulster Irish and some of the new English reinforced the pro-British and anti-American attitudes of the Loyalists. There were many charges, for example, that the schools were more American than British. In 1817 the Reverend Alexander Macdonell complained of this situation:

Boarding schools for young ladies in both the Canadas are kept principally by American women, and every book of instruction put into the hands of their pupils by these school mistresses are of American manufacture, artfully tinctured with the principles of that Government and Constitution.

G. P. Glazebrook, in whose book this appears, comments further: American textbooks were not universal but very generally used. It was said by many teachers that the books they were obliged to use in common schools were not only written from an American point of view but hardly mentioned British North America. In some districts teachers objected that the whole atmosphere was American, that even the children's voices were affected.

Life in Ontario: A Social History (1968)

The basic Americanization of the public school system was counteracted by the influence of a second-generation Loyalist, Egerton Ryerson. His family, originally Dutch, came from New York to New Brunswick, then to a Lake Erie settlement. Ryerson, Superintendent of Education in Ontario from 1844 to 1876, has undoubtedly had a profound influence upon Canada from Ontario to the West, as Walter Avis (1957) notes:

Although Ryerson's success in eliminating American influence in the schools was far from complete, his efforts and those of others with similar views have doubtless had a significant effect on the English of Canada, for the practice of "teaching British" has a long history in this country. It must be remembered that the prestige of British English has always exerted a strong influence on Canadian patterns of speech, especially among the educated.

Modern Canadians will recognize from this early history of English speech in Canada the pattern that continues to this day: a North American base, well established, with overlays of British and British dialects, especially Scottish and Irish, and many fluctuations in usage because of the continued influence of the two major dialects, and sometimes because of an innovation within Canada itself.

Some differences between the settlement of the Maritimes and that of Ontario and Quebec are clear, however. The central provinces received greater numbers of immigrants; rather than coming from the long-settled eastern seaboard towns, these Loyalist groups were more often pioneer people: from the Hudson Valley, New York State, and the middle colonies (at present, northern and midland dialect areas). Many early British settlers noticed in Upper Canada, for example, the use of the Dutch word *stoup* (or *stoop*) 'small porch', a word typical of the Hudson Valley. The Irish groups were also much more dominant in Ontario and Quebec than in the Maritimes. So there is a different basic "character" in the two regions. Yet both retain within their borders a variety of inherited speech features.

There are, for example, differences between western and eastern Ontario. Avis (1955) found that the distribution pattern of even one item clearly correlates with the main settlement differences. Of 105 informants, he found:

55—*sick to the stomach* (mostly from Toronto eastward)
40—*sick at the stomach* (mostly west of Toronto)
 7—*sick in the stomach* (all in western Ontario)
 1—either *at* or *to*
 1—*of*
 1—avoided the term as "crude"

These differences may be correlated with American usage:

sick to—northern areas, including New England
sick at—midland and southern areas, and northwest New York state
sick in or *on*—German-settled areas, and frequent in German settlements of western Ontario. (See 1972 Survey which follows.)

This differentiation has had little or no influence from SSB, as the expression is not generally heard in England (where *sick* means 'nauseated', so that a qualifying phrase is not needed). The preponderance of *sick at* west of Toronto, Avis concludes, may be from "Midland influence through Pennsylvania Loyalist settlers," and may therefore "reflect the difference in settlement history that exists between western and eastern Ontario." The expression *I want off* (*on, out*, and the like), meaning 'I want to get off' is another midland expression, and one widespread in Canada. But the source of this structure may not be midland only (see discussion on p. 11).

Results from the 1972 Survey (Grade 9 students and their parents. The figures are percentages.)

22) (A) *sick at the/my stomach*; (B) *sick to . . .*; (C) *sick in. . .*;
(D) *stomach-sick*.

| | male parents | | | | female parents | | | | male students | | | | female students | | | |
	A	B	C	D	A	B	C	D	A	B	C	D	A	B	C	D
Nfld	1	33	9	55	1	33	4	58	4	19	14	61	0	20	8	69
PEI	6	73	11	7	9	74	6	8	4	69	16	9	3	77	11	8
NS	6	81	9	4	6	84	5	4	1	81	12	6	3	88	7	2
NB	5	84	7	3	4	88	3	4	4	80	11	2	1	87	6	5
Que	6	72	15	4	4	83	7	3	3	76	16	3	2	86	7	3
Ont	13	75	9	2	15	80	2	1	5	78	8	6	3	87	5	4
Man	15	70	9	4	15	71	7	4	4	66	23	6	3	81	9	6
Sask	7	70	15	5	9	80	8	2	3	72	16	7	2	82	12	3
Alta	11	75	9	3	7	86	4	1	5	77	13	5	3	86	6	4
BC	12	74	8	3	10	82	3	1	3	74	14	4	3	83	11	2
Total	8	73	10	7	8	79	5	6	3	71	14	9	2	82	8	6

The prestige given to the speech of the cities and towns of Ontario undoubtedly helped to standardize some of the differences among the original "pockets" of settlement. The term "Old Ontario speech" is still used to refer to the older rural language of the first settlements in what is now southern Ontario. There also is a "stage dialect" for comedians depicting rural Ontario speech, often called a *back-forty accent* (the *back forty acres* being that back part of a farm most remote from the house), and some of its features may be based on fact, but much evidence for reconstructing our linguistic history is now lost.

This complex pattern of the speech patterns of the central provinces becomes even more complicated with recent developments: rapid urbanization which has shifted Canada's people, including the French Canadians, and made central Canada a place of cities; mass migration from Great Britain and Europe, making whole sections of Toronto, Montreal, and other areas Italian-speaking, Greek-speaking, and so on; events which have brought into Canada many American young people; the recent push for bilingualism and multiculturalism; and the impact of American mass media at a time when Canada's neighbor has also become an active world power. Canadian dialectologists would like to study not only the history of our language but also the rapid changes now going on—the linguistic and sociological history being made as Canadians speak and interact.

The Ottawa Valley

It is a pity that at least a generation ago dialectologists did not make an intensive study of the English spoken in the Ottawa Valley, long known as a distinctive dialect. Because of new communications, the dialect now is being replaced rapidly by "general Canadian." J. K. Chambers (1975), having worked with the limited evidence gathered from 1959 tapes and a short field-trip in 1973, believes that the dialect was never homogeneous and that it contains "both Scots and Irish elements, and perhaps some Yankee traits." Indeed, the preliminary work done by a team from Carleton University for a projected survey shows that three kinds of Hiberno-English dialects can be distinguished: an Ulster type, a non-Ulster type, and a mixed type (Pringle and Padolsky 1977). This survey, which began with a history of early settlement (see map on pp. 174-5), already suggests that the Ottawa Valley dialect may extend over a greater area than is usually held to be the case.

The most typical feature of the dialect is the low vowel [æ] (the vowel of *cat*) before [r], where most Canadian speakers use a vowel made further back in the mouth; *garden* and *far* are thus pronounced in the Valley as ['gærdən], [fær]. The pronunciation of two of the Valley place names, *Carp* and *Arnprior*, would immediately reveal the dialect speaker. The Carleton University survey, however, shows that this may be only one of a number of **a** vowels used before [r] in the Valley.

In one variety of Valley speech, based on Anglo-Irish, the **i** sounds of *night, nigh* and *hide* correspond with the diphthongs used by most Canadians, that is, changing systematically according to the voicing of the following sound (see pp. 25-6); the **ou** sound corresponds before voiceless consonants (as in *mouse, out*) but does not change before voiced sounds (as in *owl, down, loud*) or in final position (as in *cow, now*). Chambers suggests that some "impression of the 'accent' can be gained by a speaker of heartland Canadian English if he pronounces the phrase *loud shout* with the vowel sound of the word *shout* in both words." Speakers of the other variety seem to begin both the **i** and **ou** diphthongs (as in *night, hide* and *house, shout, loud*) with [æ], with no change for the following sound.

Two vocabulary or grammar items commonly found, both of which are relics of older English and heard in other rural areas are: *mind (of)* meaning 'remember', as in:

I don't mind what he did. or *I don't mind of what he did.*
'I don't remember what he did'.

and the use of *for to*, as in:

So Ralph came off the roof for to get something.

In spite of the erosion by the dominant dialect, further evidence will probably reveal that other remnants of the "Ottawa twang" remain. The news item in the margin (dated 1959) suggests that features of former dialects may linger in the English of many Canadian descendants of Irish and Scottish (and other) dialect speakers.

How Long Do Dialect Features Remain?
No one knows. Probably the answer varies with each word, each area, perhaps each person, and depends also upon how isolated and how homogeneous the settlement is, how useful or appealing the element is, how great a prestige the dialect has, and how

Some Ottawa Valley Vocabulary Items That Are Probably Irish Origin
weigh-de-buckedy or *weighdee* 'teeter-totter' (used also in parts of Newfoundland)
handshakings 'small heaps of hay in a field'
coil—Ulster term for 'haycock'
barging 'abusive scolding'
mitching 'playing truant'
moolie 'cow without horns'

He [Paddy Garvie, an Irishman who settled near Killaloe in the Ottawa Valley] named some little mountains around his land. He named all the ones he could see, like the "Natch of the Robitaille." There's something really interesting about the way these old lads used to say words, like the "natch" instead of the "notch." They still say "natch a tree." And the Swisha (*Des Joachims*). And another one is "snye." That comes from the French word "channel," but these old fellows, they still say "snye." I put that in a story I published one time back, and somebody wrote to me, and said, "No such word." And I wrote back, "Maybe not where you come from, but there is, in the Ottawa Valley."

Bernie Bedore, Ottawa Valley songwriter and storyteller, interviewed at Arnprior, Ontario, 1972; in Finnigan (1976)

". . . One of them old Milburn bought —the father of this man, d'ye mind him?"

Sara Jeanette Duncan, *The Imperialist* (1904). The speaker is a Scot.

strongly the competing forms are reinforced by both education and writing.

We have already seen that both Americans and Canadians brought over in their speech many dialect forms from the old country and that some of these have been retained. The North American child who *plays hooky* (or *hookey*) from school is using a British dialectal word, derived from *hook* 'run away'. A person who plans to go fishing or swimming in the crick is using a variant that has existed for centuries in British dialects (compare *sleek* and *slick, seek* and the command to a dog *sik 'em*). The pronunciation *crick* is widespread in northern and midland areas of the United States, but southern areas use only *creek*. Although the influence of spelling and schooling has been strongly supportive of *creek*, the variant lives on.

Creek or crick?

Here are the results (in percentages) for the Grade 9 cross-Canada survey done in 1972. The surprisingly low number of *crick* responses may be the result of a written and school-oriented survey.

73) *Creek* rhymes with (A) *lick*; (B) *leak*; (C) either way.

	male parents			female parents			male students			female students		
	A	B	C	A	B	C	A	B	C	A	B	C
Nfld	4	94	1	3	92	1	6	88	4	5	92	3
PEI	15	78	5	7	88	3	10	84	5	6	91	3
NS	7	91	2	3	94	2	6	88	5	2	96	2
NB	14	84	2	8	88	3	11	81	6	6	88	5
Que	3	89	4	3	96	1	5	91	2	2	94	2
Ont	13	81	6	10	84	4	8	82	7	5	86	9
Man	4	92	2	3	94	2	5	91	3	1	96	3
Sask	8	87	5	5	91	3	6	88	5	4	92	3
Alta	9	89	1	5	92	3	9	85	5	3	94	3
BC	4	94	2	3	97	0	6	87	6	3	92	3
Total	9	88	3	5	92	3	7	87	5	4	92	4

Most dialectal or foreign language terms that are brought in by immigrants are not used for public communication, but many linger for generations within the family circle—words for favorite foods, for household articles, for dealing with children, for emotions, for nicknames. Sometimes they serve to make a sense of intimacy, and later in life perhaps a sense of remembrance. What, for example, is your "family" colloquial word for *potatoes: taties? totties? spuds?* or another?

The newspaper report (p. 183) of R. J. Gregg's talk to dialectologists in 1959 brought a surprising number of responses from Ontarians who recognized some of their own family words, and who added to his glossary other Ulster terms that have remained within their families. Some of these are quite widely known, for many of the words listed in Gregg's original paper (1959), though they are as-

Hill Street, so named because it was one part of the town hill which led down into the valley where the Wachakwa River ran, glossy brown, shallow, narrow, more a creek than a river. They said "crick," there.

Margaret Laurence, *The Diviners* (1974). Story set in a small prairie town; the speaker has just come from Ontario.

signed to Ulster dialects, would be recognized by a Scot or northern Englishman. Some examples are:

dunch   'push someone out of the way'
loof   'palm of the hand'
pechin   'labored breathing; grunting'
sinery   'asunder; apart'
slouster   'a mess'
dwaem   'a fainting spell'
freety   'superstitious'
drunniel   'heavy burden'

Ulster Dialect Lingers Long, Educator Finds

SASKATOON (CP) June 12—An Irishman may become a Canadian but his dialect lingers on, the Canadian Linguistic Association was told yesterday.

Prof. R. J. Gregg, of the department of romance studies at the University of British Columbia, told the association that in Toronto, for example, Ulster dialect words are still used by those whose ancestors left home seven or eight generations ago.

Words such as dunt (meaning to nudge), clabber (mud), gully (large knife), spraghal (sprawl), stiaghy (an unappetizing mixture of food), switherin' (hesitating), and dailigon (twilight, or daylight gone) are used, if not publicly, at least in the family circle, Prof. Gregg said.

Prof. Gregg said it is hoped the information will help linguistic geographers in North American who are trying to trace certain North American usages to a precise spot in the British Isles.

The Montreal Star, June 12, 1959

And many Canadian children have been told they'll be *skelped* if they don't behave.

Some expressions, Gregg suggests, have survived because they express briefly what would require many words in the standard language. *To whammel*, for instance, is a neat way to say 'to turn (something) upside down'. An *oxter-coggin*, a compound using *oxter* 'armpit', means 'a friendly underarm support for someone who cannot walk by himself' (perhaps from celebrating a little too well?). Others may have survived because of some inherent expressiveness of sound: *stiaghy* (the **gh** retaining something of the original guttural sound) seems to fit its meaning of 'an unsavory, unpalatable, messy mixture of food'—a handy word to have in one's vocabulary. The strong homogenizing pressures of North American culture do not always change some of our most fundamental traits of language.

The following are some midland American words which Walter S. Avis and Raven I. McDavid, Jr. have recorded in parts of Ontario's "border" areas. How many of them do you use? How many of them do you know?

coal oil   'kerosene'
slop   'sour milk'
weatherboards   'clapboards'
overhead   'barn loft'
side meat   'salt pork'
baby buggy   'baby carriage'
sleigh   'child's sled'
blinds   'roller shades over windows'

Perhaps, suggests Walter S. Avis, the use of *blinds* in Canada has been reinforced by British usage. However, it may not be an old word, but an innovation, as older people often use *curtains*, a New England form.

coal scuttle 'coal hod'. As *coal scuttle* is normal British usage, the source may not be midland American.

Most accounts of the pioneer settlements in central Canada use some of these terms (all Canadianisms). How many do you know? Can you add to the list?

The Front	The Huron Tract	settlement-duty road
pre-Loyalist	Scotch Yankee	
Lower Colonies	back concession	
Clergy Reserves	back range (Quebec)	
school township	back lakes	
The Queen's Bush	the draw	

German-settled Areas in Ontario

"Of course you'll stay for supper," she says as she hangs up my coat on a nail. "You know we feel bad if you come for a visit and don't make out a meal."

Open buggies, two-seater and box-like dachwaegles (top buggies) came in a steady stream as the blackclad people gathered to worship. Horses pranced up to the cement stoop along one side of the building.
Edna Staebler, *Sauerkraut and Enterprise* (1969)

"Our Mennonite and old-time Waterloo County language is kind of like it but still not the same yet as the Pennsylfawnie Deutsch they talk in Pennsylvania."
Originally a Rhineland dialect that was transplanted to America in 1683, Pennsylvania Dutch speech has developed in its own delightful way, liberally borrowing English words or slightly "deutschifying" them and creating new words for modern ideas or inventions. (For example: the German word for railway is *Eisenbahn*, the Waterloo County word is *rigglevake*.)
Edna Staebler, Preface to *Food That Really Schmecks: Mennonite Country Cooking* (1968)

The Kitchener-Waterloo area of Ontario provides another example of a mixture of people speaking English yet retaining a "flavor" from its first settlement.

As early as 1786 there was a tiny settlement of German-speaking Mennonites at Twenty Mile Creek, Lake Ontario. But the large migration to Canada began in 1801 when twelve Mennonite families left their prosperous colony in Pennsylvania to make their way on foot, on horseback, or in Conestoga wagons five hundred miles north to land they had bought deep in the bush—another stage in their long search for freedom from military service. Other German settlers, many of them skilled artisans, were attracted to the area, and soon there was a prosperous settlement.

The sight was an imposing one. There were two conestogas, each drawn by two span of heavy draught horses, and covered with a white, linen, bonnet-shaped top which was supported by a half-dozen or more narrow, curved staves extending the full length of the wagon, and protecting its contents from rain and sun. The gearings were a brilliant red, presenting a striking contrast to the sky-blue of the wagon-box. There was something so whimsical, yet so substantial, about the conestogas that they seemed admirably to suit the quaint, puritanical and thrifty Pennsylvania Dutch souls they bore.

"We're on our way to Canada," sang out Benj Eby, who as they approached the Hammer Creek House, spurred on his horse that he might be in the vanguard.

Mabel Dunham, *The Trail of the Conestoga* (1942). A fictional account of the migration of many Mennonite people to the Kitchener-Waterloo area in the 1790's.

During the First World War the name of Berlin was changed to Kitchener, and the language of the shops and streets was changed from German to English. Although many nationalities eventually blended in the area, nevertheless some of the customs of the original settlers remain: its universities, its foods, the market, its music, and Saengerfests all reflect the German cultural heritage. Although it is some time since children of English parentage came home from a Kitchener-Waterloo school with the voice intonation of Pennsylvania "Dutch" and expressions such as "Come here once" or "The dinner is all already" or "I got to comb my hairs yet"—and although it is difficult to sort out whether midland American expressions (such as "I want off") have come from this group, other midland American settlers, Scots-Irish, or just a common source—nevertheless these Pennsylvania settlers have influenced the language of western Ontario and thus that of the West. Much research is yet to be done on such pockets of settlement in Canada.

The Kitchener Market is especially interesting. Edna Staebler in her delightful book *Sauerkraut and Enterprise* (1969), in which she does catch the idiom of the people, gives this description of a transaction there:

> At a table not quite midway along the left aisle downstairs, a short, plump, black-bonneted woman offers little pats of schmearkase* wrapped in waxed paper, for a nickel each. I buy a quarter's worth to take home and prepare as she tells me: "You chust mix it with a little salt and plenty sweet cream till it's real smooth, and then you put some in a nappie, pour lots of maple syrup over," she winks and smiles broadly, "and that really schmecks."

This kind of information is hardly scientific data, of course, but it does give the dialectologist some clues as to what to look for in certain areas.

German settlers made other types of cheese from their sour milk. Schmier kase is made from scalded thick sour milk. The heat separates the curds from the whey, and a sour curd cheese was the result when the whey drained out of a cloth bag. Cream was sometimes added when the cheese was ready to eat. Hand kase, or ball cheese, was prepared similarly, but was seasoned with salt and butter and rolled by hand into balls before being laid away to ripen. Pot cheese was seasoned curds packed away in a crock in a warm place, and was noted for its strong odour.

Edwin C. Guillet, *Pioneer Arts and Crafts* (1968)

* *Schmearkase*, usually spelled *smearcase* (from German *Schmierkäse*, 'spread, smear' + 'cheese') is a soft cheese, a cottage cheese. The term used in Lunenburg, Nova Scotia, is *handkase*. Some other variants in North America are: *curdcheese* (parts of New England, also British), *sour milk cheese, Dutch cheese* (all northern United States except the Hudson Valley), *pot cheese* (Hudson Valley), *clabber(ed) cheese* (southern United States), *lobbered milk* (western New England and New York), and *smear cheese*. The trade-name *cottage cheese* is making other terms obsolete.

A Kitchener

Here are some foods you can buy in the market. Match the terms in the left-hand column with the definitions in the right. The answers are below. Note that, as this is a spoken and not written dialect, the spellings of words may vary.

1. fetschpatz (literally, 'fat sparrows')
2. kochkase
3. lotvarrick
4. schnitz
5. fastnachts
6. schpeck
7. drepsley
8. rivel soup
9. Grumbara knepp
10. Hingle Potpie
11. Brotevascht mit Eppel
12. Kraut Wickel

a. 'cook cheese'—sourmilk curds, scalded and ripened
b. fat meat
c. deep-fried dumplings, eaten hot with maple syrup (the name is from the shapes they take)
d. chicken potpie
e. cabbage rolls
f. dried apple segments (dried apples would have been an important food item in pioneer days)
g. apple butter
h. dripped batter, often with soup.
i. sausages with apples
j. potato dumplings
k. doughnuts (see p. 166.)
l. crumbs (into the soup—usually buttered)

ANSWERS

1. - c   2. - a
3. - g   4. - f
5. - k   6. - b
7. - h   8. - l
9. - j   10. - d
11. - i   12. - e

Regional Vocabulary of the Central Provinces

Because Ontario English became the type of Canadian English most often transported to the areas west of that province, there are not many regionalisms as such in the central provinces, although there are probably many localisms. Nevertheless, dialectologists have uncovered a few terms that seem to be peculiar to this central region:

firereels 'fire engine, fire truck', originally from the hand-drawn vehicle with its reel of hose. The DC gives a 1966 quotation from the *Weekend Magazine* in which *hose reel* refers to the fire truck. Walter S. Avis reports that the younger generation of Toronto now does not use the term *firereels*. Edmonton seems to use *fire rig*; both *fire reel* and *fire rig* are used in Vancouver (as well, of course, as *fire truck* and *fire engine*). This would be a good item to check in various places. (Use a picture to get the response.)

dew worm 'large earthworm'. Though all the quotations for this term in the DC are from Ontario, the word has been imported recently into British Columbia.

barbot(te) 'a large catfish'

massasauga 'small rattlesnake', from the name of a river in southwestern Ontario; originally from Algonkian.

police village (or *town*)—an unincorporated village administered by an elective board of *police trustees*

pool train 'train run by more than one company' (to give service to the many cities in the central provinces).

gunk hole—(marked in the DC as a localism) 'tiny cove with deep water right to the shore'; thus to *gunk-hole* is to move from one such cove to another, fishing and idling.

There is, of course, a large vocabulary associated with the trade of the Great Lakes, *e.g. lakehead, lake boat* or *laker, bulk carrier* or *bulker*, and words related to the canals and the Seaway.

There are hundreds of terms, many now historical, that arose with the lumber trade. Some are obsolete, *e.g.* the Ottawa Valley word *keep-over*, from the British dialectal term *keep* 'to lodge, reside', meaning a "bush" inn—what in the West might be a *road house, way house, road ranche*, or, along British Columbia's Cariboo Trail, a *mile-house*, the miles being counted and marked in numbers from Lillooet.

Quebec has some of its own words, many borrowed from French. To *telegraph* a vote, for example, is a slang term meaning to 'vote more than once, by impersonating another voter', from Canadian French *télégrapher*. Better known is Quebec's *whiskey blanc*, also called *alcool*. Political terms, such as *creditiste* and *separatiste*, are nationally known. Many historical words such as *rank* (sometimes *range*, somewhat like Ontario's *concession*) remain in Quebec's special language.

There have been several short studies comparing the relative amounts of regional elements in the educated speech of Montreal and Toronto, but the results show little difference. In general, Montreal English speech is much like that of eastern Ontario

The grain elevators
Are locked on the lakehead.

Miriam Waddington, "Toronto the Golden-vaulted City" (1963)

(Hamilton, 1958): *sick to one's stomach* is the dominant form, and the percentages for other variants are about the same—though more Montrealers (in 1958) did use the American *gotten* and the phrase *in back of*, meaning 'behind'. Hamilton (1964) attributes the prevalence of the latter phrase in the Montreal area to the influence of the corresponding French phrase *en arrière de*. These surveys were made almost a generation ago, and both cities have since then greatly changed. New and larger surveys are certainly needed.

The Language of Lumbering

In the early days, Ontario and Quebec had extensive forests with huge trees, and even before 1700 the French had developed an export trade in ship-building materials. But the great development both in the central provinces and in New Brunswick took place mainly from 1808, when Napoleon's Continental System was in force, until the 1860's. Few aspects of Canadian pioneer life were more picturesque, and the special language as well as the folklore and songs, though now often historical, will long be a part of things Canadian. In the winter camps and spring "drives," the men of Canada, sometimes with Americans from Michigan and other northern states, mixed and worked together—Indian, Irish, French, Scotch Highlanders, "Loyalist" Americans, new immigrants—and developed a special occupational terminology. Edith Fowke (1963) found evidence of this mixture, important in spreading language, in the variety of folk songs (she learned to ask for "shanty songs") known by many old-timers of the Peterborough area, an Irish settlement that became a lumbering centre: the songs they sang for her were Irish, British, French Canadian, Scottish, and American— even "western" American.

Here are some Ontario words, all Canadianisms; some are now obsolete, and some have spread to other parts of Canada. These are from Joan Finnigan's collection of songs, interviews, etc., "*I Come from the Valley*" (1976).

> Paddy Garvie came there before Algonquin Park was established, and he built a sort of *stopping-place* in there on the way to Basin Depot. (63)
>> Bernie Bedore, interviewed 1972. (A *stopping-place* was an inn, where people and horses en route to the lumber camps could get a meal and be put up overnight.)

> . . . we didn't stop putting the stuff [food, hay, etc.] in the *keep-overs* until about nine o'clock at night. The keep-overs were camps to keep the stuff over until they would use it the next winter. (68)
>> Bert Horner (1899–1975), interviewed in 1972

> Archie MacAdam was *Walking Boss* on the big Egan estates *limits* at Madawaska. A Walking Boss is in charge of the whole limit. Maybe there's six or so camps, and he's in charge of all of these. (68)
>> Syd Pottinger (1890–1972), interviewed in 1972

Oh, when we get down to Quebec town,
    The girls they dance for joy,
Says one unto another one,
    "Here comes a shantyboy!"
One will treat us to a bottle,
    And another to a dram,
When the toast goes round the table
    For the jolly shantyman.

Lumberman's song: "O ye maidens of Ontario"

Well, then, other farmers would portage stuff. They called it *"cadging."* Why, right on this highway (No. 17) when I was a kid—I'm turning my 78th year, and you remember since you were five years old all right, so I can say 72 years ago—why, right on this highway, there'd be a string of teams loaded going up there, and they'd stretch for an eighth of a mile on the road, and then there would be another bunch behind that. (74)

John King (1895–), interviewed in 1972

[The origin of the word is uncertain—perhaps from the verb *cadge* 'to transport'; the DC gives several compounds.]

This one does not appear in the DC, but the context suggests the meaning:

Red birch is the choice of the *clears*. It's the board you saw off the sapwood, coming into the heart of the log. You get this lovely red birch with no knots. (144)

Syd Pottinger (1890–1972), interviewed at Renfrew in 1972

The following list is but a sampling of the many lumbering terms recorded in the DC. Some of these later were transferred to the British Columbia forest industry, which does, however, have its own rich "lumber camp" language.

shanty (also *chantie*)—'a crude hut used by the lumbermen'— from Canadian French *chantier* 'logger's cabin' (see p. 79 for a discussion of the origin of this term).

In Canada the meaning of this word has extended further to something like that of *shack*, another Canadianism (from British dialect—*shackety*, *shackling* 'rickety, rundown').

From both words have developed many compounds and phrases.

shebang 'a tavern in the bush', like *shanty*, perhaps from Canadian French *cabane* (from French 'hut'), but possibly from (or influenced by) Irish *shebeen* of similar meaning. A common term from Irish is *the whole shebang*.

river drive—and dozens of other compounds made with either *river* or *drive*

lumber raft—and many other compounds made with either word

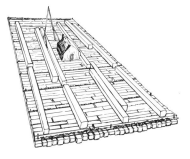

The illustrations and specimen entries on this page and the next are from the DC.

Above: Drawing of a lumber raft
Below: Photograph of a lumber raft

Notman Photographic Archives, McCord Museum

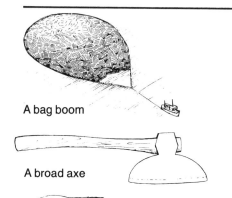

A bag boom

A broad axe

A cant hook

Robertson raft *Lumbering, Hist.* a huge, cigar-shaped raft of as many as 22,000 logs, devised by Hugh Robertson of Saint John, N.B., in 1886 and in use for several decades in the lumbering industry for transporting logs in the Atlantic and Pacific. **1965** *Canadian Wkly* 2 Jan. 15/3: [Caption] This Robertson raft on the Columbia river was so long only half of it was shown in stereoscopic picture taken in 1902. *Ibid.*: [Caption] The raft in the photograph below was a Robertson raft built in 1902. . . .

pineman, pinery 'a logger of white pine', 'a stand of pine trees'
crib 'a small raft of logs', especially one of a number making up a large lumber raft
lair 'a portable bunk' used on the raft or on shore
timber slide 'a chute constructed to by-pass rapids'—and four pages in the DC of other *timber* compounds (see also *slide* and *chute*)
make timber 'cut and trim trees ready for rafting'
bushmark 'a stamp on a log to identify the company or owner'
dram 'a hugh raft of many layers'
mast road 'a logging road along which *mast pine* were hauled to the river'

A Robertson raft

The following is a translation of one of the many folk songs sung by the lumbermen of the Ottawa River. Canada has a rich heritage of folk songs, and many have been collected and published.

Note in this folk song the Canadianisms, *By-town* 'Ottawa' (after Colonel By, the builder of the Rideau Canal), *lumber camp, shanties, log drive, portage,* and *whiskey blanc.*

2 Across By-Town,   they went, today
   To lumber camps,   they're on their way.
3 They've packed their grub,   they cannot stay,
4 They climb the Ottawa,   the livelong day,

```
 5 In bark canoes,      all weathered grey.
 6 The lumber camp      they've reached, hurray!
 7 Their axes trim,      there's no delay
 8 They're striking hard;      the tall trees sway.
 9 To give them strength      for work and play,
10 "Eat pork and beans!"      they always say;
11 Then sit and smoke      their pipes of clay.
12 The shanties close;      sing tour-a-lai.
13 The log drive starts,      the same old way.
14 Big logs they square      and drag away
15 To build the rafts,      on them to stay,
16 And float down stream      a great array.
17 The Aylmer portage      tramp so gay.
18 Their pockets jingle      with their pay.
19 They're bound to call      chez Mère Gauthier,
20 With buxom girls      to frisk and play,
21 Drink whiskey blanc,      stretch on the hay.
22 Their money gone,      they swear away,
23 A doctor call,      ah welladay!
```

Marius Barbeau, Arthur Lismer, Arthur Bourinot, *Come-a-Singing: Canadian Folk-Songs* (1963)

Maple Sugar Making

Few Canadian books about pioneer days are without some mention of the spring sugaring-off, another industry common to the eastern parts of Canada, and parts of the United States (to the envy of the westerners), and one that still thrives, though much changed. The art of making maple sugar was learned from the Indians of the eastern woodlands, and undoubtedly was a boon to the early settlers. Little wonder that the maple leaf was chosen as the Canadian emblem.

The tree that produces the sugar has various regional names. Dialectologists have collected: *hard maple, rock maple, sugar maple, sugar tree, maple tree, candy tree,* and *sweet maple*. One can quickly find many Canadian "maple sugar" expressions in the DC by looking below key words for their compounds. For example:

maple-bush	sap-boiler	sugar-boiler
-cake	-boiling	-cabin
-camp	-bucket	-grove
-grove	-bush	-house
-juice	-carrier	-hut
-molasses	-house	-orchard

There are also numerous compounds with *sugar* and *sugaring*. A non-historical term is the *sugary*, an anglicization of Canadian French *sucrerie*. Settlers would also be familiar with the Indian word *mocock* for the birch bark containers used for holding the sugar as well as berries, wild rice, and the like. Other special vocabulary grew around the industry, connected with the troughs, the *tap* (*spile*,

Reader, if you have not already tried it, don't fail to make an effort to get to a sugaring-off, and my word for it you will never regret it. . . . The wax is so sweet, so pure and pleasant, and it's all so jolly, that such experiences are always red-letter days in one's life calendar.

Thomas Conant, *Life in Canada* (1903)

No agricultural operation has ever been invested with so much glamour as the making of maple syrup and the reason is simple: none ever had so much magic.

John Kenneth Galbraith, *The Non-Potable Scotch* (1964)

Since 1949 the French Canadians of Alberta have celebrated every spring at Edmonton's *La Cabane à Sucre*, recreating (in spite of the lack of sugar maples) much of the traditional fun of the Quebec parties, including *les toquettes* (sugar on snow).

All about Maple Syrup.

Maple syrup. Canada's most delightful natural food product. And possibly the most misunderstood. Which is why we're telling the maple syrup story. So you'll know how the tradition first began and how it's changed through the centuries.

"A sap-run is the sweet goodby of winter. It is the fruit of the equal marriage of the sun and frost." John Burroughs—Signs and Seasons, 1886.

boiled to make 1 gallon of syrup. So the sugar shack is thick with the smell of smoke and maple. Once the final boiling is done, friends and neighbours (especially children) are invited to the sugaring-off party. Standard fare is "maple taffy", which is steaming hot syrup poured over fresh, clean snow. Ice-cold and chewy, it's a taste experience impossible to forget!

The Sugar Maple.

There are 4 varieties of sugar maples. They thrive on steep, rocky slopes and long, bitter winters. So they grow only in parts of southern Ontario, Quebec, the Maritimes and the New England states. And nowhere else in the world.

Sugar maples reach tappable size, under the best of conditions, in about 40 years. A carefully tapped tree will give, drop by drop, about 12 quarts of sap on a warm spring day and continue to give sap for a century.

In the beginning.

The Indians were the first to discover "sinzibuckwud" (the Algonquin word for maple syrup, meaning literally, "drawn from wood"). They would use their tomahawks to make V-shaped incisions in the trees, then insert reeds or concave pieces of bark to run the sap into birchbark buckets.

The first white settlers and fur traders introduced wooden buckets to the process, as well as iron and copper kettles. Later, they would bore holes in the trees and hang their buckets on home-made spouts.

Maple production was especially important because sugar was the principal maple product. It was as common on the table then as salt is today.

The Mystery of the sap.

Maple sap is thin, barely sweet, and as colourless as spring water. The distinctive maple taste comes only through boiling.

The sugar in sap is a bit of a mystery. It seems that each fall, the tree produces its own supply of starch to act as an antifreeze for the roots in winter. With the melting of snow, water enters the roots and begins the circulation of "sugar water" through the tree in preparation for the growing season.

As a result, sap runs—in fits and starts—from the first spring thaw until the buds turn to leaves.

Sap gathering today.

The process is the same but the equipment has changed. Taps are made of metal. Buckets are aluminum or plastic. Buckets have lids to keep the sap clean, free from snow, bark and twigs. Sap is still gathered by going from tree to tree, but in some places, elaborate tree-to-tree pipe systems are used to run the sap directly into the sugar shack.

There, the collected sap is boiled down to syrup in flat metal tanks or "evaporators". Sap must be boiled the same day it is gathered, so a hot, steady fire is kept going at all times. About 32 gallons of maple sap must be

The Old Fashioned flavour of Maple.

Aside from the better-known uses for maple syrup (on pancakes, waffles, french toast), there are many other ways to enjoy its delicate flavour.

Try it in milk, eggnogs and fruit cups. As a sweetener in pies. Or a glaze on hams, boiled carrots or baked apples. Use it in baked beans, or as a hot or cold sauce for puddings and ice cream. It's great as a base (with chopped nuts and butter) for upside-down cakes or danish buns.

100% PURE

Pure Maple Syrup. Nothing else even comes close.

or *spigot*), the various stages of boiling and sugaring, and the festivities. The excitement of the "merry sugar-making time" was partly engendered by the realization that the "sap-rising" signalled the end of the long winter, a fact reflected in the metaphors chosen by Canadians for the various runs: the first (and best) is the *robin-run*; the second is the *frog;* and the last, collected late when the buds are about to burst, is the *bud run.*

Although the maple industry has contributed only a few words to the language (there may be many still unrecorded local variations), yet it is a part of the Canadian tradition. Nearly every Canadian child has at least read references to its excitement, as in Archibald Lampman's "April" (1888):

> In the warm moon the south wind creeps and cools,
> Where the red-budded stems of maples throw
> Still tangled etchings on the amber pools,
> Quite silent now, forgetful of the slow
> Drip of the taps, the troughs, and trampled snow,
> The keen March mornings, and the silvering rime
> And mirthful labor of the sugar prime.

The Time Dimension

As long ago as the 1880's, A. F. Chamberlain, a dialectologist, was making notes on Canadian speech and vocabulary, particularly on that of Toronto and Peterborough (which he spelled Peterboro'). He noted, in Ontario, the use of many Americanisms. How many of these do you use or know?

scow—from Dutch *schouw*

mud-scow—in Peterborough, a vessel used to carry clay to brick-works

boom—probably in the sense of 'log-boom'; but perhaps he meant the sense of 'prosperous time'

coal-oil—"all over English Canada," Chamberlain states

smart—"very common"—meaning 'intelligent'

like Sam Hill—probably a euphemism for 'like hell'

so-long—"quite common now"

cows—to mean 'cattle'; also *cow pasture*

funeral card 'the printed notice of death posted on a telegraph pole'

funeral-procession—"in the sense of cortège is very common in Ontario"

gallynipper or galnipper—"a large reptile-insect, found under stones and used as bait" (*The American College Dictionary* lists it as 'a large mosquito'.)

'lunge—as an abbreviation of *muskelunge,* a Cree word for a pike-like fish

locks—the plural struck Chamberlain as odd: "At Peterboro' 'the locks' was the usual term."

to scheme school 'to play truant'; *to scheme* [ski:m] or in broad dialect [ske:m] (rhyming with *came*) is one of the normal Ulster dialect terms for 'play hookey'

"You had fun, didn't you, when we went to the sugaring? Did you like the snow candy?"

Gabrielle Roy, *The Tin Flute* (1947)

Chamberlain regrets how, in Toronto, the word *avenue* has lost "any meaning it may have had, distinct from that of *street*, although there are some cases in which the old and correct signification is apparent" (by which he probably meant a wide street or drive, usually lined with trees and forming an approach, as to an English country house). How does your area of Canada use *street, avenue, boulevard*? What distinctions of meaning are preserved?

Chamberlain also noticed words, which he classified as dialectal, that had been retained, sometimes for many years, by immigrants from Britain. How many of these do you use or know, and in what sense?

mollycoddle—"He is such a mollycoddle." ('fool')
smike—"We haven't had a smike of rain down there all summer."
squaddle—"Put your feet in your slippers. I don't like to see you squaddling about like that." ("Spoken by a native of Warwickshire who has been in Canada and the United States for eighteen years," remarks Chamberlain.)

In addition, Chamberlain noticed the special terms used by children in Peterboro in 1880. Most of these terms he considers to be Americanisms. Have you used or heard any of these?

bellywhackers—"to jump or fall *bellywhackers* is to jump from a height, *e.g.* a bridge, so as to strike the water on one's stomach."
blood-sucker (in stagnant pools)—the term is used for any creature, such as a leech or gnat, that sucks blood
bunty 'someone short and stumpy'
honey 'the yellow exudation from the grasshopper when pressed'—"called *molasses* in New England," adds an editor
minni—"a common form for *minnow*"
pissybed 'dandelion'
Jimminy Cripes! and *Jimminy Christmas!* (oaths)—The origin of the first part of these phrases is *Gemini*, the twin gods by which the Romans swore, but the additions suggest adaptation to make euphemisms for 'Jesus Christ'. [*Jimminy Crickets* is another variation.]

The OED lists pissabeds as "obsolete, except dialectal"; but the word is used in parts of England and in North America. Ray Guy (1975) uses the word to illustrate Newfoundland usage:

About the best time to visit the Awlin [Island] is in June when the dumbledores is buzzin' around the pissabeds, or as they would say upalong where the language has been watered down to a shocking extent, "when the bees are buzzing around the dandelions."

You May Know Them as Sea Urchins, Ma'am (1975)

English in the Prairie Provinces

There is nothing

nothing to stand in
the way of the eye.

Earth rolls under light
scabbed by brush.

Over water course
over slough and sand-flat

eye travels out
to rest on land's ledge.

Sky sheets down
sun-glazed air

eye open
in the space where

there is nothing.

> Peter Stevens,
> ''Prairie'' (1970)

The world is very large, the sky even larger, and you are very small. But also the world is flat, empty, nearly abstract, and in its flatness you are a challenging upright thing, as sudden as an exclamation mark, as enigmatic as a question mark.

> Wallace Stegner, *Wolf Willow* (1955). Reprinted by permission of Brandt and Brandt.

T.E. Moore Photo

William Kurelek, *Jewish Immigrants Arrive on the Prairies*

"The Laundress," trans. from
the Icelandic by Michael Patrick
O'Connor and Thorvaldur
Johnson, in *Volvox: Poetry from
the Unofficial Languages of
Canada . . . in English
Translation*, ed., Yates (1971) ▶

She worked as a housemaid, then as a laundress
in small town Winnipeg, full of émigrés speaking
every language except her own; she was Icelandic
and as she worked she sang the old Icelandic hymns
and songs: the songs had all her joy, they brought
all her peace. She kept reaching for the language
that got lost in her life. She could never speak it
again, though it always measured her breath.

Late one summer, as she lay dying, she sang again
the Icelandic hymns, sang in her mother tongue,
an other tongue for us; and as we lay her
in a foreign grave, we, who know no Icelandic,
who know then almost nothing of what she loved
and lived by, say our prayers over her in English.

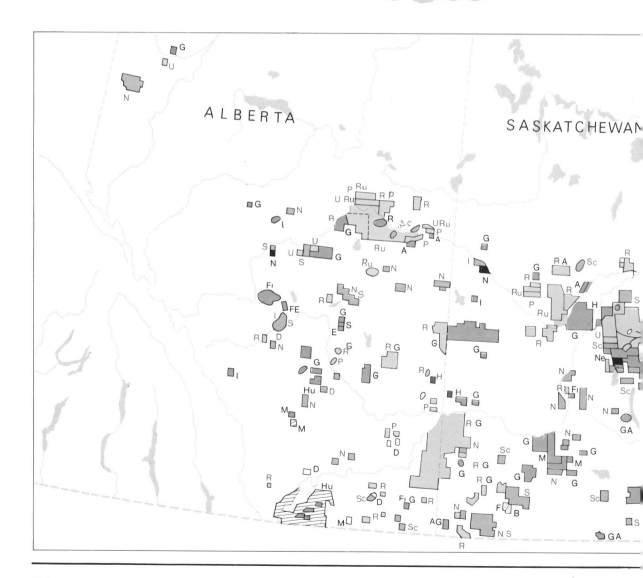

How much do you understand of the following account written by a settler in the Canadian West? How much do you think a Britisher would understand? If you know the terms well enough to define them precisely, where did you learn them: by personal experience? by hearing them? by reading? from movies or TV? Which ones can you guess at from the context? Which ones do you think would be marked "historical" in the DC or in other modern dictionaries?

The italicized words are Canadianisms, most of them from western Canada.

All quotations are from R. D. Symons' *Many Trails* (1963), a book about his adventures as a young Englishman in western Canada in the early 1900's.

Provincial Archives of Manitoba

1. Amos had filed on a quarter by the *creek*, and had a small log shack sheltered against a cut bank, a few saddle horses, and a Cripple Creek saddle. With grazing plentiful, he had contracted to run a bull herd for the ranchers; so he had a few dollars

◀ Map of European immigration to western Canada

MANITOBA

Based on Kerr (1975).

Central Europeans

Austrian	A
Finnish	Fi
German	G
Estonian	E
Hungarian	H
Hutterite (Austrian)	Hu
Italian	I
Lithuanian	L
Mennonite	M
(German-Russian)	R
Roumanian	S
Swiss	

Western Europeans

Belgian	B
Dutch	D
French	F

Scandinavian Peoples

Danish	D
Icelandic	I
Norwegian	N
Swedish	S
Undifferentiated	Sc

Slavic Peoples

Czecho-Slovak	C
Polish	P
Galician	G
Russian	R
Ruthenian	Ru
Ukrainian	U

Others

Hebrew	H
Mormon (U.S.)	M
Negro	N
Nestorian	Ne

coming in, and he could see his way, and he would have said, to running a "spread." (25)

2. Amos went to Swift Current, then the *jumping-off place* for the cattle country, of what was then Assiniboia territory. (25)

3. . . . to the south-west the triple *buttes* of the Sweetgrass Hills, to the north the timbered *coulees* and high level benches of the Cypress. (25)

4. A land of high plateaus and clear, crisp air; of balmy spring breezes and January *blizzards*. (25)

5. Fortunately, I had a little wood from the *coulee*, as well as some *cow-chips* stored up, which helped me out. (94)

6. When I filed on my homestead I didn't need to be *located*, for I knew my way around. (92)

7. He has a blanketed team drawing a *caboose* on runners. In this there is a small wood-burning sheet-iron heater . . . to keep the fish from freezing solid and so losing much of their flavour. (132)

8. . . . the hardy little trunks crack under the crushing fingers of the frost *weetigoes*.

   This is a deserted place, and the drifted snow bears no track of moccasin or *travois*. (150)

Indian woman with travois ▶

9. The grass began to get shorter and finer—real *prairie wool*. . . . (30)

10. The cowboy who was fixing a saddle cinch nearby was saying, ". . . the best I ever rode was a *buckskin* from Milk River, but these yere pintos and blues and strawberries are all right purty; ain't they now?" (45)

Settlement History

Key dates in prairie settlement

late 1700's French Canadian voyageurs settle around the Red River, the food base of the fur-trading system. The descendants of these or other white men and Indian women became the Métis.

1812–1816 Lord Selkirk's Scottish settlers at the Red River, though opposed by the fur-traders and the Métis.

1859 A steamboat on the Red River connected the settlers with St. Paul, Minnesota—a threat to British sovereignty. Upper Canadians in Red River—a threat to the Métis.

1869 Rupert's Land purchased by Canada. Rebellion in Red River Valley.

1870 Manitoba Act creates Canada's first western province.

1885 CPR completed.

1905 Provinces of Alberta and Saskatchewan created.

By 1900 Manitoba had about 250 000 people while the rest of the prairie region had fewer than 200 000. These settlers were the ones whose speech would set the pattern for the English of later immigrants. And these pioneers were mainly from Ontario. The remarkable homogeneity of Canadian speech from Ontario westward—what one could call "General Canadian"—arises from this fact and from the continued communication by train. The isolation which leads to dialectal differences did not occur to any marked degree.

When the American West began to be filled in the late 1890's, and when new types of wheat were introduced—together with new railways, elevators, lake boats, and canal systems to carry the "golden grain"—the prairie lands came into their own, and settlement was rapid. With the aid and persuasion of the remarkable Clifford Sifton, over five million immigrants came to Canada within thirty years to take up land or to help build railways in the West—immigrants speaking hundreds of different languages.

Many settlers, particularly those before 1914, settled in groups which naturally attracted others of the same language. The children learned English at the public school and, with perhaps slight differences, blended their voices into Canadian speech patterns. Only

"The West was pioneered from Ontario: it was settled by people from the ends of the earth."

A. R. M. Lower, *Colony to Nation* (1946)

Probably the great thing about a city like Winnipeg was all its contradictions and all the sounds that you heard there, all the different tones. I grew up on a street where there were Ukrainians and Poles on either side of me; there was a Scot with an incredible brogue about two houses down; a guy with the most unbelievable Raj accent, who had spent a lot of time in India, across the street; a labourer from Belgium, some Germans, some Swiss people, a Jewish tailor whose son was a violinist right out of Isaac Babel's Odessa, this kind of thing.

Jack Ludwig, in Cameron (1973)

The geographic locale in the valley of the Assiniboine River snaking west from Winnipeg through regions predominantly agricultural, the grain elevators down by the railway track, the colour and accent of cowboy-hat and blue-jeaned lope during the weeks of semi-annual fairs, mark the city's natural allegiance to the west.

However, the flavour of Old Ontario is strong in the city's architecture, its proliferation of churches, the tree-planting habits of its pioneers, its social patterns and modes of speech and thought.

Kaye Rowe, "Brandon: The Wheat City" (1969)

now, however, are Canadians beginning to realize the deep sociological effects of this remarkable migration.

In his book *Saskatchewan* (1968), Edward McCourt shows how the names of the towns within one small area in the eastern part of Saskatchewan reveal the pattern of settlement in the West:

> . . . within a radius of twenty miles we find Dubue, Bangor, Stockholm, Esterhazy, Langenburg, Thingvilla, Churchbridge—in origin French, Welsh, Swedish, Hungarian, German, Icelandic, British—intermingled with American and eastern Canadian settlements whose centres bear no distinguishing ethnic labels.

One town called Saltcoats—"originally British to the core," even to cricket—suddenly became in the 1890's "an all-nations society speaking a babel of tongues." Nearby were Gaelic-speaking Scots and the Welsh people of Bangor, a group from Patagonia who spoke Welsh and Spanish but not English.

The place names of other parts of western Canada reflect a similar polyglot background. Manitoba has at least sixteen names of Icelandic origin, including *Arborg* ('of a river' + 'town'), *Gimli* (mythological), and *Grund* ('a green field' or 'a grassy plain'). J. B. Rudnyckyj has long been researching the publishing material on Canadian Slavic namelore; *Komarno*, Manitoba, he suggests, was coined from the word *komar* 'mosquito' because of a plague of these insects; many others are descriptive of the place, *e.g. Vostok*, Alberta 'East'; *Hory*, Saskatchewan 'mountains'; *Kalyna*, Saskatchewan 'cranberry'; and *Dibrova*, Manitoba 'old forest'.

From 1907 to 1915, about forty per cent of the homestead entries by immigrants were made by Americans—many of them originally Canadians. The ranch lands of Alberta, southern Saskatchewan, and parts of British Columbia are the northern end of the great ranching belt stretching from Mexico, and the area shares a large vocabulary—much of it derived from Spanish or, as with *coyote*, from Aztec. Some of this vocabulary has been popularized by movies and television. There were also group settlements of Americans, such as the movement north in 1887 of Mormons from Utah to Cardston, Alberta. In 1954–5 M. H. Scargill found that the speech of Albertan young people was strongly American, and increasingly so with closeness to the border. His percentages would now change after the coming of American oil and gas companies and the "boom" in Edmonton and the North.

Borrowings from the United States that arise because of similar conditions or immigration may be erratic in distribution. Some people of Manitoba, for example, use the American term *sundogs* for the two spherical rainbows or "mock suns" seen on either side of the sun in very cold air (technically called *parhelia*), but many Canadians from other parts of the Prairies have never heard the term. Possibly the expression came up the old St. Paul–Red River route. The close investigation of one such term might reveal some interesting parts of Canadian settlement and social history.

The exchange of language is not always from south to north. Harold B. Allen's survey of the border area (1958) shows that the Canadianism *bluff* meaning 'grove of trees', used throughout the Canadian Prairie region, has slipped "across the Line" into North Dakota. Walter Avis states that this usage of *bluff* is so commonplace in prairie language that many French speakers have adopted it as *le bluff*. In this connection, notice how easily "sea" metaphors transfer to features of the prairie landscape: a group of trees standing out in the grasslands was earlier called an *island*, perhaps a translation from the Canadian French term *islet de bois* (similar to the Acadian French *isle d'arbres*). Alexander Henry (1809), writing about his travels of 1761, tells us that to see one was "in the phraseology of the Plains" to have "land in sight." Later, the settlers' wagon throughout the North American prairies was called a *prairie schooner*.

Allen also found that the lumbering areas of northern Minnesota and the adjacent part of Canada share a peculiar use of *tote* to refer specifically to horse-drawn vehicles: supplies were *toted* to a logging-camp by a *tote-wagon* or a *tote-sled* over a *tote-road*. The same areas use the expression *go-devil* 'a U-shaped rig for skidding logs', probably a Canadianism gone south and perhaps related to the now obsolete French Canadian *diable* (French 'porter's dolly').

Some potential borrowings never happened at all. Allen found that none of his records showed the Canadian use of the following common American terms. Do you know of any of these terms being used (not merely known) in the Prairie Provinces? Do you think the situation has changed at all since Allen's survey?

davenport	*straighten up* a room
faucet	*coffee party* or *kaffee*
hoghouse	*klatsch* or *coffee clutch*
shock (of grain)	*berm* (a regionalism) 'grass
corncrib	between sidewalk and
mush 'breakfast dish of	a paved street' (see p. 100)
corn meal'	

Bungee

Before Manitoba entered Confederation in 1870, a local language had already developed among the people of the Red River area, a *lingua franca* known as *Bungee* or *Bungay*. The origin of the name seems to lie in an Ojibwa or Cree word meaning 'little' or 'few'. The language was a simplified mixture of Cree (usually from the mother) and Scottish English (from the father and reinforced by schooling), with some addition from French. An article by S. Osborne Scott and D. A. Mulligan (1951) illustrates how sometimes the structure follows the Indian languages:

Bye me I kaykatch ('nearly') killed it two ducks with wan sot ('shot').

and at other times comes closer to Scots English (note that **sh** is often **s**):

The train clonks on and on. Through the prairies. She looks out at the flat lands, which from the train window could not ever tell you anything about what they are. The grain elevators, like stark strange towers. The small bluffs of scrub oak and poplar. In Ontario, *bluff* means something else—a ravine, a small precipice? She's never really understood that other meaning; her own is so clear. A gathering of trees, not the great hardwoods of Down East, or forests of the North, but thin tough-fibred trees that could survive on open grassland, that could live against the wind and the winter here. That was a kind of tree worth having; that was a determined kind of tree, all right.

Margaret Laurence, *The Diviners* (1974). The "speaker" is a prairie girl.

Slavs of all varieties from all provinces and speaking all dialects were there to be found: Slavs from Little Russia and from Great Russia, the alert Polak, the heavy Croatian, the haughty Magyar, and occasionally the stalwart Dalmatian from the Adriatic, in speech mostly Ruthenian, in religion orthodox Greek Catholic or Uniat or Roman Catholic. By their non-discriminating Anglo-Saxon fellow-citizens they were called Galicians, or by the unlearned, with an echo of St. Paul's Epistle in their minds, "Galatians".

Ralph Connor, *The Foreigner: A Tale of Saskatchewan* (1909)

John James Corrigal and Willie George Linklater were sooting into the marse. The canoe went apeechequanee. The watter was sallow whatefer but Willie George kept bobbin up and down callin, "O Lard save me." John James was on topside the canoe souted to Willie and sayed, "Never mind the Lard just now Willie, grab for the willows."

The phenomenon of Bungee is similar to the rise of Chinook Jargon on the west coast (see Regionalisms in British Columbia).

Here are some further examples of Bungee words:

He fell off the rock *chimmuck* in lake.   'head over heels'
keeyam   'never mind, don't bother'
neechimos   'sweetheart' (see the DC entries for *chimo* and *nitchie*)

Two examples of Scottish words used in Bungee are:

byre   'stable' (used also in the Ottawa Valley)
slock (the candle)   'put out'

Most of Bungee—a piece of the history of the Canadian people —has disappeared. But remnants linger on the tongues or in the memories of some Canadians.

Regional Vocabulary of the Prairie Provinces

Certainly some of the language of the original people of the plains still appears in the English of the region. Alberta slang, for example, has some Indian words, such as *meaks-kim* (Blackfoot), or *shinnias* (Cree), both meaning 'money'; other terms are translations, like the euphemism *gone to the sand-hills* for 'dead'. The Sand Hills are a region in southeastern Alberta, believed by Plains Indians to be the home of departed spirits.

Many prairie terms arose with the manner of settlement. Some examples are:

grid system (in Saskatchewan, *grid roads*)—roads laid out two miles apart north and south and one mile east and west (very apparent from the air when one is flying across Canada)
First Meridian—the line just west of Winnipeg from which the townships are measured and numbered
correction line—the jog every 24 miles in the north-south grid lines to make up the difference between the survey line and the true meridian

Other terms arose for specific local conditions:

local improvement district   'a district in the Prairie Provinces administered provincially because of a small population'
a pool—a co-operative grain marketing group of farms (extended in Canada to a *pool train*, meaning a train used co-operatively by two or more railway companies)
burgess—a British term used in Saskatchewan for what other Canadians call a *ratepayer* (another British term), 'owners of property who pay municipal taxes'

In good Scots tradition, the Red River children were well educated, and many spoke perfect English, yet would lapse—or relax—into the familiar dialect when everyone present knew it. One story illustrates the dangers of overteaching. A teacher proudly trained a young man to say *sure, should*, and *shall* instead of *sewer, sud*, and *sall*, then sent him off to the city church as an assistant to the rector. When the teacher next saw the rector, he asked about his pupil, telling about the **sh** drilling. The rector replied, "I think you overdid it. When he was reading the morning prayer, he said, 'God shave the Queen'."

Told in Scott and Mulligan (1951)

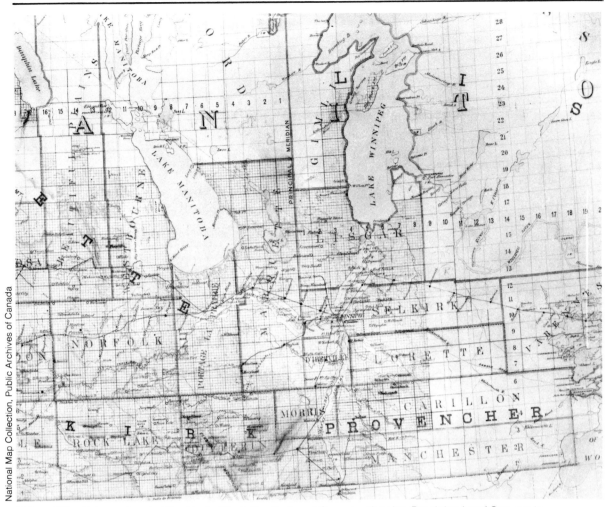

National Map Collection, Public Archives of Canada

"Map of Manitoba and part of the North-West, Territories of Canada shewing Dominion Land Surveys to December 31st, 1883 . . ."

Some local terms arise as euphemisms—attempts to make something that is unpleasant sound more pleasant by giving it a new name. A prairie example of euphemism is *nuisance grounds*— 'garbage dump'.

Because of the early interdependence between exploration and the fur trade, French Canadian words abound:

bichon   'a light bay or fawn horse'
demoiselles   'pillar-like earth formations' in Alberta
coulee   'a deep ravine or gulch' (a word that has spread south from Canada into the Dakotas, to vie with the American word *draw*)
Métis, butte, prairie itself, and hundreds of place names

Some French terms are often translated or distorted: both processes can be seen in the change of Canadian French *bois de vache*, literally 'cow wood' and meaning 'dry buffalo dung used as fuel', to *cow chips* or *buffalo chips* or to *bodewash*. Nearly every Canadian has

The town dump was known as "the nuisance grounds," a phrase fraught with weird connotations, as though the effluvia of our lives was beneath contempt but at the same time was subtly threatening to the determined and sometimes hysterical propriety of our ways.

Margaret Laurence, "Where the Wind Began" (1976)

Both the cemetery and the nuisance grounds were located, although respectably separated by a cow pasture, on land that had once been the farm of H. Stanley Ungerman.

Merna Summers, "Portulaca" in *The Skating Party* (1974)

A north Winnipeg girl
bending over water
she spent her summers at a lake
and watched the goldeye swim.

Miriam Waddington, "Things of
the World" (1965)

It was at that time, about 1908,
that Nick had set himself up as a
packer. He had had his own string
of horses and packed supplies to a
survey camp from Edson to the end
of steel in Alberta.

* * *

Only one place remained for him to
go—the benchland directly behind
and above the cabin, six miles
beyond muskeg and brule.

Howard O'Hagan, "The White
Horse" (1963)

heard of the Lake Winnipeg fish, *goldeye*; but few know or use its older name *lacaishe*, the Canadian French version of the Algonkian name *nacaishe*.

The coming of the railways, so crucial to settlement, also brought new terms: *railhead*, *end-of-steel town*, *railway lands* or *belt*, *terminal elevator*, *speeder* or *track-speeder*, and *jumping-off place* (or *point*, *spot*, *town*) are all well-used Canadianisms. A few, such as *jumping-off place* (which may go back to fur-trading days), have widened their meaning so as to have lost their connection with those important rails being slowly laid from the East to the great lands of the Canadian West.

Some western Canadian terms arise from the nature of the land, for example:

clamper (also *clumpet* and *ice clamper*) 'large chunks of ice that pile up on shore', especially in Saskatchewan (called a *clumpet* in Newfoundland)

parklands or *park belt* 'the area between open prairie and northern forests'

black blizzard 'a dust storm'

pothole—not a hole in a road, but a large circular natural depression, often with shallow water. If grass grows in it, it is a *pothole meadow*. A swampy alkali pothole may be a *slough*. A prairie farmer may be paid *pothole easement* for refraining from draining a pothole so that wildfowl may nest there.

bald-(headed) prairie (or *plains*)—the treeless grassland area

cuthill 'hill with a steep front, usually from erosion'. (The commonly used *cutbank* is general North American West.)

foothills 'rolling country between Rockies and the prairie', also termed the *high country*; Calgary is nicknamed *City of the Foothills*.

Of course, there are also scores of compounds beginning with *prairie*, *plains*, and such historically significant words as *buffalo*, *portage*, and *Hudson's Bay*.

BITAEMO
TO THE TOWN OF DAUPHIN, MANITOBA

PRINTED ON flags, flyers and posters, the word was out and all over town. And people kept saying the word. For four days last August, in a small community 220 miles northwest of Winnipeg, some 50,000 people kept saying it. The word had called them from across Canada, the US, and even South America. And as they poured into Dauphin they saw it first on the wide banner that spanned Main Street—*Bitaemo!* It's pronounced vee-*tie*-amo and means "welcome" in English. But once a year, English is not the tongue of Dauphin. It is Ukrainian.

And it was Ukrainians who thronged the streets. Ukrainians small and Ukrainians large, come to dance and sing Ukrainian, to take in Ukrainian art and food, to have one whale of a good Ukrainian time. Outside the Ukraine itself, there's only one place you can do that—at Canada's National Ukrainian Festival.

Weekend Magazine, Sept. 22, 1973

Photo: Chornomorski Kozaky Dance Ensemble

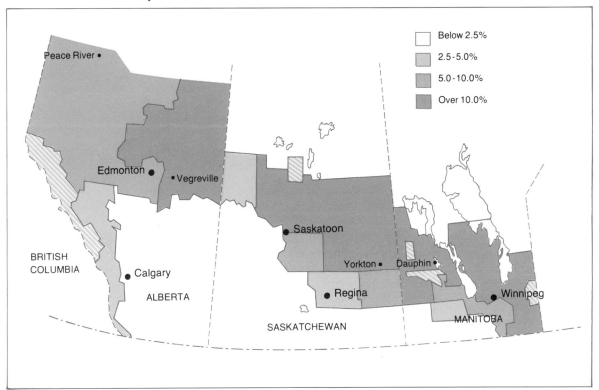

Below 2.5%

2.5-5.0%

5.0-10.0%

Over 10.0%

▲
Ukrainian speakers in
western Canada

Bilingual Communities

Except for the work on Slavic languages in Canada by J. B. Rudnyckyj, little has yet been published on the effect of mass multi-
lingualism upon the Canadian language, or that of English upon the
"home" languages. R. S. Graham's (1957) study of the German
settlement at Luseland, west central Saskatchewan, is therefore
especially valuable. He chose to study the language mixture here

because it was stable, and also limited in its contact with English speakers except through the schools. Furthermore, this town's population represented two main flows of immigrants before the Second World War: the early farmers who came about 1909 and the post- First World War group of Russo-Germans who were literate and read High German. Since the Second World War, German immigrants have entered the area, but they have been assimilated into the English-speaking community.

His findings suggest the pattern found elsewhere in North America: the first generation speaks German at home; the second is bilingual; and the third speaks English in the home and usually in the church.*

Graham found some slight interferences in the sound system similar to those recorded at Lunenburg, Nova Scotia (see Emeneau (1935) and pp. 163ff.), and other German-settled areas, all following German language rules:

(a) final [ŋ] as in *sing* is sometimes said as [ŋk] (*sink*) even by younger speakers.
(b) [b] both initially and finally can be almost [p], so *bull* and *pull* are closely alike.
(c) the two **th** sounds are sometimes produced almost as [t] or [d], so that *thick* sounds somewhat like *tick*, and *the* like *de*.
(d) even younger people unvoice [v] to [f], so *very* sounds like *ferry*.
(e) final [z] and [ʒ] are unvoiced, so that *rise* and *rice* are not distinguished one from another, and *garage* ends with a [š] (sh) sound.
(f) some speakers have trouble with [æ] so that *bad* and *bed* are alike and sound like English *bet*.

A notable feature is the German stress on the initial syllable. While most Canadians give certain compounds equal or almost equal stress, *e.g.* mínce píe, the German speakers stress the first syllable. This same stress pattern may also occur for adjective and noun groups such as *big man, first base*.

Graham also noticed some German influence on syntax (word order):

(a) the "time" adverb can be put before the "place" adverb, as in German:
    He came yesterday home.
(b) the English phrasal verb (*e.g. go out, look over*) may be separated the German way:
    I'm going with them out.
    He threw the fish in the water back.
(c) although no German loan-words persist, some semantic transfers occur in the form of *already, right away,* and *once* on

... They talked in Low German. The peculiar Russian Mennonite use of three languages caused no difficulties for there were inviolable, though unstated, conventions as to when each was spoken. High German was always used when speaking of religious matters and as a gesture of politeness towards strangers; a Low German dialect was spoken in the mundane matters of everyday living; the young people spoke English almost exclusively among themselves. Tongue and thought slipped unhesitatingly from one language to the other.

Rudy Wiebe, *Peace Shall Destroy Many* (1962). A novel about a Mennonite community in Saskatchewan at the time of the Second World War.

* This generalization may not apply to all language groups; for instance, the retention of Ukrainian in Canada is high, especially in rural areas. (See Rudnyckyj (1973) for a full discussion and interesting statistics about immigrant languages in Canada.)

the pattern of German *schon, gleich,* and *mal,* so one hears such expressions as:

He is there already yet.
Come right away quick.
Come here once.

(d) there were some other slight semantic mixtures, sometimes involving how far a word's meaning stretches in the two languages, *e.g. neck* for 'throat', *thick* to mean 'fat', and *hairs* for 'hair', in keeping with German *Hals, dick,* and *Haare.*

Curiously, the use of *all* for 'all gone', as in *The bread is all* (Das Brot ist alle), often found in German-American areas and in the Maritimes, did not appear.

Graham found that the second generation of English-speakers (that is, the fourth generation from the original settlers) have lost nearly all traces of even these "markers," and that only five German expressions were currently used in local Saskatchewan English:

Was ist los? 'What's the matter?'
Nichts kommt heraus 'Nothing comes of it.'
Komm mal hierher 'Come here at once.'
Ich bin ausgespielt 'I'm played out.'

The results of this survey of one town, indicating a gradual loss of German features over four or five generations, are probably typical of what happened in all but very isolated or socially self-isolating communities.

Certainly the English language structure may affect the German of the bilingual speaker. In the Fraser Valley, a German-speaking area of British Columbia, for instance, many young people who speak English transfer incorrectly a word or structure into the German they speak. For example, in German there are two verbs to cover the range of the English word *like,* as in: 'to *like* someone' (either *lieben* or *gernhaben*), and 'to *be like* someone' (*gleichen*); some bilinguals therefore say, incorrectly: *Ich gleiche das nicht* to express 'I don't like that' instead of *Ich liebe das nicht* or *Ich habe das nicht gern.*

One linguistic problem which seems to be little studied is the influence of the first language upon the *choice* between variant vocabulary items, particularly if the two languages are as closely related as German and English. A German-speaking person would, for instance, accept quite readily the word *icing* 'sweet covering on top of a cake', for it fits the pattern of the German language; but *frosting* does not. That is, a German person might incorporate *icing* into his or her own language structure:

Hast du den Kuchen *geeist*? (Have you iced the cake?) but he or she would not say:

Hast du den Kuchen *gefrosted*?

There may also be a conscious "mixing" of English and the original language, that is, an adoption of a mixed style to imply a close relationship or to reinforce an ethnic bond. This is a linguistic phenomenon that linguists are just beginning to study in Canada (see Urion in bibliography). Such conscious mixing of languages is much like the slight deviations any family or tightly-knit social group develops into an "in-group" code.

Much work remains to be done on these and similar aspects of the languages that lie behind the English of many Canadians—work that should reveal some of the mysteries of how languages function.

The presence of so many people to whom English is an additional language may have subtle, perhaps immeasurable, effects upon attitudes of Canadians toward language. Someone who speaks two languages is usually very conscious of language and is eager for precision in its use. One bilingual parent, for example, disliked hearing his Canadian child use *hate* in such expressions as *I hate to get up in the morning*—hardly a situation, the father thought, for such a strong verb. When his son announced at the end of a job, "I'm finished," he objected that surely the boy meant either "I have finished," or better, "The job is finished." This care with speech, together with the expectations of foreign parents for their children and for the effects of "schooling," may lie behind many North American attitudes about the role of the teacher and "proper" English—attitudes that are sometimes good but sometimes amount to intolerance of "colloquial" English or of any deviance from what is thought to be "correct."

Prairie grain elevators ▶

A box: cement, hugeness, and
   rightangles—merely the sight of
it leaning in my eyes mixes up
continents and makes a montage of
inconsequent time and
uncontiguous
   space.
   A. M. Klein, "Grain Elevator"
   (1948)

Slang of the West

The camaraderie engendered by the pioneer life of the West also gave rise to a rich "in-group" vocabulary, most of it borrowed from the major occupations of the area. Agnes Cameron, reporting in *Canadian Magazine* on the language found in Winnipeg in 1908, comments that the Britishers fresh from Oxford or Cambridge must learn more than the meanings of many North Americanisms— *coulee, canyon, gulch, corral, tepee, lariat, chaps, quirt, maverick*. They must also learn the slang: that the "three B's," for example, are *bacon, beans* and *bannock*; and that *tin-cow*, "which *might* be corned beef," may be condensed milk; and that *dope* may mean "anything from grease on a lumberman's skid-road to butter or jelly or green-gage jam."

Some expressions, she notes, go back to early customs: the drinking salutation (still heard) *Here's a Ho*, came from the starting signal "Ho" of the leader in the big community buffalo hunts; a friend who asks you to "dig up" a dollar for her may be using a term from gold-mining days, when the precious "dust" was buried in the mud floor; and the common Canadian word to *cache* something away is a French Canadian voyageur word. Another fur-trading word, *outfit*, which once meant the big annual shipment of supplies to the factories of the interior, has become, like *dope*, a catch-all term. It has been said that a westerner will never be at a loss for a word if *outfit* is in his or her vocabulary. (*The Beaver*, a periodical published by The Hudson's Bay Company in Winnipeg, still uses *outfit* to mean 'volume'.)

Other slang terms are compounds, often with duplicated sounds, or transfers of meaning based on imagery, sometimes with a sense of irony. Some have spread across Canada.

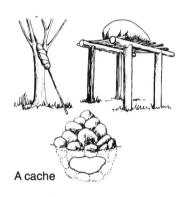

A cache

SUMMER 1972

OUTFIT 303:1

$3 A YEAR

to sodbust   'to operate a farm' (from *sod* grass-covered ground + *bust*, a dialectal variant of *burst*); thus a farmer who raises crops is a *sodbuster*

stubble-jumper   'prairie farmer'

cigarette dude   'city slicker'

grub-rider   'tramp who has the knack of arriving about meal-time'

get *a tie-pass*   'have to walk along the tracks' (by analogy with *railway pass*). A *tie* as 'wooden support for railway tracks' seems to be a Canadianism, as is *tie-camp*, where ties are cut and shaped.

scab   'saddle'

a *gunnysack* place or thing   'second rate, poorly done' (from miners and loggers). To *gunnybag* a prairie fire is to beat it out with wet sacks.

a *haywire* thing or person   'poorly done, in need of fixing, mixed up' also extended to 'slightly crazy'

This is but a sampling of the colorful colloquial language of the Canadian West. Many terms never enter the written language and therefore seldom appear in dictionaries. But there is little doubt that,

But she was sound, and if that meant that the rest of the world, especially the white world, was haywire, then the rest of the world, especially the white world, *was* haywire, and that was the way of it.

Alan Fry, *The Revenge of Anne Charlie* (1973). A story set in western Canada.

"Trapping a rhino looked like a cinch until someone handed me a lasso."

How many other cowboy expressions can you think of that are now used as metaphors in the general language?

in spite of the rapid urbanization of even the vast prairies, the spoken language of many Canadian communities retains some of the metaphors and images of the earlier days. Probably few speakers anywhere in Canada picture the origin of the metaphors when they say, "Well, I must *round up* the family and *hit the trail* for home."

Prairie Voices on Paper

A novel or story written to reflect the life in an area can be rich in regional vocabulary. W. O. Mitchell's *Jake and the Kid* (1961) tries to catch the spoken language of a small Saskatchewan town in the 1940's. Frederick Philip Grove's *Fruits of the Earth* (1933) has a different set of "voices" (written in the third person rather than the first), and attempts to reproduce the sound of the people in early Manitoba.

All of the italicized words in the following excerpts from Mitchell's book are listed in the DC as western Canadianisms. How many of them do you: (a) use in the same or similar way? (b) know but do not use? (c) not know?

Outside was spring everywhere, with a warm *Chinook* whispering along our poplar *windbreak* stirring our windmill to creaking. (3)

Still, still as water, with the sun coming kind of streaky through the *wolf willow* along her edges. (65)

I found seven skulls half-buried at the foot of the cliff where the *coulee* cuts down real sharp. (65)

He's a *buckskin* with a real light mane and a tail! (108)
Jake let a whoop out of him and jumped like a startled *jack rabbit*. (109)

It was quicker than thinking, quick as a *gopher* down a hole. (107)

He ran like the wind over the edge of the prairie—slicker than peeled *saskatoons*. (142)

Jake went right on with his *saskatoon* pie. (147)

It give everybuddy from Crocus to the *correction line* the heartburn. (3)

Jake and the Kid also has many general Canadianisms, some now slightly "dated":

I told him a *Winnipeg couch* fer when Florence come tuh stay with us. (113)

It was the time he knocked down nine grey *Canada honkers*. (184)

He is a *hay-wire* mechanic . . . who answers to the name of hardtail, *sod-buster, stubble-jumper,* hoozier, or john. (183)

Jimmy Shoelack's plane came low and fast as a scalded *coyote* over the rise of the draw. (151)*

Grove's novel reveals more general Canadianisms than westernisms. Most Canadians would recognize these:

* The word *draw* 'ravine, gully' is a western North Americanism, used also in the United States.

210

May, who up to 1897 had lived in the *county seat*. . . (3)

All these men came from south of *the Line*. (18)

They've contracted to finish the work before *freeze-up*. (25)

But the *road-allowance* was being fenced. (77)

Abe was, that winter, elected *reeve* of the municipality. (126)*

. . . the acknowledged fact that the operation of a *consolidated school* involved no more expense to the individual district than the operation of their ungraded school had done. (186)

Every farmstead was sheltered by *wind-breaks*. To the east, the *bush* fringe of the river closed the horizon. (328)

But the following is a prairie word in that it has a special meaning, 'group of trees', in that area; knowing this meaning seems essential for understanding the passage:

> . . . were shaded by tall cottonwoods which seemed to lose them-selves to the north, in what resembled a natural *bluff*—a deceptive semblance, for all trees had been planted. (5)

Provincial

My childhood
was full of people
with Russian accents
who came from
Humble Saskatchewan
or who lived in Regina
and sometimes
visited Winnipeg
to bring regards
from their frozen
snowqueen city.

In those days
all the streetcars
in the world slept
in the Elmwood
car-barns and the
Indian moundbuilders
were still wigwammed
across the river
with the birds
who sang in the bushes
of St Vital.

Since then I have
visited Paris
Moscow London
and Mexico City
I saw golden roofs
onion domes and the
most marvellous
canals, I saw people
sunning themselves
in Luxembourg Gardens
and on a London parkbench
I sat beside a man
who wore navy blue socks
and navy blue shoes
to match.

All kinds of miracles:
but I would not trade
any of them for the
empty spaces, the
snowblurred geography
of my childhood.

Miriam Waddington (1972)

* The word *reeve* is old, going back to the time of the Saxon kings, but is now only a historical word in other parts of the English-speaking world. Chaucer's *reeve* in *The Canterbury Tales* was a manager of a manor estate. Canadians (from Ontario to the West) use *reeve* with the meaning of 'chairman of the municipal, town, or village council'.

English in the Canadian North

In land so bleak and bare
a single plume of smoke
is a scroll of history.

F. R. Scott, "Mackenzie River" (1964)

Canadians, scattered thinly along the southern part of their country, are almost physically aware of the great arctic area to the north of them, the silent land stretching from the Atlantic to the Pacific.

Until recently, when air travel and a conscious effort by the federal government have made communication faster and easier, the territory was almost empty, with only eleven or twelve thousand Inuit, some Indians, Métis trappers, hunters, and traders, and a few scattered communities, each with its own mixture of modern and frontier life.

The language of the English-speaking people in this vast area reflects in part their sense of enclosure and isolation. "Civilization" is *the Outside*; to go from the Arctic to the settled areas of Canada is to *go outside* or to *come out*; the even more sparsely settled areas of the North are known as *the Inside*; and the expression *up north* as used by most Canadians, who are oriented to maps, is *down north* to northerners, who are oriented to the rivers which flow "down" to the Arctic Ocean (just as to Newfoundlanders "down" means toward the Labrador coast).

Most of the regionalisms used by the *Kabloonas* (or *Kadloonas*) 'the people of the big eyebrows', as the Inuit call the Europeans (see p. 88), are terms needed for the special kind of life there, and they are mainly borrowings from the Inuit, who taught the Kabloonas some of the tricks of surviving in that difficult climate. A few now generally known terms entered the western arctic areas through Russian, for example:

> *parka*—Russian 'hide or pelt' (originally from Samoyed)
> *tundra*—(formerly Finno-Ugric)
> *sastrugi* 'long high ridges of hard-packed snow formed by the wind'

The Danes have also left words:

> *cooney* 'wife, woman', probably from Danish *kone*, then Inuit *kuni* 'wife'
> *ice-foot* 'sea ice frozen to the coast', probably a translation of Danish *eis-fod*

And perhaps the Dutch also:

> *krang* 'whale meat' (not necessarily a Canadianism, as it is widespread), probably from Dutch *kreng* 'carcass'.

Labrador and the eastern Arctic share many words with the Newfoundlanders, many of them from older or dialectal British. Some examples are:

brin bag and *brin sack* 'large coarse sack' (related perhaps to the older British word *brins* 'colored threads used in making tapestry')

quar ice or *quar water* 'ice formed from melted water in spring' (from British dialectal *quar* 'congeal, coagulate')

The language of some Inuit in Labrador is sprinkled with German words learned from the Moravian Brethren missionaries, who were established on the coast in the eighteenth century. We are told by one researcher—who credits these heroic missionaries with saving the Labrador Inuit from extinction—that:

> Most Labrador Eskimos count in German and use German-derived names for weekdays: Sontageme, Montageme, Denestageme, Mitwokeme. It is also surprising to meet Eskimos with names like Johannes Kholmeister and Nikodemus Mentzel.
> Fred Bruemmer, "Northern Labrador" (1971)

Though the affected language is Inuit, or Inuktituk, not English, we again see evidence of a piece of Canadian history preserved in the language of a people.

Many northern words come from useful customs of the Indians. R. D. Symons (1963), telling of his adventures in the northern areas, writes:

Anyone for Ipirautaqturniq?
If you feel sympathy for National Hockey League broadcasters coping with the name of New York Rangers' Walt Tkaczuk, consider the problems of the announcers who will be doing play-by-play on such popular Eskimo games as tiliraginik qirigtagtut (jumping through the stick) and aksunaiqtug (rope gymnastics). Then, of course, the broadcasters (CBC alone is sending a 12-man crew to provide coverage in Eskimo, Indian, French and English) will be expected to give special coverage to Tautugni, the fox trapper, who set that dramatic ayagaq record at Yellowknife.

In case you aren't familiar with ayagaq, the sport is played with two bones—one long and one short—attached to each other by a short leather thong. The longer piece of bone, taken from the flipper of a bearded seal, is called a "square-flipper" and has an inch-wide hole drilled into it. It is tossed into the air and the object is to jab the short piece of bone into the hole in the "squareflipper". Tautugni, now 47, is leaving the white fox traps at Whale Cove on Hudson Bay to defend his record of seven successful flips.

Andy O'Brien, *Weekend Magazine*, Feb. 19, 1977. Article on Arctic Winter Games at Whitehorse.

We observed a Number of Trees Branched to the Top in several Places, it seems the Natives does* this close by their winter Quarters to direct one another.

Sir Alexander Mackenzie, *Exploring the Northwest Territory: Sir Alexander Mackenzie's Journal of a Voyage by Bark Canoe from Lake Athabasca to the Pacific Ocean in the Summer of 1789* (1966)

The following excerpt from the diary of Lady Frances Simpson, the wife of Sir George Simpson, shows that the device of the lobstick was well-known over 125 years ago.

25th . . . the Voyageurs agreed among themselves to cut a "May Pole" or "Lopped Stick" for me; which is a tall Pine Tree, lopped of all its branches excepting those at the top, which are cut in a round bunch: it is then barked: and mine (being a memorable one) was honored with a red feather, and streamers of purple ribband tied to a poll, and fastened to the top of the Tree, so as to be seen above every other object: the surrounding trees were then cut down, in order to leave it open to the Lake. Bernard (the Guide) then presented me with a Gun, the contents of which I discharged against the Tree, and Mr. Miles engraved my name, and the date, on the trunk, so that my "Lopped Stick" will be conspicuous as long as it stands, among the number of those to be seen along the banks of different Lakes and Rivers.

Quoted in *North*, XI. 3 (May 1964)

*This **s** form of the plural verb is a feature of northern English (which Mackenzie could use) and is very old, going back to at least the 1300's. The **s** form (*e.g. they gets*) may still be heard in the Martimes, particularly in those areas settled by Scots. Note that Mackenzie wrote his journal in 1789— about the time that many Scots were settling the Maritimes.

Lobsticks

Two blazed trees . . . will show us the *lobstick* portage. To line up the two lobsticks is a matter of minutes, and then for the open lake to receive us in friendliness to its smooth, frozen surface.

These *lobsticks* or lopsticks (sometimes called *maypoles* or *maipoles*) are tall conspicuous evergreen trees which an Indian had stripped of all except its topmost branches to serve as a monument, or tribute, to a friend, or as some kind of personal talisman. Such trees also served as a marker of a village or a route indication.

An Indian word, such as *moccasin*, can develop many compounds as its use becomes extended—*e.g. dog moccasins* (for travel over rough ice), *moccasin rubbers*, and *moccasin socks*—or as it reflects an extension of Indian custom, *e.g. moccasin telegraph*, originally 'news spread by a runner' but now merely 'news spread by word of mouth'.

Of course terms still linger from the old Hudson's Bay Company and fur-trading days:

regale—from Canadian French *régale* 'pleasure', once a special ration of rum or other liquor handed out on festive occasions or after an arduous voyage, and since then extended to any special party or 'handout'

More generally known throughout Canada are such "old" terms as the Bay's *four-pointer* 'a heavy blanket', *parla* 'a red canvas oilcloth used as a tarpaulin', and *boil up* 'stop on the trail for tea' (extended to *smoke up*). Most Canadians, too, know the term *a Hudson's Bay start*, meaning a very short first day on a long trip, designed to ensure that nothing had been forgotten and to break in the pack animals. A few know *Hudson's Bay style*, referring to a fight that is a 'free-for-all' with 'no holds barred'.

The Klondike gold rush of 1898 also popularized many terms, including—besides many mining expressions—*sourdough*, originally the fermenting dough used to "start" bread and biscuits, then broadened to mean the prospector who depended upon it and, further, to any "old hand" as opposed to a *cheechako* 'newcomer or greenhorn' (from Chinook Jargon—see pp. 226 ff.).

The people of the North have had to invent many new words or terms for peculiarities of weather and terrain. A few are:

> *grey-out*—a dreaded phenomenon when ground snow and cloud blend, so that there is no horizon
> *white-out*—a condition when features of the landscape are similarly neutralized and obliterated by a dazzling whiteness
> *a land-sky* or *water-sky*—the dark sky caused by clouds reflecting little light from unfrozen tundra or open water
> *fog-eater*—a rainbow created as fog is about to lift (a term used also in the East and West ocean regions)

Some terms which sound quite ordinary carry special meanings in the North:

> *winter ice*—is local ice, as opposed to that of the great ice-packs, and therefore less than a year old.
> *to read*—may mean *to read the water*, that is to watch for signs of shallows and snags on a river.

A cheechako may also be puzzled when asked to buy a ticket for the local *ice-pool*, a sweepstake based on the exact time that the ice moves in the spring *break-up*, a custom followed in many parts of northern Canada. Tourists may also meet the term *ice-worm*; though there is a real ice-worm found in mountain glaciers and snow, Robert Service's ice-worm, made famous by his phrase "I will meet thee when the ice-worms nest again" (from *Trail of '98*), was a mythical creature born as a practical joke in the Klondike days. In the 1949 Yukon Festival, this ice-worm was reintroduced by a song, and tourists may now order an ice-worm cocktail (bits of macaroni or spaghetti at the bottom of the glass).

Some of the local geographical terms are direct metaphors. An example is *ramparts*, transferred from its usual meaning to the high, steep banks along the rivers in the western Arctic, especially the Mackenzie, Porcupine and Yukon. In some regions, the Northern Lights are called *the merry dancers*. All such metaphors carry the power of an image, some quite simple yet effective.

A man was lying on his back, panting, in the culminating stages of violent exhaustion. . . .

"Chechaquo!" Kink Mitchell grunted, and it was the grunt of the old "sourdough" for the greenhorn, for the man who outfitted with "self-risin'" flour and used baking powder in his biscuits.

Jack London, *"Too Much Gold"* (1904)

The Mackenzie Delta has contributed one word to scientific nomenclature and that is *pingo* or ice-cored hill. Pingo means hill in Eskimo, and was so-named 30 years ago by the well known Arctic botanist, Dr. A. E. Porsild. The Mackenzie Delta pingos reach a height of 150 feet and nearly every one has grown up in a lake or partially drained lake.

J. Ross Mackay, "The Mackenzie Delta" (1969)

The earth breaks into curious blisters or blobs in the Mackenzie delta. These blisters are called pingos and rise as high as 150 feet. ▶

Everywhere
   A huge nowhere,
Underlined by a shy railway.

F. R. Scott, "Flying to Fort Smith" (1964)

Travel and communication are vital to the North. The use of *snowshoes*, commonly called *raquettes* (French) or shortened to *shoes* or *webs*, has given rise its own large vocabulary including a number of terms for *snowshoe sickness,* or *mal de raquette,* "a painful state of inflamed joints and muscles affecting snowshoers, caused by undue strain on the tendons of the leg" (DC). Air travel terms also abound. The *bush pilot* was a romantic figure in the early days and still is in the less accessible areas, particularly if needed for a *mercy flight*. Though not unique to Canada, the *cat*, a shortening of 'caterpillar tractor', is so important as a supply-line that many compounds have arisen, *e.g. cat-train, cat-swing* (from *swing* 'a train of sleighs or freight canoes moving over a regular route'), *catskinner* or *skinner* 'driver' (by analogy with *mule-skinner*), and *cat-trail*. Metaphors commonly transfer from one form of transportation to another: a northern example is *fuel-sloop*, the unit of the cat-train that carries reserve fuel.

People living so interdependently quickly develop slang, and the northerner can draw upon a large repertoire, of which these are a few examples:

moose-milk   'homebrew' or 'rum mixed with milk'
a king's steer   'moose shot out of season'
Hudson's Bay Hymn Book   the ledger recording debts
a blue ticket   'orders from the police to leave town', a term that is
      spreading into general Canadian use

Now that the North is being opened up so rapidly, many of the old regionalisms will die. Others, like the currently popular greeting *Chimo* (used in the North as a toast before drinking) will become part of the general Canadian idiom—perhaps still carrying something of the spell that the North seems to cast upon all who venture there.

Laurentian Shield

Hidden in wonder and snow, or sudden with summer,
This land stares at the sun in a huge silence
Endlessly repeating something we cannot hear.
Inarticulate, arctic,
Not written on by history, empty as paper,
It leans away from the world with songs in its lakes
Older than love, and lost in the miles.

This waiting is wanting.
It will choose its language
When it has chosen its technic,
A tongue to shape the vowels of its productivity.

A language of flesh and of roses.

Now there are pre-words,
Cabin syllables,
Nouns of settlement
Slowly forming, with steel syntax,
The long sentence of its exploitation.

The first cry was the hunter, hungry for fur,
And the digger for gold, nomad, no-man, a particle:
Then the bold command of monopolies, big with machines,
Carving its kingdoms out of the public wealth:
And now the drone of the plane, scouting the ice,
Fills all the emptiness with neighbourhood
And links our future over the vanished pole.

But a deeper note is sounding, heard in the mines,
The scattered camps and the mills, a language of life,
And what will be written in the full culture of occupation
Will come, presently, tomorrow,
From millions whose hands can turn this rock into children.

      F. R. Scott (1945)

Reprinted by permission of F.R. Scott.

English in
British Columbia

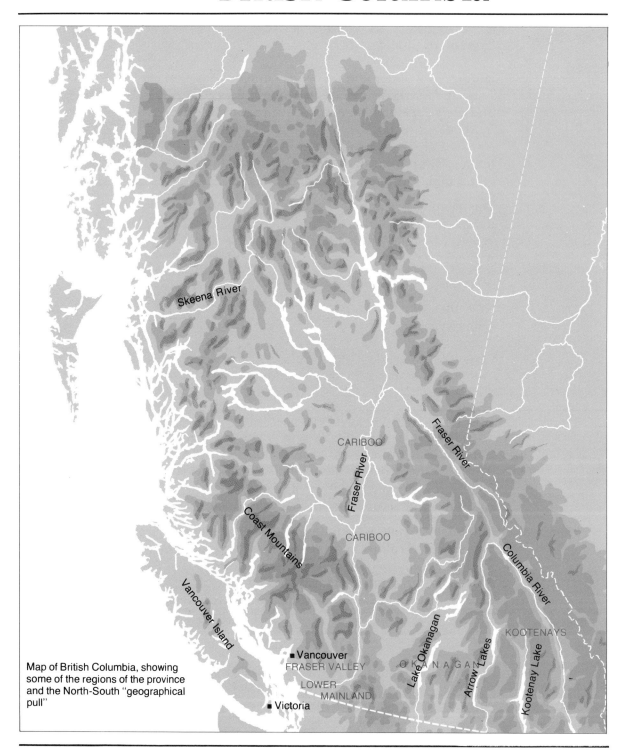

Map of British Columbia, showing
some of the regions of the province
and the North-South "geographical
pull"

Cut off from the rest of Canada by high mountains, British Columbia has developed many language features of its own. Settlements within the province, also isolated by the difficult terrain and frequently dependent upon one industry, have developed localisms, some dating back to early settlement days.

But British Columbia is not a linguistic Newfoundland. The area was settled late and very quickly, and generally the language is Ontario English.

British Columbia was a fur domain and remained practically empty until the privileges of the fur companies were challenged in 1858 by the gold rush on the Fraser. Although most of the Americans who poured into the area returned home at the end of the "rush," the fear of American annexation hurried British Columbia's entry into Confederation in 1871, and with the completion of the railway in 1886 the migration from "back East" began. The mild climate of the coastal region also attracted the British, and there is still a strong British flavor to many sections, particularly on Vancouver Island. The British element has also been strengthened after each of the two world wars.

Nevertheless, the geographic line of communication in British Columbia runs north to south. Most of the main valleys, such as the Kootenay and the Okanagan, connect to large American centres. The "American drift" in speech habits is probably stronger than most British Columbians realize.

The varying types of country have enticed different peoples: the northern section has many Scandinavians, as well as great numbers of Americans; the Cariboo is "cow country," with many Americans as well; the Okanagan fruitlands have pockets of British, as does the Shuswap area and much of Vancouver Island; the Kootenay area is the main home of the Doukhobors, many of whom still speak Russian; the Fraser Valley has attracted German- and Dutch-speaking immigrants; and some fishing areas are largely Japanese (though the main settlements were scattered during the Second World War). And in nearly every town, as well as in Vancouver, are many Chinese, first brought in to build the transcontinental railway.

Considerable work has been done on the dialects of British Columbia under the direction of R. J. Gregg of the University of British Columbia. Charles Crate and Douglas Leechman, both editors of the DC, have also studied the language of British Columbia, while the moving of M. H. Scargill and the Lexicographical Centre from Alberta to Victoria has further stimulated interest and research in this linguistically interesting region.

British Columbia Vocabulary
Charles Crate, whose work has supplied much of the material in this section, has estimated that British Columbians have coined several thousand words. Many of these, however, belong to the slang or technical language of occupations—fishing, lumbering, mining, ranching, and the like—and this special vocabulary, although known and used by particular groups or communities, has con-

A million acres of geography. History is only in the cracks and crannies.

Lister Sinclair, "Eulogy" (1958)

It was remarked by an intelligent shipmaster, whom I met in Victoria, that he had not found in any of the numerous ports he had visited during a long sea-faring career, so mixed a population as existed in that city. Though containing at present an average of only 5,000 or 6,000 inhabitants, one cannot pass along the principal thoroughfares without meeting representatives of almost every tribe and nationality under heaven. Within a limited space may be seen—of Europeans, Russians, Austrians, Poles, Hungarians, Italians, Danes, Swedes, French, Germans, Spaniards, Swiss, Scotch, English and Irish; of Africans, Negroes from the United States and the West Indies; of Asiatics, Lascars and Chinamen; of Americans, Indians, Mexicans, Chilanos, and citizens of the North American Republic; and of Polynesians, Malays from the Sandwich Islands.

Matthew Macfie, *Vancouver Island and British Columbia* (1865)

Polson's survey (1963–4) shows, with one item from his questionnaire (the name of a freshwater fish), how British Columbia is divided into valleys running north and south and cut off from each other. All the responses to this item in the Okanagan Valley and Kamloops area were *kokanee* or some variant of it; in the Kootenay-Columbia Valleys, however, most of the informants gave *redfish* or *Kamloops trout*. The lower mainland area, as to be expected, produced varied responses.

▼

tributed little to the general language. Also, Crate cautions, because British Columbia shares its early history with the rest of the Oregon Country (once a unit which included the present states of Washington, Oregon, and parts of Alaska) and is still geographically and economically similar to these areas, "it is not always safe to say on which part of the present borders a new word entered the English language."

Both mining and logging, for example, are quite different in this rough country from their counterparts in eastern Canada, and the different conditions give rise to some different practices and therefore different terms. An example may be seen in the word *slumgullion*, later shortened to *slum*. This word came from the United States,

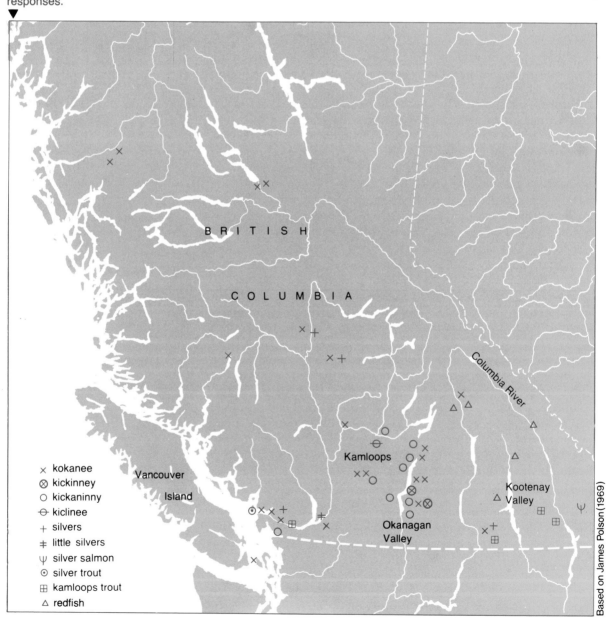

× kokanee
⊗ kickinney
○ kickaninny
⊖ kiclinee
+ silvers
‡ little silvers
ψ silver salmon
⊙ silver trout
⊞ kamloops trout
△ redfish

Based on James Polson (1969)

where the California gold rush preceded that in the Fraser River area, and originally referred to an all-inclusive stew. It probably developed from a British dialect word *gullion* 'stew'. In British Columbia the term became *Cariboo slum* and referred to the slippery mixture of clay and mud and water which always threatened to flood the gold diggings on the Fraser River. Later the word transferred back again to food, and it now refers to any poor, thin stew.

Many other terms arose to describe the peculiar conditions of mining in British Columbia. The verb to *rawhide* and the noun *rawhider*, now merely historical words, originated to describe the unique method of hauling ore in winter from diggings on a steep mountainside by wrapping the ore in untanned hides, hair out and

July 10.—Packing is one of the most lucrative employments. A train of twelve or eighteen horses and mules very soon pays the expense of first cost, and then great profits are made. The packers are principally Mexicans; there are, however, many Americans.

I met this day a train under the conduct of a very odd-looking dust-begrimed packer. He had a broken-in, slouched wide-awake. I was introduced to him. His speech showed him to be an educated English gentleman. A few years since he was a smart officer with his regiment in Canada. He came to California, where he followed 'packing'. He now packs on British soil with the best horse-pack in the colony.

Wm. Carew Hazlitt, *The Great Gold Fields of Cariboo* (1862)

head forward, and drawing these over the snow. "A first view of a rawhide train," says the Slocan *Pioneer* of 1897, "has a tendency to cause cold shivers to run up and down the spinal column, as it strikes one as looking like a long parade of dead bodies." Much research still needs to be done among old mining records, letters, and journals to uncover other linguistic innovations in this period of the West's history—a period which ended the fur traders' hold on the Oregon Country as a reserve without settlers.

Logging (the term most British Columbians use rather than *lumbering*, though both do occur) is so basic to British Columbia's economy that its special terms are widely known and used. Some are metaphorical and some are humorous. Here are a few examples of this special vocabulary:

highrigger   'a person who climbs a spar tree, cutting off branches on the way'
rigging goat   'a small donkey engine'
whistlepunk   'a person who relays signals from the workers to the donkey operator' (usually a beginner's job, so the word was often transferred to mean any young beginner; the job is now almost obsolete)

And then we are shrugging from
   skins of wet raingear—
lighting cigarettes—eating apples
   —lying a mean lick—
rattling toward warmth in the
   quitting-time crummy past killed
   machines like abandoned yellow
   elephants.

   Peter Trower, "Grease for the
   Wheels of Winter" in Geddes
   (1975). The editor, Gary Geddes,
   states that *crummy* refers to the
   'company truck or bus in which
   the logger is transported to and
   from work'.

He waited until I was in the crummy,
which is our name for the bus which
takes loggers out to their jobs in the
bush from camp. . . .

   Henry Pennier, *Chiefly Indian*
   (1972)

schoolmarm 'a tall forked tree'
log bronc (also *boom boat, boom dozer, boom scooter*) 'a small tug that controls logs in a boom'
bullpen 'the enclosed area where loggers control the logs'
bullcook 'an assistant who runs around helping the cook, making up beds, and like jobs' (then generalized so that the locomotive that switches and arranges cars is said to be *bullcooking*)

We have already discussed (p. 70) how one logging term, *skid road*, and by folk etymology *skid row*, has generalized in meaning and in area so that it may now refer to any place where the penniless congregate—not just in Vancouver or Seattle but in many cities that have no connection with logging. The term *flunkey* (like *skid row*, used also in the United States), at one time stood for the cook's helper in a logging camp and has now become part of the general language, referring to anyone who does menial chores. A similar process of generalization is now happening to the slang term *the crummy*. Probably originating in the word *crumb* 'body louse', *crummy* came to mean the old box car or caboose that was converted to transport loggers to and from camp. In many parts of British Columbia and Washington state the term is being applied, and not as slang, to the bus which transports *any* worker to his or her job, and even to school buses.

How many words or expressions in the newspaper item below are unfamiliar to you?

Vancouver Sun Photo

Chums tangle in birling

By ROGER SMITH

SQUAMISH—Two chums, Paul Herrling and Fred Wickheim, stood at opposite ends of a log in the middle of a pond Saturday, arms outstretched, concentrating intently on each other's feet.

It was the finals of the novice birling, or log-rolling, and 2,000 people attending Squamish's Loggers Sports Day watched as the two 15-year-olds tried to dump each other into the water.

'All or none at all' say fallers

By GEORGE DOBIE
Sun Labor Reporter

As if perfectly stage-managed, the first day of a week-long visit to the bush seemed to typify the testy and tense relationship existing between the boss and the workers in B.C. logging.

It was 6:30 a.m. at the Franklin River marshalling yards near Port Alberni. An overnight snowfall in the mountains and continuing cold spring weather would make it more difficult to work.

But the logging crews, assembled from the nearby camp and their own homes down the mountain, boarded the crummies and headed for their appointed jobs. All except a small and contentious group of men, the fallers.

The tension suddenly sliced the crisp air and left bare one of those grey areas of disagreement between labor and management that can keep an industry constantly off balance.

The trouble this day was brief but symptomatic. It was over an unwritten understanding that there will be work for all or work for none of the fallers except in cases of emergency.

One of the MacMillan Bloedel company's bullbuckers (foremen) had checked the weather office and then driven into the bush on a dawn patrol. The side hills were slippery and the tree branches heavily weighted with snow.

When the bull returned he posted a sign on the chalkboard in the cookhouse and in front of the office of the marshalling yards. There would be no falling this day because of the weather.

Aubrey Price, camp chairman of the International Woodworkers of America, emerged from a melee of grumbling fallers and headed straight for the offices of Bob Hicks, bull of the woods, more formally known as the general foreman, mumbling: "What the hell's going on here?"

Six senior fallers were called to work in the Sarita area near where the Alberni Canal heads into the sea.

The Vancouver Sun, April 20, 1972

Briticisms in British Columbia

Many communities in British Columbia preserve some dialect features of the original settlers. The Comox Valley and Nanaimo areas were settled early because of the coal mines, and still show traces of the original British and Welsh dialects. Victoria and Duncan on Vancouver Island and parts of the Okanagan are also ''British'' centres. The Polson (1963–4) survey gives evidence that many speakers of these areas, unlike those in the rest of the province, keep the distinction between *caught* and *cot* (see p. 28); and the responses on Vancouver Island from even young students to test items such as the pronunciation of *vase, rather,* and *tomato* (see p. 27) tend to be more British than those in Vancouver or some ''interior'' towns. The secondary school students questioned also seem to be more familiar with British usage; an example may be seen in the replies to the question:

What do you call the vehicle that you wheel babies in?

The answer *baby carriage* and *baby buggy* (the latter the Midland American preference) were equally popular in all areas, but in Victoria a significant number offered the British term *pram* as second choice.

Plain, unpretentious Canadian is a lost language in Victoria.

W. E. Walsh, *The Canadian Forum* (1923)

''. . . I tell you we're just over for the ▶ day from Victoria . . .''

The Vancouver Province

Because of the relative isolation of the west coast, a number of old British geographical terms linger. A *canal*, now archaic in British English to mean 'fiord' or 'long inlet of the sea', is still used in British Columbia, as in *Portland Canal* (a source of confusion for some American boaters). Short channels between islands are called not *outs* or *gaps*, as in the East, but *passages* and *passes*.

Other English words have been adapted or coined for the different conditions: a *gut* in the interior of British Columbia is not a twisting channel as in Nova Scotia, but a long, narrow, steep ravine. The word *dry belt* seems to have originated in British Columbia. Also commonly found in the West are the terms *blind valley* 'a valley blocked on all sides by hills', and *blind slough* 'an old river channel now blocked'. (This term *slough*, as discussed previously (pp. 113, 115), is itself an archaism in England.)

"Ethnic" Groups

The Chinese have long been part of the cultural background of British Columbia, where every small town has a Chinese café and had, at one time, a Chinese laundry. Charles Crate suggests (though the DC does not support this) that the dish *chop suey*, a now almost universally known term, was invented in Victoria about 1892 in honor of a visiting dignitary. The popular slang term *Wobbly Wobbly* for the IWW (Industrial Workers of the World) is said to have arisen from a loyal Chinese member's mispronunciation of the name of the letter **W**. Only those who could answer "Yes" to his question "You,

I Wobble Wobble?" were granted credit at his restaurant.

The presence of many immigrants from India and their descendants necessitated the creation of the redundant term *native Indians* to separate the Canadian "Amerindians" from those known locally as "East Indians" or, even more incorrectly as it is a religious classification, as "Hindus."

Much work has yet to be done in areas with other language backgrounds, for example, the effects of Scandinavian languages in northern British Columbia, of German in parts of the Fraser Valley, and of Russian in the Doukhobor areas of the Kootenays.

An example of what may occur can be seen in a small way in the speech of five high school students (out of 246) in Vancouver, all of whom consistently pronounced the **g** of the -**ng** in such words as *singing, sung, hang, hanging, long* and *lung* (that is, as [ŋg], as in *finger* rather than as in *singer*). Although none of the informants themselves spoke anything but English, three had parents who spoke Japanese, one had parents who spoke Ukrainian, and the other's parents spoke Czech. As this survey (also by Polson) was from a printed sheet, the spelling form may have influenced the oral responses, so an oral follow-up would be necessary to establish what seems, in each case, to be a connection with the home language.

A dialectologist in British Columbia, therefore, must make many samplings and choose informants and towns carefully, becoming aware not only of settlement history but also, because many small villages were once important boom towns, of the oldest occupations associated with each area. Such surveys should reveal a great deal about how older history and cultures may linger in a people's language.

Fish Tips

Tyee chinook run under way

The Britannia-Squamish tyee chinook run has started and several saltchuckers took good hauls, most of them on the weekend.

The *Vancouver Sun*, July 8, 1976

Indian Influence

The languages of the native Indians have contributed hundreds of place names and some regionalisms. Among the latter are names of fish, which often have quite different names in the bordering American states. The best known are:

sockeye—from Salish *suk-tegh* 'red fish' and changed by folk etymology to "English" elements

chinook or *quinnat*—also called *king salmon* (especially in Alaska) or, when mature, *spring salmon* (the B.C. term)

chum—also called *dog salmon* or *keta*, the latter from the scientific Russian name and adopted to make the fish more saleable (see also p. 230)

coho—probably from Interior Salish, also known as *fall fish* (and, in the U.S., as *silver salmon*)

kokanee—also from Interior Salish, the landlocked salmon of the large interior lakes

Many terms related to the life of the Indians are slowly becoming merely parts of British Columbia history, as, for example, are the old *grease trails*, age-old routes between the coast and the Interior Indians, along which was transported the valuable oil of the *oolichan* 'candlefish'.

The most noticeable contribution of the Indian languages to the regional vocabulary of British Columbia is that made by the Chinook Jargon of the west coast—a contribution so interesting that it has been given a section of its own.

Contributions of the Chinook Jargon

The conversations in the margins of this page and the next use expressions from a language once spoken along the Pacific coast from Alaska to the mouth of the Columbia River. It was no one's first language, but an auxiliary trade language that came to be called the Chinook Jargon. From this trade language have come some interesting regionalisms of the west coast. Most British Columbians know and perhaps use the following terms, for example:

skookum 'big, strong'

chuck 'water'

saltchuck 'ocean'

klahowya 'hello' or 'goodbye'

tyee 'chief'—now used mainly for a huge salmon (over 13 kg)

tillicum 'people' or 'person', extended to 'friend'

Boy but I was slowing down though and I fell in to the chuck quite a bit but of course you weren't a boom man if you didn't fall in once in a while.

Henry Pennier, *Chiefly Indian* (1972)

Kokanee to stock B.C. lakes

Sun Victoria Bureau

VICTORIA — Approximately 24 million Kokanee (landlocked salmon) will be released in B.C. lakes this year, Recreation and Conservation Minister Jack Randford told the legislature, Thursday.

Fish 'N' Game Tips

Fishermen have choice— rivers or saltchuck

The *Vancouver Sun*, February 5, 1976

OOLICHANS START RUN, JOIN HIGHER PRICES

The oolichans arrived in the Fraser during the weekend.

The annual run of the oily, but tasty, little silver fish began Friday, according to Delta fisherman Frank Adam, who said he took 25 pounds on the first day. Sunday, his catch increased to 100 pounds.

The run should continue for at least three or four more weeks as the fish make their way to spawning grounds near Mission.

Roadside stands have been set up along the river, where net-caught fish are selling at 40 to 50 cents a pound—up from last year's price of 30 to 35 cents.

The *Vancouver Sun*, April 15, 1974

"You Boston man?" asked the Indian, meaning American as I quickly learnt.

"You King George man?"

"Yes, King George men," replied Captain Macdonell. To our visitor there was evidently a difference between a Boston man and a King George man but a difference also between a Nor'-Wester and a King George man for he remarked: "King George man more good than Nor'-West."

Frederick Niven, *Mine Inheritance* (1940). A historical novel about Lord Selkirk's settlement on the Red River.

Many old-timers in British Columbia can still speak Chinook, or remember some of it; however, in the 1870's and 1880's probably a hundred thousand people used it daily: miners going to the Fraser River gold rush, often carrying guidebooks printed in New York or San Francisco, which included dictionaires of the Jargon; Hudson's Bay Company traders, known in the Jargon as *kin chotsch-men* 'King George men'; Americans, *Boston-men*; French traders, known in the Jargon as *passioks*, derived from Chinook *pasisi* 'blanket' and a suffix **-uks** denoting 'living things', thus 'blanket-men'; Russian traders,

227

who may have contributed a few words to the Jargon; Indian agents; loggers; Chinese, who came as cooks, launderers, placer miners, and railroad workers, and who often preferred the Jargon to attempting to speak English; missionaries, who translated sermons, hymns, and prayers into Chinook to reach their flocks; and, of course, the Indians themselves when dealing with either the European invaders or other Indians who spoke a different language. Pauline Johnson, a native of Ontario and a Mohawk, found that she could converse with Chief Joe Capilano and other British Columbian chiefs when they met at Buckingham Palace in 1906 because she had learned the Chinook Jargon. In her Foreword to *Legends of Vancouver* (1911) she tells how this knowledge of Chinook and this friendship enabled her to record the legends of British Columbia Indians as told to her by Chief Joe Capilano and other coastal "tillicums."

Some scholars maintain that the Jargon existed long before the coming of the white traders and developed among the tribes themselves, as they spoke over a hundred mutually unintelligible languages. Certainly the base of the Jargon is, as the name suggests, the language of the Chinook Indians, a powerful trading nation at the mouth of the Columbia River and the "middlemen" between the south and the north, and between the coast and the interior. Many words are from Nootka, the language of the important warlike tribe on the stormy west coast of Vancouver Island, who controlled the prized dentilia shells; and other words are from Salish and Kwakiutl. To these rudiments of an already established trade language were added words picked up from the English and the French. This theory is disputed by those who claim that the Jargon was first stimulated by the white maritime traders who, thinking that all the Coast Indians spoke the same language, helped to spread key Indian words.

Whatever its origin, the Chinook Jargon illustrates some basic principles of language. Like all languages developed from several languages and for a restricted use, it has an extremely simple grammar, one that can be learned quickly. There are, for example, almost no inflections: either an actual number or repetition of the word can express plural, so *hyas* 'big one' can become *hyashyas* 'big ones'; there are no tenses, the time distinction being either inferred from the context or expressed by a few adverbs such as *alta* 'now' or *alki* 'soon'; a word can function as any part of speech, and a change of meaning can be signalled simply by a change in word order, a device used also in English:

Mika	*kumtux*	*Chinook*	*wawa?*
'you'	'understand'	'Chinook'	'talk'?

meaning: Do you understand Chinook?

Mika	*kumtux*	*wawa*	*Chinook?*

meaning: Do you know how to talk Chinook?

The vocabulary is limited, probably having only 500 words at its maximum. Supporting the theory that the language developed before the arrival of European traders is the fact that the language of

Dictionary

OF THE

Chinook Jargon,

OR

Indian Trade Language,

OF THE

North Pacific Coast.

T. N. HIBBEN & CO,
PUBLISHERS.
GOVERNMENT ST., VICTORIA, B. C.

John Barnsley & Co.,

➤➤IMPORTERS OF◄◄

Fire Arms Etc.,
Kodacs, Safes.

Agents for Str. Boscowitz.   *Gun Repairs.*
115 Government St.,   Victoria, B. C.

the Chinook nation supplied not only half of this vocabulary but also the most basic terms and the structure words, such as the numerals, the pronouns, the interrogatives, and the word *kopa*, the catch-all preposition meaning 'to', 'for', 'by', 'from', and others according to the context. Nootka also supplied some basic words, for example: *mamook* 'do' or 'make'; *chako* 'come' or 'become'; *kumtux* 'understand, know', *potlatch* 'give'. Others came from Salish and other coastal tribes. According to some authorities, a few entered from the Polynesian language of Hawaii, because the early European seatraders went on from the west coast to the South Seas, and we know that the Hudson's Bay fort at Astoria contained a village of South Sea Islanders, and both Vancouver and the Gulf Islands had settlements of "Kanakas" (Polynesian for 'man').

For the rest of the vocabulary, some is from French and English: for example, *capo* (Fr. *capot*) 'coat'; *Mah-sie* (Fr. *merci*) 'thanks', extended to 'pray' and 'prayer'; *la puss* 'cat', the *la* from French; *book*, *boat*, *cole* 'cold', and *mama*. Other words are onomatopoeic, formed in imitation of a natural sound: *tik-tik* 'watch', extended later to the telegraph; *poo* 'shoot'; *tumtum* 'heart', 'emotion', 'love', and so on, supposedly coined from the sound of the heartbeat; and *chik-chik* 'wagon' or 'wheel', in imitation of the creaking of the wheels.

As is usual when borrowing from languages, each speaker adapted the Jargon words to the sound system of his or her own language. Most Indians, for example, found the pronunciation of **f** and **r** difficult, so either substituted **p** for **f** or **l** for **r** or omitted the sounds altogether: so *fish* became *pish* in the Jargon, *coffee* is *caupy*, and French *courir* 'to run' is *couley*. A **v** often becomes a **w**, and the English sound -**dge** is pronounced something like -**tsh**, accounting for 'King George man' being rendered as *kin chotsch-man* and the French *sauvage* as *Siwash*, which meant any Indian and not, as some people think, a particular tribe. The Japanese of British Columbia, in turn, have converted *Siwash* to *Sibushi*, to fit their tongues. Similarly **n** and -**ing** sounds were difficult for the Indians, and the unfamiliar **d** was often omitted, so that English *handkerchief* becomes *hak-at-shum*.

By the same principle, Europeans had great difficulty with some Indian sequences of consonants, including the velar "clucking" sound used in most Indian languages, a sound resembling a **tl** and exploding with a simultaneous stop somewhat like a **k** but made by the tongue pressing against the roof of the mouth. The word *tillicum*, for instance, began with a **tl** sequence which the Europeans separated with **i**; and the Chinook word *klkwu-shala* became reduced to *salal* (a glossy evergreen shrub common in the Pacific coast area); possibly, too, the name of the *chum* salmon is derived from the Jargon term *tzum* 'spotted'.

These phonological changes, however, were fairly systematic and did not destroy the intelligibility of the Jargon while it remained oral. But when the language came to be written down, the spelling of a Jargon word could vary greatly. Using a Jargon dictionary can involve much searching.

The skilful speaker of Chinook Jargon can extend the limited vocabulary to express many complex, even abstract, ideas by using the linguistic ability and the imagination common to all human beings. One's main linguistic devices, besides those of word order and flexibility in parts of speech, are metaphor and compounding. A seal, for example, is *siwash cosho*, literally 'Indian pig' (the second word from French *cochon*); rather than making a separate word for 'moose', the Jargon uses *hyas* 'big' with *mowitch* 'deer'; *hyas Sunday* conveys the idea of 'holiday'; 'rapids' can be expressed as *skookumchuk* 'strong water' (now a common place name in British Columbia); and *colechuck* 'cold water' is 'ice'.

Some phrases are euphonious and hard to replace. One still hears in British Columbia the phrase, "I'm going for a *cultus coulee*" (from

Huge upturned stumps necessitated detours through hard-leafed sallal bushes and skunk cabbage bogs.

Emily Carr, *Klee Wyck* (1941)

Cultus coulee . . . means that if you see a deer track, you're free to leave the trail and follow it.

R. D. Symons, *Many Trails* (1963)

Hyack Festival (New Westminister, May 15 to 25) For the 105th time, the Royal City puts up its bunting and polishes its brass buttons for the annual event. **May 17** Intrepid canoeists start from Hope at 8 a.m. to run the Hyack Marathon, arriving, wet or dry, at King Neptune Dock somewhere between 3 and 5 p.m. Those who prefer a more sedate aquatic pace can take a river cruise, leaving the same dock at 1, 2:30 and 4 p.m. **May 18** Four-wheeled travelers have a chance to test their skills at the Hyack Canyon Car Rally,

leaving Queens Park at 7:30 a.m. and heading off toward Kelowna. **May 19** One of the most revered of Hyack traditions takes place with a bang at noon, when the Honourable Hyack Anvil Battery sets off its gunless 21-boom salute using anvils and gun powder. For those whose eardrums are still intact, a band concert follows at 1 p.m. **May 20** A carnival sets a festive air at Canada Games Pool in the afternoon and evening. **May 21** The big day for New Westminster school children sees the crowning of May Queen Katharine and colorful may pole

dancing. 1 p.m. **May 23** Nostalgia pairs with skill at a penny farthing bicycle race in Sapperton at 7 p.m., while at the Canada Games Pool swimmers ply the water at the Hyack Invitational Swim Meet. **May 24** No festival is complete without a parade, which in Hyack version is usually an impressive gathering of floats, bands and clowns. 11 a.m. For full schedule details call 522-6894.

Vancouver Calendar Magazine (1975)

cultus 'useless', 'of no purpose' and *courir* French 'run'), meaning a stroll or ride for pleasure with no set destination, as opposed to *go klatawa* 'to go to visit at a special place'. (A long journey is a *hyas klatawa*.) Similar to *cultus coulee* is *cultus potlatch* 'a little gift of no value, and nothing expected in return'.

Sometimes a metaphor is amusing: a knife is *opitsah*, so a fork is *opitsah sikh* 'knife friend'. A volunteer fire fighter was called a *hyack* 'hurry', a term preserved in the "Honourable Hyack Battery" of New Westminster, British Columbia, and now in the local spring festival. Similar economy can be seen in naming the days of the week: only one word, *Sunday*, is needed, the others being numbered from it as 'first day', 'second day', and so on.

Abstract nouns can be expressed in concrete terms: 'courage', for example, can be *skookum tumtum* 'strong heart'. To express 'God', the missionaries combined *tyee* 'chief' and *saghalie* 'above' to make *Saghalie Tyee*, often run together as is *Sockalee*; while the addition of *yaka book* 'his book' expresses 'Bible'.

Causative verbs, such as *mamook*, originally 'to fish' but extended in the Jargon to any 'doing' or 'making', are valuable to extend the vocabulary's range:

Touching religious matters, the Bishop of Columbia, in his *Journal* (1860), says:

"Most of the Indians profess to know of the Sackally Tyhee Papa, Great Chief Father. They point upwards; they say He sees all, is all-wise, and strong and good, and never dies. I found out to-day, from two Indians of this place, that Skatyatkeitlah is the same as Squaquash Suokum, or the sun. The sun is the Sackally Tyhee Papa. Klanampton, the moon, is his wife, and the stars their children."

Quoted in Hazlitt (1862)

mamook tumtum can express many subjective actions: 'make up one's mind', 'decide', 'plan', and the like

sick tumtum can mean 'to be sorry', 'to feel sad'

cultus mamook is both 'to do wrong' and 'to do something badly'

mamook kumtux, literally 'make understand' does for the concept 'to teach'

High Muckamuck

A two-foot-high wooden bear with a salmon grasped in its jaws stands at the entrance to Muckamuck (Chinook *patois*, meaning "to eat"), a two-year-old, subterranean restaurant in Vancouver's West End. Inside, newly scrubbed pebbles on the floor give a customer the impression of walking along a rocky beach. . . .

Pemmican and the meat dishes of Plains Indians are not on Muckamuck's bill of fare, since B.C.

coastal Indians are largely fish eaters by custom. Nor is venison, which is so protected by game laws that the restaurant would have to import it from Norway. But there is duck soup, loaded with dark meat and vegetables, and salmon egg soup, and barbecued oysters, plus, of course, salmon (barbecued, poached or cured for up to eight days in a smokehouse). Main courses are served in hand-carved and painted Haida-style feast bowls of red cedar, on a bed of fresh cedar fronds. For vegetables, Mucka-

muck serves fresh fern shoots, chocolate lily bulbs, steamed stinging nettle, or a salad of water cress, spinach, dill weed and onion. For dessert, there is raspberry soup, soapberries (Indian ice cream) or fresh apple sauce, washed down with tea made from Labrador leaves (*Ledum groenlandicum*), which can be slightly narcotic and is recommended "only in the evening, when the relaxing effect won't cause any problems."

Time, Nov. 18, 1974

Outside, the night was surprisingly bland for the middle of May, the moist chinook breathing against his cheek, carrying the smell of damp earth.

W. O. Mitchell, *The Kite* (1962). Setting: the Prairies.

Often he spends days siwashing, inching toward a herd of sheep only to have a squirrely wind carry his scent to them.

Michael Yates, "The Hunter who Loses his Human Scent" in Wainwright (1969)

Gesture and intonation can also add to the meaning desired: *siah* 'far', for instance, is extended in sound *sia-a-a-ah* to suggest 'far, far away'. All these linguistic devices we can see at work in our own language as well.

As with the vocabulary of any living language, the meaning of many Chinook Jargon terms changed with extended use and with borrowings by different cultures. One phrase, *hyas muckamuck* 'big food' or 'plenty to eat', entered the slang of England in the form of *high muckamuck*, a derogatory term for leaders of society. The word *Chinook* itself, besides being transferred from a tribe and its language to the Jargon was given the warm southwest wind which quickly melts the snow of Oregon, Washington, British Columbia, and Alberta; and the name is now being generalized to refer to any such warming and drying wind. The term *Siwash* 'Indian' became extended as a verb to mean either to sleep out without shelter, *to siwash it*, or to be interdicted (what an eastern Canadian would express as "to be put on the Indian list"), that is, to be prohibited from buying alcoholic drink (now made "historical" in British Columbia by new laws which allow Indians to purchase liquor). When *siwash* began to gather derogatory connotations, the Indians naturally resented the term and sensitive people no longer use it. Thus the famous raw wool sweaters made on Vancouver Island, originally called *Siwash sweaters*, are now called *Cowichan sweaters* in the West, though the former term might still be found in eastern Canada, where the unfavorable connotations of *Siwash* have not become established.

The term *skookum* is used so commonly on the west coast that its basic meaning may become lost (as, in general English, the original meaning of *awful* is lost); frequently heard as slang is "Everything is skookum," meaning 'satisfactory', a weakening of the original meaning of 'strong, fine, good'. In the Cariboo, however, the humor of the Indian and white keeps the older meaning in the slang expression *skookum house* 'jail'—similar to the retention in the same area of the Chinook *tee-hee house* for 'theatre' or 'vaudeville house'.

Some words have become shortened with use: *klootchman* 'woman', from Nootka *lhutsma* and not related to English *man*, has become in the North *klootch*, usually referring to any Indian woman living common-law with a white man; then, by mistaken etymology, the whole word *klootchman* has come to refer to the man living in this way.

When a word is borrowed from the Jargon, English word-forming methods take over: for example, the English **-er** has been added to the Jargon word *saltchuck* 'sea' to make *saltchucker*, a common term for anyone who fishes in the sea for sport; this in turn is now often shortened to *chucker*.

Eventually, Chinook Jargon became a written language. Père Le Jeune, a missionary priest, succeeded in an interesting experiment: he found that he could easily teach the Indians of British Columbia to learn and read Chinook by using a phonetic script

". . . Two of them was too far gone when I got there. I shot them right where I found them. But that other old cow looked a little more skookum, so I broke a trail out for her. . . .

Paul St. Pierre, *Breaking Smith's Quarter Horse* (1966)

There too was the skookum box—that is, the *strong* room or lock-up. To it the first mate of the *Cassiar* is wont to shoot too noisy drunks, pushing them before him at arm's length, with that fine collar-and-trouserseat grip of his that is so much admired.

M. A. Grainger, *Woodsmen of the West* (1908)

. . . at eleven-thirty A.M. he went up to the skookum house to retrieve Ol Antoine.

Paul St. Pierre, *Breaking Smith's Quarter Horse* (1966)

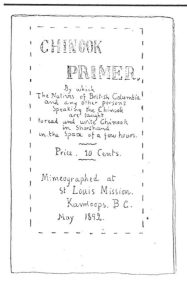

CHINOOK

PRIMER,

By which
The Natives of British Columbia
and any other persons
Speaking the Chinook
are taught
to read and write Chinook
in Shorthand
in the space of a few hours.

Price. 10 Cents.

Mimeographed at
St Louis Mission.
Kamloops. B.C.
May 1892.

based on the Sloan-Duployer Shorthand which he had learned in France. His small newspaper, the Kamloops *Wawa*, was first issued in 1891 and for several years gave the Indians hymns, Bible stories, and church history as well as news in a common language.

Whoosham
They call it Indian icecream, that stuff!
Whoosham, whoosham, made from the soapolallie bush.
Made from little red berries.

I boil them without sugar, without sugar.
I put it in a sack and strain it.
The pure juice you get, yes, the pure juice
And you beat it up with sugar.

But you've got to watch, yes.
Everything must be clean—no grease
Or you won't have good luck.
You won't have *whoosham*!

> *Soapolallie*—Chinook Jargon 'soap' + *olallie* 'berry', 'soapberry'—from *The Days of Augusta*, ed. Jean Speare (1973)

One day I found the Douse family all sitting round on the floor. In the centre of the group was Lizzie. She was beating something in a pail, beating it with her hands; her arms were blobbed with pink froth to the elbows. Everyone stuck his hand into Lizzie's pail and hooked out some of the froth in the crook of his fingers, then took long delicious licks. It was "soperlallie", or soap berry. It grows in the woods; when you beat the berry it froths up and has a queer bitter taste. The Indians love it.

> Emily Carr, *Klee Wyck* (1941). Written in the 1920's at Kitwancool, an Indian village in the Skeena Valley of British Columbia.

"You make cultus wawa in that court, you will be in real trouble. You understand that thing? Real trouble. More bigger trouble than you had already."

> Paul St. Pierre, *Breaking Smith's Quarter Horse* (1966)

We dwell in our own landscape,
The terrain, a bit of water
In our thoughts:
A creek or a splinter
Of one saltchuck.

> Charles Lillard, "Landscape" in Geddes (1975)

The study of this short-lived trade language is, in miniature, a study of many processes taking place within any language. And, as are many other languages, the Jargon is rapidly disappearing. Occasionally a Chinook word is given artificial life when adopted by public media, as *klahanie* 'great outdoors' has been popularized by a Vancouver-based television program. But generally, the Chinook Jargon, so rich in allusions to the history of the early traders and settlers on the Pacific coast and their relationships with the Indians, has been replaced by *Kinchautch wawa* (English) as the new lingua franca. Probably only a few terms will remain in Canadian English even as regionalisms—and these are not fully Canadian as they are shared with parts of the American coast.

Yet traces are preserved in place names. How many B.C. saltchuckers going by a *Mamaloos* Island (there are several) know that the word is Chinook Jargon for 'dead', 'to die', and that the little island was an ancient and sacred burial place? How many people seeing on a map of British Columbia *Canim Lake* 'canoe', *Skookumchuck*, *Cultus Lake* 'worthless, bad', *Siwash Rock* (near which is Pauline Johnson's memorial), *Chickamin Mountain* 'metal' and extended to 'money', *Tyee Lake*, *Mowitch* 'deer', or *Mesachie* 'evil', can visualize some of the human history—with human imagination, humor, and linguistic ability—that lies behind the names? In our language lingers something of those who went before us, and to know something about our language can make our lives a little richer.

Vol. I. No. 1.   *Kamloops Wawa.*   2. May 1891.

Ookook Pepa iaka nem :
Kamloops Wawa. — Chi alta
iaka chako tanaz. Msaika
alke tlap iaka kanawe
Sunday. Iaka alke kwane-
sem lolo tlous wawa kopa
msaika. Iaka help msai-
ka pous aiak chako Kom-
tax pepa : kaltash pous
msaika tkop man, kaltash
pous msaika sawaj telikom.

Pous msaika kwanesem
eskom ookouk pepa, msai-
ka dret aiak chako Kom-
tax mamook ookouk tsem.

Wek aiaz makook ook-
ouk pepa : Kopet iht
tala kopa iht snow, iht
kwata kopa tloon moon.
Elo Jã Bone : Kopet pous
ilep msaika patlach
Chikmin, pi msaika tlap
ookouk pepa.

Pous wek msaika aiak
eskom ookouk pepa, msai-
aioo lost.

Tlous nanich ookouk pe-
pa : wek iaka kaltash.
Pous wek msaika tlous na-
nich ookouk pepa, alke iaka chako sick msaika
Tomtom.

This paper is named:
Kamloops Wawa. — It is born
just now. You will receive it
every Sunday.

It will always carry good
words to you. It will help
you to learn to read.
No matter if you be
white people or Indians.

If you always take
this paper, you will soon
learn to write this Phono=
graphy.

This paper will not cost
you very much : only one
Dollar a year, one quar=
ter every three months.
No credit : you have first
to pay cash; and then you
will receive this paper.

If you do not subscribe
for this paper at once, you
loose very much.
Take care of this paper:
it is not a useless one.
If you do not take care of
this paper, you will after=
wards be very sorry for
it.

Traduction de ce qui précède en Français.

A Chinook Jargon Test

1. The following is an Indian folk song, sung in Vancouver and Victoria about 1886 by the Indians and one of a number collected by the anthropologist Franz Boas. Can you translate it? Do not use the gloss unless you must—first see what you can do without it. All the other words are within the text.

> Cultus kopa nika,
> Spose mika mash nika.
> Hiyu puty boys cooley kopa town
> Alki weght nika iskum
> Wake kull kopa nika.

Gloss:

> *mash* 'go', 'go away' (Fr. *marche*)
> *nika* 'I', 'me'
> *weght* 'take'
> *iskum* 'another'
> *wake* 'negative'
> *kull* 'hard', 'difficult'

Translation

> I don't care
> If you desert me
> Many pretty boys are in town
> Soon I shall take another
> That is not hard for me.
>   Douglas Leechman (1926)

2. In his book *Many Trails* (1963) R. D. Symons gives some examples of Chinook Jargon as used by Chilcotin Indians (in the interior of British Columbia) to talk to whites.

An Indian friend used to tell Symons about the *Ankiti Siwashes*, the Indian giants who lived in bygone days at Chilko Lake and who, the Indians believe, still turn up unexpectedly. Here is Symons' account. Can you understand it?

> "One tam," Jack told me, "me see um that Ankiti Siwash—my hyu scare—all he dlaid hyu tall—he helo shirt his back; he helo mocassin his feet; helo hat his head stop—just plenty hair like bush. Me no savvy see-um that fellow before—me hyu cumtux him Ankiti Siwash! Me go way that place all same cultus coulee."

◄ Fisherman with oolichans

Some "everyday" west coast words from Chinook Jargon, used in Margaret Craven's novel *I Heard the Owl Call My Name* (1967):

1. Indian delicacies, berry sprouts cooked with alder and *salal*, and salmon eggs baked with milk-weed, topped with fern. (77)

2. In late March the tribe prepared for the coming of the *oolachon*, the candlefish. . . .(65)
   They [children returning from boarding schools] are ashamed to dip their food in the oil of the *oolachon*, which we call gleena. (52)

3. In the social hall Chief Eddy found the old men waiting to play the ancient guessing game of *La-hell*, the benches in place, the bones on the floor. (22)

4. The mountains were snow-tipped above the timber-line. When they passed the *potlatch* paintings and reached the muskeg near the mouth of the river, the hand of the Welcome totem rose above the trees. . . . (15)

5. They tugged, pulled, shoved and lifted—the young vicar trying awkwardly to help, afraid the canoes would tip over and the organ end in the *salt chuck*. (14–15)
   Another interesting term (see the picture on p. 256) is:

6. He knew the young hand-logger who took his four children in a little open boat to the school at Echo Bay each morning and home again each afternoon, and sometimes he shared dinner with him and his fine brood at their *float house* on the edge of the chuck. (45)

Not in the DC, but formed on the same pattern, is *float store*:
   They had been to the float store to pick up a load of plywood. . . . (34)

Quiz

Canadian Regionalisms in Literature:

"When we speak of a recognizably Canadian poet we usually mean a regional poet who uses the distinctive objects and actions of his locality as poetic materials."

Milton Wilson, "Other Canadians and After" (1962)

Do you know what the italicized words mean and can you identify the regions? (See pp. 240-241 for the answers and sources.) If you do know the word, where did you learn it?

1. The trail winds round, for it is a logging trail, leading to the best *bluffs* which are ruthlessly cut down by the fuel-hunters.
2. These are the simple facts of the case, and I guess I ought to know. They say that the stranger was crazed with *hooch*, and I'm not denying it's so.
   I'm not so wise as the lawyer guys, but strictly between us two—
   The woman that kissed him—and *pinched his poke*—was the lady that's known as Lou.
3. *Rinding* being over, they next rebuild their *fishing-stages*, and repair their *flakes*; then go to the merchant's store for their spring supply.
4. Marie outdid herself cooking piles of golden *bannocks*.
5. Mother had made a blueberry *fungy*.
6. Both the cemetery and the *nuisance grounds* were located, although respectably separated by a cow pasture, on land that had once been the farm of H. Stanley Ungerman.
7. In the first quarter of this century there were plenty of colorful characters in . . .: old *Klondikers*, *beachcombers*, *remittance men*; frantic solitary men who got *bushed* and stayed behind. . . .
8. A sandpit poked its slender finger into the ocean almost in the shadow of one of the *pingoes*.
9. There was a *lahelle* game at the Indian camp on the *stampede grounds* as Ol Antoine approached and the chant of the gamblers fell pleasantly upon his ear.
10. After weddings *salutings* broke with a bang that split the night.
11. A *gopher* jumps from a round cave, sprints furtively, spurts under fence, is gone.
12.   the slipping tide,
    Round the dun rocks and wattled *fisheries*,
    Creeps murmuring in.
13. the air constantly alive with the cloven sticks of *rock maple* hurtling towards the pile like gleaming Indian clubs.

14. He waded through the waxy-green *salal* to his waist and came into the grove.

15. He found the nest by a clump of *buffalo beans*.

16. The trail to where she had been painting for the previous three days was rough and overgrown, sometimes thick with salmon-berry bush and *devil's club*. . . a decaying *windfall* . . . blocked her passage.

17. Ralph was born and raised on a little clearing in the woods seven miles back from the river, and had married an *Acadian* girl, a Doucette from somewhere down the *North Shore*. He worked on the drive in the spring and cut pulp on contract most of the winter.

18. He told us that . . . where he fished there were two kinds of ice, *blue* and white: live and dead. (*blue ice*)

19. "I guess life hasn't been easy up here *in the sticks*," he said.

20. . . . they hail from everywhere, *upper lakers*, tankers, the few remaining canalers, ocean-going freighters . . .

21. Well now, he's got four sons. He set aside *half-sections* for each of em.

22. "Ye tell yer father that any man as sets foot on the Simms place betwix now an' tomorrow noon is liable to be shot like a *swile* on the *whelpin' ice*."

23. . . . at the age of eleven she was plucked out of school and put to work in the merchant's lobster canning factory, where all hands wore a stiff apron made from a material known as *brin bag*.

24. The grain elevators Are locked on the *lakehead*.

25. . . . he told me that no fewer than twenty-two teams had that very morning come in with cordwood from the northern *correction line*.

26. We'd go by boat as far as the *barachois* at the mouth of Wolf Pond Brook. . . . There's an old *tilt* there.

27. The *sloven* moved north onto Barrington Street as the horses were pulled in to a walk. Traffic slowed down behind it . . . .

28. It was easy to arrange matters so as to carry home a companion; and whether it was *junk* for shingles, staves, axe handles, or any other use, my shoulders never grumbled.

29. . . . like a sylph she wanders through its *bluffs* and *coulees*, across its haylands, its alkali flats, its gumbo stretches, its gopher meadows.

30. True, coast dwellers and *down-easterners* are likely to be contemptuous of such water attractions as the region has to offer.

31. "We searched everywhere," she said, "up in the meetinghouse, back in the *blueberry barrens*—we even looked in the well."

32. Partly because of the storm and cold and snow, but partly also because of these dim memories, the Indians of Chilko Lake never penetrate that far; to them it is a *cultus* place.

Answers to Quiz on Canadian Regionalisms

1. Prairies: from Frederick Philip Grove, *Over Prairie Trails* (1922); 'grove of trees'.
2. Northwest and North: Robert W. Service, "The Shooting of Dan McGrew" (1907); 'homebrew or cheap liquor'; 'stole his bag of gold-dust', also used in U.S.
3. Newfoundland: William Wilson, *Newfoundland and Its Missionaries* (1866); 'covering piles of fish with bark strips'; 'wooden racks to dry fish on'.
4. Esp. North: Farley Mowat, *Lost in the Barrens* (1956); 'a pancake made of flour, lard or pemmican grease, and baking powder'; derived from Scots Gaelic *bannach* 'thin oatmeal cake'.
5. Nova Scotia: Ernest Buckler, *Ox Bells and Fireflies* (1968); 'a deep pie of berries'; (origin unknown).
6. West, esp. prairies: Merna Summers, "Portulaca," in *The Skating Party: Stories by Merna Summers* (1974); a prairie euphemism for 'town dump'.
7. West and northwest: George Whalley, *The Legend of John Hornby* (1962); 'men taking part in the Klondike gold rush'; 'men eking out an existence as trappers along Arctic coast and living with Eskimo women'; 'person living off money sent from his family in the Old Country and paid to stay away'; 'good-for-nothings who live in the wilderness by choice'.
8. North: Pierre Berton, *The Mysterious North* (1956); Berton describes them as "odd cone-shaped mounds, 100 feet or so high . . . covered with lake-bottom vegetation, and their core is solid blue ice."
9. West (B.C.): Paul St. Pierre, *Breaking Smith's Quarter Horse* (1966); *lahelle* (or *lahel*) is an Indian gambler's game which has various forms; *stampede ground* is the place where rodeos are held.
10. Maritimes: Ernest Buckler, *Ox Bells and Fireflies* (1968); 'shivaree; noisy greeting to a newly married couple on their wedding night'.
11. West: Anne Marriott, "A Prairie Graveyard" (1945); 'a ground squirrel'; originally *gaufres*, from Canadian French *gaufre gris*; *gaufre* means 'honeycomb', from the shape of the burrow.
12. Probably Maritimes: Archibald Lampman, "A Sunset at Les Eboulements" (1900); 'an area for fishing, often including buildings'; (no region given in this sense by the DC, but probably Maritimes only).
13. Maritimes: Ernest Buckler, *Ox Bells and Fireflies* (1968); 'the sugar maple or its wood'.
14. Pacific coast: Alan Phillips, "The Presence in the Grove" (1952); 'a small evergreen shrub that grows everywhere on the Pacific coast'; from Chinook Jargon, derived from Chinook *Klkwa-shala*.
15. Prairies: Jean Howarth, "The Novitiate" (1952); 'a wild pea with yellow blossoms and a large brown pod'.
16. West (B.C. coast): William McConnell, "Totem" (1952); 'a shrub with huge leaves and a very prickly stem'; at one time called *le bois picant*, Canadian French 'prickly wood'; the word *windfall*, 'tree blown down by the wind', is a general Canadianism.

17. New Brunswick: Hugh Garner, "One Mile of Ice" (1952); *Acadian* is general Maritimes (and widely known elsewhere) 'a descendant of the early French settlers in what is now the Maritimes'; 'the eastern part of N.B.'; possibly the phrase *to cut pulp* is a Canadianism, even eastern Canadianism, but it is not listed in the DC.

18. North: Malcolm Lowry, "The Forest Path to the Spring" (1961). The rest of the quotation illuminates the meaning: "The white was dead so could not climb. But the blue ice would come and ravish an island of all her beauty of trees and moss, bleed her lichen to the rock, and leave her bare. . . ."

19. West: Robert Harlow, *Royal Murdoch* (1962); from Chinook Jargon *stick* 'wood, tree' and extended to the woods or bush; thus slang for any place distant from a city.

20. Ontario and St. Lawrence region: Hugh Hood, "Three Halves of a House" (1962); 'boats that ply the Upper Lakes, *i.e.* Lake Superior'.

21. West: Earle Birney, "Prairie Counterpoint." A section is 640 acres, a square mile.

22. Newfoundland: Harold Horwood, *Tomorrow Will Be Sunday* (1966); 'a seal'; *whelping ice* is a smooth, white ice come down from the Labrador coast, where the seals usually give birth to their pups.

23. Labrador and east Arctic: Percy Janes, *House of Hate*; 'burlap'.

24. Ontario: Miriam Waddington, "Toronto the Golden-vaulted City" (1972); 'the twin cities of Port Arthur and Fort William, and the surrounding region on Lake Superior'.

25. Prairies: Frederick Philip Grove, *Over Prairie Trails* (1922); 'a jog every 24 miles along the survey line to match up with the true meridians'.

26. Atlantic Provinces: Harold Horwood, *Tomorrow Will Be Sunday* (1966); *barachois* (also *barrasway*) is from Canadian French, meaning 'sand bar', and has come to mean either a 'small pond near the sea' or the 'narrow causeway separating the pond from the sea'.

27. Atlantic Provinces: Hugh MacLennan, *Barometer Rising* (1941); 'a long low wagon'.

28. East: Thomas McCulloch *The Stepsure Letters*, in the Halifax *Acadian Recorder* (1821); 'a length of sawn wood' (a variant of *chunk*)

29. Prairies: Paul Hiebert, *Sarah Binks* (1947); a mock biography of a "poet," in which the juxtaposition of traditional "poetic" language and Canadian regional expressions is turned to comic effect. For *bluff* see No. 1; a *coulee* is 'the dry bed of a stream, deeply cut'.

30. Prairies: Edward McCourt, *Saskatchewan* (1968); by *coast dwellers* he probably means the Pacific coast, and *down-easterners* usually means, for Canadians, 'Maritimers', while *back East* means Ontario or Quebec to most westerners.

31. Maritimes: Ernest Buckler, "Penny in the Dust" (1948); 'tract of untillable land on which blueberries flourish'.

32. British Columbia: R. D. Symons, *Many Trails* (1963); *cultus* is a Chinook Jargon word meaning 'bad'.

Summary

In this section we have seen something of the variety and richness of English as used in the different regions of Canada—the vigorous oral tradition of Newfoundland and the Maritimes with its echoes of the voices of ancestors many generations ago, the pockets of older speech patterns surviving even in the highly urbanized heartland of Canada, the creations and borrowings needed by those who settled and farmed the Prairies, and the specialized language of ranchers, loggers, and fishermen as well as that developed in each area by Canadians as they formed their own institutions, political systems, and customs. Does such wealth and diversity mean that Canadian English is really only a mixture of regional varieties? (Should the title of this book have been *Our Own Voices*—in the plural?) The answer is no. In spite of these regional differences (which lie mainly in vocabulary) Canadians share many more features that set their language apart from other varieties of English. A Canadian can usually identify another speaker as Canadian whether the person is from St. John's, Saint John, Toronto, Winnipeg, Moose Jaw, Edmonton, or Vancouver. The homogeneity of Canadian English is more striking than the internal differences.

Will these regional differences persist? Can they survive the pressures toward uniformity that result from urbanization, population mixture, mass media, universal public education, and the influence of an English-speaking world power as a close neighbor? Part of the answer depends, of course, on the political future of Canada and the future centres of power and prestige. Partly, too, it depends upon how the people of Canada (which is still a very young country) come to view themselves—how they see themselves as belonging or (perhaps more important) *not* belonging to certain groups. There is little doubt that most Canadians have a sense of being Canadian (that identity, the search for which has become a national cliché), and that they are becoming increasingly conscious that certain features in their language are neither British nor American, but their own. Yet most Canadians also have a feeling of belonging to a region with its own physical features, industries, customs, and history. Many Canadian writers—one thinks of Ernest Buckler, W. O. Mitchell, Hugh Hood, Margaret Laurence, Rudy Wiebe, Charles Bruce, Harold Horwood, Paul St. Pierre, to name only a few—not only draw strength from a sense of place but also seem to be trying consciously to capture the oral language of particular regions. Some regional vocabulary will persist because it carries this strong sense of identity with the land.

One remembers, too, how long features of a "home" language can survive—as in the Ottawa Valley—for three or four generations. A few regionalisms will spread and become general Canadianisms (*hydro* is an example), or perhaps move into general English. Some terms will remain as regionalisms because they are needed in one area: British Columbians will probably continue to speak of *sockeye, coho*, and *oolichan*; Alberta people will look for a *chinook arch*, and in Saskatchewan and Manitoba people will point to a clump of trees and call it a *bluff*; Ontario speakers will know what a *laker* and a *lakerman* are; and Maritimers will recognize an *aboideau* and continue to have *a time*. Other regional words will linger only in the specialized language of small groups—as signals of belonging: hunters in central British Columbia will probably use *mowitch* to refer to a deer, and sport fishermen back East will continue to cast for *muskies*. Thousands of other words, however, will die, victims of time and changing customs.

But new words and phrases and new pronunciations, both regional and national, will also appear. For, like any variety of English, Canadian English is subject to slow internal changes in all the sub-systems of the language. And Canadians, like any speakers of English, will continue to use the almost unlimited resources of their language to create new terms or to change the meaning of old terms in order to meet the need of naming new objects and expressing new concepts. The recent discussions concerning the BNA Act, for example, have led to the coinage of the word *patriate* (from *repatriate*), a word formed in response to a national situation and one that may stay in the language. New editions of *A Dictionary of Canadianisms* will grow in size, and dialectologists will continue to observe Canadian speech and writing to see how Canadians adapt the English language to fit Canadians ways.

KROETSCH: . . . You know, American writers in the nineteenth century had a choice between their own voices and a literary voice, with Longfellow electing to work within the convention, while Whitman dared to sing himself. I see Canadian writers facing the same choice. There are very tempting other voices around us. The American voice is one of them, and it may be the most obvious temptation. It has authority, it has directness, it has confidence. But Canadians still have to elect for this relatively unknown voice that is theirs, and make literature out of that. . . .

CAMERON: Do you find it an exhilarating experience writing and working with that voice?

KROETSCH: Yes, I do, because I guess I'm a frontiersman and I like the sense of its newness.

Robert Kroetsch, in Cameron (1973)

Acknowledgments

Our Own Voice owes its existence to the work of the scholars who over the years have investigated and written about Canadian English. Among these, special acknowledgment goes to Walter S. Avis, Robert Gregg, G. M. Story, H. R. Wilson, Frederic G. Cassidy, A. Murray Kinloch, Connie Cullen, James Polson, and Howard Woods. These have generously given me material and answered my questions.

For particular contributions, my thanks go to Lilita Rodman, Sandra Djwa, and Isla Penner. In the early stages, I could not have done without the editorial help of Philip Penner and Roy Bentley. Professor Penner also contributed much of the material about German-speaking Canadians. Special thanks go to Dorothy Palmarche, who read the manuscript with a teacher's eye and gave constructive criticism; also to Judith Penner and Maria MacKay for their intelligent collating and typing.

The quality of a book owes much to the kind of editing it gets. I consider myself especially fortunate to have had Patrick Drysdale as editor.

R. E. McConnell
1978

In addition to the items below, the author and publisher are grateful to all those who have given permission to reprint copyrighted material. For a comprehensive listing see the bibliographies. Page 59 Photo of "mystery pickets," courtesy of The *Vancouver Province* and Wayne Leidenfrost. Page 69 Excerpt from *Sunshine Sketches of a Little Town* by Stephen Leacock, by permission of Dodd, Mead & Company. Page 138 Map reproduced from Iona and Peter Opie, *The Lore and Language of Schoolchildren* (Oxford, 1959). Page 88 Map based on J. Garth Taylor, *The Canadian Eskimos* (Toronto: Royal Ontario Museum, 1971). Pages 136, 190, and 198 Reproduced by permission of the Minister of Supply and Services, Canada. Page 205 Map adapted from J. B. Rudnyckyj, "Un cas de bilinguisme régionale: le bilinguisme anglo-ukrainien au Canada," *Studies in Slavic Linguistics and Poetics in Honor of Boris O. Unbegaun* (New York/London, 1968).

General Bibliography on Canadian English and Dialectology

This bibliography is intended to serve two purposes: to give particulars of works referred to in the text, and to suggest materials for further reading. Because full bibliographies of writings on Canadian English already exist (see Avis 1965 and Bahr 1977), this listing is not comprehensive. For similar reasons, the references concerning the study of dialectology in general and those regarding the English used in other regions are limited to major works and to titles cited in the text.

The author and publisher wish to thank copyright holders for permission to reprint copyrighted material.

Adams, G.B., and others, editors
1964   *Ulster Dialects: An Introductory Symposium.* Holywood: Ulster Folk Museum.

Akrigg, G. P. V., and Helen B. Akrigg
1970   *1001 British Columbia Place Names.* 3rd ed. Vancouver: Discovery Press. (Done in dictionary style, with some interesting background stories.)

Alexander, Henry
1939   "Charting Canadian Speech." *Journal of Education* (Nova Scotia), 4th Series, 10, 457-8.
1940   "Linguistic Geography." *Queen's Quarterly* 47, 38-47. (About his field work in Nova Scotia.)
1941   "Collecting Canadian Speech." *Queen's Review* 15, 45-47.
1951   "The English Language in Canada: An Essay Prepared for the Royal Commission on National Development in the Arts and Sciences." ("Massey Report") In *Royal Commission Studies,* 13-24. Ottawa: King's Printer.
1955   "Is There a Canadian Language?" *CBC Times,* Feb. 27, 2-3.

Allen, Harold B.
1959   "Canadian-American Speech Differences Along the Middle Border." *Journal of the Canadian Linguistic Association* 5, 17-24.

(Shows both differences and instances of borrowing.) Reprinted in Chambers 1975.
1971   "Some Problems in Editing the Linguistic Atlas of the Upper Midwest." In Burghardt 1971.
1973-76 *Linguistic Atlas of the Upper Midwest of the United States.* Minneapolis: University of Minnesota Press. Vol 1, *Introduction and Lexicon,* 1973; Vol. 2, *The Grammar,* 1975; Vol. 3, *The Pronunciation,* 1976.

Allen, Harold B., and Garry N. Underwood, editors
1971   *Readings in American Dialectology.* New York: Appleton-Century-Crofts. (An excellent collection of scholarly articles; for advanced students, but provides also a bibliography and an index of sounds, words, and phrases studied.)

The American Heritage Dictionary
1969-70 See Morris.

American Dialect Dictionary
1944   See Wentworth.

Anonymous
1962   "Speaking as a Canadian." *Canada Council Bulletin* 13, 1-5. Ottawa: Queen's Printer.

Armstrong, G. H.
1930   *The Origin and Meaning of Place Names in Canada.* 2nd ed., 1972. Toronto: Macmillan.

Atwood, E. Bagby
1953   *A Survey of Verb Forms in the Eastern United States.* Ann Arbor: University of Michigan Press. (Based on the early surveys for the *Linguistic Atlas of New England.*)

Avis, Walter S.
1954-6 "Speech Differences Along the Ontario-United States Border." *Journal of the Canadian Linguistic Association.* "1. Vocabulary," 1:1 (1954), 13-18; "2. Grammar and Syntax," 1:1 (regular series, 1955), 14-19; "3. Pronunciation," 2:2 (1956), 41-59. Reprinted in Chambers 1975.

1957 "Canadian English Merits a Dictionary." *Culture* 18, 245-6.

1960 "Canadian English and Native Dictionaries." *Education* 3:4, 15-19. Toronto: Gage.

1963 "Canadian English." In *Funk and Wagnall's Standard College Dictionary*, New York/Toronto. Reprinted in subsequent editions, including revised Canadian Edition. Toronto: Fitzhenry & Whiteside, 1976. Also in *Funk and Wagnall's Standard Dictionary* (International Edition), 1965.

1965a "Problems in the Study of Canadian English." In *Communications et rapports du Premier congrès international de dialectologie générale*, 181-191. Louvain.

1965b *A Bibliography of Writings in Canadian English 1857–1965.* Toronto: Gage. (The bibliography is often updated as a Canadian English section of "Linguistica canadiana" in *The Canadian Journal of Linguistics, e.g.* 15:1, Fall 1969.

1966a "Canadian Spoken Here." In Scargill and Penner. (Includes a glossary of Canadianisms cited.)

1966b "Why a Canadian Dictionary?" *Speaking of Dictionaries* 1. Toronto: Gage. (First of a series of pamphlets on dictionaries and Canadian material.)

1967a "Canadian English." In Avis, Drysdale, Gregg, Scargill 1967, 1973. (A revision of the preceding.)

1967b "Slang" (in part). In *Encyclopaedia Britannica* 20, 625. (List of contemporary Canadian slang terms.)

1972a "The Phonemic Segments of an Edmonton Idiolect." In Lawrence M. Davis 1972. Reprinted in Chambers 1975.

1972b "So *eh?* is Canadian, eh?" *Canadian Journal of Linguistics* 17:2, 89-104.

1973a "The English Language in Canada: A Report." In Sebeok 1973. 40-74.

1973b "Eskimo Words in Canadian English." In *Lexicography and Dialect Geography* (Festgabe für Hans Kurath), 25-36. Edited by Harald Scholler. Wiesbaden: Franz Steiner.

1973c "Problems in Editing a Canadian Dictionary: Phonology." In *Annals of the New York Academy of Science (Lexicography in English)* 211, 110-114.

1975 "Some French-Canadian Loanwords in Canadian English." In *Signum* 2:1 (January). (Royal Military College of Canada.)

Avis, Walter S., C. Crate, P. Drysdale, D. Leechman, M. H. Scargill, C. J. Lovell, editors
1967 *A Dictionary of Canadianisms on Historical Principles.* Toronto: Gage. (DC)
1972 *Concise Dictionary of Canadianisms.* Toronto: Gage. (A concise edition of the 1967 dictionary, with some regionalisms and less well known words omitted.)

Avis, Walter S., P. D. Drysdale, R. J. Gregg, M. H. Scargill, editors
1967 *The Senior Dictionary.* Toronto: Gage. Revised and updated 1973. (Third in the Dictionary of Canadian English series, based on the Thorndike-Barnhart dictionaries, thoroughly revised for Canadian use, and augmented with material from files of some 30 000 words gathered by the Dictionary Committee of the Canadian Linguistic Association.)
1973 *Gage Canadian Dictionary.* Toronto: Gage. (Alternative title of revision of *The Senior Dictionary*.)

Avis, Walter S., R. J. Gregg, C. J. Lovell, M. H. Scargill, editors
1962 *The Beginning Dictionary.* Toronto: Gage. (An English-language dictionary for Grades 4 and 5; first book of the Dictionary of Canadian English series.)

Avis, Walter S., R. J. Gregg, and M. H. Scargill, editors
1963 *The Intermediate Dictionary.* Toronto: Gage. (Second book of the Dictionary of Canadian English series, for Grades 6 to 9.)
1977 *Canadian Junior Dictionary.* Toronto: Gage. (A revision and expansion of *The Beginning Dictionary*, for Grades 4 to 6.)

Babcock, C. Merton, editor
1961 *The Ordeal of American English.* Boston: Houghton Mifflin. (Articles and early comments about American English.)

Bähr, Dieter
1977 *A Bibliography of Writings on the English Language in Canada: From 1857–1976.* Heidelberg: Carl Winter Universitätsverlag.

Bailey, Charles-James N., and Roger W. Shuy, editors
1973 *New Ways of Analyzing Variation in English.* Washington: Georgetown University Press. (Describes the move toward unified

grammars rather than atomistic studies; advanced.)

Bailey, Richard W., and Jay L. Robinson, editors
1973 *Varieties of Present-Day English*. New York: Macmillan. (Articles on dialects, especially social dialects as related to education.)

Baker, Sidney
1966 *The Australian Language*. 2nd ed. Sydney: Currawong Press; San Francisco: Tri-Ocean Books.

Barbeau, Marius
1960 "Legend and History in the Oldest Geographical Names of the St. Lawrence." *Canadian Geographical Journal* 61:1 (July), 2-9.

Barber, Charles
1964 *Linguistic Change in Present-Day English*. London: Oliver & Boyd; University, Alabama: University of Alabama Press.

Bennett, J. A. W.
1943 "English as it is Spoken in New Zealand." *American Speech* 18, 81-95. (A good short survey.)

Bloomfield, Leonard
1933 *Language*. New York: Holt, Rinehart and Winston. (One section gives an excellent account of early dialectology in Europe and America.)

Bloomfield, Morton W.
1948 "Canadian English and its Relation to Eighteenth Century American Speech." *Journal of English and Germanic Philology* 47, 59-67. Reprinted in Chambers 1975.

Boas, Franz
1888 "Chinook Songs." *Journal of American Folklore* 1, 222-226.
1911 "Chinook." *Bulletin of Bureau of American Ethnology* 40:1, 559-677 and "Introduction."
1933 "Notes on the Chinook Jargon." *Language* 9, 208-213.

Brook, G. L.
1965 *English Dialects*. 2nd ed. London: Deutsch. (An introduction to British dialects.)
1973 *Varieties of English*. London: Macmillan. (A general account of dialects and selected social and functional differences in British English.)

Brooks, Cleanth
1937 "The English Language of the South." In

Williamson and Burke 1971.

Bruemmer, Fred
1966 "The Mummers." *The Beaver*, Outfit 297, 24-5. (A short photographic essay about this ancient European custom as practised along the north shore of the Gulf of St. Lawrence.)

Burghardt, Lorraine Hall, editor
1971 *Dialectology: Problems and Perspectives*. Knoxville: University of Tennessee. (Papers for a 1970 conference, featuring Harold Orton, director of the British dialect surveys; advanced.)

Burstynsky, E. N.
1971 "Language in Contact: Ukrainian and English." In *Slavs in Canada* 3, 149-255. (How English influences Canadian Ukrainian; advanced.)

Canada
1964-9 *Immigration, Migration, and Ethnic Groups in Canada: A Bibliography of Research*. Ottawa: Department of Citizenship and Immigration.
1970 *Linguistic and Cultural Affiliations of Canadian Indian Bands*. Ottawa: Department of Indian Affairs and Northern Development. (Gives maps of each province, with location of bands, and other statistics. The department also has maps for each province and region.)
1974 *Indian-Inuit Authors: An Annotated Bibliography*. Ottawa: Information Canada.
1976 *Profile Studies: Language in Canada*. Ottawa: Statistics Canada. (A 75-page booklet, based on the 1971 census.)
1970 *Report of the Royal Commission on Bilingualism and Biculturalism*. 4. *The Cultural Contribution of the Other Ethnic Groups*. Ottawa: Queen's Printer.
1969 *Canadian Ethnic Studies*. University of Calgary. (Issued semi-annually. Carries bibliographies and articles. Vol. 7:2, 1975, focuses on "Ethnic Folklore in Canada.")

Cassidy, F. G.
1953 "A Method for Collecting Dialect." *Publications of the American Dialect Society* 20.
1970 "Collecting the Lexicon of American Regional English." In *Promise of English: N.C.T.E. Distinguished Lectures*. Champaign, Illinois: National Council of Teachers of English. (Describes the methods

being used to get data for the *Dictionary of American Regional English*.)

1973 "Of Matters Lexicographical: The Meaning of 'Regional' in DARE." *American Speech* 48:3-4, 282-289. (Discusses and gives examples of types of regionalisms.)

Cassidy, F. G., editor
Dictionary of American Regional English (DARE). (In preparation.)

Cassidy, F. G., and R. B. Le Page, editors
1967 *Dictionary of Jamaican English*. Cambridge University Press. (Now being revised.)

Chamberlain, Alexander F.
1890 "Dialect Research in Canada." *Dialect Notes* 1, 43-56. (Gives word lists of Canadian French and Canadian English, details about settlements, and many suggestions for research.)

Chambers, J. K.
1973 "Canadian Raising." *The Canadian Journal of Linguistics* 18, 113-135. Reprinted, with revisions, in Chambers 1975. (An analysis of the Canadian vowel sounds as in *house* and *wife*.)
1975 "Ottawa Valley Twang." In Chambers, editor, 1975, 55-60.

Chambers, J. K., editor
1975 *Canadian English: Origins and Structures*. Toronto: Methuen. (Reprints of key scholarly articles, and some new studies of regional dialects within Canada.)

Colombo, John Robert, editor
1974 *Colombo's Canadian Quotations*. Edmonton: Hurtig. (An interesting source book.)
1976 *Colombo's Canadian References*. Toronto: Oxford University Press. (A wide-ranging collection of information, including items relating to authors, titles, and language.)

Cotnam, Jacques, editor
1973 *Contemporary Quebec: An Analytical Bibliography*. Toronto: McClelland and Stewart. (Lists articles, bibliographies, books, and research studies by topic, concentrating on those written since 1953; includes language, education, history, folklore, and literature.)

Cowan, Helen I.
1961 *British Emigration to British North America: The First Hundred Years*. Revised and enlarged edition. University of Toronto Press. (Also gives a good bibliography.)

Craig, Gerald M.
1963 *Upper Canada: The Formative Years 1784-1841*. Toronto: McClelland and Stewart. (Good bibliographies.)

Craigie, W. A., and James R. Hulbert, editors
1938-44 *A Dictionary of American English on Historical Principles*. (DAE) 4 vols. University of Chicago Press.

Cullen, Connie
1971 "Dialect Research on Prince Edward Island." *English Quarterly* 4:3, 51-53. (A preliminary report.)

Darnell, Regna, editor
1971 *Linguistic Diversity in Canadian Society*. Edmonton: Linguistic Research. (Articles, mainly detailed sociolinguistic studies; advanced.)
1973 *Canadian Languages in their Social Context*. Edmonton: Linguistic Research. (Articles on sociolinguistics; advanced.)

Davis, A. L., editor
1969 *American Dialects for English Teachers*. Champaign, Illinois: Illinois State-Wide Curriculum Study Center. (Material and suggestions for study.)
1972 *Culture, Class, and Language Variety: A Resource Book for Teachers*. Revised ed. Champaign, Illinois: National Council of Teachers of English.

Davis, A. L., and L. M. Davis, editors
1969 "Recording of Standard English Questionnaire." *Orbis* 18, 385-404. (Methods and materials in tape-recording standard English.)

Davis, A. L., and Raven I. McDavid, Jr.
1949 "Shivaree: An Example of Cultural Diffusion." *American Speech* 24, 249-255. Reprinted in Allen and Underwood 1971. (How this French-Canadian word spread.)

Davis, A. L., Raven I. McDavid, Jr., and Virginia G. McDavid, editors
1969 *A Compilation of the Work Sheets of the Linguistic Atlas of the United States and Canada and Associated Projects*. 2nd ed. University of Chicago Press. (The words, phrases, etc. used in surveys.)

Davis, Lawrence M., editor
1972 *Studies in Linguistics: In Honor of Raven I. McDavid, Jr.* University, Alabama: Uni-

versity of Alabama Press. (Has some Canadian material.)

Deighton, Lee C.
1972 *A Comparative Study of Spellings in Four Major Collegiate Dictionaries.* Pleasantville, New York: Hardscrabble Press.

Dempsey, H. A.
1956 "Blackfeet Place Names." *Alberta Historical Review* 4, 29-30.

Devine, P. K.
1937 *Devine's Folklore of Newfoundland in Old Words, Phrases, and Expressions.* St. John's: Robinson.

A Dictionary of American English on Historical Principles. (DAE)
1938-44 See Craigie and Hulbert.

A Dictionary of Americanisms on Historical Principles. (DA)
1951 See Mathews.

A Dictionary of Canadianisms on Historical Principles. (DC)
1967 See Avis, Crate, Drysdale, Leechman, Scargill.

Dictionnaire canadien—The Canadian Dictionary.
1962 See Vinay.

Dictionary of the Chinook Jargon, or Indian Trade Language of the North Pacific Coast
1889 Victoria, B.C.: T. N. Hibben. Reprinted Vancouver: K. Lang, 1972. (Typical of several reprints of the dictionaries used in the early days.)

Dorion, Henri, and Christian Morissoneau, editors
1972 *Place Names and Language Contact.* Quebec: Les Presses de l'Université Laval. (Excellent scholarly material, about one-half on Canada.)

Drysdale, P. D.
1959 "A First Approach to Newfoundland Phonemics." *Canadian Journal of Linguistics* 5:1, 25-34.
1966 "Why a High-School Dictionary?" *Speaking of Dictionaries* 2. Toronto: Gage. (One of a series of pamphlets on dictionaries and, especially, Canadian dictionaries.)
1971 "Her Parkee, Made of Caribou . . . Using a Dictionary as a Sourcebook." *English Quarterly* 4:3, 47-50.

Dulong, Gaston
1968 *Dictionnaire correctif du français au Canada.*

Quebec: Les Presses de l'Université Laval. (The book gives evidence of lexical borrowings by Canadian French from English.)

Eagleson, Robert D.
1967 "The Nature and Study of Australian English." *Journal of English Linguistics* 1, 11-23.

Ekwall, Eilert
1960 *The Concise Oxford Dictionary of English Place-Names.* 4th ed. Oxford University Press.

Emeneau, M. B.
1935-40 "The Dialect of Lunenburg, Nova Scotia." *"Language* 11 (1935), 140-147; 16 (1940) 214-215. (The first article concerns the influence of German upon the English spoken; the second is a note about Belsnickels at Christmas time.) The first is reprinted in Chambers 1975.

Emery, Donald W.
1973 *Variant Spellings in Modern American Dictionaries.* Revised ed. Champaign, Illinois: National Council of Teachers of English. (Gives 2400 instances of variant spellings in five recent major desk dictionairies.)

Encyclopedia Canadiana
1957- 10 vols. Ottawa: Grolier. Frequent revisions. (See *Language, Ethnic origins,* and similar headings.)

England, George Allen
1925 "Newfoundland Dialect Items." *Dialect Notes* 5, 322-346. (A glossary—gives about a thousand items, each defined.)

English Usage in Southern Africa
1970- University of South Africa. (Issued twice yearly.)

ERIC Clearinghouse for Linguistics
1969- *A Preliminary Bibliography of American English Dialects.* Washington, D.C. (A computerized bibliography, periodically updated.)

Evans, Mary S.
1930 "Terms from the Labrador Coast." *American Speech* 6, 56-58.

Fee, Chester A.
1941 "Oregon's Historical Esperanto—the Chinook Jargon." *Oregon Historical Quarterly* 42, 116-185.

Fee, Margery, Gail Donald, and Ruth Cawker, editors
1975 *Canadian Fiction: An Annotated Bibliography.* Toronto: Peter Martin. (Lists and briefly describes every novel, short story collection, and biographical or critical study by and about Canadian writers published to the end of 1974.)

Fishman, Joshua A., and others
1966 *Language Loyalty in the United States: The Maintenance and Perpetuation of non-English Mother Tongues by American Ethnic and Religious Groups.* Introduction by Einar Haugen. The Hague: Mouton. (Based on original research; has relevance to Canada.)

Foster, Brian
1968 *The Changing English Language.* New York: St. Martin's; Toronto: Macmillan. (Has material about recent American-British influences; little about Canadian usage.)

Fowke, Edith
1970 *Sally Go Round the Sun.* Book and record. Toronto: McClelland and Stewart. (The oral songs, games, spells, etc. used by young Canadian children.)
1976 *Folklore of Canada.* Toronto: McClelland and Stewart. (A rich collection of tales, legends, jokes, myths, songs, etc., representing Canada's diverse folk traditions. Excellent bibliography.)
1977 *Ring Around the Moon: 200 Songs, Tongue-Twisters, Riddles and Rhymes of Canadian Children.* Toronto: McClelland and Stewart. (The oral songs, games, etc., used by Canadian children aged six to 11.)

Fowler, H. W.
1940 *A Dictionary of Modern English Usage.* Oxford: Clarendon Press. (First published 1926. 2nd ed., revised by Sir Ernest Gowers, 1965.)

Francis, W. Nelson
1959 "Some Dialect Isoglosses in England." *American Speech* 34, 243-257. Reprinted in Allen and Underwood 1961. (Points out some possible relationships between British and American dialects.)

Funk & Wagnall's Standard College Dictionary
1973 Canadian ed. New and updated ed. 1976. Toronto: Fitzhenry & Whiteside. (Many Canadian words.)

Geikie, A. S.
1857 "Canadian English." *Canadian Journal* 2, 344-355. (Some early observations of Canadian speech.)

Gibbon, John Murray
1938 *Canadian Mosaic: The Making of a Northern Nation.* Toronto: McClelland and Stewart. (Historical and literary study, which uses poetry and art to illustrate the spirit of the ethnic groups in Canada; a popular rather than scholarly work, but a source of interesting information.)

Giglioli, Pier Paolo, editor
1972 *Language and Social Context.* Penguin Modern Sociology Readings. London: Penguin. (Excellent collection; advanced.)

Gilbert, Glenn G., editor
1971 *The German Language in America: A Symposium.* Austin: University of Texas Press.

Gill, George K., with W. C. Chaltin
1884 *Dictionary of the Chinook Jargon with Examples of its Use in Conversation.* 10th ed. Portland, Oregon: J. K. Gill.

Gimson, A. C.
1970 *An Introduction to the Pronunciation of English.* 2nd ed. London: Edward Arnold. (Within the framework of general phonetics; British.)

Gledhill, Christopher, editor
1975 *Folk Songs of Prince Edward Island.* Rev. ed. Charlottetown: Square Deal.

Goossens, Maria
1973 "Degree of Bilingualism among Dutch Immigrants in Calgary." In Darnell 1973.

Gove, Philip B., editor
1961 *Webster's Third New International Dictionary of the English Language.* Springfield, Massachusetts: G. & C. Merriam.

Gowers, Sir Ernest
1954 *The Complete Plain Words.* London: H. M. Stationery Office; reprinted Pelican 1962. 2nd ed. 1973. (An amalgamation of his two books, *Plain Words*, 1948, and *The ABC of Plain Words*, 1951.)

Graham, Robert Somerville
1955 "The Anglicization of German Family Names in Western Canada." *American Speech* 30, 260-264.
1957 "The Transition from German to English in the German Settlements of Saskatche-

wan." *Journal of the Canadian Linguistic Association* 3:1, 9-13.

Grant, Rena V.
1944 "The Chinook Jargon, Past and Present." *California Folklore Quarterly* 3, 259-276.
1945 "Chinook Jargon." *International Journal of American Linguistics* 11, 225-233. (An excellent account.)

Gregg, Robert J.
1957a "Notes on the Pronunciation of Canadian English as Spoken in Vancouver, B.C." *"Journal of the Canadian Linguistic Association* 3:1, 20-26. (Detailed account.)
1957b "Neutralization and Fusion of Vocalic Phonemes in Canadian English as Spoken in the Vancouver Area." *Journal of the Canadian Linguistic Association* 3:2, 78-83. (A revised version of these two articles is reprinted in Chambers 1975.)
1959 Paper on Ulster dialect, presented to Canadian Linguistic Association, Saskatoon. Unpublished.
1973a "The Dipthongs əi and ɑɪ in Scottish, Scotch-Irish, and Canadian English." *Canadian Journal of Linguistics* 18:2, 136-145.
1973b "The Linguistic Survey of British Columbia: The Kootenay Region." In Darnell 1973. (Describes the survey and discusses some of the results.)

Gregorovich, Andrew
1972a *Canadian Ethnic Groups Bibliography.* Toronto: Department of the Provincial Secretary and Citizenship. (A selected bibliography, with emphasis on Ontario.)
1972b *Ukrainian Canadian History and Culture: A Selected and Annotated Bibliography.* Toronto: Ukrainian Canadian Research Foundation.

Hale, Kenneth
1965 "On the Use of Informants in Field-work." *Canadian Journal of Linguistics* 10, 108-119. (A non-technical article on the relationship between a linguist and the informant.)

Hall, Robert A., Jr.
1966 *Pidgin and Creole Languages.* Ithaca: Cornell University Press. (A full discussion, with a good bibliography.)

Halpert, Herbert, and G. M. Story, editors
1969 *Christmas Mumming in Newfoundland.* University of Toronto Press. (Articles about this ancient custom.)

Hamilton, Donald E.
1958 "Notes on Montreal English." *Journal of the Canadian Linguistic Association* 4:2, 70-79. Reprinted in Chambers 1975. (How it differs from that of Toronto, as well as from American and British English.)
1964 "Standard Canadian English: Pronunciation." In *Proceedings of Ninth International Congress of Linguists*, 456-459. Edited by Horace G. Lunt. The Hague: Mouton.

Hamilton, William B.
1974 *Local History in Atlantic Canada.* Toronto: Macmillan. (Excellent. Has a good 12-page chapter on place-name research.)
1977 *The Macmillan Book of Canadian Place Names.* Toronto: Macmillan.

Hansen, Marcus Lee
1940 *The Mingling of the Canadian and American Peoples.* New Haven: Yale University Press. (Historical background.)

Hardwick, Francis C., editor
1971-74 *Canadian Culture Series.* Vancouver: Tantalus Research. 1. *The Helping Hand: Indian Canadians and Explorers* (1971; 2nd ed. 1973); 2. *When Strangers Meet: Meeting of Indian Canadians and Anglo-Canadian Cultures* (1972); 3. *To the Promised Land: Contributions of Ukrainians to Canadian Society* (1973); 4. *From Far Beyond the Western Horizon: East Indian Canadians* (1974); 5. *From the Oldest Civilization: Chinese Canadians* (1974); 6. *The Return of the Vikings: Scandinavians in Canada* (1974). (A series of source books designed for secondary students; excellent original materials.)

Harney, Robert F., and Harold Troper
1975 *Immigrants: A Portrait of the Urban Experience, 1890-1930.* Toronto: Van Nostrand Reinhold. (Photographs and essay, based on the lives of immigrants in Toronto; excellent background material.)

Harrington, Lynn
1958 "Chinook Jargon." *The Beaver*, Outfit 289, 26-29. (A short survey.)

Harris, Barbara P., and Joseph K. Kess
1975 "Salmon Fishing Terms in British Columbia." *Names* 23:2, 61-66. (Shows sources of terms, compares with American terms, etc.)

Haugen, Einar
1953 *The Norwegian Language in America: A Study*

in Bilingual Behavior. Philadelphia: University of Pennsylvania Press.

1956 *Bilingualism in the Americas: A Bibliography and Research Guide*. University, Alabama: University of Alabama Press. 2nd printing 1964.

1972 *The Ecology of Language*. Language Science and National Development Series, 4. Palo Alto: Stanford University Press. (Essays by Haugen on language contact and bilingualism; the title means language interacting with its environment.)

Higinbotham, John D.
1962 "Western Vernacular." *Alberta Historical Review* 10, 9-17.

Holmgren, Eric J., and Patricia M. Holmgren
1973 *Over 2000 Place Names of Alberta*. Rev. ed., with supplement. Saskatoon: Prairie Books. (Well researched; gives the stories behind the names.)

Howay, F. W.
1942 "Origin of the Chinook Jargon." *British Columbia Historical Quarterly* 6, 225-250. Reprinted in *Oregon Historical Quarterly* 44 (1943), 27-55.

Hungerford, Harold, Jay Robinson, and James Sledd, editors
1970 "Dialectology." Part II of *English Linguistics: An Introductory Reader*. Glenview, Illinois: Scott, Foresman. (Excellent selection of articles by Sapir, Orton, Atwood, Weinreich, Sledd, and Labov.)

Hunter, A. F.
1901 "The Ethnographical Element of Ontario." *Ontario Historical Society Papers and Records* 3, 180-199. (A detailed listing by districts and counties of Ontario ethnic groups in 1900.)

Hymes, Dell
1969 "Linguistic Theory and the Functions of Speech." In *The Second International Congress of Social Sciences of the Luigi Institute*. Rome.

Innis, Hugh R., editor
1973 *Bilingualism and Biculturalism: An Abridged Version of the Royal Commission Report*. Toronto: McClelland and Stewart.

Jacobs, Melville
1932 "Notes on the Structure of Chinook Jargon." *Language* 8, 27-50. (A good article; advanced.)

1936 "Texts in Chinook Jargon." *University of Washington Publications in Anthropology* 7, 1-27.

1937 "Historical Perspectives in Indian Languages of Oregon and Washington." *Pacific Northwest Quarterly* 28, 55-74. (Material on Chinook Jargon.)

Jenness, Diamond
1963 *The Indians of Canada*. 6th ed. Ottawa: National Museum. Reprinted 1972. (One of the best references.)

Joos, Martin
1942 "A Phonological Dilemma in Canadian English." *Language* 18, 141-144. Reprinted in Chambers 1975. (An early discussion of the Canadian vowel system.)

Karpeles, M.
1971 *Folk Songs from Newfoundland*. New Haven: Yale University Press.

Kaye, Vladmir J.
1964 *Early Ukrainian Settlements in Canada*. University of Toronto Press.

Kenyon, John S.
1961 *American Pronunciation*. 10th ed. Ann Arbor: George Wahr.

Kerr, D.G.G.
1975 *A Historical Atlas of Canada*. 3rd ed. Toronto: Nelson.

Kerr, D. G. G., and R. I. K. Davidson, editors
1966 *Canada: A Visual History*. Toronto: Nelson. (Photographs from archives, giving a historical perspective; interesting background material.)

Key, Mary Ritchie
1975 *Male/Female Language, with a Comprehensive Bibliography*. Methuen, N.J.: Scarecrow Press. (Many examples of differences in usage.)

Kinlock, A. M.
1971 "The Survey of Canadian English: Possible Evidence for Pronunciation." *English Quarterly* 4:4, 59-65.

1972-3 "The Survey of Canadian English: A First Look at New Brunswick Results." *English Quarterly* 5:4, 41-49.

Kinloch, A. M., H. R. Wilson, and T. J. O'Neil
1973 "Classroom Uses of the Survey of Canadian English." *English Quarterly* 6:4, 369-372.

Kirschbaum, Joseph M.
1967 *Slovaks in Canada.* Toronto: Canadian Ethnic Press Association of Ontario. (A history.)

Kirwin, William
1960 "Labrador, St. John's and Newfoundland: Some Pronunciations." *Journal of the Canadian Linguistic Association* 6:2, 115-116.
1965 "Lines, Coves, and Squares in Newfoundland [Street] Names." *American Speech* 40, 163-170.
1968 "Bibliography of Writings on Newfoundland English." *Regional Language Studies—Newfoundland* 1, 4-7.
1974 "Newfoundland Usage in the 'Survey of Canadian English'." *Regional Language Studies—Newfoundland* 5, 9-14.

Kirwin, William, editor
1968- *Regional Language Studies—Newfoundland.* St. John's: Memorial University. (An informal and occasional publication giving information about linguistic research being done in and concerning Newfoundland.)
1975 "The Growth of the 'Dictionary of Newfoundland English'." Special issue of *Regional Language Studies—Newfoundland* 6. (Articles by G. M. Story, Kirwin, and J. D. A. Widdowson, and some sample entries.)

Klinck, Carl F., and others, editors
1976 *Literary History of Canada: Canadian Literature in English.* 2nd ed. 3 vols. University of Toronto Press. (Vol. 1, to 1920; Vol. 2, 1920-1960; Vol. 3, 1960-1974; good reference.)

Klymasz, Robert
1963 "The Canadianization of Slavic Surnames: A Study in Language Contact." *Names* 11, 81-105, 182-195, 229-253.

Kratz, Henry and Humphrey Miles
1953 "Kitchener German: A Pennslyvania German Dialect." *Modern Language Quarterly.* Vol. 14, pp. 184-98, 274-83.

Kurath, Hans
1949 *A Word Geography of the Eastern United States.* Ann Arbor: University of Michigan Press. Reprinted 1966. (Based on the first surveys; gives maps.)
1964a "British Sources of Selected Features of American Pronunciation: Problems and Methods." In *In Honor of Daniel Jones,* edited by D. Abercrombie and others. London: Longmans Green, 146-255. Reprinted in Allen and Underwood 1971.
1964b "Interrelation Between Regional and Social Dialects." In *Proceedings of the Ninth International Congress of Linguists,* 134-144. Edited by Horace G. Lunt. The Hague: Mouton. (Especially about how a prestige form may spread.)
1965 "Some Aspects of Atlantic Seaboard English Considered in Their Connections with British English." In *Communications et rapports du Premier congrès international de dialectologie générale,* 239-240. Louvain. Reprinted in Williamson and Burke 1971.
1970a *Contributions of British Folk Speech to American Pronunciation.* Leeds Studies in English. University of Leeds.
1970b "English Sources of Some American Words." *American Speech* 45, 60-68.
1972a "Relics of English Folk Speech in American English." In *Studies in Linguistics: In Honor of Raven I. McDavid, Jr.,* 367-375. Edited by Lawrence M. Davis. University, Alabama: University of Alabama Press.
1972b *Studies in Area Linguistics.* Bloomington: Indiana University Press. (Methodology, with examples from North American and British English; advanced.)

Kurath, Hans, editor
1939 *Handbook of the Linguistic Geography of New England.* Providence: American Council of Learned Societies. Reprinted Washington, 1954. 2nd ed., with a new introduction, word-index, and inventory of LANE maps and commentary by Audrey R. Duckert, and a reverse index of LANE maps to worksheets by Raven I. McDavid, Jr. New York: AMS Press, 1973.

Kurath, Hans, and Bernard Bloch, editors
1939-43 *Linguistic Atlas of New England.* 3 vols. in 6 parts. Providence: Brown University Press. Reprinted, with 300 pages of new materials, New York: AMS Press, 1972.

Kurath, Hans, and Raven I. McDavid, Jr., editors
1961 *The Pronunciation of English in the Atlantic*

States. Ann Arbor: University of Michigan Press.

Labov, William
1970 *The Study of Nonstandard English*. Champaign, Illinois: National Council of Teachers of English.
1972 *Sociolinguistic Patterns*. Philadelphia: University of Pennsylvania Press. (A systematic account of the study of language variation in a social setting; advanced.)

Laird, Charlton
1970 *Language in America*. New York: Prentice-Hall. Prism paperback 1973. (An historical account of the languages spoken on the American continents; little about Canadian English; interesting material on Indian languages.)

Lanham, L. W.
1967 *The Pronunciation of South African English*. Johannesburg: Witwatersrand University Press.

Leechman, Douglas
1926 "The Chinook Jargon." *American Speech* 1, 531-534.
1956 *Native Tribes of Canada*. Toronto: Gage. (Introductory; well illustrated.)

Lehn, Walter
1959 "Vowel Contrasts in a Saskatchewan English Dialect." *Journal of the Canadian Linguistic Association* 5:2, 90-98. Reprinted in Chambers 1975.

Léon, P. R., and P. Martin, editors
1976 *Toronto English: Studies in Phonetics and Phonology*. Unpublished MS. (Analyses of various aspects of the speech of 17 teenagers of Toronto; advanced.)

Logan, Robert A.
1951 "The Precise Speakers." *The Beaver*, Outfit 282, 40-43. (Short article about the Cree language.)

Long, Frederick J., compiler
1969 *Dictionary of the Chinook Jargon*. Seattle: Lowman & Hanford.

Lovell, Charles J.
1955 "Lexicographic Challenges of Canadian English." *Journal of the Canadian Linguistic Association* 1:1 (regular series), 2-5.
1955-6 "Whys and Hows of Collecting for the Dictionary of Canadian English." *Journal of the Canadian Linguistic Association*. Part 1, 1:2 (1955), 3-8; Part 2, 2:1 (1956), 23-32.
1958 "A sampling of Material for a Dictionary of Canadian English Based on Historical Principles." *Journal of the Canadian Linguistic Association* 4:1, 7-33.

McAtee, W. L.
1955 "Bird Names with Animal or Plant Components." *American Speech* 30, 176-185. (Gives many Canadian distributions; terms such as *bullbird, pussy owl*, etc.)

McDavid, Raven I., Jr.
1951 "Midland and Canadian Words in Upstate New York." *American Speech* 26, 248-256.
1954 "Linguistic Geography in Canada: An Introduction." *Journal of the Canadian Linguistic Association* 1:1, 3-8.
1958 "The Dialects of American English." Chapter 9 of W. Nelson Francis, *The Structure of American English*. New York: Ronald. (An excellent overview.)
1960 "The Second Round in Dialectology of North American English." *Journal of the Canadian Linguistic Association* 6:2, 108-115.
1969 "Dialects: British and American Standard and Nonstandard." In *Linguistics Today*. Edited by Archibald Hill. New York/London: Basic Books, 79-88.
1972 "Some Notes on Acadian English." In *Culture, Class, and Language Variety*. Edited by A. L. Davis. Urbana, Illinois: National Council of Teachers of English. (Acadians of southwest Louisiana, French-speaking emigrants from Nova Scotia in the eighteenth century.)

MacInnes, Tom
1926 *Chinook Days*. Vancouver: Sun Publishing. The essay on Chinook is reprinted in A. J. M. Smith, editor, *The Canadian Century: English-Canadian Writing Since Confederation*. Toronto: Gage, 1973.

McIntosh, Angus
1952 *Introduction to a Survey of Scottish Dialects*. Edinburgh University Press. Reprinted 1961.

Malmstrom, Jean
1973 *Language in Society*. 2nd ed. New York: Hayden. (Overview of language in a world society, and specific aspects of social dialects in the U.S.A.; designed for beginners. First published 1965.)

Malmstrom, Jean, and Annabel Ashley
1963 *Dialects—U.S.A.* Champaign, Illinois: National Council of Teachers of English. (An introduction for American students.)

Marckwardt, Albert H.
1957 "Principal and Subsidiary Dialect Areas in the North-Central States." *Publications of the American Dialect Society* 27, 3-15. Reprinted in Allen and Underwood 1971.
1958 *American English.* New York: Oxford University Press. (A brief historical outline.)
1971 "The Concept of Standard English." In *The Discovery of English.* Urbana, Illinois: National Council of Teachers of English. (A discussion of the historical development of a standard dialect in England and the social forces that shaped it.)

Marckwardt, Albert H., and Randolph Quirk
1964 *A Common Language: British and American English.* London: BBC and the United States Government. (A series of radio discussions between these two linguists.)

Mardon, Ernest G.
1973 *Community Names of Alberta.* University of Lethbridge.

Mather, J. Y., and H. M. Speitel, editors
1975 *The Linguistic Atlas of Scotland.* Vol. 1. New York: Shoestring Press. (The first of three volumes; gives maps, spellings, population density, etc. for Lowland Scotland, Orkney, Shetland, Northern Ireland, Northumberland, and Cumberland.)

Mathews, Mitford M., editor
1931 *The Beginnings of American English: Essays and Comments.* University of Chicago Press. Phoenix paperback, 1963.
1951 *A Dictionary of Americanisms on Historical Principles.* (DA) University of Chicago Press.
1966 *Americanisms: A Dictionary of Selected Americanisms on Historical Principles.* University of Chicago Press. (An abridgement of 1951).

Mencken, H. L.
1963 *The American Language: An Inquiry into the Development of English in the United States.* 4th ed. and 2 supplements, abridged, with annotations and new material by Raven I. McDavid, Jr., and David W. Maurer. New York: Knopf. Paperback ed. 1977. (An updating of a classic.)

Miffin, Robert James
1956 "Some French Place Names of Newfoundland." *American Speech* 31, 79-80.

Mitchell, A. G., and Arth. Delbridge
1965 *The Pronunciation of English in Australia.* 2nd ed. Sydney: Angus & Robertson.
1965 *The Speech of Australian Adolescents.* Sydney: Angus & Robertson.

Moon, Barbara
1962 "Does Anyone Here Speak Canadian?" *Maclean's,* June 2.

Morley, William F. E., editor
1967 *The Atlantic Provinces.* Canadian Local Histories to 1950: Bibliography, Vol. 1. University of Toronto Press.

Morris, William, editor
1969-70 *The American Heritage Dictionary of the English Language.* Boston: American Heritage/Houghton Mifflin. (Good introductory material on dialects, usage, spelling, history of English; excellent etymological material.)

Moss, Norman
1973 *What's the Difference? A British/American Dictionary.* New York/London: Harper & Row.

Muri, John T., and Raven I. McDavid, Jr., editors
1967 *Americans Speaking: A Dialect Recording Prepared for the National Council of Teachers of English.* Champaign, Illinois: National Council of Teachers of English. (Recording and pamphlet; voices from Inland, Northern, Brooklyn, Eastern New England, South Midland, Delaware Valley, and Southern Plantation.)

Norris, John, editor
1972 *Strangers Entertained: A History of the Ethnic Groups of British Columbia.* Vancouver Centennial '71 Committee.

Noseworthy, Ronald G.
1974 "Fishing Supplement: Linguistic Atlas of Newfoundland Dialect Questionnaire." *Regional Language Studies—Newfoundland* 5, 18-21.

Orkin, Mark M.

1970 *Speaking Canadian English: An Informal Account of the English Language in Canada.* Toronto: General. (Interesting material; has a bibliography.)

Orton, Harold, and others, editors

1962 *Survey of English Dialects: Introduction.* Leeds: E. J. Arnold, for the University of Leeds. (Describes how the survey was made, gives the questionnaire.)

1962-71 *Survey of English Dialects.* 4 vols. Leeds: E. J. Arnold, for the University of Leeds. (Gives an introduction and results of the survey by regions.)

Orton, Harold, and Nathalia Wright

1972 *Questionnaire for the Investigation of American Regional English Based on the Worksheets of the Linguistic Atlas of the United States and Canada.* Knoxville: University of Tennessee. (Provides question frames to elicit responses, and a six-page Introduction about field techniques.)

1974 *A Word Geography of England.* London: Seminar Press. (Survey results.)

Oxford English Dictionary. (OED) 12 vols. plus Supplement. Oxford University Press, 1933. (Originally published as *A New English Dictionary on Historical Principles.* 10 vols. 1884-1928.) The first two of four new supplements are A-G, 1974; H-N, 1976.

Paddock, Harold J.

1975 "The Folk Grammar of Carbonear, Newfoundland." In Chambers 1975. (Originally "Some Notes on Grammar," Chapter 1 of following entry.)

1976 *A Dialect Survey of Carbonear, Newfoundland.* In *Publications of the American Dialect Society* 65. See also 1975. (Based on his 1966 survey and unpublished M.A. thesis.)

Padolsky, Enoch, and Ian Pringle

1977 "Reflexes of M.E. Vowels before /r/ in Ottawa Valley Dialects of Hiberno-English Types." Unpublished paper presented to Canadian Linguistic Association, Fredericton.

Palmer, Howard

1972 *Land of the Second Chance: A History of Ethnic Groups in Southern Alberta.* The Lethbridge Herald. (Gives a bibliography.)

Partridge, Eric

1970 *A Dictionary of Slang and Unconventional English.* 7th ed. London: Routledge & Kegan Paul; New York: Macmillan.

Partridge, Eric, and John W. Clark

1951 *British and American English since 1900.* London: Andrew Dakers. Reprinted New York: Greenwood, 1968. (Also gives a short account of Canadian English, by F. E. L. Priestley, and of other "Englishes".)

Patterson, G.

1895-97 "Notes on the Dialect of the People of Newfoundland." *Journal of American Folklore* 8 (1895), 27-40; 9 (1896), 19-37; 10 (1897), 203-213. Summarized in *Proceedings and Transactions of the Nova Scotian Institute of Natural Sciences* 9 (1894-98), 44-77.

Peacock, F. W.

1974 "Languages in Contact in Labrador." *Regional Language Studies—Newfoundland* 5, 1-3. (Influence of English and German, the latter from Moravian missionaries of the eighteenth century, upon Eskimo speech.)

Pilling, James Constantine

1893 *Bibliography of the Chinookan Languages (Including the Chinook Jargon).* Bulletin No. 15. Washington: Bureau of Ethnology. (Excellent, fully annotated, bibliography and some illustrations.)

Polson, James

1969 "A Linguistic Questionnaire for British Columbia: A Plan for a Postal Survey of Dialectal Variation in B.C., with an Account of Recent Research." Unpublished M.A. thesis. University of British Columbia.

Porter, Bernard H.

1963 "A Newfoundland Vocabulary." *American Speech* 38, 297-301. (A list, with meanings; many terms, he claims, spread from Newfoundland to Maine.)

Potter, Simeon

1969 *Changing English.* London: Deutsch. (Good recent material.)

Priestley, F. E. L.

1957 "English Language." In *Encyclopedia Canadiana.* (*i.e.* English Language in Canada.)

1968 "Canadian English." In Partridge and

Clark 1951, 72-79.

Principles of the International Phonetic Association.
1974   London.

Pyles, Thomas
1952   *Words and Ways of American English*. New York: Random House.
1964   *The Origin and Development of the English Language*. New York: Harcourt, Brace & World. (Excellent material on American/British differences, as well as on historical background.)
1972   "The Auditory Mass Media and U." In Lawrence M. Davis 1972, 425-433. (Material on some social differentiations in American pronunciation.)

Quirk, Randolph
1972   *The English Language and Images of Matter*. Oxford University Press.

Ramsay, Sterling
1973   *Folklore of Prince Edward Island*. Charlottetown: Square Deal.

Ransom, W. S.
1966   *Australian English: An Historical Study of the Vocabulary 1788-1898*. Canberra: Australian National University Press.

Ransom, W. S., editor
1970   *English Transported: Essays on Australian English*. Canberra: Australian National University Press. (Includes a bibliography compiled by David Blair.)

Rayburn, Alan
1967a   "Geographical Names of Amerindian Origin in Canada." *Names* 15, 203-215.
1967b   *Geographical Names of Renfrew County, Ontario*. Geographical Paper No. 40. Ottawa: Department of Energy, Mines, and Resources.
1973   *Geographical Names of Prince Edward Island*. Ottawa: Surveys and Mapping Branch, Department of Energy, Mines and Resources. (Gives historical data and the origins of names. Similar material is being prepared for other provinces.)
1975   *Geographical Names of New Brunswick*. Ottawa: Surveys and Mapping Branch, Department of Energy, Mines and Resources. (Gives historical data and origins of names.)

Read, Allan Walker
1973   "Approaches to Lexicography and Semantics." In Sebeok 1973, 145-206.

Reamon, George Elmore
1965   *The Trail of the Black Walnut*. 2nd ed. Toronto: McClelland and Stewart. First published 1957. (Story of Pennsylvania Germans, U.E.L.'s and other groups who came to Ontario during the American Revolution; gives maps and bibliography.)

Reed, Carroll E.
1961   "The Pronunciation of English in the Pacific Northwest." *Language* 37, 559-564. Reprinted in Allen and Underwood 1971 and in Williamson and Burke 1971. (Useful for comparisons.)
1973   *Dialects of American English*. Amherst: University of Massachusetts Press. (First published Cleveland: World Book Company, 1967.) (A concise survey of American English regional dialects based on the Linguistic Atlas, with maps and bibliography. Foreword by Raven I. McDavid, Jr.)

Reed, Carroll E., and L. W. Siefert, editors
1948   "A Study of the Pennsylvania German Spoken in the Counties of Lehigh and Berks." *Modern Language Quarterly*, 9 (Dec.), pp. 448-66.
1961   "Double Dialect Geography." *Orbis*, 10 (June), pp. 308-19.

Reed, David W.
1954   "Eastern Dialect Words in California." *Publications of American Dialect Society* 21, 5-6. Reprinted in Allen and Underwood 1971. (Includes discussion of the word *chesterfield*.)

Regional Language Studies—Newfoundland
1968-   See Kirwin, editor.

Reid, Robie L.
1942   "The Chinook Jargon." *British Columbia Historical Quarterly* 6, 1-11.

Rodman, Lilita
1974-5   "Characteristics of B.C. English." *English Quarterly* 7:4, 49-82. (Further analysis of the 1971 survey.)

Rodman, Lilita, and Ingrida Deglavs-Brenzinger
1973   "Aspects of English-Latvian Language Contact: Part 1, Nouns." In Darnell 1973. (Advanced.)

Rogers, P. W.
1970 "Unlocking the Canadian Word Hoard." *Queen's Quarterly* 77, 111-123. (A review article on Canadian dictionaries.)

Royick, Alexander
1968 "Ukrainian Settlement in Alberta." *Canadian Slavonic Papers* 10:3, 278-279.

Rudnyckyj, J. B.
1957 *Canadian Place Names of Ukrainian Origin*. (*Onomastica* 2.) 3rd ed. Winnipeg: Ukrainian National Home Association.
1970 *Manitoba: Mosaic of Place Names*. Winnipeg: Canadian Institute of Onomastic Science.
1973 "Immigrant Languages, Language Contact, and Bilingualism in Canada." In Sebeok 1973, 592-652.
1974 *Mosaic of Winnipeg Street Names*. (*Onomastica* 48.) Winnipeg: University of Manitoba.

Russell, E. T., editor
1974 *What's in a Name? Travelling through Saskatchewan with the Story behind 1600 Place-names*. 2nd ed. Saskatoon: Western Producer Book Service. (A book done as a project by the students of Henry Kelsey School in Saskatoon; gives stories and reminiscences of pioneers as well as the origins of names.)

Samarin, William I.
1967 *Field Linguistics: A Guide to Linguistic Field Work*. New York: Holt, Rinehart and Winston. (A guide on collecting data.)

Sandilands, John
1912 *Western Canadian Dictionary and Phrase-Book: Things a Newcomer Wants to Know*. Winnipeg: Telegram Job Printers. Reprinted Edmonton: University of Alberta Press, 1977.

Scargill, M. H.
1954 "A Pilot Study of Alberta Speech: Vocabulary." *Journal of the Canadian Linguistic Association* 1:1, 21-22.
1955 "Canadian English and Canadian Culture in Alberta." *Journal of the Canadian Linguistic Association* 1:1 (regular series) 26-29.
1956 "Eighteenth Century English in Nova Scotia." *Journal of Canadian Linguistic Association* 2:1, 3.
1957 "The Sources of Canadian English." *Journal of English and Germanic Philology* 56, 610-614. Reprinted in Chambers 1975.

1960 "Canadian Dictionary Projects." *Education* III, 79-87. Toronto: Gage.
1965a "The Growth of Canadian English." In Klinck 1976, Vol. 1, 265-273.
1965b "Making a Canadian Dictionary." Unpublished paper.
1968 "Canadianisms from Western Canada, with Special Reference to British Columbia." *Transactions of the Royal Society of Canada*, Vol. 6, Series 4, 181-185.
1973a "Is Riz, Some Hot, Clumb, and Other Canadianisms." *English Quarterly* 6:2, 115-121. (Assesses some results of the 1971 Survey of Canadian English.)
1973b "Using the Historical Dictionary: A Concise Dictionary of Canadianisms." *Speaking of Dictionaries*, No. 4. Pamphlet. Toronto: Gage.
1974 *Modern Canadian English Usage: Linguistic Change and Reconstruction*. Toronto: McClelland and Stewart. (Gives results of the 1971 Survey of Canadian English and comments upon them.)
1977 *A Short History of Canadian English*. Victoria: Sono Nis Press.

Scargill, M. H., and P. G. Penner, editors
1966 *Looking at Language*. Toronto: Gage. (A collection of essays about language, designed for Canadian secondary schools.)

Scargill, M. H., and H. J. Warkentyne
1972 "The Survey of Canadian English: A Report." *English Quarterly* 5:3, 47-104.

Scott, S. O., and D. A. Mulligan
1951 "The Red River Dialect." *The Beaver*, Outfit 282, 42-45. Partly reprinted in Chambers 1975.

Sealock, Richard B., and Pauline A. Seeley, compilers
1967 *Bibliography of Place-Name Literature: United States and Canada*. 2nd ed. Chicago: American Library Association. (Supplements appear in *Names*; the third Supplement, 1973, carries a large section on Canadian place names.)

Seary, E. R.
1958 "The French Element in Newfoundland Place Names," *Journal of the Canadian Linguistic Association* 4:2, 63-69.
1962 "Linguistic Variety in the Place Names of Newfoundland." *Canadian Geographical Journal* 65, 146-155.
1971 *Place Names of the Avalon Peninsula of the*

Island of Newfoundland. (Memorial University Series 2.) University of Toronto Press. (A scholarly collection and interpretation of the names known over five centuries.)

Seary, E. R., G. M. Story, and W. J. Kirwin
1968 *The Avalon Peninsula of Newfoundland: An Ethno-linguistic Survey*. National Museum of Canada, *Bulletin No. 219*, Anthropological Series 81. Ottawa: Queen's Printer. (Results of an intensive survey done 1957-1961.)

Sebeok, Thomas A., editor
1973 *Current Trends in Linguistics: 10. Linguistics in North America*. 2 vols. The Hague: Mouton. (Has material on languages of Indians, Inuit, and English-speaking Canadians.)

Shaw, George C.
1909 *The Chinook Jargon and How to Use It*. Seattle: Rainier Printing. Facsimile reprint. Seattle: Shorey Book Store, 1955.

Sheffe, Norman, editor
1975 *Many Cultures: Many Heritages*. Toronto: McGraw-Hill. (A school text about the Canadian people, illustrated and with historical material.)

Shores, David L., editor
1972 *Contemporary English: Change and Variation*. Philadelphia/Toronto: Lippincott. (Various articles.)

Shuy, Roger W.
1967 *Discovering American Dialects*. Champaign, Illinois: National Council of Teachers of English. (A brief survey.)

Shuy, Roger W., and Ralph W. Fasold, editors
1973 *Language Attitudes: Current Trends and Prospects*. Washington: Georgetown University Press. (A focus on subjective reactions to varieties of language, *e.g.* dialects; also on stereotypes, teachers' attitudes, etc.)

Shuy, Roger W., Walter A. Wolfram, and William K. Riley
1968 *Field Techniques in an Urban Language Study*. Washington: Georgetown University Press. (A report on the methodology used in a survey of Detroit speech; a descriptive work; advanced.)

Sledd, James
1973 "Bidialectalism: A New Book and Some Old Issues." *American Speech* 48:3-4, 258-269. (About the value of standard English.)

Stevenson, Roberta C.
1977 "The Pronunciation of English in British Columbia: An Analysis of the Responses to the Phonological Section of the Gregg-Polson Postal Questionnaire for B.C., with Suggestions for Further Dialect Investigation in the Province." Unpublished M.A. thesis. University of British Columbia.

Stewart, George R.
1967 *Names on the Land*. Boston: Houghton Mifflin. (How American places were named; some parts useful to Canadians doing similar investigations.)

Story, G. M.
1957a "Newfoundland English Usage." In *Encyclopedia Canadiana* 7, 321-322.
1957b "Research in the Language and Place-Names of Newfoundland." *Journal of the Canadian Linguistics Association* 3, 47-55.
1959a "Newfoundland Dialect." In *The Story of Newfoundland*, edited by A. B. Perlin, 68-70. St. John's: Guardian Limited.
1959b *A Newfoundland Dialect Questionnaire: The Avalon Peninsula. 1: Vocabulary*. St. John's: Memorial University.
1965 "Newfoundland Dialect: An Historical View." *Canadian Geographical Journal* 70, 127-131. Reprinted in Chambers 1975. (Excellent material.)
1969 See Halpert and Story.
1971 "The St. John's Balladeers." *English Quarterly* 4:4, 49-58.

Story, G. M., and W. Kirwin
1974 "The Dictionary of Newfoundland English: Progress and Promise." *Regional Language Studies—Newfoundland* 5, 15-17.

Story, G. M., W. Kirwin, and J. D. A. Widdowson
1973 "Collecting for *The Dictionary of Newfoundland English*." *Annals of the New York Academy of Sciences* 211, 104-108.

Story, Norah
1967 *The Oxford Companion to Canadian History and Literature*. Toronto: Oxford University Press. *Supplement 1967-1972*, edited by William Toye, 1973.

Strevens, Peter
1972 *British and American English*. London: Collier-Macmillan. (Discusses differences and how they came to be.)

Thomas, Edward H.

1970 *Chinook: A History and Dictionary of the Northwest Coast Trade Jargon.* 2nd ed. Portland, Oregon: Metropolitan Press. (Gives a good bibliography.)

Turner, G. W.

1966 *The English Language in Australia and New Zealand.* London: Longmans.

Urion, C.

1971 "A German-English Interlingual 'Key'." In Darnell 1971, 223-230.

Vallins, G. H.

1965 *Spelling.* 2nd ed., with revisions by D. G. Scragg and with a chapter on American spelling by John W. Clark. London: Deutsch. (Excellent material.)

Vinay, Jean-Paul, Pierre Daviault, and Henry Alexander, editors

1962 *Dictionnaire canadien—The Canadian Dictionary.* Concise Edition. Toronto: McClelland and Stewart. (A bilingual dictionary for Canada, from work done at the Lexicographic Research Centre at the University of Montreal.)

Wakelin, Martyn F.

1972 *English Dialects: An Introduction.* London: Athlone Press. (Dialects within England; based on H. Orton's survey; also has a good bibliography.)

Wakelin, Martyn F., editor

1971 *Patterns in the Folk Speech of the British Isles.* London: Athlone Press. (Nine essays by experts; advanced.)

Walker, Douglas C.

1975 "Another Edmonton Idiolect: Comments on an Article by Professor Avis." In Chambers 1975. (Comments on Avis 1972a, which is also in Chambers.)

Wall, Arnold

1959 *New Zealand English.* 3rd ed. Christchurch, N.Z.: Whitcombe & Tombs.

Wanamaker, M. G.

1959 "Canadian English: Whence? Whither?" *Journal of Education* (Nova Scotia), 5th series, 9, 22-26.

1966 "Your Dialect is Showing." In Scargill and Penner 1966.

1976-77 "Who Controls Writing Standards?" *English Quarterly* 9:4, 45-52. (Results of an enquiry into spelling and punctuation policies of Canadian publishers.)

Warkentyne, H. J.

1971 "Contemporary Canadian Usage: A Report on the Survey of Canadian English." *American Speech,* 46:3-4, 193-199.

Watters, Reginald Eyre

1972 *A Checklist of Canadian Literature and Background Materials 1628-1960.* 2nd ed., revised and enlarged. University of Toronto Press. (First edition 1959.)

Webster's Third New International Dictionary

1961 See Gove.

Weinreich, Uriel

1953 *Languages in Contact: Findings and Problems.* The Hague: Mouton. Reprinted 1963. Text ed. 1964. (What happens when languages mingle; advanced.)

Wentworth, Harold, editor

1944 *American Dialect Dictionary.* New York: Crowell.

Wentworth, Harold, and Stuart Berg Flexner, editors

1975 *Dictionary of American Slang.* 2nd ed. New York: Crowell.

Widdowson, J. D. A.

1964 "Some Items of a Central Newfoundland Dialect." *Canadian Journal of Linguistics* 10:1, 37-46.

Williamson, Juanita V., and V. M. Burke, editors

1971 *A Various Language: Perspectives on American Dialects.* New York: Holt, Rinehart and Winston. (Excellent collection of material; generally advanced.)

Wilson, H. Rex

1956 "The Implication of Tape Recording in the Field of Dialect Geography." *Journal of the Canadian Linguistic Association* 2:1, 17-21. (How he used tape recording in collecting data for his dialect research in Nova Scotia—an early use of this device.)

1958 "The Dialect of Lunenburg County, Nova Scotia." Ph.D. dissertation (on microfilm). University of Michigan. See also 1975.

1973 "Dialect Literature: A Two-Way Street?" *Canadian Journal of Linguistics* 18:2, 157-162.

1975 "Lunenburg Dutch: Fact and Folklore." In Chambers 1975. (An article based on his 1958 dissertation and later research.)

Winks, Robin W.

1971 *The Blacks in Canada: A History.* Montreal: McGill-Queen's University Press. (The most complete and authoritative book on the subject; gives maps and bibliography.)

Wintemberg, W. J.
1950 *Folk-lore of Waterloo County, Ontario*. Ottawa: Department of Resources and Development.

Wolfart, C. H., and Janet F. Carroll
1973 *Meet Cree: A Practical Guide to the Cree Language*. Edmonton: University of Alberta Press.

Wolfram, Walt, and Ralph W. Fasold
1974 *The Study of Social Dialects in American English*. Englewood Cliffs, N.J.: Prentice-Hall.

Wright, Joseph
1905 *The English Dialect Grammar*. Oxford University Press. Reprinted 1968. (Also published 1905 as part of Vol. 6 of following entry.)

Wright, Joseph, editor
1898-1905 *The English Dialect Dictionary*. 6 vols. London: Henry Frowde. Reprinted Oxford University Press, 1968. (Volume 6, 1905, includes *The English Dialect Grammar*. See previous entry.)

Bibliography of Literary and Historical Sources quoted

This list includes only those literary and historical materials cited in the text. Because the original sources of some poems, stories, and articles are now rather inaccessible, the list also supplies cross references to a few major collections of Canadian material.

References relating to Canadian English and to dialectology are given in a separate bibliography.

The author and publisher wish to thank the copyright holders for permission to reprint copyrighted material, including the editors of the following:

The Beaver	*Time*
Canadian Magazine	*The Vancouver Province*
The Canadian Forum	*The Vancouver Sun*
Maclean's	*Weekend Magazine*
North	

Acorn, Milton
1975   *The Island Means Minago: Poems from Prince Edward Island.* Toronto: N C Press.

Allan, Ted
"Lies My Father Told Me." In Weaver and James 1952.

Annett, William S.
"The Relic." In Weaver and James 1952.

Armour, Richard
1955   "Mother Tongue." *The New Yorker.*

Atwood, Margaret
1972   *Survival: A Thematic Guide To Canadian Literature.* Toronto: Anasi.

Baird, P. D.
1950   "Baffin Island Expedition, 1950." *Arctic III* (December).

Barbeau, Marius, Arthur Lismer, Arthur Bourinot, editors
1963   *Come-a-Singing! Canadian Folk Songs.* National Museum of Canada, *Bulletin No. 107,* Anthropological Series 26. Ottawa: Information Canada. Reprinted 1973.

Berton, Pierre
1956   *The Mysterious North.* Toronto/Montreal: McClelland and Stewart.

Birney, Earle
1947   "Prairie Counterpoint." In *The Strait of Anian: Selected Poems.* Toronto: Ryerson.
1952   "Bushed" and "Maritime Faces." In *Trial of a City and Other Verse.* Toronto: Ryerson. Reprinted in *Selected Poems 1940-1966.* Toronto: McClelland and Stewart, 1966.
1955   *Down the Long Table.* Toronto: McClelland and Stewart.

Bowering, George
"Time and Again." In Geddes 1975.

Broadfoot, Barry
1973   *Ten Lost Years, 1929–1939: Memories of Canadians Who Survived the Depression.* Toronto: Doubleday. Paperback ed. Don Mills: General Publishing, 1975.

Brooke, Frances
1769   *The History of Emily Montague.* London: T. Dodsley. Reprinted Toronto: McClelland and Stewart, 1961.

Bruce, Charles
1957   *The Channel Shore.* Toronto: Macmillan.

Bruce, Harry
1968   *The Short Happy Walks of Max MacPherson.* Toronto: Macmillan.

Bruemmer, Fred
1971   "Northern Labrador." *Canadian Geographical Journal* LXXXII (May).

Buck, Ruth Matheson
1974   *The Doctor Rode Side-Saddle.* Toronto: McClelland and Stewart.

Buckle, Daphne
"The Sea-Haven." In Rimanelli and Roberto 1966.

Buckler, Ernest
1948   "Penny in the Dust." *Maclean's* LXI (Dec. 15).
1952   *The Mountain and the Valley.* New York: Henry Holt. Reprinted Signet, 1954.

1968　*Ox Bells and Fireflies*. Toronto: McClelland and Stewart.

Cameron, Agnes Deans
1908　"New Words with Crops of Yellow Wheat."*Canadian Magazine* XXXI, 141-143.

Cameron, Donald, editor
1973　*Conversations with Canadian Novelists*. Toronto: Macmillan.

Campbell, Majorie Wilkins
1959　"The Prairie Provinces." In *The Face of Canada*. Toronto: Clarke, Irwin.

Canada
1962　*Royal Commission on Bilingualism and Biculturalism: The Official Languages*. Ottawa: Queen's Printer.

Canuel, Alfred
1976　"The Voyageur Belt." *Heritage* (Government of Alberta), May/June.

Careless, J. M. S., editor
1968　*The Pioneers: An Illustrated History of Early Settlement in Canada*. Rev. ed. 1973. Toronto: McClelland and Stewart.

Carman, Bliss
1929　"A Bluebird in March." In *Sanctuary*. Toronto: McClelland and Stewart.

Carr, Emily
1941　*Klee Wyck*. Toronto: Oxford. Reprinted Clarke, Irwin, 1951. Paperback ed. 1962.

Cary, Thomas
1789　*Abram's Plains: A Poem*. In *Three Early Poems from Lower Canada*. Edited by Michael Gnarowski. Montreal: McGill, 1969.

Chappell, Lieut. Edward, R.N.
1817　*Narrative of a Voyage to Hudson's Bay in His Majesty's Ship Rosamond*. London. Facsimile reprint. Toronto: Coles, 1970.

Cogswell, Fred
1967　"The Development of Writing" [in New Brunswick]. In R. A. Tweedie, Fred Cogswell, W. Stewart MacNutt, editors. *Arts in New Brunswick*. Fredericton: University Press of New Brunswick.

Conant, Thomas
1903　*Life in Canada*. Toronto: Briggs.

Connor, Ralph [pseudonym for Rev. C. W. Gordon]
1901　*The Man from Glengarry*. Chicago: F. H. Revell. Reprinted Toronto: McClelland and Stewart, 1965.

1902　*Glengarry Schooldays*. Toronto: Westminster.Reprinted McClelland and Stewart, 1963, 1975.

1909　*The Foreigner: A Tale of Saskatchewan*. Toronto: Westminster.

Craig, John
1975　*The Clearing*. London: Constable; Toronto: Longman.

Craven, Margaret
1967　*I Heard the Owl Call My Name*. Toronto/Vancouver: Clarke, Irwin. Reprinted 1970.

Creighton, Helen
1950　*Folklore of Lunenburg, County, Nova Scotia*. Department of Resources and Development, National Museum of Canada, *Bulletin No. 117*, Anthropology Series 29. Ottawa: Queen's Printer. Reprinted Toronto: McGraw-Hill Ryerson, 1976.

Cronin, Fergus
1965　"Do You Speak Canadian?" *Canadian Weekly*. 27 Feb.

Crowe, Keith J.
1974　*A History of the Original Peoples of Northern Canada*.Montreal: McGill-Queen's University Press.

Currie, Margaret Gill
1900　"By the St. John." In Theodore H. Rand, editor. *A Treasury of Canadian Verse*. Freeport,New York: Books for Libraries Press. Reprinted Granger Index Reprint Series, 1969.

Davies, Robertson
1969　"The Poetry of a People." In Wainwright 1969.

1970　*Fifth Business*. New York: Viking. Reprinted Signet, 1970.

Day, David, and Marilyn Bowering, editors
1977　*Many Voices*. Vancouver: J. J. Douglas.

Demers, James
1974　*The God Tree*. Don Mills: Musson.

Dewdney, Selwyn
1946　*Wind Without Rain*. Toronto: Copp Clark. Reprinted McClelland and Stewart, 1974.

Dickens, Charles
1864-65　*Our Mutual Friend*. London: Chapman and Hall.

Dobbs, Kildare
1962　*Running to Paradise*. Toronto: Oxford. Re-

printed in part as "Views of Venice" in Weaver and Toye 1972.

Duncan, Sara Jeanette
1904 *The Imperialist.* Toronto: Copp Clark. Reprinted Toronto: McClelland and Stewart, 1961.

Dunham, Mabel
1942 *The Trail of the Conestoga.* Toronto/Montreal: McClelland and Stewart. Reprinted 1947, 1960.

England, George Allan
1924 *Vikings of the Ice.* New York: Doubleday. Reprinted as *The Greatest Hunt in the World.* Montreal: Tundra, 1969.

English, L. E. F., editor.
1969 *Historic Newfoundland.* 2nd ed. St. John's: The Newfoundland Tourist Development Division.

Filion, Gerard
1959 "La Vieille Province." In *The Face of Canada.* Toronto: Clarke, Irwin.

Finnigan, Joan
1976 *"I Come from the Valley."* Photographs by Erik Christensen. Toronto: N C Press.

Fowke, Edith
1963 "Folk Songs in Ontario." *Canadian Literature* XVI, 27-42.

Fraser, Simon
See Lamb 1960.

Fry, Alan
1973 *The Revenge of Annie Charlie.* Toronto: Doubleday.

Frye, Northrop
1971 *The Bush Garden: Essays on the Canadian Imagination.* Toronto: Anansi.

Galbraith, John Kenneth
1964 *The Non-Potable Scotch: A Memoir on the Clansmen in Canada.* Boston: Houghton-Mifflin. Alternative title *The Scotch.* Also published as *Made to Last.* London: Hamish Hamilton. Reprinted Penguin, 1967.

Garner, Hugh
1952 "One Mile of Ice." In *The Yellow Sweater and Other Stories.* Toronto: Collins. Also in Weaver and James 1952.
1968 *Cabbagetown.* Toronto: Ryerson.

Geddes, Gary, editor
1975 *Skookum Wawa: Writings of the Canadian Northwest.* Toronto: Oxford University Press.

Geike, John Cunningham
1864 *George Stanley; or, Life in the Woods.* London: Routledge, Warne, and Routledge. Reprinted as *Life in the Woods.* London: Strahan, 1873; and as *Adventures in Canada.* Philadelphia: Porter, 1882.

George, Chief Dan, and Helmut Hirnschell
1974 *My Heart Soars.* Saanichton, B.C.: Hancock House.

Gerrard, Elisabeth
1967 *We Came to Canada.* Toronto: Longman.

Glassco, John
1962 "A Season in Limbo." *Tamarack Review.* Reprinted in Smith 1973a.

Glazebrook, G. P. de T.
1968 *Life in Ontario: A Social History.* University of Toronto Press.

Grainger, M. Allerdale
1908 *Woodsmen of the West.* Toronto: Musson. Reprinted Toronto: McClelland and Stewart, 1964.

Greenough, William Parker
1897 *Canadian Folk-Life and Folk-Lore.* New York: Geo. H. Richmond. Reprinted Coles, 1971.

Grove Frederick Philip
1922 *Over Prairie Trails.* Toronto: McClelland and Stewart. Reprinted 1969.
1930 *The Yoke of Life.* Toronto: Macmillan.
1933 *Fruits of the Earth.* Toronto: Dent. Reprinted McClelland and Stewart, 1965.

Guillet, Edwin C.
1940 *Pioneer Arts and Crafts.* Toronto: Ontario Publishing Company. New ed. University of Toronto Press, 1968.

Gustafson, Ralph, editor
1944 *Canadian Accent: A Collection of Stories and Poems by Contemporary Writers from Canada.* New York: Penguin.
1958 *The Penguin Book of Canadian Verse.* London: Penguin.

Guy, Ray
1974 "Newfoundlanders and Mainlanders." *The Canadian Forum*, March.
1975 *You May Know Them As Sea Urchins, Ma'am.* Edited by Eric Norman. Portugal Cove, Nfld.: Breakwater Books.

Haig-Brown, Roderick
1950   "Autumn." In *The Measure of the Year*. Toronto: Collins.

Haliburton, Thomas Chandler
1836-40 *The Clockmaker; or, The Sayings and Doings of Samuel Slick of Slickville*. 3 vols. First series, Halifax: Joseph Howe, 1836. First-Third series, London: Bentley, 1837-40. First series reprinted Toronto: McClelland and Stewart, 1958.
1849   "Seeing the Devil." In *The Old Judge*. London: Colburn; New York: Stringer & Townsend. Reprinted Toronto: Clarke, Irwin, 1968.

Hamilton, Robert M., compiler
1952   *Canadian Quotations and Phrases Literary and Historical*. Toronto: McClelland and Stewart. Paperback ed. 1965.

Harker, Herbert
1972   *Goldenrod*. New York: Random.

Harlow, Robert
1962   *Royal Murdoch*. Toronto: Macmillan.

Hart, Ann
1976   "The Friday Everything Changed." *Chatelaine* XLIX (April).

Hayball, Gwen
1973   "Historic Lobsticks and Others." *Canadian Geographical Journal* 85 (Feb.), 62-65.

Hayman, Robert
1628   *Quodlibets: Lately Come Over from New Britaniola, Old Newfound-Land. Epigrams and Other Small Parcels: Both Morall and Divine*. London: Mitchell.

Hazlitt, William Carew
1862   *The Great Gold Fields of Cariboo with an authentic description brought down to the latest period of British Columbia and Vancouver Island with an Authentic map*. London: Routledge, Warne, and Routledge. New edition, with foreword by Barry M. Gough. Vancouver: Klanak Press, 1974.

Head, Sir George
1829   *Forest Scenes and Incidents in the Wilds of North America*. London: John Murray. Facsimile reprint. Toronto: Coles, 1970.

Henry, Alexander ("The Elder")
1809   *Travels and Adventures in Canada and the Indian Territories, Between the Years 1760 and 1776*. New York: I. Riley. New ed., with notes by James Bain, Toronto: Morang, 1901. Reprinted Edmonton: Hurtig, 1969.

Hiebert, Paul G.
1947   *Sarah Binks*. Toronto: Macmillan.

Hillen, Ernest
1973   "*Bitaemo* to the Town of Dauphin, Manitoba." *Weekend Magazine*, Sept. 22.

Hood, Hugh
1962   "The End of It" and "Three Halves of a House." In *Flying a Red Kite*. Toronto: Ryerson.

Hopwood, Victor G., editor
1971   *David Thompson: Travels in Western North America 1784-1812*. Toronto: Macmillan.

Horwood, Harold
1966   *Tomorrow Will Be Sunday*. New York: Doubleday. Paperback ed. Toronto: PaperJacks, 1975.
1969   *Newfoundland*. New York: St. Martin's.

Howarth, Jean
       "The Novitiate." In Weaver and James 1952.

Howe, Joseph
1839   Letter to Lord John Russell. Reprinted in Smith 1973b.

Hutchinson, Sybil
       "Second Sight." In Gustafson 1944.

Janes, Percy
1970   *House of Hate*. Toronto/Montreal: McClelland and Stewart.

Johnson, E. Pauline (Tekahionwake)
1911   *Legends of Vancouver*. 3rd ed. Vancouver: Thomson Stationery Company.

Johnson, Samuel
1755   *A Dictionary of the English Language*. London: W. Strahan. Facsimile reprint New York: Ams Press, 1967. *A Modern Selection*, by E. L. McAdam Jr. and George Milne. London: Gollancz, 1963.

Kennedy, H. A.
1925   *Book of the West: The Story of Western Canada, its Birth & Early Adventures, its Present Ways*. Toronto: Ryerson.

Kilbourn, William, editor
1970   *Canada: A Guide to the Peaceable Kingdom*. Toronto: Macmillan.

Klein, A. M.
1948   "Grain Elevator." In *The Rocking Chair & Other Poems*. Toronto: Ryerson. Reprinted in *Collected Poems of A. M. Klein*. Toronto: McGraw-Hill Ryerson, 1974.

Klinck, Carl F., and R. E. Watters, editors
1966   *Canadian Anthology*. Revised ed. Toronto: Gage. 3rd ed., 1974.

Kroetsch, Robert
1973   In Cameron, *Conversations with Canadian Novelists*.

Lamb, W. Kaye, editor
1960   *Simon Fraser: Letters & Journals, 1806-1808*. Toronto: Macmillan.

Lampman, Archibald
1888   "April." In *Among the Millet, and Other Poems*. Ottawa: Durie.
1900   "A Sunset at Les Eboulements." In *The Poems of Archibald Lampman*. Edited and with a memoir by Duncan Campbell Scott. Toronto: Morang. Also in *Lyrics of Earth: Sonnets and Ballads*. Toronto: Musson, 1925.

Laurence, Margaret
1964   *The Stone Angel*. Toronto: McClelland and Stewart. Paperback ed. 1968.
1965   "The Mask of the Bear." In *A Bird in the House*. Toronto: McClelland and Stewart, 1970. Paperback ed. McClelland and Stewart, 1974. Reprinted in Klinck and Watters 1974.
1966   *A Jest of God*. Toronto: McClelland and Stewart. Reprinted 1974. U.S. paperback and movie title *Rachel, Rachel.* New York: Popular Library, 1966.
1973   In Cameron, *Conversations with Canadian Novelists*.
1974   *The Diviners*. Toronto: McClelland and Stewart. Reprinted Bantam, 1975.
1976   "Where the Wind Began." In *Heart of a Stranger*. Toronto: McClelland and Stewart.

Leacock, Stephen
1912   "The Speculations of Jefferson Thorpe." In *Sunshine Sketches of a Little Town*. London: John Lane. Paperback ed. Toronto: McClelland and Stewart, 1960.
1936   "I'll Stay in Canada." In *Funny Pieces: A Book of Random Sketches*. New York: Dodd Mead.
1943   "Good and Bad Language." In *How to Write*. New York: Dodd Mead.

Le Pan, Douglas
1953   "Canoe-Trip." In *The Net and the Sword*. Toronto: Clarke, Irwin. Reprinted in Klinck and Watters 1974.

Lillard, Charles
1975   "Landscape." Masset, Queen Charlottes: Sono Nis Press. Reprinted in Geddes 1975.

London, Jack
1899   "From Dawson to the Sea." In *Buffalo Express*, June 4. Reprinted in *Jack London's Tales of Adventure*. Edited by Irving Shepard. Garden City, New York: Hanover House, 1956.
1904   "Too Much Gold." In *Faith of Men and Other Stories*. New York: Macmillan.

Lower, A. R. M.
1946   *Colony to Nation: A History of Canada*. Toronto/New York: Longman.

Lowry, Malcolm
1961   "The Forest Path to the Spring." In *Hear Us O Lord from Heaven Thy Dwelling Place*. Philadelphia/New York: Lippincott.

Lucas, Alec, editor
1971   *Great Canadian Short Stories*. New York: Dell.

Ludwig, Jack
1973   In Cameron, *Conversations with Canadian Novelists*.

Macfie, Matthew
1865   *Vancouver Island and British Columbia: Their History, Resources, and Prospects*. London: Longman. Facsimile reprint Toronto: Coles, 1972.

Mackay, J. Ross
1969   "The Mackenzie Delta." *Canadian Geographical Journal* LXXVIII (May).

MacKay, L. A.
1936   "Frankie Went Down to the Corner." *The Canadian Forum*. Reprinted in Scott and Smith 1957.

Mackenzie, Sir Alexander
1789   See T. H. McDonald 1966.

Mackenzie, William Lyon
1837   "The Navy Island Proclamation." Reprinted in Smith 1973b.

MacLennan, Hugh
1941   *Barometer Rising*. Toronto: Collins. Paperback ed. Toronto: McClelland and Stewart, 1958.

1959 *The Watch That Ends the Night*. Toronto: Macmillan. Paperback ed. Macmillan, 1975.

1960 "The People Behind This Peculiar Nation." In George E. Nelson, editor, *Northern Lights*. New York: Doubleday.

1961 "The Rivers That Made a Nation." From *Seven Rivers of Canada*. Toronto: Macmillan.

MacLeod, Alistair
1976 *The Lost Salt Gift of Blood*. Toronto: McClelland and Stewart.

McConnell, William
"Totem." In Weaver and James 1952.

McCourt, Edward
1947 *Music at the Close*. Toronto: Ryerson. Reprinted McClelland and Stewart, 1966.

1968 *Saskatchewan*. Toronto: Macmillan.

McCulloch, Thomas
1960 *The Stepsure Letters*. Toronto: McClelland and Stewart. Formerly *Letters of Mephibosheth Stepsure*. Halifax: Blackader, 1860 (1862). Originally published as letters to the *Acadian Recorder*, 1821-22.

McDonald, Archibald
1828 *Peace River: A Canoe Voyage From Hudson's Bay to the Pacific by the late George Simpson. . .in 1828; Journal of the Chief Factor, Archibald McDonald*. Ottawa: Durie, 1872. Reprinted Toronto: Coles, 1972.

McDonald, T. H., editor
1966 *Exploring the Northwest Territory: Sir Alexander Mackenzie's Journal of a Voyage by Bark Canoe from Lake Athabaska to the Pacific Ocean in the Summer of 1789*. Norman: University of Oklahoma Press.

Mair, Charles
1886 *Tecumseh: A Drama*. Toronto: Hunter Rose.

Major, Kevin, editor
1974 *Doryloads: Newfoundland Writings and Art Selected and Edited for Young People*. Portugal Cove, Nfld: Breakwater Books.

Marlatt, Daphne
1974 "A By-Channel; A Small Backwater." In *Steveston*. Vancouver: Talonbooks.

Marlyn, John
1957 *Under the Ribs of Death*. Toronto: McClelland and Stewart. Paperback ed. 1964.

Marriott, Anne
1939 *The Wind Our Enemy*. Toronto: Ryerson.

1945 "Prairie Graveyard." In *Sandstone and Other Poems*. Toronto: Ryerson. Reprinted in Gustafson 1958.

Marryat, Captain Frederick
1839 *Diary in America with Remarks on its Institutions*. Philadelphia. Reprinted New York: Knopf, 1962. Quoted in Mathews 1963.

Marshall, Joyce
"The Old Woman." In Weaver and James 1952.

Marshall, Mel
1971 *Cooking Over Coals*. Illus. Joe Boren. New York: Winchester Press.

Mathews, M. M., editor
1931 *The Beginnings of American English*. Chicago: Phoenix Books. Reprinted 1963.

Metayer, Maurice, translator
1966 *I. Nuligak*. Translated from Eskimo. Toronto: Peter Martin.

Mitchell, W. O.
1947 *Who Has Seen the Wind?* Toronto: Macmillan. Paperback ed. 1960.

1961 *Jake and the Kid*. Toronto: Macmillan. Paperback ed. 1974.

1962 *The Kite*. Toronto: Macmillan. Paperback ed. 1974.

1973 *The Vanishing Point*. Toronto: Macmillan.

Moodie, Susanna
1852 *Roughing it in the Bush*. London: Bentley. Reprinted Toronto: McClelland and Stewart, 1923 and 1962. Reprinted Toronto: Coles, 1974.

Mowat, Farley
1956 *Lost in the Barrens*. Toronto: McClelland and Stewart.

Munro, Alice
1968 "Boys and Girls" and "Walker Brothers Cowboy." In *Dance of the Happy Shades*. Toronto: Ryerson. "Walker Brothers Cowboy" is reprinted in Weaver and Toye 1973.

Nash, Ogden
1945 *Many Long Years Ago*. Boston: Little Brown.

Newlove, John
1968 "The Pride." In *Black Night Window*. Toronto: McClelland and Stewart. Reprinted in Klinck and Watters 1974 and in Weaver and Toye 1973.

Niven, Frederick
1935 *The Flying Years*. London: Collins. Paperback ed. Toronto: McClelland and Stewart, 1974.

1940 *Mine Inheritance*. London: Collins.

Nowlan, Alden
1968   "The Girl Who Went to Mexico." From *Miracle at Indian River*. Toronto: Clarke, Irwin.
1973   *Various Persons Named Kevin O'Brien: A Fictional Memoir*. Toronto/Vancouver: Clarke, Irwin.

Nuligak
1966   See Metayer.

O'Brien, Andy
1972   "Anyone for Ipirautaqturniq?" *Weekend Magazine*, Feb. 19.

O'Connor, Michael Patrick, and Thorvaldur Johnson, translators
"The Laundress." Yates 1971.

O'Hagan, Howard
1963   "The White Horse." In *The Woman Who Got On at Jasper Station and Other Stories*. Denver: A. Swallow. Reprinted in Geddes 1975.

Opie, Iona and Peter
1959   *The Lore and Language of Schoolchildren*. London: Oxford.

Pennier, Henry
1972   *Chiefly Indian: The Warm and Witty Story of a British Columbia Half Breed Logger*. Edited by Herbert L. McDonald. West Vancouver: Graydonald Graphics.

Perrault, E. G.
"The Silver King." In Weaver and James 1952.

Phillips, Alan
"The Presence in the Grove." In Weaver and James 1952.

Pinsent, Gordon
1974   *John & the Missus*. Toronto: McGraw-Hill Ryerson.

Pitseolak
1971   *Pitseolak: Pictures Out of My Life*. Toronto: Design Collaborative Books in association with Oxford University Press.

Pollett, Ron
1956   "The Tongue That Never Told a Lie." In *The Ocean At My Door*. St. John's: Guardian. Reprinted in Major 1974.

Pratt. E. J.
1935   *The Titanic*. Toronto: Macmillan. Reprinted in *Collected Poems*. Toronto: Macmillan, 1944; 2nd ed. 1958.

1936   "Memories of Newfoundland." In Joseph R. Smallwood, ed. *The Book of Newfoundland*. Vol. 2. St. John's: Newfoundland Book Publishers, 1937. (Quoted in Reid 1973.)

Pryde, Duncan
1971   *Nunaga: My Land, My Country*.Edmonton: Hurtig. Paperback ed. *Nunaga: Ten Years of Eskimo Life*. New York: Bantam, 1973.

Purdy, Alfred
1967   "Innuit." In *North of Summer*. Toronto: McClelland and Stewart. Reprinted in Klinck and Watters 1974.
1974   *In Search of Owen Roblin*. Toronto: McClelland and Stewart.

Raddall, Thomas H.
1959   "A Harp in the Willows." In *At the Tide's Turn and Other Stories*. Toronto: McClelland and Stewart. Reprinted 1971.

Reaney, James
1964   "A Grain of Local Sand." *Edge*, Autumn 1964. Reprinted in Kilbourn 1970.

Reid, Raymond, compiler
1973   *The Canadian Style: Today and Yesterday in Love, Work, Play, and Politics*. Toronto: Fitzhenry & Whiteside.

Richler, Mordecai
1959   *The Apprenticeship of Duddy Kravitz*. Don Mills, Ont.: Deutsch. New ed. Toronto: McClelland and Stewart, 1974. Paperback ed. McClelland and Stewart, 1969.

Richler, Mordecai, editor
1970   *Creative Writing Today*. Penguin.

Rimanelli, Giose, and Roberto Ruberto, editors
1966   *Modern Canadian Stories*. Toronto: Ryerson.

Ringuet [pseudonym for Dr. Philippe Panneton]
1938   *Thirty Acres*. Paris: Flammarion. Translated into English by Felix and Dorothea Walker. Toronto: Macmillan, 1940. Reprinted Toronto: McClelland and Stewart, 1960.

Roberts, T. G.
1934   "The Wreckers' Prayer." In *The Leather Bottle*. Toronto: Ryerson.

Robertson, Heather
1973   *Grass Roots*. Toronto: James Lewis & Samuel.

Robertson, Heather, editor
1974   *Salt of the Earth: The Story of the Homesteaders*

in Western Canada. Toronto: James Lorimer.

Rose, Carol
1976 "La Cabane à sucre." *Heritage* (Government of Alberta), May/June, 9.

Ross, Malcolm, editor
1954 *Our Sense of Identity*. Toronto: Ryerson.

Rowe, Kaye
1969 "Brandon: The Wheat City." *Canadian Geographical Journal* LXXVIII, May.

Roy, Gabrielle
1947 *The Tin Flute*. Translated by Hannah Josephson. Toronto/Montreal: McClelland and Stewart. Reprinted 1958. Paperback ed. 1969.

Rudnyckyi, J. B.
1967 "Separate Statement." In the *Report of the Royal Commission on Bilingualism and Biculturalism: Book One, General Introduction*. Ottawa: Queen's Printer.

Russell, Franklin
1965 *The Secret Islands: An Exploration*. Toronto/Montreal: McClelland and Stewart.

Russell, Ted
"Smokeroom on the Kyle." In Major 1974.

St. Pierre, Paul
1966 *Breaking Smith's Quarter Horse*. Toronto: Ryerson.

Scott, Duncan Campell
1947 "At Gull Lake," "The Height of Land," and "Indian Names." In *Selected Poems of Duncan Campbell Scott*. Toronto: Ryerson.

Scott, F. R.
1945 "Laurentian Shield." In *Overtures: Poems*. Toronto: Ryerson.
1964 "Flying to Fort Smith" and "Mackenzie River." In *Signature*. Vancouver: Klanak Press.
1966 "Trans Canada." In *Selected Poems*. Toronto: Oxford University Press. Reprinted in Klinck and Watters 1974 and in Weaver and Toye 1973.

Scott, F. R., and A. J. M. Smith, editors
1957 *The Blasted Pine—An Anthology of Satire, Invective & Disrespectful Verse Chiefly by Canadian Writers*. Toronto: Macmillan. Revised and enlarged 1967.

Scott, S. Osborne, and D. A. Mulligan
1951 "The Red River Dialect." *The Beaver*. Reprinted in P. G. Penner and J. McGechaen,

editors. *Canadian Reflections: An Anthology of Canadian Prose*. Toronto: Macmillan, 1964.

Service, Robert. W.
1907 "The Shooting of Dan McGrew." In *Songs of a Sourdough*. Toronto: Briggs.

Simpson, Lady Frances
1964 *Journal*. Quoted in *North* XI:3 (May).

Sinclair, Lister
1949 "The Canadian Idiom," *Here and Now*, No. 4 (June). Reprinted in Ross 1954.
1958 "Eulogy." In R. E. Watters, *British Columbia: A Centennial Anthology*. Toronto: McClelland and Stewart, 1958.

Slater, Patrick [pseudonym for John Mitchell]
1933 *The Yellow Briar: A Story of the Irish on the Canadian Countryside*. Toronto: Macmillan. Reprinted 1970.

Smith, A. J. M., editor
1958 *Masks of Poetry: Canadian Critics on Canadian Verse*. Toronto: McClelland and Stewart.
1973a *The Canadian Century: English-Canadian Writing Since Confederation*. Toronto: Gage. (Vol. 2 of *The Book of Canadian Prose*.)
1973b *The Colonial Century: English-Canadian Writing Before Confederation*. Toronto: Gage. (Vol. 1 of *The Book of Canadian Prose*. First issued with that title 1965.)

Smith, I. Norman, editor
1964 *The Unbelievable Land: 29 Experts Bring Us Closer to the Arctic*. Department of Northern Affairs and National Resources. Ottawa: Queen's Printer.

Speare, Jean E., editor
1973 *The Days of Augusta*. Vancouver: J. J. Douglas.

Staebler, Edna
1968 *Food That Really Schmecks: Mennonite Country Cooking*. Toronto: Ryerson.
1969 *Sauerkraut and Enterprise*. Revised edition. Toronto/Montreal: McClelland and Stewart.
1972 *Cape Breton Harbour*. Toronto: McClelland and Stewart.

Stegner, Wallace
1955 *Wolf Willow: A History, A Story, and A Memory of the Last Plains Frontier*. New York: Viking. Reprinted 1966.

Stevens, Peter
1970 "Prairie." In *A Few Myths*. Vancouver: Talonbooks.

Stoddart, Jack
1970 Introduction to reissue of *The 1901 Editions of the T. Eaton Co. Limited Catalogues*. Toronto: Musson.

Strachan, Bishop John
Quoted in Hamilton 1952.

Summers, Merna
1974 *The Skating Party: Stories by Merna Summers*. Ottawa: Oberon.

Symons, R. D.
1963 *Many Trails*. Toronto: Longman.
1973 *Where the Wagon Led: One Man's Memories of the Cowboy's Life in the Old West*. Toronto: Doubleday.

Taylor, J. Garth
1971 *The Canadian Eskimos*. Toronto: Royal Ontario Museum.

Thompson, David
See Victor G. Hopwood 1971.

Thompson, Samuel
1884 *Reminiscences of a Canadian Pioneer for the Last Fifty Years (1833-1883): An Autobiography*. Toronto: Hunter Rose. Reprinted Toronto: McClelland and Stewart, 1968.

Traill, Catherine Parr
1836 *The Backwoods of Canada*. London: C. Knight. Reprinted Toronto: McClelland and Stewart, 1929.

Trower, Peter
1974 "Grease for the Wheels of Winter." In *Between the Sky and the Splinters*. Toronto: Nelson. Reprinted in Geddes 1975.

Valgardson, W. D.
1973 *Bloodflowers: The Stories*. Ottawa: Oberon.

Waddington, Miriam
1972 "Provincial," "Things of the World," and "Toronto the Golden-vaulted city." In *Driving Home*. Toronto: Oxford University Press.

Wainwright, Andy, editor
1969 *Notes for a Native Land: A New Encounter with Canada*. Ottawa: Oberon.

Waite, P. B., editor
1965 *Pre-Confederation*. Canadian Historical Documents Series, Vol. II. Scarborough: Prentice Hall.

Watters, R. E., editor
1958 *British Columbia: A Centennial Anthology*. Toronto: McClelland and Stewart.

Weaver, Robert, editor
1968 *Canadian Short Stories*. Second series. Toronto: Oxford University Press.

Weaver, Robert, and Helen James, editors
1952 *Canadian Short Stories*. Toronto: Oxford University Press.

Weaver, Robert, and William Toye, editors
1973 *The Oxford Anthology of Canadian Literature*. Toronto: Oxford University Press.

Whalley, George
1962 *The Legend of John Hornby*. London: John Murray; Toronto: Macmillan.

Whitman, Walt
1888 Quotation from *November Boughs*. Philadelphia: David McKay.

Wiebe, Rudy Henry
1962 *Peace Shall Destroy Many*. Toronto: McClelland and Stewart.

Wilde, Oscar
1883 *Notes on a Tour of the United States*. Quoted in Mathews 1931, 1963.

Wilson, Ethel
1961 "Mrs. Golightly's First Convention." In *Mrs. Golightly and Other Stories*. Toronto: Oxford. Reprinted in Lucas 1971 and in Weaver and James 1952.
1954 *Swamp Angel*. Toronto: Macmillan. Reprinted Toronto: McClelland and Stewart, 1962.

Wilson, Milton
1962 "Other Canadians and After." In Smith 1958.

Wilson, William
1866 *Newfoundland and Its Missionaries*. Cambridge, Mass.: Dakin and Metcalf.

Wintemberg, W. J.
1950 *Folk-Lore of Waterloo County, Ontario*. National Museum of Canada, *Bulletin No. 116*, Anthropological Series No. 28. Ottawa: King's Printer.

Yates, Michael
"The Hunter Who Loses his Human Scent." In Wainwright 1969.

Yates, Michael, editor
1971 *Volvox: Poetry from the Unofficial Languages of Canada. . .in English Translation*. Queen Charlotte Islands, B.C.: Sono Nis Press.

General Index

[a], [aː], in Standard Southern British, 22-3, 27; in Canadian English, 26-7, 154
Acadia, Acadians, 80, 162, 164, 168-9
Acorn, Milton, *quoted*, 171
acronyms, 65; punctuating, 50
[aɪ] / [ʌɪ], 25-6
Alexander, Henry, 6, 12-3, 115, 120, 162, 164, 166; *quoted*, 164, 166
Allen, Harold B., 145; *quoted*, 201
Allen, Ted, *quoted*, 124
American English, and dictionaries, 126; influence on Canadian English, 3-4, 8-10, 35-6, 176-180, 182, 183-4, 193-4, 200-1, 220-1, 226; map of dialects, 116; phonology of, 26-34; regional dialects of, 8, 38, 116-7, 138-9. *See also* Canadian/American differences; North American English; spelling; Southern U.S.; Midland U.S.; Northern U.S.; New England; Pennsylvania; New York.
The American Heritage Dictionary, iv, 30
archaisms. *See* relic forms; historical forms.
Armour, Richard, *quoted*, 17
attitudes to dialects, 27, 28-31, 97-100, 104-5, 112, 118, 120, 123, 164
Atwood, Margaret, *quoted*, 92
[aʊ]/[ʌʊ] (ou), 2-3, 25-6, 28, 154-5, 181
aunt, map of, 115
Australian English, 14-5, 56-7, 69
The Authors' and Printers' Dictionary, 42
Avalon Peninsula, Newfoundland, survey of, 153-5
Avis, Walter S., 32, 43, 88, 102, 113, 115, 119, 125, 127, 183, 201; *quoted*, 30-1, 32, 33, 42, 119, 178, 179, 183-4
Aztec, 200

Babcock, C. Merton, *quoted*, 126
Bacon, Lord, *quoted*, 148
Baker, R. J., 171
ballads. *See* folklore.
Barbeau, Marius, Arthur Lismer, and Arthur Bourinot, *quoted*, 190-1
Basque, in place names, 176
The Beaver, 209
Bedore, Bernie, *quoted*, 181, 188

Bennett, R. B., 128
Berton, Pierre, *quoted*, 238, 240
Bible (1611), 40, 95
bilingual communities, 119-20, 125, 165-6, 205-8, 225-6. *See also* German; Ukrainian; etc.
Birney, Earle, 57; *quoted*, 28, 124, 161, 239, 241
Bishop of Columbia, *quoted*, 231
blends, 63-4
Bloomfield, Morton, *quoted*, 168
Boas, Franz, 234-5
borrowing to make Canadianisms, 68-71; and folk etymology, 69-70; loan translations, 70-1. *See also* French; Indian languages; Inuit; German; Dutch; Spanish; Chinook Jargon.
Bowering, George, *quoted*, 99
British Columbia, English in, 3, 130, 145-6, 187, 200, 218-37, 242-3. *See also* Chinook Jargon.
British English, grammar and idioms of, 35-8; phonology of, 21-34; prestige in Canada, 19, 224; punctuation, 51; recent changes in, 37-8, 50-1; spelling of, 41-50; terms lost in colonies, 15. *See also* Standard Southern British; North American/British differences; Canadian/British; standard English.
British/North American differences, 12-5, 17, 101-2, 131-2, 146; grammatical, 35-8, 40; intonation and stress, 23-5; phonology, 21-7; punctuation, 50-1; in semantic range, 16-8
British, regional variants in Canada, 2, 9-10, 11, 28, 37-8, 39, 102, 133, 140, 146, 150-2, 154-5, 162, 168, 169, 182, 187, 194, 213, 221. *See also* Irish; Scots Irish; Scots; Ulster; etc.
Broadfoot, Barry, *quoted*, 55, 129, 165
Brooke, Frances, *quoted*, 79
Brooks, Cleanth, *quoted*, 8
Bruce, Charles, 242; *quoted*, 13, 70
Bruce, Harry, *quoted*, 61
Bruemmer, Fred, *quoted*, 213
Buck, Ruth Matheson, *quoted*, 75, 86, 130
Buckler, Ernest, 242; *quoted*, 39, 100, 106, 126, 131, 136, 172, 173, 238, 240, 241
Bungee (Bungay), 201-2

Bunyan, Paul, 135, 170
Burke, Johnny, 137
By, Colonel John, 190-1
Byron, Lord George, *quoted*, 12

Cameron, Agnes Deans, *quoted*, 200, 209
Cameron, Donald, *quoted*, 243
Campbell, Marjorie Wilkins, *quoted*, 144
Canadian English, early history and examples of, 8-11, 45, 105, 176-9; grammatical variations, 37-8; phonology, 1, 4, 21, 23-36; spelling, 45-51; vocabulary, 1, 4, 13, 38-9, 52 ff. *See also Dictionary of Canadianisms*; relic forms; the individual regions.
Canadian/American differences, 2, 3-4, 9, 19-20, 23-36, 38, 41-9, 101-2, 131-2, 145-6. *See also* American English; British/North American differences.
Cajuns. *See* Acadians.
Calgary, 144, 145-6
Canada, Canadian, meanings of, 8-9, 55, 176
Canadian Council of Teachers of English (CCTE), 119
Canadianism, defined, 127, 150; and regionalisms, 141 ff. *See also Dictionary of Canadianisms*.
Canadian Linguistic Association (CLA), 6, 42, 119, 126
"Canadian ou sound," 2-3, 25-6, 154-5, 181
Cape Breton Island, 8, 144, 162, 165
Capilano, Chief Joe, 228
Carbonear, survey of, 103
Carleton University, 181
Carman, Bliss, *quoted*, 170
Carr, Emily, *quoted*, 230, 234
Cartier, Jacques, 76
Cartwright, George, 148
Cary, Thomas, *quoted*, 174
Cassidy, F. G., 114, 138-9
catalogues, as sources, 131-3
caught/cot, pronunciation of, 28, 154
Caxton, William, 95
Central Canada, 8-9, 174-94. *See also* Ontario; Quebec.
Chamberlain, A. F., 6, 60; *quoted*, 60, 136, 193-4
Chambers, J. K., 180-1; *quoted*, 181
Champlain, Samuel, 76, 127, 171

271

Garner, Hugh, *quoted*, 129-30, 239, 241
"The Gay Raftsmen," 190-1
Geddes, Gary, *quoted*, 222
Geikie, John C., *quoted*, 1
geographical dialects, 100, 102, 109; how studied, 109 ff. *See also* regional variations.
German, borrowings from, 11, 38; in Canada, 9, 136, 165-7, 176, 179, 184-7, 205-8, 213, 219, 225-6. *See also* Pennsylvania Dutch.
Gerrard, Elisabeth, *quoted*, 106, 113
Glasier, John B., 170
Glazebrook, G. P. de T., *quoted*, 178
Gowers, Sir Ernest, 36
Graham, R. S., *quoted*, 205-7
Grainger, M. A., *quoted*, 60, 70, 233
grammatical shift, 67-8, 152, 228
Gregg, R. J., iv, 145, 219; *quoted*, 27, 183
Grove, Frederick Philip, *quoted*, 128, 130, 210-1, 238, 241
Guillet, Edwin C., *quoted*, 185
Guy, Ray, *quoted*, 38, 152, 160, 194

Haig-Brown, Roderick, *quoted*, 61
Hakluyt, Richard, *quoted*, 127
Haliburton, Thomas, *quoted*, 70, 162
Hamilton, Donald E., 187-8
Hancock, W. K., *quoted*, 15
Harker, Herbert, *quoted*, 124
Harlow, Robert, *quoted*, 14, 92-3, 239, 241
Hart, Ann, *quoted*, 70
Hay, Robert, *quoted*, 148
Hayman, Robert, *quoted*, 147
Hazlitt, William Carew, *quoted*, 107, 221
Head, Sir George, *quoted*, 14, 177
Henry, Alexander ("The Elder"), *quoted*, 85
Hiebert, Paul, *quoted*, 239, 241
historical forms, 106-7, 122-3, 188-9. *See also* time dimension; fur trade vocabulary.
Hood, Hugh, 242; *quoted*, 61, 239, 241
Horwood, Harold, 242; *quoted*, 146, 158-60, 169, 239, 241
House, A. B., 120
Howarth, Jean, *quoted*, 239-40
Hudson's Bay. *See* fur trade vocabulary.
hyphen, changes in use, 50-1

Icelandic, 196, 200
idiolect, 99

-*ile*, pronunciation of, 30
Indian languages, borrowings from, 13, 81-7, 106-7, 122, 130-1, 168, 201-2, 215; Chinook Jargon, 71, 81, 86, 226-37; distortion of, 81, 84; map and names of tribal groups, 82-4
-*ine*, pronunciation of, 30
-*ing*, pronunciation of, 39, 126
International Phonetic Alphabet (IPA), viii, 21-2
intonation, 24-5
Inuit, borrowings from, 87-91; folk etymology and, 88-9; map of, 88; quiz on, 90, 91
Irish, in North America, 9-10, 12, 21, 36, 38, 150-1, 154-64, 167, 172, 177, 179, 181-3, 188-91. *See also* Gaelic; Scots Irish; Ulster; Ottawa Valley.
isogloss, 115

Janes, Percy, *quoted*, 99, 106, 239, 241
Japanese, 226, 230
Johnson, E. Pauline, 228, 234; *quoted*, 228
Johnson, Samuel, 95; *quoted*, 103
Johnson, Thorvaldur, *quoted*, 196

Kamloops, B.C., 220, 234-5
Kennedy, H. A., *quoted*, 106
Kinloch, A. M., 115, 120, 164; *quoted*, 170-1
Kirwin, W. J., 153-5
Klein, A. M., *quoted*, 208
Klondike, vocabulary of, 215
Kootenays, B.C., 27, 101, 145, 219, 220, 225
Kroetsch, Robert, *quoted*, 243
Kurath, Hans, 111-2, 116, 162, 164

Labrador, 212, 213. *See also* Newfoundland.
Lamb, W. Kaye, 122
Lampman, Archibald, *quoted*, 193, 238, 240
Late Loyalists, 176
Laurence, Margaret, 242; *quoted*, 14, 56, 107, 131, 182, 201, 203
Leacock, Stephen, *quoted*, 29, 69, 176
Leechman, Douglas, 127, 219; *quoted*, 236
Le Jeune, Père, 233-4
LePan, Douglas, *quoted*, 66, 73
lexicography. *See* dictionaries.

Lillard, Charles, *quoted*, 234
Linguistic Atlas of the United States and Canada, 111-7, 119, 162, 164
loan translations. *See* borrowing.
localisms, 100-1, 106, 113. *See also* regional variations.
London, Jack, *quoted*, 61, 215
Lovell, Charles J., 127
Lower, A. R. M., *quoted*, 8, 165, 199
Lower Canada. *See* Quebec.
Lowman, Guy S., *quoted*, 164
Lowry, Malcolm, *quoted*, 239, 241
Loyalists. *See* United Empire Loyalists; Late Loyalists.
Ludwig, Jack, *quoted*, 199
lumbering terms, 1, 78-9, 103-4, 135-6, 170, 187, 188-91, 201, 220-3
Lunenburg, N.S., 136, 163, 165-7, 185, 206

McConnell, William, *quoted*, 239-40
McCourt, Edward, *quoted*, 29, 124, 200, 239, 241
McCulloch, Thomas, *quoted*, 102, 170, 239, 241
McDavid, Raven I., Jr., 171; *quoted*, 183
McDonald, Archibald, *quoted*, 73
Macdonell, Rev. Alexander, *quoted*, 178
Macfie, Matthew, *quoted*, 60, 219
McIntosh, Angus, 119
Mackay, J. Ross, *quoted*, 216
MacKay, L. A., *quoted*, 62
Mackenzie, Sir Alexander, 39; *quoted*, 214
MacLennan, Hugh, *quoted*, 58, 73, 81, 93, 124, 146, 239, 241
Mair, Charles, *quoted*, 81
maple sugar, vocabulary of, 80, 191-3
Marckwardt, Albert H., *quoted*, 98
Maritimes, English in, 21, 32, 39, 40, 55, 60, 70, 85, 104, 111, 113, 120, 144-6, 161-73, 179-80, 243; French in, 80; surveys in, 119. *See also* Cape Breton; New Brunswick; Nova Scotia; Prince Edward Island.
Marlyn, John, *quoted*, 124
Marriott, Anne, *quoted*, 238, 240
Marryat, Captain F., *quoted*, 30, 164
Marshall, Joyce, *quoted*, 57
Marshall, Mel, *quoted*, 10
Mary, merry, marry, pronunciation of, 28
Mathews, Mitford M., 126
Memorial University, 150
Mennonites, 176, 184, 206